Radical Mandarin:
The Memoirs of Escott Reid

UNIVERSITY OF TORONTO PRESS
Toronto Buffalo London

© University of Toronto Press 1989
Toronto Buffalo London
Printed in Canada

ISBN 0-8020-5811-6

∞

Printed on acid-free paper

Canadian Cataloguing in Publication Data

Reid, Escott
  Radical Mandarin

  Includes index.
  ISBN 0-8020-5811-6

  1. Reid, Escott. 2. Canada – Foreign relations –
  1918-1945.* 3. Canada – Foreign relations –
  1945–   . 4. Diplomats – Canada – Biography.
  I. Title.

  FC601.R4A3 1989   327.2'092'4   C89-094280-3
  F1034.3R4A3 1989

To Ruth and Morna

Contents

viii Contents

*P*reface

I ask myself as I complete these memoirs of my public life why I have devoted so many hours over so many years to writing them. The main reason is that I enjoy writing. Writing has since 1969 been my principal diversion, my profession, my final career. In that time I have written five books, many essays, and these memoirs. This activity has enabled me to describe myself in biographical notes for who's whos as 'writer' not as 'retired,' a description from which I recoil. There are other reasons for writing my memoirs. I hope they will throw light on some aspects of twentieth-century history. I hope they will bring pleasure to some readers. I have the desire which Graham Greene speaks of in his memoirs, the 'desire to reduce a chaos of experience to some sort of order, and a hungry curiosity' about myself. In my old age I like to think that the memoirs will keep memory of me alive for a few years after my death and, most important of all, I hope they will help me to live in the memories of my children, grandchildren, and great-grandchildren. Finally, I agree with Graham Greene that 'writing is a form of therapy; sometimes I wonder how all those who do not write, compose or paint can manage to escape the madness, the melancholia, the panic fear which is inherent in the human situation.'

George Orwell has said that 'a man who gives a good account of himself is probably lying, since any life when viewed from the inside, is simply a series of defeats.' I fear that these memoirs are more concerned with my successes than with my defeats, frustrations, and disappointments, which were many. When I survey my public career over the last half-century I echo what Dean Acheson said of his years in the State Department: 'Yet an account of the experience, despite its successes, inevitably leaves a sense of disappointment and frustration, for the achievements fell short of both hope and need.' And the essays in persuasion I have written have not been nearly so persuasive as I hoped they might be in influencing for the better the development of the United Nations, the North Atlantic alliance, and the relations between rich and poor countries.

Mr St Laurent once told me that when Mr King asked him in December 1941 to leave his law practice in Quebec City and become his second-in-command in the government of Ottawa, he consulted Cardinal Villeneuve. The cardinal advised him to accept and then said: 'I have one word of advice to you. The good God does not expect you to bear the whole burden of the world on your shoulders. He expects you to bear only your fair share of the burden.'

In an essay I wrote in 1967 on the conscience of a diplomat I said that a diplomat who examined his conscience would ask himself whether, when he had had an opportunity to increase the likelihood of his government pursuing a wise course on an issue of foreign policy, large or small, he had done all he could to help the government make the wisest possible decision. Or had he failed because he had been too lazy to work hard at understanding the issue, or had refrained from expressing his honest opinion for fear of endangering his prospects for promotion, or had been unwilling to weigh carefully enough the views of his colleagues, or had not brought to bear on his task the most informed, disciplined, subtle, imaginative, creative, sympathetic judgment of which he was capable? The writing of these memoirs has been for me an examination of conscience in which I have sought to reassure myself that I have tried to bear my fair share of the burden.

I am conscious of the difficulty of recalling accurately feelings and thoughts and actions over a long life. I am impressed by a recent study which shows that the collective image of the past can impose itself on and even erase individual recollections. Survivors of the London blitz, who had kept nightly diaries at the time, were asked thirty-four years later to rewrite from memory what they felt and did then. 'There is usually little or no logical relation between the two sets of accounts ... Memory has glossified and sanctified these "finest hours".'[1] In order to lessen the danger that the collective image of the past might impose itself on or even erase my recollections or that my memory might glossify and sanctify my 'finest hours,' I have in writing these memoirs relied mainly on

---

1 Robert Hewison, *Under Siege: Literary Life in London 1939–1945* (Newton Abbott: Readers Union 1978), 36–7

what I wrote at the time in letters, articles, speeches, an infrequent diary, and my memoranda and despatches while in the foreign service. These papers and the copies I have made of other documents I cite in this book are in my papers in the National Archives of Canada and I give few footnote references to them.

My excuse for calling myself a radical mandarin is that this is how Cranford Pratt described me in his review of my book on the World Bank. This seems to me a great compliment.

E.R.
February 1989

Escott Reid at six years old with his mother at the Rectory, Campbellford,
August 1911

Escott Reid, aged sixteen, Toronto

Escott Reid and Ruth, August 1929

Escott Reid, Ottawa, August 1947

Escott Reid, chairman of the Committee on Procedures and Organization of the U.N. General Assembly, New York, September 1947
Credit: National Archives of Canada

Opposite

Escott Reid, Indira Gandhi, Louis St Laurent, Madelaine O'Donnell (St Laurent's daughter), Nehru, Ruth, Jean-Paul (St Laurent's son). Dinner at the Canadian High Commission, New Delhi, February 1954

Timothy, Ruth, Escott, Morna, and Patrick trekking in the Himalayas, summer 1954

Escott Reid and Nehru at the signing of the agreement on the Canada-India Reactor Project, New Delhi, April 1956. On the left in Homi Bhabha, India's leading nuclear physicist.

Krishna Menon and Escott Reid at the New Delhi airport, February 1957. 'If the Canadian government want to protest, let them protest.'

Escott and Ruth waving farewell from the train at the New Delhi railway
station, April 1957

Escott Reid with Willy Brant, Berlin, April 1962

Escott and René Lévesque, Glendon College, 1968

Escott Reid, 1983

RADICAL MANDARIN

*F*orefathers and Foremothers

We must all of us be puzzled by what it was in the genes we inherited from our forbears, in our upbringing at home, in our education, our work, our family and friends, that has made us what we are.

Like most English-speaking Canadians of my generation, most of my immediate forbears were immigrants from the British Isles. My father came to Canada from England in 1885. My mother was born in Canada but her father came to Canada from Ireland in 1841. Her mother, descended from United Empire Loyalists, was the only one of my grandparents to be born in Canada.

My mother's father, Edmund Meredith, was born in 1817 in Ardtrea, in the County of Tyrone, where his father was rector of the Anglican church. His father was a fellow of Trinity College, Dublin, and his mother was a daughter of Dean Richard Graves, also a fellow of Trinity College, and he himself went to Trinity. He came to Canada in 1841, was appointed unpaid principal of McGill University, Montreal, in 1846, and served until 1849. He was a member of the Canadian civil service for thirty-one years from 1847 to 1878. When I was deputy under-secretary of state for external affairs from 1948 to 1952 I had an office in the East Block of the Parliament Buildings which I afterwards discovered was the office my grandfather had occupied in 1867 at the time of Confederation when he was assistant secretary of state for the provinces. He was then one of nine deputy ministers at a time when the entire civil service in Ottawa consisted of only about 350 officers and clerks. They lived in a 'sub-arctic lumber village transformed by a stroke of Victoria's pen into a cockpit of malodorous politics' – John Stevenson's version of Goldwin Smith's description of Ottawa.

In 1984 my grandfather was resurrected by Sandra Gwyn in her book

The Private Capital. Sandra Gwyn wrote to me shortly before the book was published:

Meredith – a 'Pioneer Mandarin' ... is the central character of the entire first half of the book, covering the years 1865–1879, when he left Ottawa. He and his wife Fanny, and their children, are the 'prisms of history', in Barbara Tuchman's phrase, through whose point of view I have been able to recreate the world of immediate post-Confederation Ottawa ...

I became enormously fond of your grandfather, who time and again struck me as having been a man about three-quarters of a century ahead of his time: as an 'Ottawa man' of the 1930's and 1940's his energy and intellect and sense of public service would have ensured him great success, but in the inert, patronage-ridden civil service of the day, he was constantly at logger-heads with John A. [Macdonald]. Even so, he left his mark; as a prison reformer; as a founder of the Literary and Scientific Society; as one of those who pushed to establish the National Gallery.

Edmund Meredith was fortunate in living in what was for the better-off classes in the western world the best period in the last three centuries or more – a period in which there were no great wars, a period of progress, and increasing prosperity. He was born two years after the end of the Napoleonic wars and died in January 1899, nine months before the outbreak of the Boer War demonstrated that Britain had succumbed to the disease of jingoism. We who have witnessed one tragedy in world affairs after another find it hard to comprehend that for him there was only one such tragedy – the condition of his beloved native country, Ireland. My mother told me that he would sometimes mutter to himself, 'My unhappy country!'

Like many Victorian upper-class intellectuals, he had doubts about some Christian doctrines. Once when in my early twenties I had been standing beside my mother in church when the Nicene creed was being recited, she said to me after the service, 'You were silent at the very same passages my father would never recite,' and she wrote to me, 'I know he never recited the denunciatory verses of the Psalms or concurred in the cruel judgements of the Commination Service; and I think he remained silent during the reading of the Athanasian Creed.'

A century later his church has in its prayer-book almost caught up with him. The worst of the denunciatory verses of the psalms is the conclusion of the otherwise lovely 'By the waters of Babylon we sat down and wept when we remembered thee, O Sion.' This ends with 'O daughter of Babylon ... blessed shall he be that taketh thy children and throweth them against the stones.' In most modern Anglican prayer-books this and other such passages in the psalms are omitted. (What could generations of pious Christians have been thinking of when they recited in church this beatitude of the devil?) The commination service which was a 'denouncing of God's anger and judgments against sinners' is now 'a penitential service' and the curses on sinners are omitted. The second verse of the Athanasian creed which asserts that 'except every one do keep [the Catholick Faith] whole and undefiled without doubt he shall perish everlastingly' is still in the prayer-book of the Anglican Church in Canada but the prayer-books of other branches of the Anglican church state that this verse may be omitted when the creed is recited.

My mother's mother was descended from two of the founding families of Toronto (then York), the Powells and the Jarvises. They were United Empire Loyalists and members of the Family Compact which dominated the government of Ontario (then Upper Canada) until the rebellion of 1837, led by William Lyon Mackenzie, the grandfather of W.L. Mackenzie King. William Dummer Powell, my mother's great-great-grandfather, was born in Boston in 1755. He was 'descended on both sides of his family from 17th-century emigrants to Massachusetts from England. His maternal grandfather, William Dummer, had been lieutenant-governor of the colony ... He served in arms, although probably not in action, as a volunteer with the British garrison [in Boston in 1775]. With open rebellion approaching and his opposition to it established beyond any chance of compromise' he left Boston for England in 1775. In 1779 he moved to Montreal to practise law. Ten years later he was appointed a judge with his headquarters at Detroit, Detroit being held by the British until 1796. He was granted land in York when it was founded in 1793 and became chief justice of Upper Canada in 1816. According to the *Dictionary of Canadian Biography*, 'No one else ... put such sustained effort and such shrewd intelligence into the government of Upper Canada.'[1]

My mother's maternal grandfather, William Botsford Jarvis, was sheriff in Toronto at the time of the rebellion of 1837. His daughter Fanny, my grandmother, was seven years old then. She remembered being taken from the family home, 'Rosedale,' then about two miles north of the Toronto city limits, to safety in a ship in the harbour. She also tells the story that the rebels rushed down Yonge Street calling out, 'Down with the sheriff! Down with Jarvis!' and would have burned 'Rosedale' if Samuel Lount, a rebel leader who was hanged for treason, had not

1 *Dictionary of Canadian Biography*, vol. VI (Toronto: University of Toronto Press 1987), 605–13

stopped them by saying that if they did, he would leave them, that he was not there to fight women and sick children. The sheriff headed a picket of twenty-seven men which on 5 December met at the outskirts of Toronto at Carlton and Yonge streets a group of eight hundred rebels moving south to seize Toronto. Both sides fired a volley and both sides then fled – all except the sheriff and a few rebel riflemen under Lount. By fleeing, the rebels lost their last chance to seize Toronto.

William Jarvis's father Stephen had likewise fought rebels but not so successfully. He was a farmer's son from Danbury, Connecticut, born in 1756, and in the American Revolutionary War he fought in the loyalist forces, first as a sergeant in the Queen's Rangers and then as a lieutenant in the 17th Light Dragoons. In his memoirs[2] he states that as soon as peace was proclaimed in 1783 he went back to his father's house in Danbury 'to the great joy of my aged parents and here I met the Young Lady to whom I was engaged and whom I the next day married.' The bitterness in the neighbourhood against Tories who had fought against the rebels was profound and on the night of his wedding the local militia besieged the house. Fortunately for him there was in Danbury a regiment of dragoons of the American army. Jarvis's brother sought protection for him from the colonel of the regiment. The colonel came to the Jarvis house, 'went to his Regiment and sent a sergeant and twelve Dragoons for my Protection.' After the wedding Jarvis returned to his regiment and sailed with it from St Augustine, Florida, to Halifax, Nova Scotia, where it was disbanded and he became a half-pay officer. Meanwhile his wife had gone back to Danbury. Since he feared he might have difficulty reaching her as she was, as he wrote, 'among my Enemies,' he went to New York and made his way to General Washington's headquarters. The next day he was introduced to Washington by General Alexander Hamilton. 'I communicated to him my business and asked him for a Passport to go into the Country. He received me very civilly but declined complying with my request as his Command had ceased and Civil Government was again in operation, but at the same time said, there was no difficulty, that I was perfectly safe under the Treaty of Peace to travel and transact my business, reporting myself to the authority of the Place to which I was bound.'

Jarvis and his wife were able to remain peaceably at his father's house during the winter. They 'were visited by all the most respectable Inhab-

2 'Narrative of Colonel Stephen Jarvis', in *Loyalist Narratives from Upper Canada*, Publications of the Champlain Society XXVII (Toronto: The Champlain Society 1946), 149–266

itants of the place' and they visited 'those Families from whom we had received Civilities.' But in the spring a mob again attacked the house and again he was protected by the American army. A few months later he and his wife and their child settled in Fredericton, New Brunswick, where they stayed until 1809 when they moved to York (Toronto). By this time he had become a colonel. The last position he held was 'Gentleman Usher of the Black Rod' in the Parliament of Upper Canada. He was the last man in Canada to give up the style of hairdressing in peruke.

My father was born in Newport, Shropshire, in 1861 and was brought up in Little Bowden, just outside Market Harborough in Leicestershire, where his father Thomas was supervisor of inland revenue in the English revenue service. Thomas had been born in 1809 in Kinsale, near Cork, in Ireland. My father's mother was a Siderfin from Knowle Farm in Minehead, Somerset. Her mother was an Escott and that is how I got my given name. I was told by one of my father's sisters that I was the youngest son, of the youngest son, of the youngest son, of the youngest son. This must be a rare distinction. When my father was thirteen his father retired from the revenue service and the family income shrank to such an extent that he could not afford to send his son to the Market Harborough grammar school. Fortunately the rector of the parish church was impressed by the boy's abilities and coached him for the scholarship examinations and later for the theological college of St Augustine's in Canterbury. If the rector had not taken this interest in my father he would not have become a curate at the church my mother's family attended in Toronto, he would not have married her, and I would not have existed.

My father served in a wide variety of Anglican churches in Canada, first as curate in Moncton and Saint John, New Brunswick, and at St Luke's in Toronto; then as rector in Nelson, British Columbia; Bathurst, New Brunswick; Uxbridge, north of Toronto; Clayton in New York State; Campbellford, Ontario, from 1901 to 1911; and finally as rector or rector emeritus of St Chad's, Toronto, until his death in 1957.

My father knew from his work in Canada something of the lives of the poor – poor farmers, poor loggers, poor industrial workers. He knew of the terrifying insecurity of the poor in the days before unemployment insurance, health insurance, children's allowances, and old age pensions, and he refused to believe that this insecurity was compatible with Christianity. I have been told that he might have been appointed the rector of a well-to-do church in a prosperous small town in southern

Ontario had he not in his sermon referred to the tremendous difference he had noticed in Toronto between the condition of life of the wealthy and of the poor. Certainly his career in the church suffered from his outspokenness. I did not realize until he was ninety-four that he brooded on this – indeed, perhaps he had not brooded on it until then. I was staying with my parents in Toronto in the summer of 1955 and was about to call on the bishop of Toronto, whose brother in India, also a bishop, was a friend, when my father took me aside and said, 'If there is an opportunity could you say to the bishop how hurt I am that men much younger than I have been made canons and I have not.' If I have at times damaged my career by being too outspoken, I come by the fault honestly.

My father loved the Anglican prayer-book, the music of its words, the beauty of its ceremonies, the magic of its mysteries, and he strove to create at St Chad's a reflection of this music and beauty and magic. His thoughtful voice as he read the services still echoes in my inner ear. I hear him speaking the 'comfortable words' of Jesus, 'Come unto me all that travail and are heavy laden, and I will refresh you,' and the climax of the prologue of the Gospel of John. 'And the Word was made flesh, and dwelt among us (and we beheld his glory, the glory of the only-begotten of the Father) full of grace and truth.' When he was a very old man and read this passage in church his voice would break with emotion. I have sometimes been told that I have an English accent and that I must have acquired it at Oxford. My accent, however, was the same before Oxford as afterwards, and if my accent is English it is probably because I subconsciously modelled it on my father's because of my admiration for his voice.

My father was a good man, a very good man, a devout Christian, compassionate, something of a Christian socialist. He had been brought up at a time when many, perhaps most, good Christians believed in a literal hell of fire in which sinners would be tortured eternally. The first theological discussion I remember hearing at home – I was seven at the time – was about this doctrine which Northrop Frye rightly terms foul. I remember my father saying that he could not believe that God would do such a thing even to Judas Iscariot. My father was saved from such beliefs not by his intellect but by his loving heart; he knew that what God required of him was to do justice but to love mercy and that what God required of him, God would himself perform, that God would temper justice with mercy.

He believed in prayer – congregational prayer, family prayer, personal prayer. Every weekday evening at home we moved immediately after dinner from the dining-room to the living-room for family prayer. My father prayed on his knees twice a day, as soon as he got up in the morning and just before he went to bed at night. He was ninety-one when I went to India as high commissioner. Just after we left he wrote my wife and me a farewell letter: 'Day by day twice every day unless too "bewildered by the way" I pray for all my family and grandchildren – and so far, though most unworthy, God has most graciously heard my prayers. You will need my poor, affectionate thoughts and prayers more than ever now and I promise to try not to fail you.' And he was promising us the support of his prayers not only for his lifetime on earth but beyond, for he had written me five years before: 'You will be surrounded by prayer not only by dear ones here on earth but by the loving dear ones in God's nearer world.' Perhaps when he wrote me about prayer he was unconsciously echoing what Lancelot Andrewes, bishop in the time of James I, had written: 'Prayer is the guardian of the sleeping, the confidence of the waking. We think him not safe who is undefended by the arms and the guard of prayer.'

At the International Civil Aviation Conference in Chicago in 1944 I told Adolf Berle, the chairman of the conference, that my father was praying for the success of the conference, adding, 'The prayer of a righteous man availeth much.' Twenty-one years later he recalled this incorrectly. He wrote in his diary that I, his 'old friend', prayed before giving lectures at his college 'as he did before Foreign Office conferences.' He added that he 'is a wonderful man though sometimes I think unrealistic in his judgment of events.'[3] I had, when he wrote this, ceased to pray for at least thirty years except at occasional church services. One of the tribulations of minor actors on the public stage is to be referred to inaccurately in the writings of leading actors, with the result that if we are mentioned in a history of some aspect of the period it is likely to be in a misleading footnote.

In a letter to my father on his ninetieth birthday in September 1951 I said that a person who had reached his ninetieth birthday 'should have the privilege of having the truth told to him – even if it embarrasses him ... I have been privileged to know a half dozen people who have in them some element of greatness. It is a rare quality. But what is even rarer is to know some one who has in him some element of sainthood ... I want you to know how much I admire your combination of belief and tolerance, your refusal to close your mind to new ideas decades after most men's minds have become impermeable, your constant interest in

3 Adolf A. Berle, *Navigating the Rapids: 1918–1971* (New York: Harcourt Brace Jovanovich 1973), 815

life. I am proud of you and very grateful to the good God that you are my father and that I have known you for half of your life.'

By my mid-twenties I had ceased to be a regular churchgoer and my religious beliefs had become nebulous – I called myself a wistful agnostic – but I had absorbed much from my father: his social gospel, his hatred of poverty, his contempt for lavish expenditure by the rich, and for parents who physically chastised their children. His own father was authoritarian and had beaten his children; he never struck a child. I followed his example.

My mother, Morna Meredith, was intelligent, well-read, animated, and full of nervous energy. She was brought up in Rosedale, Toronto, to which her father moved in 1879 after resigning from the civil service in Ottawa. She was then eight years old. The house in Rosedale was a spacious, white-brick house of twenty-two rooms, built on what had been the apple orchard of the original 'Rosedale,' the house in which her mother had lived before her marriage. My mother was twenty-two when she married my father, then a penniless, earnest clergyman of thirty-two. Within a week of the high-society wedding she was precipitated from the gracious comfort of Rosedale to a 'vilely uncomfortable' boarding-house in Bathurst, New Brunswick, where 'we were cold, poorly fed and bewildered.' (They found on arrival at Bathurst that the rectory was uninhabitable and that they could not afford to live in Bathurst's one hotel.) She once said that her misery in Bathurst was so great that she would have left her husband and gone home if she had not been so terribly sorry for him. Fortunately they stayed in Bathurst for only seven months, their doctor having advised them to return to a drier climate on account of my father's 'recurrent alarming throat trouble.'

My mother took refuge from the tribulations of the wife of a poor parson in books. There were always books in our living-room, our own and borrowed from libraries. She wrote of the wife of a clergyman in New Brunswick. 'On principle I like and admire women, but a woman who has no time for reading or love of books is too queer for me.'

My mother was a sceptic about things temporal; she despised Winston Churchill because she felt that he enjoyed running the war, unlike one of her few heroes, Abraham Lincoln, who was torn by pity and sorrow for the sufferings of the Civil War. She refused to accept the adulation of the Old Testament patriarchs common among good Christians in her time; she had special contempt for Jacob and David. Her sympathies were with Esau because Jacob and his mother had tricked Isaac into giving his blessing to Jacob instead of to Esau. She loathed David for ordering that his neighbour, the valiant soldier Uriah, be treacherously killed in battle so that he might marry his wife, Bathsheba. In her day the Anglican prayer-book's title for the psalms was 'The Psalms of David' and she could not understand how such a despicable person could have written the psalms. Now the heading in the prayer-book is 'The Psalter' and it is generally agreed that David wrote very few or none of the psalms. It is a pity she did not know that. Her doubts on Christian doctrine did not extend to the resurrection of the dead, and the life of the world to come. She wrote to me on the death of her closest friend, 'I hope she is happy in some lovely place.' When in her thirties she was near death from illness, she saw her father waiting to welcome her on the other shore.

I have a letter from her which must have been in reply to some newspaper questionnaire I had sent her. She wrote:

I like beautiful words beautifully used in conversation or literature, nature in gentle mood, the trees, birds and flowers of early autumn, the simplicity of the Quaker faith, and people of courage. I dislike high winds, angry loud arguments, coercion in family circles or in religious life, tyranny over children or animals, and men who call their wives, 'the wife' or 'mother' ... I consider my strongest characteristic the ability to keep intact a world apart from the material one, where 'the loved and lost', the flowers of yesteryear, and memories of great affections, constitute a happy haven.

She wrote some 'recollections' from which I have quoted. In the preface to them she said: 'These self-centred recollections are written by an Irish-Canadian which is a tricky mixture, I am afraid. Such a person is rather like a hot moss-covered Muskoka rock, rub off the warm soft surface and you will touch something cold and hard.' In 1945 a close friend of my mother, one of her bridesmaids in 1893, died. In a letter to me my mother gave a description of her. I wrote back, 'Your description of her sounds so much like yourself, "lovely to look at, and very intellectual and charming, with a curious fibre of cynicism in her gentle, aristocratic character".'

I cherish the New Year's message she sent me in 1959:

God's benison go with you, and with those
That would make good of bad, and friends of foes.

2

*B*eginnings

1905–1923

I have only vague memories of the first six years of my life, from 1905 to 1911, spent at the Anglican rectory in Campbellford, a small town in the lovely Trent Valley about one-third of the way from Toronto to Ottawa. The rectory grounds seemed to me to be enormous and they did consist of ten acres on the top of a hill a little outside the town. I had two older brothers and two older sisters, and together we played the usual childhood games in the rectory grounds: hide-and-seek, run-sheep-run, still-waters-no-more-moving. Once a year in the summer the church garden party was held in the rectory grounds, and I remember being entranced by the Chinese lanterns hung in the trees. The next day we children went carefully over the lawn looking for pennies, nickels, and dimes that had been dropped, and we always found a few. The first movie I went to, probably the only movie I saw in Campbellford, was of the coronation of George v. In 1910 I went to my first school, the Campbellford jail school. The kindergarten that year was held in the jail because the school buildings in the town were too crowded to accommodate it. I remember that one day when my sister and I arrived at the school there was a man in the cell, probably the town drunk, and we were all sent home.

During the first year after we moved to Toronto in 1911 we lived in a rented house. The next year we moved into a distinguished-looking house on the hill above Davenport Road at Lansdowne Avenue which was, I think, built in about 1850. This was to be the family home for fifty years until my mother died in 1962, five years after my father. The house overlooked the huge establishment of the Canada Foundry, and it was probably this disadvantage which made the house cheap enough for my father to be able to buy with, of course, a large mortgage. When the Canada Foundry was making munitions during the war the noise from it was constant, night and day.

I remember that in the summer of 1913 my father and sister and I, armed with hoes, would rush at the burdocks under the lilac bushes as if we were bayoneting enemy soldiers and we would cry out, 'There goes another Bulgar!' Why we were anti-Bulgar in the Second Balkan War I do not know. It was probably in 1913 that I was taken to an amateur theatrical performance where an actor dressed in golfing costume recited in a strong English accent:

> I was playing golf one day
> When the Germans landed.
> All our troops were far away.
> All our ships were stranded.
> And the thought of England's shame
> Nearly put me off my game.

And another actor, portraying this time an Englishman in Canada, recited a poem containing the following lines:

> Made in Canada.
> By Jove. Upon my word.
> I thought things were imported here.
> At least that's what I heard.

My father's church, St Chad's, was about twenty minutes' walk from our house. It was just north of St Clair and Dufferin, the centre of the district of Earlscourt, which at that time was on the northwest outskirts of Toronto. Toronto has now grown miles beyond it. It had been settled mainly by immigrants from England who had come to Canada between 1908 and 1914, when over half a million English emigrated to Canada. It was called shacktown when my father first knew it since most of the houses were tar-papered shacks. The First World War brought prosperity to Earlscourt: a large number of the men enlisted and many of the women got jobs in the munitions factories; the houses were improved and Earlscourt ceased to be shacktown. A few Italians moved into the area just before the war and many years later Earlscourt became a predominantly Italian community. I remember the first demonstration of Italian influence: the drab English greengrocers near us on St Clair Avenue were superseded by attractive Italian fruit and vegetable shops.

In those days a rector of a poor parish such as St Chad's had a very small income. I do not, however, recall as a child being conscious of our lack of money. My father never owned a car, but few middle-class people did then. Chicken was an expensive meat in those days and we seldom could afford it; when we had cold roast pork for dinner someone always said, 'It tastes just like chicken.' My mother was constantly embarrassed when ordering from the neighbourhood grocer because we had run up a big bill and did not have the money to pay it. Every little while my father would give the grocer something on account.

A housewife in a city like Toronto before most people had cars and shopped in supermarkets had a less lonely life than the housewife today. The milkman and the bread man called every morning at the house. The iceman delivered ice for the icebox; and the coalman lugged heavy sacks of coal up the long, steep steps to the house. All four of them came in horse-drawn carts and the unwrapped bread had a faint smell of horse. The Chinese laundry man picked up the laundry and brought it back and at Christmas he brought us a present of dried lichees. My mother phoned her daily order to the neighbourhood grocery shop half a block away, and the grocery boy delivered her order. All these people and the postman were to my mother close acquaintances. She chatted with them about their families and in the winter she would give the coalman cups of tea.

In my first year in Toronto I went to the Western Avenue public school and the next year (1912–13) to the Earlscourt Public School opposite my father's church. One of my most vivid memories of the school is of the horrid water-closets. One sat in a cubicle that had no door and underneath was a mass of sewage, for the whole row of w.c.'s was connected to the same water tank that automatically flushed from time to time. My guess is that my father, with his egalitarian principles and his desire not to offend his congregation, considered that I should go to the school to which the children of his parishioners went, whereas my mother with her elitist principles would have liked me to go to a private school if only there had been enough money to pay the fees. One evening Mother discovered lice in my scalp; I had obviously picked them up at school. This tipped the scales against egalitarianism and I was sent the next autumn to the Toronto Model School in downtown Toronto fifty minutes by streetcar from our house. The Ryerson Polytechnical Institute now occupies the site.

The Model School cost my father two dollars a month for fees and a dollar a month for streetcar tickets at ten for twenty-five cents. The school had a first-rate teaching staff, much better than that at ordinary public school, for it was a model for the teachers in training at the adjoining Normal School. I am grateful to the Earlscourt lice which sent me to the Model School.

In the summer of 1914 I found the newspapers especially interesting. My sister Jocelyn, who was a little over a year older than I, could not understand what the international crisis was all about. So one Sunday morning when we were walking home together from church I explained to her about the assassination at Sarajevo and that the Austrians had made demands on the Serbians and that they were quite right in so doing. In the evenings just before the outbreak of war our father took us downtown to see the bulletins put up outside the newspaper offices – the only way in those pre-radio and pre-television days to keep abreast of rapid developments. I wish I could recall the actual declaration of war but I cannot. I only know that I was chagrined because I had told my sister that the Austrians were in the right in making their demands on Serbia and now we were going in to the war on the side of the Serbians and it was they who were in the right.

At school in the first winter of the war our teacher, Mr Mustard, put charts on the walls of the comparative strength of the armies and navies of the Triple Entente of Britain, France, and Russia and of the Triple Alliance of Germany, Austria, and Italy. The total enemy strength seemed very large but Mr Mustard reassured us by saying that Italy would probably come into the war on our side. He also pinned up newspaper clippings on the war. One clipping which remained up for a long time showed how the frontiers of the world would look if Germany won and how they would look if the Allies won. The shifts in the boundaries from the existing ones were profound, but Mr Mustard said that we should not take the maps at their face value. We sang at school the national anthems of our allies, France, Russia, and Belgium, all in English until our final year when we sang the Marseillaise in French. I still remember the Russian national anthem, sung to the tune of the hymn 'God the all terrible':

God save our lord the Czar, noble and strong,
Lead him to victory, his power prolong.
O Ruler mild and good, our church's shield,
God is thy sole defence in court and field.

I remember seeing a parade in 1915 of a contingent of soldiers going off to war. The streets were crowded but silent. My mother said that the newspapers thought that the crowds ought to cheer the men on their way to the front but she did not see how the crowd could do anything else but be silent. So the khaki line of soldiers marched up Yonge Street and turned left along Bloor Street through ranks of silence. Later, after the United States had entered the war, there were parades in Toronto in which Canadian soldiers were joined by a contingent of American soldiers. People said they hated these parades because the Americans, fresh to the war, were enlisting the pick of their men while we had to accept recruits of poor physique and the contrast in physical appearance between the Canadian and American soldiers was painful to behold. We did not like the Americans in 1917 and 1918 because they had come into the war three years too late. We agreed with Kipling:

> At the eleventh hour he came,
> But his wages were the same
> As ours who all day long had trod
> The wine-press of the Wrath of God.

By the time the war came to an end we had learnt how to make comparisons between our losses in the war and the American losses. About 52,000 members of our armed forces had been killed in action or died of wounds. Since the population of the United States was twelve and a half times Canada's (one hundred million to eight million) the United States would have had to lose 650,000 men in action to make an equivalent sacrifice to Canada's but their losses were only about the same as ours.

Being nine when the war broke out and thirteen when it ended, it is not surprising that I swallowed wartime propaganda whole. In 1915 I picked up from a table in our living-room the Bryce report on German atrocities in Belgium and read with mingled horror and fascination the stories of Belgian women having their breasts cut off by German soldiers and being raped by them. I scorned people who did not believe in the story of the angels who appeared at Mons in 1914 to support the British soldiers. Then there were the stories spread to make the Kaiser look silly. I remember one statement attributed to him: 'The ice-cold haberdashers of the Thames yearn for our holiest things.' Presumably this was a malicious mistranslation of something the Kaiser had said about a nation of shopkeepers. It must have been in the summer of 1917 that my brother Lionel and I were sitting on our lawn looking at pictures in a magazine showing piles of naked corpses ready to be carted away to the German corpse factories, where they would be turned into feed for pigs which the Germans then ate. My brother explained that the pictures were not photographs as I had thought but drawings by the artist in accordance with the descriptions of eyewitnesses.

My secondary school was Oakwood Collegiate Institute, which I went to from 1917 to 1921. It was a new high school at St Clair and Oakwood, established in 1908. Once again I was fortunate in the high quality of most of the teachers. They demanded much of their students; they gave more than they demanded. I did well at the Model School and at Oakwood Collegiate, being always either first or second in my class. In the seven years from 1910 when I joined the kindergarten school in Campbellford to 1917 when I entered Oakwood I had been to five schools. In all five I knew none of my classmates when I enrolled at the school. I was shy and found it hard to make new friends, so entering a new school was an ordeal which I dreaded.

My recollection is that in my class at Oakwood all the students were of British descent except for three Jews and a girl of Dutch descent.

Our term examination in Canadian history in December 1917 came soon after the 1917 general election fought between the Union government which favoured conscription and the Laurier Liberals who were opposed. One of the questions in the examination was: 'Which party would you have voted for in the election? Give reasons for your choice.' The key sentence in my answer was: 'The Unionists because they are The Win the War Party.' In my mind's eye at the time was the election poster which the Union government had used, a Canadian soldier standing among graves in a field of poppies and the lines of John McCrae's poem:

If ye break faith with us who die
We shall not sleep, though poppies blow
In Flanders fields.

We had to keep faith and the way to keep faith was to elect a government which would put forth every effort to win the war and, above all, would bring in conscription to catch the 'slackers.'

The influenza epidemic burst out in September 1918 shortly after school had started. It was so bad that the schools were closed at the beginning of October and we were sent home with instructions on the school work we were to do while school was shut. One of the tasks assigned to everyone in the school was to write an essay on why Canadians should buy Victory bonds. The first sentence of my essay demonstrated the effect on me of wartime propaganda: 'It is four years now since Canada pledged all her resources to aid in overcoming the great German military machine which threatened to overrun the world, and to establish over us an autocracy, which would have forever banished Freedom.'

I started doing what was called war work in the summer of 1917. My sister Jocelyn and I picked strawberries at a fruit farm west of Toronto at Lorne Park. We got up at six, took the streetcar to Sunnyside and the radial car to the Lorne Park station, where a wagon took us to the farm. The next year Jocelyn and I graduated to living at a farmhouse in the Niagara peninsula and picking fruit there for two weeks. I was proud of my fortnight's fruit picking. It proved to me that I had passed out of child-hood; I was living away from home; my earnings after paying for board and lodging averaged $1.10 a day, exactly the same as that of a private soldier, a coincidence which pleased me. For my war work picking fruit I was awarded the Ontario government's decoration, Soldier of the Soil.

I find it hard to believe that in the spring of 1918 I assumed that the war would still be going on five years later, that I would enlist then, and that I planned what I would do in the intervening five years with that in mind. I did not want to be a private, so in September 1918 I handed in my name at school for the officers' training corps. I was told that if I joined the OTC I would be a sergeant in the high school cadet corps in the spring of 1919 and a lieutenant the next year. Rising to the rank of lieutenant in the cadet corps would mean that I would be a sergeant in the army when I enlisted. I might do even better: if I passed the math-ematics examination in my honour matriculation in 1922 I could become a lieutenant in the artillery or a pilot in the air force. We all at high school knew that Canadians were particularly good at being fighter pi-lots. I had waited outside Timothy Eaton Memorial Church to see the great Canadian air force hero, Colonel Billy Bishop, come out after his wedding.

Within a week or so of the armistice I resigned from the officers' training corps and the cadet corps.

I was downtown on the afternoon of Friday, 8 November 1918, when the *Toronto Star* came out with the front-page headline: 'Tell Kaiser to quit. German majority parties hold final caucus. Abdication due tomor-row.' Two days later at the Sunday morning church service my father announced that if the armistice took effect the next day there would be a thanksgiving service at the church. So on Monday the eleventh all our family trooped to church. I could not sit in the pew with them because the boy who blew the organ had not turned up and I had to take his place. I was disappointed because I wanted to stand with the rest of the congregation and sing 'O God, our help in ages past.' After the service we went downtown to see the celebrations. People threw talcum powder all over the place and the streets were littered with brokers' tapes and confetti. Mother thought the celebration was too rowdy.

The main change which the armistice made at school was in the speeches at the daily school assembly at nine in the morning. They were no longer about the need for soldiers of the soil and we no longer had read to us letters from old boys in the armed forces containing reminiscences of their school-days and flattering messages to their former teachers. Now the speeches were on a theme which made necessary every few minutes the use of the words 'the dawn of a new era.' We had purchased by our sacrifices in the war a better world; we had fought to make the world safe for democracy; we had fought for freedom, justice, and the rights of small nations; we were now going to make a peace founded on those principles; the League of Nations was going to make war in the future impossible. The war had made the world a better place. As for Canada, it had become a nation. It had sent an army overseas larger than Britain had ever raised before 1914. The army had fought gallantly. The Canadian prime minister, Sir Robert Borden, had sat in the Imperial War Cabinet. Canada was represented by its own delegation at the Paris Peace Conference. Canada was a member of the new League of Nations. 'Canada, a nation' was the title of speech after speech delivered at the high school assembly by visitors, old boys, and the principal. Half the participants in the annual oratorical contest in the spring of 1919 spoke on 'Canada, a nation.'

In February 1921 a service was held at the school in memory of former teachers and students who had died in the war. The principal speech was given by Archdeacon H.J. Cody, later minister of education of Ontario and president of the University of Toronto. His speech was, I think, typical of speeches on the war given at that time to schools in English Canada. It moved me greatly. I reported the speech for the school paper. This is in part what I reported Archdeacon Cody as saying:

When we review the war it is just as though every crisis were marked by some brave deed of the Canadian Contingent. In 1915, at Ypres the fiendish gas was let loose but the Canadians stood their ground ... In 1918, the last great 'Hundred Days', far greater than Napoleon's, took place from Amiens on the 8th of August to Mons on the 11th of November. Not for nothing was it that the cubs of the old lion had entered the city of Mons on the 11th of November, that city from which in 1914 the 'Old Contemptibles' had made such a gallant retreat ... They who died had vindicated the principles of right and truth, the intentions of good faith, and the sovereign power of goodness; they had punished those who ruthlessly trampled under foot international good will; they had challenged those at home to take their places and win the great victories of peace ... In a world such as this, of blended good and ill, there has been no great advance except by sacrifice. 'Without the shedding of blood, there is no remission of sins.'

My reaction to this kind of emotional appeal and to the wartime propaganda I had swallowed came quickly. In 1919 my oldest brother Anthony, ten years older than I, started studying engineering at the University of Toronto. He had been a captain in the Canadian Engineers, had been wounded, and had been awarded a Military Cross for gallantry. At the end of his first term in university he attended a convention of the Student Christian Volunteer Movement at Des Moines, Iowa, and came back with ugly stories about the lies of wartime propaganda and the evil behaviour of the Allies after the war. All I can remember is something about the reason for the first, deliberately misleading, account of the battle of Jutland and that the Allies had, by the magnitude of their demands on Germany for reparations, broken the terms on which Germany had agreed to the armistice. My brother Lionel, five years older than I, was studying art at the Toronto Technical School. Some of his fellow students were returned soldiers. They told him that it was not just the Germans who had committed atrocities; they themselves had thrown bombs at German soldiers inside the barbed wire of prisoner-of-war camps, and they had often taken no prisoners in an attack.

And passages from Cody's speech kept reverberating in my head. What did he mean by saying about the deaths of our soldiers in the war, 'Without the shedding of blood there is no remission of sins'? Did he think the shedding of blood had been desirable? Necessary, I still believed it to be, but desirable? Did he think it necessary and desirable that there should be shedding of blood in future wars so that the stains of the world's sins should again be washed away? And what about 'the cubs of the old lion' entering the city of Mons on the 11th of November? This sounded more forced, more false, the oftener the words occurred to me.

A speech I gave at the annual oratorical contest at my high school in the spring of 1921, my last year at Oakwood Collegiate, throws light on my intellectual development and may help in an understanding of the intellectual development of my contemporaries: bright boys of British descent, born in the early years of the century and brought up in a middle-class family in English-speaking Canada. I was awarded the second prize in the oratorical contest. My friend Wallace McCutcheon got the first prize for a speech in praise of Lloyd George.

I said in my speech that Canada should become an absolutely independent nation under the British crown; Canada and the other dominions would be separate kingdoms under the same king as Great Britain. To secure this 'the British Parliament should repudiate the three nominal powers over us which it still possesses, that of overriding our laws, cancelling our constitution, and abolishing our parliaments. These of course exist in name only but a far more important fact is that we cannot amend our own constitution. This restriction should immediately be removed as abhorrent to our national pride.' Appeals from Canadian courts to the British Privy Council should be abolished 'for it is absurd to think that Canada is too young and inexperienced to manage her own legal affairs.' We should 'strive for independence in our foreign relations and the right to appoint our own ambassadors.'

I made these proposals at the age of sixteen; I was seventy-seven before they had all been brought into effect. In 1927 Canada opened its first diplomatic mission to a foreign country, the legation to the United States. In 1931 the British Parliament surrendered its power to legislate for Canada, subject to one exception made at Canada's request: it retained the power to amend the Canadian constitution until Canada could reach agreement on how to amend it within Canada. In 1949 Canada abolished appeals to the British Privy Council. In 1953 the Queen became Queen of Canada and Her other Realms and Territories, a formal recognition that those realms were separate kingdoms under the same monarch. In 1982 Canada secured the power to amend its own constitution. The obstacles to our moving faster to nationhood had not been in Britain but within Canada.

In my speech I went on to say that political independence was not enough: 'It is necessary to guard against an Americanization of our people. Independence must be our aim not only politically but also intellectually. Already our fashions, our movies, our slang and our prohibition orators originate in the United States and we are fast developing from a British into an American people. It is mainly for our schools to counteract this movement and to build up a separate Canadian nationality with a distinctive national thought and feeling.'

I was forthright about domestic economic and social policy. 'On the one hand are the poor, crowded into slums and unsanitary dwellings, on the other hand the wealthy flaunting their riches by their extravagance.' 'Is it,' I asked, 'any wonder that there is unrest, even fear of violent revolution?' I advocated laws to prevent 'the squandering of our forest wealth by rapacious corporations.' All our natural resources should be so protected by law that 'no few men or group of men only will derive benefit from them but the people as a whole to whom they rightfully belong.' The worker should be protected by security against unemployment, by a guaranteed living wage, by proper housing, and by reasonable leisure.

My guess is that I derived these views on economic and social policy mainly from the pamphlets of the Social Service Council of Canada which my father received. But my views were not derived only from reading. I had had glimpses of the misery of the poor from the age of eight. I remember that in 1913, when there was a recession, people came to our house for vouchers entitling them to free bread and milk and coal. The clergy at that time were distributors of these vouchers. An Italian man came to the house one day with another Italian who could speak little English. He said to my father, 'I found this gentleman crying on your doorstep.' In 1913 and 1914, on my way to school I would pass long lines of men outside the Gerrard Street Mission waiting for a free meal. The pamphlets of the Social Service Council told me that charity was not enough; there had to be a new social order.

I do not know the source of my belief that Canada should become an absolutely independent nation under the British crown. It certainly did not come from the histories of Canada which I studied at public school and high school. They did not even hint that such a development was a possibility. Instead they were rhetorical about the unity of the Empire and their authors would have repudiated with contempt any suggestion that an empire composed of independent nations could possibly be called united. The textbook on the history of Canada which I studied at public school (published in 1910) emphasized the closeness of the ties which bound Canada to the Empire and how these ties had been strengthened by the Diamond Jubilee of Queen Victoria in 1897, by Canadian participation in the Boer War, and by the presence of the Prince of Wales at the tercentenary of Quebec in 1908. When the Boer War broke out, 'it was felt that the destiny of all parts of the Empire lay in their permanent alliance, and an enthusiastic desire to aid the motherland displayed itself ... The eagerness with which the colonies came to the aid of the motherland in the Boer War proved the unity of the British Empire.'

The concluding paragraph of my high school history of Canada (published in 1914) urged every Canadian to love his municipality, his province, and Canada. 'And beyond even Canada we must love the worldwide Empire of whose people an English poet has said:

We sailed wherever ship could sail,
We founded many a mighty state.
Pray God our greatness may not fail
Through craven fear of being great.'

I am appalled now by the absence from my speech of any reference to French Canada. I was certainly aware, only four years after the bitter conscription crisis of 1917 which pitted French Canadians against English Canadians, of the division of Canada between these two groups, because I referred at the beginning of my speech to Canada as a country divided by 'racial strife.' Could I possibly have believed that the French Canadians would in my lifetime become anglicized? But if I did not, what did I mean when I said that my vision of the future was of 'a great Canada supporting no longer a population of less than nine million ... but with a population of from thirty to forty million of ... British people' and that 'immigration flowing into the country must be such that the nation remain predominantly British. For it is unthinkable that our country should ever be inhabited by a polyglot race, speaking a babble of tongues and not possessing British ideals.' I am slightly relieved that these words are followed by a statement that 'whatever is valuable in the national life [of non-British immigrants] must be incorporated in ours to develop a great Canadian race even as the British race sprang from such distinct peoples as the Celt, Saxon, Dane and Norman.'

I can perhaps put some of the blame for ignoring the existence of French Canada on the patriotic songs we learned at school. The leading patriotic song in Ontario, and I assume in the rest of English-speaking Canada, was not 'O Canada' but 'The Maple Leaf,' which has no reference to French Canada. 'The thistle, shamrock, rose entwine the maple leaf forever.' (My brother Lionel insisted that when he was at public school in Campbellford the children sang, 'the thistle, shamrock, rose, and twine.') There is no fleur de lys. It was 'at Queenston Heights and Lundy's Lane' that 'our brave fathers' – all English-speaking Canadians – 'firmly stood and nobly died' repelling the American invader in 1812. There is no mention of Chateauguay where in 1813 French Canadians, outnumbered four to one, drove the Americans back. Kind heaven was asked to smile on 'merry England' and God was asked to bless 'old Scotland' and 'Ireland's emerald isle,' but neither heaven nor God was asked to bless the other Canadian motherland, France. 'The Maple Leaf' was not a Canadian national song; it was a song for English-speaking Canada.

'O Canada' did not mention any ethnic groups in Canada or any motherlands, and the version which we sang at school was closer to the original French version than the now authorized version:

Beneath the shade of the holy cross
Our fathers owned their birth ...
Almighty God, on thee we call
Defend our rights, forefend this nation's thrall.

A third patriotic song, 'Men of the North,' was more aggressively anti-American than 'The Maple Leaf.' 'The Maple Leaf' extolled Canadian victories over American invaders; 'Men of the North' called on us to be ready once again to repel the Americans:

Come if you dare
To the north man's lair.
The tramp of your armies
Shall not shake us.
Shout as you will
We are free men still.
Words cannot break us.

'Men of the North' did not disregard the French Canadians, for it went on to declare:

For we have the brain
And the brawn and the blood
Of the Saxon and the Celt and the Gaul.

Virtually all the books I read up to the age of sixteen ignored the existence of French Canada. At Christmas my brother Lionel would be given the bound annual volume of *Chums* and I the volume of the *Boys' Own Paper* and between Christmas and New Year's we would devour these volumes full of stories of British wars, past and future, and of British boarding-schools. I read all of G.M. Henty's books. At high school I read every novel by Kipling, Robert Louis Stevenson, and Sir Walter Scott that the school library contained, and many by Dickens and Thackeray. These British novels far outnumbered the American novels I read. The American writers were, I think, Horatio Alger, O. Henry, Louisa M. Alcott, and Mark Twain. Dumas was probably the only French novelist I read. As for Canadian books, they were few. I can recall only *The Golden Dog, The Seats of the Mighty, Wild Animals I Have Known,* and books by Ralph Connor. I enjoyed reading novels. They were the source of much of my education; they stimulated my imagination, increased my vocabulary, and subconsciously taught me something about style in writing. But since most of the novels were by British authors, they increased my feeling of kinship with Britain and things British, and taught me little about English-speaking Canada and virtually nothing about French-speaking Canada.

Until I was sixteen and started working I faithfully performed all the observances then expected of a rector's son who was supposed to set an example to the other boys of his age in his father's congregation. At family prayers my father read the prayers, and I one of the psalms for the day. On Sundays I went to church once, sometimes twice; during Lent I went to church on Wednesday evenings; I went to Sunday school; I sang in the choir. When I became old enough to graduate from being a pupil at Sunday school to being a teacher I escaped by taking on the job of administrative officer of the Sunday school, which consisted mainly of counting the collection. When my father gave one of his sermons which I had heard many times I would open my prayer-book and study the Latin at the beginning of each psalm or the Elizabethan thirty-nine articles of religion of 1563 or the table of kindred and affinity which interested me by stating among other things that a man might not marry his grandmother or his deceased wife's sister's daughter. It was not till many years later that I realized that the thirty-nine articles are models for draftsmen at international conferences. When the authors wanted to leave no doubt about the meaning of the political articles they used the fewest possible words: 'The Bishop of Rome hath no jurisdiction in this Realm of England'; 'It is lawful for Christian men, at the commandment of the Magistrate, to wear weapons and serve in the wars.' When in the interest of the wise Elizabethan compromise between Protestantism and Catholicism their objective was a formula which blurred theological differences, they were wordy and ambiguous. They adhered to the cardinal rule for draftsmen: never be ambiguous except intentionally.

In the spring of 1921 I had to decide whether to stay for a fifth year at high school and take my honour matriculation or go to work in order to save money to pay my way at university, since I knew my father could not afford to pay my university expenses. I decided to work and to take my honour matriculation by going to night school for two years at Harbord and Jarvis collegiates. I had already worked as a bank clerk in the summer of 1920 at $50 a month. In September 1921 I started work as a trainee in the Harris Abattoir at $15 a week. The hours were seven in the morning to five in the afternoon with an hour off for lunch and five hours on Saturday. I soon discovered that I could not work fifty hours a week at the abattoir, go to high school three nights a week, and study two nights a week, so I left after three weeks for a nine-to-five job as a clerk in the Audit Department of the Ontario government. The head of the department was a member of my father's congregation. I started at $750 a year and went up to $900 a year. By the end of August 1923, when I was about to go to university, I had saved $1,000. In those days tuition fees at the university and board and lodging at Trinity College cost only $415 a year; now they are over $6,000. So $1,000 in 1923 had a purchasing power at university of about $14,000 in 1988. My marks in the honour matriculation examinations were very high and Trinity College gave me a small scholarship ('other things being equal sons of the clergy preferred'), which was increased the next year to enable me to live in residence. I also won university scholarships. Working during the day and studying at night from 1921 to 1923 meant that when I was sixteen, seventeen, and eighteen I worked too hard and played too little, a vice to which I have been addicted most of my life.

3

The University of Toronto
1923–1927

I was fortunate to get my university education at Toronto in the mid-twenties. The University of Toronto had reached what to my mind is the ideal size for a university, about five thousand students (now it has over twenty-eight thousand full-time students on its main campus). Classes were small and the teaching staff in the subjects I was interested in was excellent. I participated in two vibrant activities, the Student Christian Movement and the Hart House Debating Union. I combined membership in a large university with the close communal life of a small residential Anglican college, Trinity, which had only one hundred and sixty-five students, all but twenty-seven living in residence. (Now Trinity has eleven hundred full-time students of whom only four hundred live in residence.) I was able to get interesting work in the summer.

When I entered the University of Toronto in the autumn of 1923, at the age of eighteen, I was a socialist, a Canadian nationalist, and a fervent believer in the League of Nations. In my first term at the university I joined a Student Christian Movement (SCM) study group on Christianity and war which met on the university campus on Sunday afternoons and I was an active member of the SCM during my four years at the university. In the twenties most leading radicals at universities in Canada who had been brought up as Protestants and were interested in international affairs were active in the SCM. Some critics said of it that it was neither student, Christian, nor a movement. The SCM made fun of its right-wing critics by singing at its meetings a song by Davidson Ketchum with the refrain:

Poisoning the student mind, poisoning the student mind,
Bad men, bold men, villains double-dyed

'Neath their smiling countenances hide
Spiritual arsenic, moral cyanide,
For poisoning the student, poisoning the student,
Poisoning the student mind.

In November of my first term I attended an SCM meeting at Hart House in the university addressed by Paul Blanchard, an organizer for the United States' socialist organization, the League for Industrial Democracy (LID). The league was a sort of Fabian Society for the United States. Indeed, the title of American Fabian Society was considered when it was founded in 1921 as the successor to the Intercollegiate Socialist Society, which had been founded in 1905 by Upton Sinclair and supported by Clarence Darrow and Jack London, the society's first president. Jack London coined an apt phrase in 1905 when he said that the ISS was a reaction against 'the passionless pursuit of passionless intelligence' at American universities, an accusation echoed sixty years later by student radicals at universities in the United States and Canada. The League for Social Reconstruction, founded in Canada in 1932, eleven years after the foundation of the LID, felt such a close kinship with the LID that it considered calling itself the League for Economic Democracy.

On 8 January I went to a meeting called to discuss whether we should establish a branch of the league at the university. About a dozen men students were at the meeting – no women. Women attended SCM conferences, but women students were not invited to meetings such as that on the LID and I cannot recall anyone, teacher or student, suggesting they should be. The only decision we made was to hold weekly meetings, and it was not until four weeks later that we decided to petition the university authorities for permission to establish a university chapter of the LID. We authorized a delegation to call on Sir Robert Falconer, the president of the university, to present the petition.

From 21 December on, Colonel J.B. Maclean, the president of the influential *Financial Post*, had been attacking the LID in the *Post* as an agency for spreading Red propaganda and the *Toronto Telegram* had joined in the attack. The articles in the *Post*, which were displayed prominently on its front page, continued until 15 February 1924. When I read them now I am amazed by their venom and their low intellectual level.

The first attack by the *Financial Post* on the LID began as follows: 'The foreign campaign against Canadianism and capitalism in the colleges, and particularly in Toronto University, keeps up. It was inaugurated by John Rothschild [later identified as a young German-Russian] and his group of young German, Polish and Russian students – some of whose vicious moral ideas were admittedly contrary to those taught in all decent Canadian homes.' The article went on to say that the LID was 'one of the many subsidiaries of a foreign organization with headquarters in New York operating particularly against Great Britain, the United States and France. It ... was under the direction of a notorious personage known as Mrs. Florence Nightingale Kelly. Mrs. Kelly's real name is Mrs. Wischnewetzky.' It was linked with 'the Rand School for Science, in which Scott Nearing was a leading light. The school was raided by the United States government about five years ago, because of its immoral teachings.' Scott Nearing 'had been in German pay during the war.' His 'promoters [were] the Soviet Bureau, New York – which is the old Central German War Council which carried on espionage in the United States and Canada.'

According to a later article in the *Financial Post*, the League for Industrial Democracy was a subsidiary of the Worker's Party, which, in turn, was the United States' and Canadian end of the Third Internationale of Moscow. 'The men really back of the whole movement are the same men who are directing the Soviet campaign on the continent – the same men who, during the war, were aiding and abetting German activities in Canada and the United States.'

Paul Blanchard was, the *Post* said, the author of an article 'distributed quietly among young men and women in Toronto colleges' which put forward 'views that are not usually permitted in well-regulated Sunday schools.' The writer must have had his tongue in his cheek and must have counted on Colonel Maclean being so stupid that he would not realize he was employing a fifth columnist with a liking for satire. The views which were not usually permitted in well-regulated Sunday schools were probably the kind of views disseminated in the 'literature' mentioned in the *Post's* first article on the LID, 'literature which advocates sex and other standards of such a nature that they dare not reveal them to the police authorities.' This material was distributed by the Worker's Party of which the LID was a subsidiary. The Worker's Party taught that the first step was the destruction of religion and the churches, especially the Roman Catholic Church; that marriage was an institution of capitalists; that desire to live together expressed before a registrar and to part in the same way were the only necessities of marriage and divorce; that there would be no restrictions on the number of lovers on either side.

As a result of these articles, when our delegation called on Sir Robert Falconer he advised us not to press our petition until the row between the LID and the *Post* was cleared up. It was his opinion that, as matters stood, the university authorities would not grant the petition. I commented in my diary that, though one might agree with the president thus far, what he added showed a lamentable state of affairs at the university, for he said that the university officials were virtually civil servants and had to be careful not to offend the government at Queen's Park: 'It is a disgrace that a university which is supposed to be a centre of inquiry into the truth, should have to consider the feelings and inclinations of any government.' I would not have been so surprised at Falconer's dictum if I had known that a year or so before he had in a public speech said that a university professor, 'like a judge or a great civil servant ... has high functions the exercise of which may make it wise for him not to perform all the offices of an ordinary citizen,' and that it was 'expedient' that someone teaching in a state university should neither be active in 'party politics' nor express himself on 'burning political questions.'

Three years later, the poet A.J.M. Smith satirized the views of the kind of businessman exemplified by Colonel Maclean in his poem 'College $pirit' published in the *McGill Fortnightly Review* under the pseudonym 'Vincent Starr':

Suffer the little children
To come unto me,
Said the Big Business Man
As he endowed a University ...

We shall instruct our students in
The value of discipline:
Esprit de corps
Won the war,
Did it not?

We shall preach the divine right
Of Capital to its dividends,
For here economics begins
And ends;

And our students shall grow God-fearing.
That is, respectful of money,
And learn to distrust Scott Nearing,
And think Poets funny ...

In the twenties and thirties most of the big business men in the English-speaking communities of Canada professed great admiration for Britain and British traditions yet many, possibly most of them, advocated for Canada curbs on freedom of speech repugnant to British traditions. Probably they thought that freedom of speech, particularly at universities, would endanger their material interests. French radical-socialists in the thirties were said to have their hearts on their left and their purses on their right. These big business men had pro-British sentiments on their left and their material interests on their right.

At the beginning of my second year at the university a Hart House debating union was established modelled on the Oxford and Cambridge unions, and I soon became prominent in its debates. At the first debate on 13 November 1924 Paul Martin was the first speaker. According to my diary he 'was a little heavy ... tended to be too thundering,' and a succeeding speaker, Maurice Cody, 'was much like Martin.' A few months later I, for the first time, led off a debate. In my diary I said: 'In leading the debate I believe that I gave the best speech I have yet given at Hart House. The reports published before the debate which said that I was noted for my break with the traditions of public speaking in Canada, believing that in order to convince an audience one had first to make them laugh and stating that I used epigrammatic sallies – though largely unfounded yet did me good by putting me on my mettle.'

My desire to be bright in my speeches at Hart House led me onto dangerous ground. In a debate in October 1925 I contended that Arthur Meighen, the leader of the Conservative party, was probably more radical than the Liberal prime minister, Mackenzie King, and went on to say, in words borrowed from an article in the *Canadian Forum*, 'Mr. King's chief claim to distinction is that he is the grandson of a rebel. He could never be the grandfather of one.' I had interpreted the statement in an intellectual sense. My audience was less naive. I was surprised by the laughter and applause.

When my application for a Rhodes scholarship was being considered by the selection committee in the autumn of 1926 the secretary of the committee, Roland Michener, attended a Hart House debate at which I was a principal speaker. His report to the committee on my debating abilities was, I am sure, one of the reasons I was chosen as a Rhodes scholar. The committee probably hoped that I would become the first Canadian president of the Oxford Union. I didn't. David Lewis did in 1934.

I was fortunate to be studying political economy at the University of

Toronto from 1923 to 1927 because at that time the teaching staff in political economy and related departments was first-rate and stimulating: R.M. MacIver, G.M. Wrong, W.P.M. Kennedy, C.R. Fay, Harold Innis, Vincent Bladen, Norman (Larry) MacKenzie, Forrester Davison, and Gilbert Jackson. Kennedy's lectures on the constitutional history of Canada were sometimes dramatic. I remember the final words of his lecture on the rebellion of 1837: 'A nation that has no rebellion in its history has no soul,' and with this curtain line he flicked his gown and strode out of the lecture hall. Innis, on the other hand, could scarcely have been more pedestrian in the way he delivered his lectures. If students had at that time published critiques of their lecturers, Innis, one of Canada's most creative scholars, would have been castigated for his lectures and this might have dangerously weakened his self-confidence.

MacIver had the most influence on me. His best book, *The Modern State*, was just about to be published and his lectures were a dress rehearsal for the book. One technique he used was to spend one lecture expounding a leading theory of the state in such a way as to make it sound utterly convincing and to spend the next lecture demolishing it. Having expounded and demolished half a dozen theories of the state he expounded his own. That lecture was not followed by a demolition.

MacIver happily urged us to read Walter Lippmann's *The Phantom Public* and *Public Opinion*. In my last year at Toronto, Forrester Davison introduced me to books on jurisprudence by Roscoe Pound and Benjamin Cardozo. These books gave me new insights into political theory and since my tutors and examiners at Oxford had not read Pound and Cardozo, they were impressed by the originality of my views. (I have sometimes wondered whether Harold Laski did not make his early reputation in much the same way by his *A Grammar of Politics*.) I thank Innis for introducing me to Thorstein Veblen's *The Engineer and the Price System*, *The Instinct of Workmanship*, and *The Theory of the Leisure Class*. Bladen said to me that R.H. Tawney had said in lucid English in one short book, *The Acquisitive Society*, what Veblen had said turgidly in three books, and Tawney's book influenced me more than any other book I read at the University of Toronto. This book, written at the end of the First World War, moved me by its eloquent appeal to workers by hand and by brain to build a new social order. I do not know who recommended to me two books which made me for a time a guild socialist: *The Guild State* by G.R.S. Taylor and *Guild Socialism Restated* by G.D.H. Cole. In my first term at the university I became so enthusiastic a guild socialist that I wrote an article for the college magazine in which I contended that guild socialism was no new thing. It was a mistake to think that progress was always the invention of something new; it was frequently the rediscovery of something old. Guild socialism was based on the democratization not only of political but of industrial and economic affairs and involved representation of the people by their function in society, not by their geographical location. The desire of the movement was to catch the spirit of the medieval guild which imbued its members with a craftmen's love for his art, not an automaton's hatred for his machine. Ramsay MacDonald's *Socialism: Critical and Constructive*, which I read a year later, brought me back to the mainstream of British socialist thought from the modified syndicalism of the guild socialists.

My approach to international affairs when I was at the University of Toronto was, I think, much the same as that of most intellectuals in the western world, especially those under thirty. In my first year at the university I put my views in the form of an article on Woodrow Wilson, who had just died. The United States should, I wrote, have remained neutral in the war. Its entry into the conflict lengthened the war since it could no longer put pressure on the Allies to make a compromise peace in August 1917 and February 1918. 'In both cases the Allies refused to consider terms because their ignoble demands [set forth in their secret treaties with Italy and Romania] could only be obtained from a prostrate foe.' The truth of Woodrow Wilson's assertion that 'it must be a peace without victory' had been shown only too clearly by the six years' misery following Germany's decisive defeat: 'The victor always dictates an unjust peace to the vanquished. The "fight to the knock-out blow" ended in the inevitable peace of vengeance ... The peace which was concluded was not Wilsonian but Carthaginian, not reconstructive but revengeful, a peace not to end war but to breed war.'

In my last year at the University of Toronto I was angered by the sermon given at the annual memorial day service in the Trinity College chapel by a visiting clergyman, Canon H.F.D. Woodcock. I was editor of the college magazine, the *Trinity University Review*, and I wrote a brief editorial entitled 'Armistice Day 1926' which vigorously attacked the views Woodcock had put forward in his sermon without mentioning his name or the memorial service. He replied in a thousand-word letter to the *Review* and I countered with a fifteen-hundred-word editorial.

My first editorial began as follows:

Each recurring Armistice Day finds our hearts more bitter. The old platitudes can no longer console us. It is not only the tragedy of the years from 1914 to 1918 that oppresses, it is the greater tragedy of the years that followed – the years of disenchantment. Our once comforting creed has forsaken us. No longer can we believe in Germany's sole responsibility for the war; in her sole violations of rules of warfare and of international morality. The history of nineteenth century foreign policy is too obscure yet for any final judgment to be passed on war guilt but we know enough not to speak hysterically [as Woodcock had in his sermon] of Germany as a 'nation running amok.'

I had by 1926 come to believe – a belief I still adhere to – that the cause of war is international anarchy. I had been greatly influenced by the thesis advanced by G. Lowes Dickinson in his *The International Anarchy 1904–1914* that the cause of the First World War was 'the anarchy of armed States pursuing by war the maintenance or the extension of power.' Salvador de Madariaga put the same thought in another way when, writing about disarmament, he said, 'The problem of disarmament is not the problem of disarmament. It is the problem of the setting up and the organization of the world community.' In my second editorial I said that 'the condition of European anarchy [had] made war inevitable in 1914 or a few years later.'

In this ultimate [war] guilt all the Great Powers must take their share of responsibility, responsibility for 'the general situation which grouped the Powers of the Entente against those of the Triple Alliance; the armaments and counter-armaments; the colonial and economic rivalry; the racial and national problems in South East Europe; and the long series of previous crises, in each case tidied over, but leaving behind, every one of them, a legacy of fresh mistrust and fear, which made every new crisis worse than the one before.

And what was my prescription for world peace? I quoted with approval what Sir Edward Grey, the foreign minister of Britain in August 1914, had recently written in his memoirs: 'No enduring security can be found in competing armaments and in separate alliances.' I said that arbitration, security, and disarmament were inseparable, the thesis of the abortive Geneva Protocol of 1924: 'There can be no disarmament unless the nations find security elsewhere than in national armies; there can be no security unless each nation binds itself to accept the decisions of arbitral courts.' It was the duty of governments to submit their disputes with other countries to an arbitral court and to accept the decision of the court. It was the duty of every citizen to take the pledge which COPEC had recommended to the Christian churches. (COPEC was the inter-denominational Conference on Politics, Economics and Citizenship held in England in 1924. William Temple, the archbishop of Canterbury, was its leading spirit.) The COPEC pledge was that the Christian churches 'should unreservedly condemn, and refuse to support in any way, a war waged before the matter in dispute has been submitted to an arbitral tribunal, or in defiance of the decision of such a tribunal.'

At that time I did not realize that arbitration had to be accompanied by peaceful change if it were to provide an alternative to war as a method of settling international disputes. Arbitration under the Geneva Protocol meant the settlement of international disputes on the basis of existing rights as set forth in treaties and international law. But almost all dangerous international disputes are not over what are the existing rights of the nations which are parties to the dispute, but over what changes, if any, should be made in existing rights. By the late twenties it was evident that the principal discontented powers, Germany, Japan, and Italy, had legitimate grievances which could not be settled by arbitration on the basis of the status quo but required making article 19 of the League of Nations covenant effective. This was the article which spoke of revising treaties and changing 'international conditions whose continuance might endanger the peace of the world.'

The importance of the COPEC pledge of 1924 and the similar appeal in 1929 of the World Alliance of Churches lay not so much in their advocacy of arbitration as in their insistence that the good citizen had the duty to disobey his government if it embarked on an unjust war. In my editorial supporting this doctrine I said that by disobeying a government which refused to accept arbitration under the auspices of the League the citizen would be putting the decision of the League above the decision of his national government.

In my first summer at the University of Toronto I went back to work in the Audit Department of the Ontario government. In my second summer I tried something completely different and a good deal more remunerative; I worked as a guide or spieler on a sightseeing bus in Toronto. This was the first time university students were employed as spielers in Toronto. Some of our non-university predecessors had earned the disfavour of the civic authorities by using too much imagination in their description of the route. Thus they would point out as their home a mansion in the most fashionable part of Toronto, Rosedale; if the owner was present and heard this he might protest to the authorities. Another jest to which exception was taken was also perpetrated in Rosedale. The spieler would point at a very handsome house and say it belonged to a man who had made millions as a taxi driver before meters were invented.

Our customers were mainly Americans. I thought they should know much more about Canada than they did and I was annoyed by their ignorance. It was only with great difficulty that I could persuade them that the provincial parliament buildings in Toronto were not the parliament buildings of Canada. Many of them would ask me with bated breath, as if it were a terrible secret, whether it was true that Roman Catholics constituted a majority of the population of Canada. I was always surprised by their belief in the acceptance of American stamps on mail posted in Canada. The aspect of Toronto which interested them most depended on their place of residence in the United States: if from the south it was the absence of negroes; if from the west, the absence of wooden buildings; if from New York they would make some remark about Toronto's slums and suggest, as if almost proud of it, that I should see the much worse ones in New York. The most fascinating place in Toronto for any visitor, no matter where he came from, was the birthplace of Mary Pickford. On every trip we would make a special stop, the only stop on the tour, beside that famous house, 212 University Avenue, so that all could gaze at the insignificant dwelling where the great movie star had been born. We used this stop to sell picture postcards of Toronto to our captive customers. I would say that the profits on the sale of the postcards went to the widows and orphans; 'the driver is the widow and I am the orphan.' Our customers were charged one dollar for the tour. We were paid $20 a week for a seven-day week and we made about another $10 a week from tips and the sale of postcards. In three months I made $400, the equivalent in purchasing power of about $3,000 in 1988 dollars.

I was first with first-class honours in the honours course of political science in my four years at the university; indeed, I secured first-class honours in every subject in every examination. I received prizes for academic achievement. I was prominent in college and university debates. I was editor of the Trinity College magazine and acted in the college dramatic society. All this marked me as a potential Rhodes scholar. But one of the requirements for the scholarship was that the applicant have physical vigour, demonstrated by participation in athletics or in other ways. I was no good at athletics so I demonstrated my physical vigour by working in the summer of 1926 as a trackman on a Canadian National Railway extra gang in Muskoka. At night I taught the other labourers as a Frontier College instructor. I was awarded a Rhodes scholarship that autumn.

The extra gang consisted of about ninety men. More than half were recent immigrants from Slavic countries: Ukraine, Czechoslovakia, Poland, and Bulgaria. There was one Italian, one Dutchman, and one French Canadian. The others were of British origin. The British, plus one Ukrainian, lived in one boarding-car, the others in the other boarding-car. The British group said they liked their Ukrainian because he was so clean and because on Sundays he would sweep their car out; also he would never speak to anyone but in the evening he would sit by himself on the side of the railway car staring out into the woods or the fields, brooding. One Sunday evening when I had succeeded in striking up a conversation with him I said I was surprised he spoke English so well when he had been in Canada for only two years. 'Oh,' he said, 'I was here before the war from 1906 to 1912. I was only sixteen when I came over with my elder brother.' He had made his 'stake' and had returned to his home in the Austrian Ukraine to see his parents. He was conscripted into the Austrian army and fought for five years. His village on the Russian border was invaded and held for three years by the Russians. For four years he fought without a word from home. Shortly after his return home he found that his savings in the bank had become worthless as the result of inflation. Now he had nothing to show for his twelve years working in Canada and fighting in the Austrian army. It was no wonder he brooded.

Mike Levkus, a Czechoslovak, had also been drafted into the Austrian army in 1917. He was still in training when the morale of the Austrian army collapsed early in 1918. He deserted and went home but a week later the police dragged him and the other deserters in his village back to the army. They deserted again and again and the farce of forced return to the army continued. Desertion had become so common that it was no longer possible to treat it as a serious offence. Then came the revolution and Thomas Masaryk became president at Prague.

My work as a Frontier College instructor centred on the class in English which I held in the evening in the dining-car four times a week. The achievement which gave me the greatest pleasure was teaching our one Italian workman, Frank Molasso, to sign his name. He was so proud when he finally succeeded. One evening when I had been giving the class for about two months I asked the men to come early to class the next day so that I could have someone take our picture. At 7:15 one man came in but it was not until 7:40, ten minutes after the regular hour for beginning the class, that a second man appeared. He had on his white Sunday shirt. He was late because he had been dressing for the occasion. From then on the men dribbled in: one with a new blue shirt buttoned at the neck, all with their usually tumbled hair combed and plastered down with water. I apologized for causing them so much trouble and the class went on its ordinary way. At ten minutes after eight a ripple of amusement disturbed the routine. George Jenzik entered the far door of the car attired in trousers with a crease, a vest, a white shirt, a tie, and a stiff white collar, his full-dress clothes.

One of my students wrote a poem for me entitled 'Summer Evening':

It was a summer evening
And pleasant was day
When we were working
At railway to gether won day.
You know how it was here
Because you saw that all.
It is golden summer
For us and every won.

The foreman on my railway extra gang said that my given name was impossible and decreed that I should be called Scotty not Escott. Lester Pearson, when his colleagues in the air force decided that he should be called Mike and not Lester, kept Mike for the rest of his life. Perhaps he would not have become prime minister if he had not done so. If I had been as wise I would have kept Scotty. It might have helped me disguise my arrogance just as Mike helped Pearson disguise his ambition.

My membership in the railway gang increased my command of language. One man said of a talkative colleague: 'He would talk the hind legs off the Lamb of God.' Another, contending that when you are in the army there are worse things than fighting, said: 'When ye's fighting, ye ain't marching.' The government employment office was 'the slave market.' When we had prunes at a meal, they were called 'C.P.R. strawberries.' Figs were 'C.P.R. raspberries.' Baked beans were 'musical fruit.' When life became too difficult for our sole French Canadian he would explode with one long word, ending with a rising note on the last syllable: goddamsonnovabitchsonnovahooerkoksukair. When similarly tried, my Slav colleagues would say something like kihinskykuyamelinkybum. I have never had the courage to ask a Slav what this meant.

Towards the end of my time at the University of Toronto one of the professors of theology at Trinity urged me to consider becoming a clergyman. I would, he said, be a bishop in no time. I had by then lost much of my faith and I was not tempted by this vision of ecclesiastical glory. If I had not been awarded a Rhodes scholarship I would probably have gone to Osgoode Hall Law School and have practised law in Toronto. I would not have met Ruth Herriot at Oxford who became my wife. I am most grateful to the Rhodes scholarship selection committee.

4

Oxford

1927–1930

One of the wisest decisions I have made in my life was not to go straight to Oxford, as almost all North American Rhodes scholars did, but to borrow money from my father to finance a two-month-long trip by way of New York, Naples, Rome, Florence, Milan, Geneva, Paris, and London. I had up till then never been more than about a hundred miles from Toronto. Making Naples my first European city gave me a stimulating culture shock which I would not have got from landing in England and my first experience of the special beauties of the Mediterranean was Capri, Sorrento, and Amalfi. I am fortunate I was born early enough to see them before mass holiday travel made them accessible to over eighty thousand tourists a year but diminished their enchantment.

In Rome I had my first experience of participating in an international conference. I represented the newly established National Federation of Canadian University Students at the annual meeting of the Conféderation Internationale des Etudiants at which the NFCUS was admitted to the CIE. The struggles for power within the CIE, the bitter personal disputes, the back-stabbing, the national animosities, and the accompanying political intrigues were a revelation to me. There were two blocs within the CIE – the French bloc, and the Anglo-Saxon bloc to which the countries which had been neutral in the Great War adhered. The French bloc had been losing influence but the two groups were still evenly enough balanced to provide the basis for hard-fought struggles. I was not impressed by the CIE. In my report to the NFCUS I suggested that we might try for at least a year or so to see what could be done to turn it into an organization which would effectively promote international understanding and friendship. That I was beginning to comprehend something about the nature of Canada and of the part which French Canadians could play in Canada's international relations was indicated by my recommendation that the NFCUS should send to the next annual meeting of the CIE at least two delegates, one of whom should be a French Canadian and the other able to speak French: 'I am optimistic enough to hope that a French Canadian might be a link between the French and English points of view in the meetings of the CIE. Canada is frequently spoken of as an interpreter between the United States and Great Britain but I believe it is even more important in the CIE for her to serve as an interpreter of England to France.'

At the conference I learned the necessity of travelling with a dinner jacket if you were attending an international conference in Europe, even a student one. The Italians gave a dinner for the conference and I had to put together a dinner jacket: the coat and waistcoat came from a Dutchman and the shirt and collar from a South African. I supplemented these with my own tie and dark blue trousers.

I wrote an article for the Toronto *Star Weekly* on my impressions of fascist Italy. I said I had visited a little beer parlour near the Colosseum. On the wall was a placard with the words, 'It is forbidden in this place to blaspheme or to discuss politics.' In my concluding paragraph I said: 'Naples, Rome, Florence, Milan, on the docks, railways, streets, stations, everywhere, armed men. Soldiers of all kinds, fascisti in their black shirts, the national army, carabiniere, other policemen, and then more black shirts, special fascist military police, everywhere in Italy, armed men. Armed for what? For display, for civil uprising, or for international war?' I was delighted to receive fifteen dollars for the article, the first time I had made money out of writing.

In Geneva I attended a conference of university students from the British Commonwealth at Alfred Zimmern's school of international studies. There were lectures by Zimmern and by leaders of Commonwealth delegations to the annual Assembly of the League of Nations which was then meeting and we were constant attendants at sessions of the League Council and Assembly. At the Assembly I heard Briand, Stresemann, and Austen Chamberlain speak. This was the second assembly at which Germany was represented.

Briand's speech was a masterpiece of French oratory. It was the first time I had heard such oratory and I was impressed. I wrote in my diary: 'The gestures, the voice, the face – all took part in the dramatic nature of the speech. At times he shouted, at times he whispered. He wept over the sufferings of France. He had a very curious gesture of clenching both hands and then moving them up and down above the table without touching it. At another time he gave the Fascist salute for about five minutes ... He theatrically accepted the hand of Germany.'

The Assembly applauded loudly when Stresemann in his speech announced Germany's adherence to the optional clause of the statute of the Permanent Court of International Justice. Briand's speech was delivered in the intervals between bursts of applause. Chamberlain's speech was received in almost complete silence. Once during it an Australian clapped and once a Canadian but that was all. He spoke as a schoolmaster to his pupils, and they were unintelligent pupils. It was a lecture, a dressing down of the Assembly, which had misbehaved itself and was on the mat before Sir Austen. On the one side was the British Commonwealth; on the other the Assembly. He used the anomalous constitution of the Commonwealth as a cloak to escape criticism for Britain's non-adherence to the optional clause and the Geneva Protocol. My comment on this in my diary was that the constitution of the Commonwealth should be changed 'so that every Commonwealth government can be held responsible for its own inaction or misdeeds.' The dominions had a responsibility to the Assembly as full members of it. 'They should accept the full responsibility themselves and not allow Great Britain to use them as an excuse for herself escaping her responsibilities.'

O.D. Skelton, who had been made head of the fledgling Canadian Department of External Affairs two years before, was in Geneva as a member of the Canadian delegation. He invited me to lunch. I expected him to look like my idea of a polished diplomat, and instead he looked like a college professor, which is what he had been until two years before. I asked him when Mr Mackenzie King would be coming to Geneva and he replied 'that King had said he would never attend another conference – the Imperial Conference [of 1926] had been too much for him.'

Before I left Toronto my teachers at the university and Burgon Bickersteth, the warden of Hart House, had given me letters of introduction. One was to the Dean of Windsor, who invited me for a weekend at the deanery. A fellow guest at dinner was Sir Clive Wigram, assistant private secretary to George V. He said that the king was much annoyed at the recent complaint by Arnold Bennett that no member of the royal family had attended the funeral of Thomas Hardy. 'It is amazing the fuss that was made about that man. It just shows what can be done to a man if the newspapers take him up.'

Immediately after my appointment to a Rhodes scholarship Bickersteth persuaded me that the college I should go to in Oxford was not Balliol, where so many Canadian Rhodes scholars went, but his college,

Christ Church, and he cabled Christ Church asking that I be admitted to the college and be given rooms 'not in Meadows.' I was given ground-floor rooms in Peckwater quad. Bickersteth's prejudice against the Meadow buildings could have been based on the 'bastard Gothic ugliness' of that Victorian building contrasted with the architectural glories of the rest of the college, but my guess is that it was based on his belief that Meadows was full of dull, hard-working, middle-class students and that the undergraduates worth knowing, including those with titles or wealth or both, lived in other parts of the college. I was therefore surprised when, many years later, I found that Evelyn Waugh, in his *Brideshead Revisited*, had placed the wealthy aristocrat Sebastian Flyte in rooms in Meadows.

When I came to Oxford in the autumn of 1927 the standard of living in the western world was higher than before the First World War which meant that it was higher than it had ever been and it was generally assumed that it would continue to go up year after year. My first two years at Oxford were passed in what seems to me now, six decades later, a carefree world. That world ended in the autumn of 1929 with the onset of the great depression followed by a second world war and a perilous peace. Oxford in my time, especially Christ Church, was still very much what it had been at the beginning of the century. Public school men, the Oxford accent, and well-to-do undergraduates set the tone. When someone at my college complained about the size of his term bills the bursar was reported to have exploded that no one should come to Christ Church who had to worry about the expense of living there. Expenses at Christ Church were high, partly because we not only had breakfast served to us in our rooms but we could have lunch and tea served there and we could give lunch and tea parties in our rooms.

During the day most of us wore plus-fours (golf trousers) and Harris tweed jackets. When we went to dinner in the great hall we pulled grey flannel trousers over our plus-fours. It was a strange sight to see students doing this as they walked up the impressive grand staircase to the great hall. Our wardrobe had to include not only a dinner jacket but also formal evening dress – tailcoat, stiff white shirt, white tie – which we wore to special dinners and balls and when a principal speaker in a debate at the Oxford Union.

In my first year I had to borrow from my father to supplement my income of £400 a year from the Rhodes Trust. Fortunately in my second and third years I won prizes and scholarships amounting to over £300 and for the first time in my life I had money for luxuries – good clothes, books, and travel. I loved Oxford and London and the English countryside. I revelled in the Oxford system of going to almost no lectures and of having in my first two undergraduate years two tutorials a week and three essays every two weeks.

I was fortunate in my tutors. I had Roy Harrod in economics, Keith Feiling in history, W.G.S. Adams in political science, and Humphrey Sumner on the development of international relations since 1815. My tutor in philosophy was one of the last of the old-style Oxford academics – a brilliant scholar who, I believe, never published anything, not even a book review. He used to make obscure noises all the time during a tutorial and he was forever quoting Latin which I did not understand. He bore with me even though philosophy was my weak subject. At the end of my first term with him he uttered a typical Oxford judgment: 'Many of your essays for the term were second-class but they were the second-class work of a first-class mind.' Oxford tutors prided themselves on their ability, early in an encounter with a student, to discern whether he had a first-class mind, a second-class, or third-class. Knowing my limitations, he gave me the sound advice that in my final examination on the history of philosophy I should not try to display too great a knowledge of philosophers after Kant. I took his advice and confined my answers to questions about Descartes, Leibniz, and Berkeley.

Humphrey Sumner's brilliance made him an intimidating tutor. In my second tutorial with him he asked me, 'Are you a Near Eastern expert?' and 'Are you strong on Italy?' When I had painstakingly prepared an essay for him on some crisis in international relations in the nineteenth century, he would, after I had read it to him, come out with some such criticism as, 'But Reid, you failed to mention the despatch of 16 April 1885 from the British ambassador in Vienna.'

I have discovered in my papers some of the essays I wrote for Harrod on economics. In one I stated my approach to economics: 'The value of economics is in guiding society in the task of improving itself and to do this it must have an ethical basis ... We are concerned with that production and distribution of goods and services which will make for the greatest social good ... The concept of social costs and social utilities should form the basis of economic theory.' I have not deviated from that view, an example of the truth of Maynard Keynes's statement that 'in the field of economic and political philosophy there are not many who are influenced by new theories after they are twenty-five or thirty years of age.'

Roy Harrod, after having been my tutor for a year, told Harold Acton that I was 'charming and bland.' Marjorie Perham, a tutor at St Hugh's, whom I had met in Geneva in September 1927 and saw a half-dozen times in my first year, told one of her students that I was 'an engaging youth but a butterfly.' I said at the time in a letter home that 'it is the proper thing at Oxford to pretend to be a butterfly, but I'm not certain that I'm glad the pose has been convincing,' and I didn't like the thought that I was a bland butterfly.

I debated in the Oxford Union, I was treasurer of the university Labour Club, and secretary and then president of the English Club. The committee of the English Club when I was president included Stephen Spender and Elizabeth Harman (later Elizabeth Longford) who had the well-deserved reputation of being the most distinguished intellectual among the women undergraduates. The membership fee for the club was low but we had hundreds of members and the revenue from fees was sufficient to pay for excellent dinners at which the committee entertained themselves and the speaker of the evening. The only record I have of a conversation with Stephen Spender is that he told me in May 1930 that he was able to understand a good deal of the new poem by T.S. Eliot, 'Ash Wednesday.'

As secretary of the club I wrote to D.H. Lawrence in 1928 asking him to speak. He replied from the south of France: 'No, I'm sorry I can't come and address your English club. My health is a genuine curse, lately, and won't let me come to England, especially in winter. All I can do is to swear into the void of the Mediterranean. But perhaps it will chirp up one day.' He died two years later.

The letters declining invitations to speak were rich in polite formulas. A.P. Herbert's formula was, 'I'm so behindhand with so many things that I really must not take on anything more.' Sheila Kaye-Smith wrote, 'I have given up lecturing for the moment, finding that it interferes unduly with my work.' Havelock Ellis was firmer: 'This is the kind of thing I never do for it clashes with my proper work as a writer.' Arnold Bennett's formula was, 'I never give lectures or speak in public. This kind of activity is quite outside my field of work.' My collection of polite formulas encouraged me a few years ago to invent one for the use of my friend John Holmes, who suffered from the generous weakness of an inability to refuse requests for his help even though acceptance interfered with his proper work of writing books on Canadian foreign policy. I told him that I would, if he agreed, have a thousand postcards printed reading as follows:

I greatly appreciate your invitation to
   attend a conference.
   write an article.

do a book review.
give a speech.
read your manuscript.
give an interview.

I regret I cannot accept. I am desperately trying to finish a difficult book on Canadian foreign policy and I have to spend my whole time on that.

All he would have to do would be to sign the thousand postcards and give them to his secretary; whenever a request for his help came in she would tick the appropriate clause, date the postcard, and mail it.

Harold Acton was one of the speakers at the English Club in 1928. He had been notorious in Oxford a few years before as an aesthete and a homosexual. After the meeting we had drinks in the rooms of the president of the club. That lasted till 11:30 when he decided he wanted to call on an undergraduate friend who lived on Merton Street. The young man had gone to bed but Acton woke him up and we stayed there till 12:15 and got back to Christ Church just before the gates closed at 12:30. He then woke up his host, Roy Harrod. When I left him in Harrod's rooms he presented me with the book he had been quoting from in his lecture, D.H. Lawrence's *The Woman Who Rode Away*. He inscribed it 'To dear Escott Reid with every hope that this will affect his libido, and with lots of love from Harold Acton.' I had no idea I had aroused his affection.

Harold Nicolson was the speaker at the last meeting of the club in June 1930 at which I presided as president. At the dinner with the executive of the club before the meeting he told me a story of his interview with Beaverbrook when they were discussing whether he should leave the diplomatic service and write for the *Daily Express*. It had been a very businesslike discussion until he remarked that the room looked so different from its appearance in Lady Beaverbrook's time. Beaverbrook burst into tears. Nicolson said that he thought that Beaverbrook's Empire campaign was to a certain extent to salve his sense of sin and to perpetuate the memory of Lady Beaverbrook because she was always saying that all he cared for was money, money, whereas this campaign would certainly cost him money. In his paper at the club Nicolson said that he was fascinated by the psychology of modern Germany. The Germans suffered from an inferiority complex and were in consequence self-assertive and yet diffident. They believed in knowledge for knowledge's sake. They thought that if a thing was difficult to understand it was therefore worth understanding. The favourable thing about the German character was that they had thrown aside convention. That was the pleasant obverse to their lack of tradition. They had come to some reasonable way of thinking about sex. The Reichstag had amended the code to bring it into line with modern thought on sex. They had discussed matters which it would embarrass him even to mention.

Nicolson was asked whether he believed that there was an analogy between the unpleasant sides of the German character and of the American. He replied that he would not comment on this since he had never visited the United States but when he was walking back with me to my lodgings after the meeting he said to me that there was probably an analogy. I wondered whether this might mean that American diplomacy would consequently be as stupid as German diplomacy before the war. He thought not because the Americans would not be so terrified as the Germans had been, but should they become fearful of a European coalition against them they would probably be as stupid. At present they were stupid enough in their diplomacy and were successful only on such rare occasions as when they sent Dwight Morrow to Mexico as ambassador.

What, I asked, did he think was the distinction between the old and the new diplomacy; was there really any difference or was it not true that behind the façade of the League of Nations there was the old balance of power? He thought that the League made just the difference because if it had existed in 1914 Austria could not have refused to come to a meeting of the League Council to which Serbia had appealed. Germany would not have supported her in such a refusal. England would have said that whichever country broke the League covenant would have to fight her or rather that she would perform her obligations under the covenant. Sir Edward Grey failed because he could not get the powers to a conference. It also had to be remembered that in England at the end of July 1914 seven out of every ten people wanted war. They thought it would give the country a chance to show its courage and so on. Now that was changed because we had learnt from the lesson of the last war. I wanted to say that I thought the generation just younger than I had not learnt anything but by this time we were at my rooms and I had to serve lemon squash and gin to some dozen people.

As treasurer of the Labour Club I had occasionally to write letters to members of the club. I had come across a copy of a letter from a leading conservative trade union leader of the Labour party, J.R. Clynes, which had ended with, 'Yours for the revolution.' When writing to one of the more conservative members of the Labour Club I, with my tongue in my cheek, ended my letter, 'Yours for the revolution, Escott Reid.' The two strains in the British Labour party, the internationalist Marxist and the

England-centred Christian socialist, were exemplified in the songs we sang at meetings of the club: 'The Red Flag' and Blake's 'Jerusalem.'

One of the most interesting speakers in my last term at the club was W.J. Brown, who spoke at the end of May 1930. He was then a Labour MP and was in the left wing of the party. He came not from an industrial trade union but from the Civil Service Clerical Association of which he was general secretary. What he said foreshadowed his support for Oswald Mosley a few months later when Mosley resigned from the Labour cabinet. He, Nye Bevan, and John Strachey were for a short time the brains of the Mosley movement. All three left Mosley when his fascist tendencies became apparent. Brown was obsessed by the parallels between the existing situation in England and the Russian revolution. He called the present period the Kerensky regime. He foresaw the defeat of the Labour government if it should go to the country now or within a year, the return of a Conservative government, the industrial condition becoming worse and worse, and so to an overthrow of the parliamentary regime and the establishment of a dictatorship, Churchill having already pre-empted a claim, and then civil war to which he did not look forward, being a physical coward. The leaders of the Labour party, who had been trained in the trade union movement, had been accustomed all their life to petty compromises and in consequence they were unable to take decisions on matters of high policy. The result was that the civil servants had it their own way. What the Labour party needed was an influx of aristocratic renegades like Oswald Mosley and converts from the middle class. The phrase he used was 'a sprinkling of aristocrats.' They could be used to go part way on the road of revolution and then could be thrust aside.

I was a member of the Oxford University Dramatic Society (OUDS) during one of its best periods. The presidents of the club in my time were John Fernald, Peter Fleming, and Brewster Morgan. I did not rise to the heights of acting in an OUDS production but I was given by Fernald the exhausting jobs of rehearsals manager and property manager for the production of *The Fourteenth of July* in February 1928. My tasks included making noises by playing records of cheering crowd, angry mob, angelus bell, anvils, and bombardment. The other side of the bombardment record was 'large puppy, puppy dog, cat' so that I was in a constant state of terror that I would put the wrong side of the record on and have cats howling at the storming of the Bastille. At the dress rehearsal I was at the gramophone for the first time and was constantly putting wrong things on at the wrong time or too loudly, with the result that at one particularly horrible noise Theodore Komisarjevsky, the producer, jumped six rows of seats and rushed across the stage to the back of the theatre to make me stop. At the opening performance the only mistake I made was at the beginning when I played 'God Save the King' so fast that many members of the audience failed to recognize the signal to stand up.

As a member of the house committee of the OUDS I learned a trick in salesmanship. We had a large stock of a low-priced burgundy which almost no one would order. We made it the second most expensive burgundy on our wine list and it sold quickly. Members who did not know what burgundy to choose rejected the most expensive and chose the second most expensive.

An Indian student whom I did not know asked me to propose him for membership. I invited him to lunch with me at the club. Afterwards I spoke to a friend on the membership committee about my intention to propose the Indian for membership. He said, 'Until you brought the Indian to lunch there had never been an Indian in our dining-room. But now you've done that I suppose we can drop the bar against Indian members.' This is not the only time I have been blind to the existence of racial discriminations. Once many years ago in talking to a member of the Rideau Club in Ottawa I criticized the club for barring Jews from membership. (The club now has Jewish members.) He said, 'But you were a member of the University Club in Toronto in the thirties and it had no Jewish members.' I had never realized this.

My contemporaries in debates at the Oxford Union included future British politicians: Quintin Hogg, Dingle Foot, Michael Stewart, J.A. Boyd-Carpenter, J.P.W. Mallalieu, E.M. Lustgarten, D.C. Walker-Smith, James MacColl. I was elected secretary of the Union and was twice defeated for the presidency, once by Lustgarten and once by Mallalieu. I spoke in debates against such distinguished visitors as Neville Chamberlain and Winston Churchill. The critic of Union debates in one issue of the undergraduate magazine *The Isis* said that I was a speaker whom he had always admired and that I had 'less of a "pamphlet mind" than any other politician now prominent in the Union.' Another critic in *The Isis* later balanced this praise by stating: 'Mr. Reid was a sarcastic chap; he ought to be heard again but not by us.'

Shortly after my arrival in Oxford Eugene Forsey, whom I had met at the conference in Geneva and who was in his second year at Oxford, invited me to tea at his college, Balliol. I wrote in a letter home: 'He looks rather delicate, is highly strung and probably excitable and he possesses brains to rather an alarming degree.' We became good friends and spent two spring vacations together, walking and reading for examinations, one in Provence, the other on the French Riviera. Those were the days to travel in France. The franc cost four cents. In Les Baux in Provence, which then had only eighty inhabitants, we stayed at the Hotel de la Reine Jeanne and paid $1.40 a day for a pleasant room and three delicious meals.

In May 1930 Paul Martin, who was studying at Cambridge, had dinner with me at Christ Church. Two years before, at the age of twenty-five, he had been the unsuccessful Liberal candidate in a provincial by-election in his home constituency of Renfrew North. Martin said that just before the by-election he had asked Mackenzie King what the difference was between Conservatives and Liberals and King had replied 'that there was fundamentally none, but that Canada needed a two-party system and that was the justification for having two parties.'

My love of Oxford and of England was not blind. At the end of my time there I was closely interrogated about Oxford by a Canadian student who was at Cambridge. Most Rhodes scholars would, I said, gladly go home at the end of their first term. One knows no one. There seems no possibility of knowing anyone. The men on your staircase do not speak to you. If you meet a man at lunch one day he will cut you on the street the next. Many Rhodes scholars give up the struggle and say the Englishman is not worth knowing and from then on consort only with their own nationals or with other Rhodes scholars. Gradually you get to know a few Englishmen through games or the Union or the OUDS and from then on all goes well. You are elected to clubs and you will be accepted at somewhere near your proper valuation. You recognize that the cutting or the non-recognition of people on the street is quite a good idea as otherwise one would be continually having to nod at men as you passed them.

In answer to his question about homosexuality at Oxford I said that there was a set in Oxford who practised it, that there were many others who pretended to, that it was impossible to tell how widespread it was, that it played the same part in dirty stories here as heterosexual copulation did at home, that it had its base in the public schools, that from the stories one heard no one but the raconteur or the raconteur's brother had remained a virgin in his house in Eton, that perhaps it was traceable to the influence of the classics in upper-class education, that it was definitely an upper-class practice, and that I could not say what its effects were.

As to snobbery, it bit deep into the English character and permeated all classes. It was shown, for example, in the attitude of Oxford to the provincial universities. I hated English snobbery, but it was useless to expect the Englishman one met not to be a snob and consequently one had to accept him, snobbery and all. In England there were two distinct races, the upper and the lower classes, who differed in physique and in features; this was due to the effects of the industrial revolution in the nineteenth century when the poor had been herded into slums where they had been underfed and overworked and this had been accentuated by the war. To my interlocutor's remark that no one in England worked hard enough, I replied that the present evils in England were due to the very policy which he admired so much in modern Canada – working hard, increasing the wealth of the country, and investing capital in machinery instead of in the health and education of the citizens. Nineteenth-century England should have worked shorter hours and spent more time in thinking. What I admired in modern England was that they were making some attempt to establish a system of social justice which we were not doing in Canada. What depressed me in England was the almost hopeless fight they had to wage because of their evil inheritance. Nevertheless, I thought that perhaps in a generation England would be a better country to live in than Canada because, though it would have a smaller population than now, though it would have less wealth than now, it would be a country founded upon principles of social justice.

In my last term at Oxford my friend Angus Malcolm invited me to be his guest at the annual dinner of the Bullingdon Club. After gathering at Christ Church for cocktails we went by bus to Bullingdon where the village children were lined up to give us what Angus called a feudal welcome. As soon as the dinner started the noise commenced. Our end of the table was quiet but elsewhere everyone was yelling some one's name until he had to rise in his place and drain his wine glass. There was a concerted attempt against the sobriety of Angus Graham, the president of the Club, without much effect except that he must have been got up five times. I was warned that I would have to reply for the guests and I accepted on the understanding that I would only have to say a few words. The president toasted each guest in turn and each rose in his seat and drank with him. Most of the remarks had an undercurrent of homosexuality about them. Angus Graham quoted Osbert Lancaster, 'Scratch a hearty and you find a tart.' About me he said that he had not the pleasure of knowing me but that he had heard that I was a Canadian and a socialist and some joke about that. I had to think of something in reply. I appealed to Angus Malcolm but in vain except that he said I ought to turn the remark about being a socialist. I stood on my chair and said: 'I have to thank you, Mr. President, on behalf of the guests for the kind remarks you have made about them. You remarked about me that I am a socialist. (Cries of why?) I am a socialist because I believe in equality of consumption.' Loud and prolonged laughter from an audience made generous by much wine.

The annual dinner of the Ralegh Club in May 1930 was more sedate. I sat between the prime minister, Ramsay MacDonald, and the secretary of state for India, Wedgwood Benn. What struck me about the prime minister was that he was a tired man. His voice was listless, his face worn, his appetite poor. He ate only soup, a little bit of salmon, the inside of his vol au vent, a few potatoes, and the sweet. He brightened when he spoke to Wedgwood Benn with whom he appeared to be on terms of intimate friendship. He asked me some questions about the club. I mentioned that Patrick McGilligan, foreign minister of the Irish Free State, had come to the club the previous November and had very persuasively put the case for the Free State government in pressing for the removal of all legal limitations on their sovereignty because of their position vis-à-vis the claims of the de Valera party. The prime minister said bitterly: 'To save their face they break up the Empire.' Timothy Smiddy, the Irish high commissioner in London, asked him how Chequers was looking. He waxed enthusiastic over its loveliness, he had never seen it looking more beautiful. The meadowsweet was particularly delightful. He had done a good deal of clearing since he was there. Baldwin had done nothing and as a result the forget-me-nots had to push their way through undergrowth so that they had spindly stems so long – putting his hands about a foot apart. In his after-dinner speech he spoke of the difficulties of the government of colonies and mandates. To understand the difficulties we ought to read a volume of war speeches by British statesmen and consider the propaganda that we used in the war: propaganda about nationalism, self-government, free peoples. In Palestine, for example, we had during the war made absolutely incompatible pledges to Jew and Arab. 'The Arabs send delegations and prove by documentary evidence that they are in the right. The Jews send delegations and prove by documentary evidence that they are in the right.' The Empire was in danger of dissolving into its several parts. Its condition reminded him of his house, 10 Downing Street. 'It was built in 1740. It has stood therefore for nearly 200 years. The walls are bulging. The mortar has decayed away between the bricks. Some new mortar is necessary. So with the Empire. Unless some binding force is found the Empire would not be a building but a pile of bricks.'

Lionel Curtis, the founder of the Round Table group, who had for years advocated a federal union of the British Empire, said to me that what had struck him in MacDonald's speech was the use of the words 'organic union' of the Commonwealth, the first time a British prime minister dared to use the phrase – and it came from a Labour prime minister. Curtis, however, discounted its meaning as he thought MacDonald was using the expression loosely to express his desire for greater unity of the Commonwealth. Curtis said that he himself was in favour of a structure similar to the League of Nations: a Commonwealth council and an assembly in which both governments and oppositions would be represented. What was needed was to create an informed public opinion in the Empire on imperial questions. At present that was impossible because the imperial conferences were held in secret.

A few days before, in a speech to the Bryce Club, Curtis had said: 'This is a sick world, gentlemen. I have not been so depressed, no, not during the worst years of the war.' In a letter to my mother I reported what Curtis had said and commented: 'I am afraid he is right. The public haven't realized it yet but this is the worst international economic crisis since the 1890's – even worse than 1921. Some people prophesy it will last two years and that unemployment in Britain will go up to 2,500,000.' The international economic crisis lasted ten years and unemployment in Britain went up to three million.

An article on 'Canada on the [League] Council' which I wrote in the autumn of 1927 for the *Canadian Forum*, the first of many articles of mine in that journal, reflected the views I had reached on international affairs at the University of Toronto sharpened by my experiences the preceding summer at the conference in Rome of the Confédération Internationale des Etudiants and the Zimmern seminar at Geneva. At the League Assembly that year Canada had for the first time been elected to the League Council. In this article I put forward arguments which I was constantly to repeat over many decades: 'Canada may play a great part in the solution of the problems which threaten the peace of the world or she may be a non-entity at the Council table ... It depends on the representative she appoints to the meetings of the Council ... [Canada's] delegations to the Assembly have on the whole been notoriously weak. We do not wish the Dominion representation on the Council to gain that same notoriety.'

I urged that the prime minister himself, in his capacity of secretary of state for external affairs, should attend the annual League Assembly and the council meeting which preceded it. There were two members of the Liberal party, either of whom would be a suitable representative at the other three annual meetings of the council and a suitable second-in-command of the delegation to the Assembly – Vincent Massey and Newton Rowell. 'If the Prime Minister finds it impossible to be the first delegate of Canada to the Council and the Assembly then he ought to request either Mr. Massey or Mr. Rowell to accept the position of Secretary of State for External Affairs. The Secretary of State would then be the first delegate of Canada.' Massey and Rowell were the two most influential members of the Canadian Institute of International Affairs in 1932 when J.W. Dafoe suggested to them that I be appointed national secretary of the Institute. Perhaps my tribute to them in this article helped to persuade them of the soundness of my views. It was not long after my appointment that they realized they had been mistaken.

I went on in my article to urge that the Department of External Affairs be enlarged 'to cope with the new situation in which international affairs are becoming increasingly important to Canada and Canada increasingly important in international affairs.' I concluded by dealing with what was then a delicate question, the necessity of Canada being prepared to oppose Britain publicly at Geneva when British policy was misguided. To do so the Canadian delegates must be in possession of sufficient knowledge to know when it was misguided, and have competent expert advice to assist them in stating their opposition at the private meetings at Geneva of the delegations to the Assembly of the six members of the British Commonwealth. 'We must hope that on grave issues the spokesmen of the Commonwealth at the League of Nations are not divided, but, if they are, then we must make sure from the calibre of our foreign office and of our delegates that Canada supports that policy which is in the interest of the peace of the world.'

After I had been a little over a year at Oxford I developed my views on Canada's status and functions in international affairs in an article in the *New Ambassador* published by the British Universities League of Nations Union. The article was a review of *Canada and World Politics* by Percy Corbett and H.A. Smith. It is hard now to comprehend how two such intelligent Canadian intellectuals could have argued in 1928 that there should be a common foreign policy for the British Empire, 'a single controlling authority with the power of final and binding decision over all the component parts [of the Empire] in all questions of major foreign policy.' The effect of this, the authors acknowledged, would be that the policy of the British government would prevail: 'The final control on matters of general and vital interest shall remain where it is now' and 'where it is now' was in Great Britain. The reason the authors gave for believing that Britain in 1928 still controlled Canadian foreign policy was not convincing; it was that the king could not ratify a treaty on the request of his Canadian ministers until the British foreign secretary had authorized the use of the great seal of Great Britain. According to Corbett and Smith the conflict between those who believed in Canadian autonomy in international affairs and those who insisted on a united Empire foreign policy was between the 'disruptive tendencies of the new nationalism' and 'the unifying tendency of the League and the Court [the Permanent Court of International Justice].'

In my criticism I insisted, as I had eight years before in my speech at high school, that the British Empire must become 'a personal union, that is a union of independent states under the Crown.' In defence of the right of Canada to be neutral in a British war I put forward an argument which was to become popular in discussions in Canada from about 1933 to the outbreak of the Second World War. It was indeed the thesis generally accepted at the unofficial British Commonwealth Relations Conference in Toronto in 1933. I said that if the British government entered no war unless it was one which accorded with its obligations under the League covenant and the Kellogg Pact, no question of Canadian neutrality could arise because Canada's international obligations were derived from these same two instruments. The question of neutrality would arise only when Great Britain was considering the waging of a 'private war.' Then the possibility of Canadian neutrality would have a beneficial effect, for the British government's knowledge that entry into war would break the unity of the Empire on so serious a matter would be one more deterrent to taking such a step.

The other argument I brought up against the Corbett-Smith advocacy of a common foreign policy for the British Commonwealth was that it made it 'possible for members of the Commonwealth to shuffle off responsibility for their action or inaction on each other.' I listed five recent decisions by the British government which it had indicated had been taken in part at least because of the views of the Dominions: the rejection of the Geneva Protocol, the break with Soviet Russia, the reservations on the Kellogg Pact, the long delay in signing a new Anglo-American arbitration treaty, and the failure to sign the optional clause of the statute of the Permanent Court of International Justice. Who, I asked, was responsible for these acts? We did not know since British and Dominion statesmen were always able in defence of their conduct to plead, whether explicitly or by implication, the desires of some other member of the Empire and the necessity of preserving a common foreign policy. Responsibility could not be fixed and without the allocation of responsibility there could be no effective exercise of control.

In a talk on Armistice Sunday 1929 in a village church near Oxford I preached the doctrine of the duty of civil disobedience (what Gandhi called non-violent non-co-operation) which I had advocated in my editorials in the *Trinity University Review* three years before. The Oxford

University League of Nations Union provided undergraduates as speakers on Armistice Sunday to churches in and near Oxford and I had agreed to be a speaker. When I arrived at the church I said to the rector that I supposed I would not wear a surplice and that I would speak not from the pulpit but from the chancel steps. He said that the congregation would not understand this. So to my dismay I was clothed in cassock and surplice and spoke from the pulpit. My early years of church attendance enabled me to give the benediction before the sermon and the ascription afterwards and even to provide a text for my address, though I could not give chapter and verse for it. My text was 'Render unto Caesar the things that are Caesar's and unto God the things that are God's.'

When some years ago I unearthed my notes for this address I was apprehensive that I would discover that I had talked down to these parents and wives and children of the men from the parish who had been killed in the war and that I might have said something that would wound them. I was relieved to discover that I had not. I did say that a Christian service of commemoration of the sacrifices of the war could have no national boundaries: 'We remember today all those on whatever side they fought who lost their lives in the war. French or English, Germans or Russians, Turks or Italians, they all died in a common tragedy.' The greatest of all war memorials to the dead would be the creation of a just and lasting peace. 'The task seems hopeless to us at times. Individually we feel so helpless before the great forces that made the last war, and are even now making another war: the forces of greed, of pride, of stupidity. What can we as individuals do to fight these forces?' My answer was that we could support the League of Nations. The League 'is only a tool in the hands of the governments of the world.' I then made the point I was to make again five years later in an address in Ottawa, that the only government on which we could exert direct pressure was our own government. We could have little or no influence on the attitude of the French government, or the Italian government, but we did have influence on the policy of our own government. 'Our duty is to make sure that the government of this country does everything in its power to support the League in its work for world peace.'

I concluded my talk with the statement that the country to which we owed loyalty was 'a country devoted to justice and fair dealings among the nations, a country willing to accept sacrifices in the interest of peace ... If my country acts wrongly I no longer owe it loyalty. We owe it disloyalty.' I was on safe ground in making this statement in a church for, only two months before, the management committee of the World Alliance of Churches had appealed 'to the respective authorities of all Christian communions to declare in unmistakeable terms that they will not countenance or assist in any way in any war with regard to which the Government of their country has refused a *bona fide* offer to submit the dispute to arbitration.'

In those days I believed that the exercise of the right of private judgment meant that one should refuse to help the government of one's country if it were waging an unjust war – the belief twenty-five years before of British who opposed the Boer War, the belief forty years later of Americans who opposed the Vietnam War. That was the extent of the disloyalty which I advocated. I did not then contemplate that the exercise of the right of private judgment would, in the tragic mid-thirties, lead some young people of conscience and intelligence in the west to conclude that their first loyalty was to the Soviet government, not their own government.

My general approach to domestic and foreign policy did not change much while I was at Oxford. This was the period before Hitler, and the depression broke only in my final year. It was, up to the autumn of 1929, a period of great hope for continued economic and social progress and for international co-operation. I was at Geneva during the League of Nations Assembly in the autumn of 1929, the Assembly dominated by the three men whom we considered to be the statesmen of peace and reconciliation – Ramsay MacDonald, Briand, and Stresemann. The first twenty-four years of my life were spent in a hopeful world. No one born since 1929 has been born into a hopeful world. This is what separates my generation from the generations of our children, grandchildren, and great-grandchildren.

The generation born in the late eighteen eighties was even more fortunate than my generation. My friend and guru, Frank Underhill, said in his speech on his eightieth birthday in 1969 that 'he or she who was not born soon enough to grow up in that delectable quarter century before 1914 can never know what the sweetness of life is.' Underhill was born in 1889, a vintage year. It produced Jawaharlal Nehru, Arnold Toynbee, Water Lippmann, and G.D.H. Cole – and many others who were killed in the First World War. It was a rare wine that was spilt in that war.

I crowned my career at Oxford with two speeches, given in June 1930 just before I returned to Canada. One was at the Christ Church Gaudy where I gave the annual oration in honour of a former member of the college. Being a North American I decided it would be appropriate for me to choose someone who had an association with North America, and

I chose William Penn, whose portrait hangs in Cardinal Wolsey's great hall of Christ Church. Two weeks before I was to deliver the oration I was honoured by being invited to dine at high table in the college. The historian Keith Feiling was there and I took advantage of the opportunity to ask him for information about Penn. I suppose, I said, that I would find the chief books about him noted in the *Dictionary of National Biography*. 'What', he exclaimed, 'haven't you started work on that yet? That's supposed to be a polished essay, Reid.' I promised to begin in two days. (Thirty years later Feiling published a polished essay on Penn in his book *In Christ Church Hall*.)

In my oration I said that there was only one Quaker in all the gallery of portraits in Christ Church hall and he was the only man in armour. At the age of twenty-two he had done some fighting in Ireland in the quelling of a mutiny, was successful, had enjoyed it, was offered the command of a company, and, in anticipation of his military rank, had had this portrait painted. The next year he became a Quaker. In the draft of my oration (which I was required to show to one of the canons of Christ Church) I said that Penn was the only nonconformist to have his portrait in the great hall. The canon thought it would be inappropriate to mention this.

Delivering the oration was a strain. The dean and canons of Christ Church and some seventy others gathered in the thirteenth-century Chapter House, all in evening dress with decorations. I waited outside until the dean nodded to me. I strode up the aisle, passed the reading desk; the dean stood; we bowed, I went back to the desk, put down my mortarboard cap (I was in academic costume over evening dress), opened my typescript, and read the speech. I bowed to the Dean, went up to him, shook his outstretched hand in my nervousness, gave him the oration, walked out, picking up my cap as I passed the desk. The dean and canons and the seventy others filed out. All this without a word spoken except by me.

My other speech was at the annual dinner given by the Rhodes trustees to the Rhodes scholars who were completing their time at Oxford. I was chosen to 'act for the colonials' in replying to the toast to the Rhodes scholars. My friend Brewster Morgan spoke for the United States. In my speech I chided the Rhodes scholarship authorities for still calling the Dominions colonies, when even the Royal Colonial Institute, 'that last refuge of an obscurantist imperialism,' had changed its name to the Royal Empire Society. I began my speech by saying that since I was speaking as a representative Rhodes scholar my speech would be composed of what Cecil Rhodes had considered to be the ingredients of a representative Rhodes scholar: 'two parts of smugness (that is Rhodes's name for intellect), one part of brutality, one part tact, and one part unctuous rectitude.'

I said that I had recently seen a film, *White Cargo*, which had to do with the degeneration of a young Englishman on the Gold Coast because of the damp rot – a degeneration which ended with his going native. I said that I was going to write a play about Oxford modelled on *White Cargo*:

The first scene in the play will take place in the rooms I used to have in Peckwater Quadrangle before if was refaced. I shall be in my third year and a newly arrived Rhodes Scholar will come to see me. I shall be sitting by the window drinking a whisky and soda. He will tell me of everything he intends doing. He is going to row for his college, to produce a play for the Dramatic Society, to take Modern Greats in two years and also write actuarial exams at the same time. I shall laugh sardonically and, leaning out of the window, will put my hand in the stone wall and, taking a piece of the stone away, will crumble it between my fingers and say 'Damp rot! – the damp rot will get you.' The later scene will show the young man degenerating until finally he 'goes native.' When a man on the Gold Coast goes native, he takes a native wife; when a Rhodes Scholar goes native he consorts only with his fellow countrymen.

This, I said, happened to some Rhodes scholars who had every intention when they came to Oxford of living up to Rhodes's ideas about the scholarship, who tried for a term or two to get to know their English fellow students, and then gave up the task as hopeless and went native.

I proceeded with unctuous rectitude to give advice to the Rhodes trustees on what might be done to make it less likely that Rhodes scholars would go native. The English student was usually only nineteen when he came to Oxford. The present tendency was to appoint Rhodes scholars who were twenty-three when they came up. Some Rhodes scholars had told me they did not think it worth their while to get to know Englishmen four years their junior. Rhodes scholars should therefore be not more than twenty-one when they came to Oxford. At that age they would be likely to do undergraduate, not graduate work, and as a rule graduate students did not get to know the English. Rhodes had determined in 1900 that the scholarship should be sufficient to enable his scholars, as he put it, to rub shoulders with all classes at Oxford and he had set the scholarship at £300 a year. This was the equivalent of £516 in 1930 and the scholarship should now be increased to £500 from its present level of £400. I suggested that the Rhodes trustees could find the money to do this if they did not spend money on activities never mentioned in Rhodes's will, such as 'sending Oxford dons on trips around the world or arranging for people to give in London lectures on the British Empire which had much better not be delivered.'

I was supposed in this speech to pay tribute to the retiring Oxford secretary of the Rhodes Trust, Sir Francis Wylie. I displayed a lack of generosity and good manners by failing to do so. But I was relieved the next day to read an account of my speech in the newspapers which said only that this was what I had done. Rhodes trustees were expert in dealing with the press.

Now when I read that speech I realize that it had too much smugness, brutality, and unctuous rectitude and not enough tact. John Flynn, an Australian Rhodes scholar, told me afterwards that it was amusing to watch the effect of the speech on the audience: Peacock, the chairman of the Rhodes Trust, was annoyed; Lord Lothian (Philip Kerr) was amused; Count Bernstorff, a former German Rhodes scholar, who was sitting next to Flynn, was delighted. Afterwards Lothian and Wylie showed their generosity and good manners by joking with me about the speech, so I felt better. A Canadian Rhodes scholar, A.E. (Dal) Grauer, told me that he and other Canadians at Oxford had despised me slightly because they thought I had become anglicized but that the speech had put everything right and they didn't know I had it in me.

My years at Oxford gave me more self-confidence. I sharpened my ability to suck the marrow out of books quickly, to write essays quickly and clearly, and to speak in public persuasively and sometimes with wit. I acquired more social poise. I became aware that the social-democratic views I professed, which were in Canada held by few, were in Britain the conventional wisdom of probably more than half the intelligentsia. I won the coveted award of a first class in my final examinations in Modern Greats (philosophy, politics, and economics), and I was immensely flattered by the comments on my examination papers of Cannan, one of the two principal examiners, which my tutor, Roy Harrod, passed on to me: 'Reid's average was almost the best in the whole examination ... I thought better of his economics theory paper than my colleague did ... and I marked his economic history paper as high as any on that subject which was generally bad. I thought his paper on economics books voluminous and good.' I believe that Hume Wrong, Douglas LePan, and Gordon Robertson were the only contemporaries of mine in the Canadian External Affairs service to have been awarded a first class at Oxford or its equivalent. This no doubt accentuated my tendency to intellectual arrogance.

It was not until a quarter of a century later, when I had been living in India for two or three years, that I realized how limited my education had been at Toronto and at Oxford. I thought I had been studying economics, politics, and philosophy when in fact I had been studying the economics, politics, and philosophy of the western world. There was nothing in my courses of study on the economic problems of poor countries such as India and China, on the special political problems of poor countries, on the philosophies of the great non-western civilizations of India, China, and the Muslim world. Of the 114 questions in my final examinations at Oxford only three had anything to do with the non-western world, and of these one was Eurocentric: 'If the population of Asia and Africa were to grow very rapidly, what effect might this be expected to produce on the prosperity of Western Europe?' The other two questions were about 'the introduction of the elective element into the Government of India,' and whether towards the end of the nineteenth century 'the question of the Far East became of much greater moment than that of the Near East.'

My years at Oxford made my work as a diplomat easier since when I had to deal with a fellow Oxbridge graduate – whether British or American or Australian or Indian – it usually was as if from our first meeting we were old acquaintances. I now think, though I did not realize it consciously at the time, that this helped me greatly when I was Canadian high commissioner to India in making friends with senior Indian members of the Indian Civil Service who were likewise from Oxbridge and who, as one Indian reviewer of my book on India said, felt closer to me than to most of their fellow countrymen. My Oxford years plus my social-democratic views also helped me to get along with and understand Jawaharlal Nehru since he was a Cambridge graduate and a social democrat.

I was not at all certain in my last year at Oxford what I wanted to do at the end of the year. In December 1929 I wrote about my future to Norman (Larry) MacKenzie from a reading-skiing vacation in Switzerland. I began by congratulating him on his contribution to a Hart House debate on Toronto's intolerance and went on to say that if the police in Toronto continued their practices I should be afraid to return to Toronto (the police had since the beginning of 1929 been preventing or breaking up meetings which they deemed to be communistic). 'I had rather face the prospect of being stoned by the left-wing [of the Labour party] in England for being a moderate than be kicked by the police in Toronto for being a socialist.' I ended my letter by asking MacKenzie, who had been a senior official in the International Labour Organisation (ILO), for advice on how I might go about trying to get a good appointment to the secretariat of the League of Nations or the ILO. 'Two and a half years in Oxford have not succeeded in killing all my enthusiasms. I am still enthusiastic about doing something for international peace.' I am not now certain about what happened as a result of this inquiry. I vaguely recall one of my tutors in Oxford advising me not to apply for one job in the ILO which was available because, he said, it was not good enough for me.

In the spring of 1930 I was offered a fellowship at Hertford College. I turned it down for three reasons: I wanted to get married; I wanted to return to Canada; I did not want to go into university work. At the beginning of June I wrote to my mother:

Keith Feiling whom I like best of the Christ Church dons ... thinks I am perfectly right in not staying in Oxford any longer and in particular in not taking the Hertford fellowship. He says that if I thought that economics was the thing that mattered most of all to me and if I decided to give up Canada and live in England then it would be all right but if I am returning to Canada and am not going into university work the sooner I return the better. I ought to spend a year on my thesis and then go into business preparatory to entering politics. I suggested the Canadian National Railways and he was enthusiastic. I can be a socialist in the CNR and no one can object [because it was owned by the government] ... My pose [in applying to the CNR] will have to be as an economics expert though I am supremely cynical about economics. I shall be glad to get back to Canada. I am getting bored with England. At the same time I am just beginning this term to feel at home in England. Hitherto I have always felt a foreigner. Perhaps that is an additional argument for leaving the country.

At a lecture on Kant by the master of Balliol, A.D. Lindsay, early in 1928 I saw across the lecture hall a remarkably beautiful and vivacious young woman. I found out that she was Ruth Herriot from Winnipeg who was studying at St Hugh's College. We have now been married for fifty-nine years.

I did not know when I left England at the beginning of July 1930 how I was going to support myself, much less a wife. I had applied for a research fellowship from the Rockefeller Foundation to pursue my studies of Canadian political parties but I had not received the Foundation's decision. When I arrived in New York and called at the Foundation office I was told that I had been granted a fellowship at $1,800 at year. I wired to Ruth Herriot: 'Awarded Rockefeller fellowship. Let's get married.' We were married on 30 August.

5

Studies of Canadian Political Parties 1930–1932

For two years from 1930 to 1932 I studied the development and nature of Canadian political parties since 1867. On my travels across Canada I kept a record of my interviews with active and retired politicians. I made no notes during the interviews but as soon as possible after an interview I would type out an account of it while it was fresh in my mind. My record of interviews runs to about one hundred thousand words. I spent much time analysing the voting in general elections from 1867 on – too much time for I became overwhelmed by the statistics I compiled – and never completed my doctoral thesis for Oxford. But I did write six essays on Canadian political parties for learned journals. I am ashamed of my failure to complete my thesis but I take comfort in Jack Granatstein's statement in his book on the Ottawa mandarins that my record of my interviews 'was the first systematic oral history project by a Canadian scholar' and that the essays 'were brilliant examples of political analysis to which students half a century later are still referred.'[1]

Oxford appointed Frank Underhill of the history department of the University of Toronto as director of my studies. This was the beginning of a rewarding friendship. I was at Harvard one winter studying under the direction of Arthur Holcombe of the department of government. His book, *The Political Parties of Today*, and *The American Party System* by C.E. Merriam and H.F. Gosnell, greatly influenced my approach to an evaluation of the Canadian party system. In the reading-room of the lovely Parliamentary Library in Ottawa I immersed myself in newspaper accounts of electoral campaigns in the first thirty years of Confederation.

1 J.L. Granatstein, *The Ottawa Men: The Civil Service Mandarins 1935–1957*
(Toronto: Oxford University Press 1982), 239

The newspapers had become brittle and since then, in order to keep them from falling to pieces, they have been microfilmed and students no longer have access to the original newspapers. I am glad that this happened after my time because there was something about turning over old yellowing newspapers which made it easier for me to relive past political conflicts.

Of my six essays, the one I am fondest of is on the Saskatchewan Liberal machine before 1929. It did not require so much work as most of the others, being based on about a dozen interviews I had in Saskatchewan in July and August 1931. It may be the first detailed, realistic description of a Canadian political machine. I said that most of the staff of the Liberal party organization in Saskatchewan were employees of the provincial government: highway inspectors, road supervisors, sanitary inspectors, the men in charge of the provincial liquor stores. Each constituency had an organizer who drew the boundaries of the polling subdivisions and located the polling stations where they would be most convenient to the Liberal voters. He and his assistants divided the voters into Liberals, Conservatives, and doubtfuls, and as the day of the general election drew near the force of the whole organization was turned on the doubtfuls, the party organizer sending to each doubtful voter whichever of his workers might be expected to have the most influence on him. According to the organizers it was this man-to-man argument that determined the result of the election, not public meetings or party pamphlets except in so far as these inspired the party workers to greater efforts or furnished them with convincing arguments. One organizer said to me: 'Public meetings don't change no votes but they're customary.' The organizer for the province paid particular attention to the 'dumb' Liberal members of the provincial legislature and the 'dumb' Liberal candidates and if they were arousing opposition in any part of their constituency by some foolish action he would let them know. A former provincial cabinet minister told me a story about a very reputable citizen who had been chosen as Liberal candidate. He went in to see the provincial organizer and, when asked how things were getting on, replied: 'All the decent citizens in the constituency are going to vote for me.' The organizer's comment was: 'That's bad. You can't get in on the vote of the decent citizens.' And he didn't.

The patronage system gave the Liberal party the votes in both federal and provincial elections of practically all the employees of the provincial government. In the federal general election of 1921 the Liberals got less than one-third of the vote in one constituency but at the provincial hospital in the constituency, where only the staff were eligible to vote, they got 141 out of 162 votes. In the federal general election of 1925 the vote in one provincial hospital was 135 for the Liberal candidate, 5 for the Conservative, and 1 for the Progressive, while in the constituency as a whole the Liberals got only 55 per cent of the vote. The party also got good value out of its use of the pork barrel. Legally the planning of the roads was in the hands of the highways department, but actually the constituency organizer put the roads where they would do the party the most good. One organizer asked the Liberal reeve of one municipality for advice on how to spend highways money in his municipality. The reeve's reply was: 'Spend it somewhere else where it will do some good. The sons of bitches here are all going to vote Conservative and nothing will stop them.' The *Canadian Journal of Economics and Political Science* which published the article was doubtful about the propriety of printing the word 'bitches' but decided to take the risk of offending some readers.

T.C. (Tommy) Davis had been a Liberal member of the Saskatchewan legislature from 1925 to 1939 and a cabinet minister in the Liberal government of the province from 1926 to 1929 and 1934 to 1939 when he was made a judge. He served on the bench for only two years and in 1941 he came to Ottawa as deputy minister of the department of national war services. In those days most External Affairs officers lunched in the Chateau Laurier cafeteria. One day when I was making my way out of the cafeteria after having had lunch, Norman Robertson, who was sitting at another table, beckoned me to come over. He introduced me to the man he was lunching with, Tommy Davis. Davis said: 'I've long wanted to meet you to thank you for your article on the Saskatchewan Liberal machine. Whenever the CCF couldn't think of anything else to do in the legislature they would read extracts from your article. They could have been doing much more damaging things to us.'

In my essay on the rise of national parties in Canada I contended that it took almost thirty years after Confederation before the Liberals and the Conservatives became national parties. I emphasized the importance in those years of candidates in general elections who refused to commit themselves to any party until it was clear which party was going to form the government; they would then if elected join that party. These candidates had the interests of their constituency at heart and did not want its chances of obtaining a new post office, wharf, or railway spoilt by being represented in Parliament by a member of the opposition. These political realists constituted an important part of all the early parliaments. John A. Macdonald called them 'loose fish'; George Brown, 'the shaky fellows'; and Richard Cartwright, 'waiters on Providence.' In my article I called them 'ministerialists' because their politics were to support not a party but a ministry and any ministry would do. They were inverted Irishman; they were always 'agin' the opposition. Their counterpart in ecclesiastical politics was the Vicar of Bray. By 1878 a two-party system had been pretty firmly established in Ontario, Quebec, and the maritime provinces but Manitoba remained ministerialist until 1882 or 1887, British Columbia until 1891 or 1896.

The essay which embodied the most painstaking research was on the economic and racial bases of Conservatism and Liberalism in 1930 as demonstrated by the voting in the general election that year in which the Conservatives defeated the Liberals. This essay was replete with statistical tables. It may be not only the first but perhaps for many years the only detailed study of voting in a Canadian general election. Constituencies in which at least 80 per cent of the population was of French origin I called French-speaking; those with 21 per cent to 79 per cent of French origin, bilingual; the others I called English-speaking. Constituencies in which a party received at least 52.5 per cent of the votes I called safe constituencies for that party.

My studies showed that the Liberals in the general election of 1930 had won over three times as many French-speaking constituencies as the Conservatives, the Conservatives over twice as many English-speaking constituencies as the Liberals. French and bilingual constituencies made up three-fifths of all Liberal constituencies and three-quarters of its safe seats. English-speaking constituencies made up three-quarters of all Conservative constituencies and the same proportion of its safe seats. Within their racial homelands the parties made a greater appeal to the urban population than to the rural; outside their racial homelands to the rural population. The Conservative party was more urban than the Liberal; it got 42 per cent of its support in Parliament from urban areas, the Liberals 31 per cent. These generalizations constituted a great over-simplification of the real divisions between the two parties, for there were many other issues which cut across the two main ones which alone had been analysed. The English-speaking population, for example, was divided by religious differences; on certain issues Roman Catholics, whether Irish, German, or Polish, would unite with their French co-religionists and the conflicts of race and economics would, for the moment, be forgotten. Moreover, the English-speaking population was composed not of one race but of many and between these races there were often violent antagonisms. Thus an ambitious and realistic politician might form a party based on English-speaking farmers, continental immigrants, French Canadians, and Roman Catholics – a not inaccurate description of the Saskatchewan Liberal party in the heyday of its prosperity – and the opposition would be composed in the main of townspeople, native English-speaking Canadians, British immigrants, and Protestants, with a sprinkling of English-speaking farmers who disliked continental immigrants or Roman Catholics or French Canadians more than townspeople, or Roman Catholics who disliked English-speaking farmers, French Canadians, and continental immigrants more than Protestants – and so on. Neither a purely economic nor a purely racial interpretation nor yet a combination of the two would fit all the complexities of Canadian politics. Nevertheless, a racio-economic interpretation would fit many facts and would cast some light on the obscure realities of the Canadian party system.

Two of the most interesting politicians I interviewed in my travels in 1931 and 1932 were Henri Bourassa, the distinguished leader of French-Canadian nationalism, and his one-time lieutenant, Armand Lavergne. Bourassa was on his summer holidays at a charming little hotel on the Ile d'Orléans, a ferry-boat ride from Quebec City. He was then sixty-four years old. We talked about the three nationalist movements in the province of Quebec: Jetté in 1872, Mercier in 1885, and his own in 1900. He said that the first two were nationalist in the sense that they aimed to protect the rights of the French-Canadian nation against the English Canadians, the rights of the church, and the rights of the race. His nationalist movement arose out of the struggle over whether Canada should help Britain in the Boer War; its purpose was to protect the national rights of Canada as a whole against the British imperialists under Joseph Chamberlain. He had not wanted his movement to become a political party. In the election of 1911 he was opposed to Laurier's naval policy but he was also opposed to Borden's naval policy. This was the line he had wanted the nationalist candidates in Quebec to follow in the election. After the election most of those who had been elected as nationalists went over to the Conservative party and this lent colour to the Liberal charge that they had been bought by the Conservatives. He did not know until after the election that the nationalist candidates had accepted money for their campaign expenses from a special fund raised for them by Hugh Graham (later Lord Atholstan), a leading Conservative.

The day after my talk with Bourassa I had lunch with Armand Lavergne and his wife at their apartment in Quebec City. He said that after the 1911 election Borden had offered Bourassa and himself seats in the cabinet. Bourassa refused and he also refused, for he was only thirty-one and he felt he could not go into the cabinet without Bourassa's support. The result was that the Quebec delegation in the Borden cabinet was weak. Bourassa was wrong in not entering the cabinet, since if he had the Conservative government would not have tried to carry out its naval policy of giving the British government an emergency contribution of $35 million for the construction of three dreadnoughts, and, what was more important, the situation at the outbreak of the war in 1914 might have been different. He himself as a member of cabinet would not have supported Canada's entry into the war unless it had been clearly demonstrated that Canada's direct interests were involved in the struggle. The Borden government did not attempt to demonstrate this to the French Canadians but instead appealed to them to support the war on the ground that the interests of France as well as of England were at stake; but this had nothing to do with the French Canadians. He defended himself against his inconsistency in supporting Meighen in the Chanak crisis in 1922 when Meighen wanted Canada to send troops to help Britain by saying that if Canada were to take part in imperial wars, a war against the infidel Turk was the best war it could take part in. Meighen, he said, had been converted by 1926 to his view that the only way to keep Canada from becoming so Americanized that it would ultimately be absorbed by the United States was to make it bilingual. Lavergne died in 1935. In his will he said, 'Canada will be bilingual, or it will be American.'

The day after my talk with Lavergne I wrote to Ruth:

Lavergne appears to have respect for no politician in Quebec since LaFontaine [who had retired from public life eighty years before]. The rest are all bitches and WHO's. He calls them that and I presume he means whores. Laurier is a nefaste WHO and later he said that the translation he wanted for nefaste was nefarious. In the Borden cabinet of 1911 there was only one honest man and only one Canadian, Sam Hughes. And apparently the Bennett cabinet is very little better. Bennett is going to lose all but seven seats in the province of Quebec in the next election [he lost all but five] when all that he need do to win 60 is to appoint intelligent men (naturellement that means Armand Lavergne) to his cabinet and make the money bilingual. (Look at your dollar bills and notice, if you are like me, for the first time that they are not bilingual.)

Years later I learned that many people believed that Lavergne was Laurier's son. Sandra Gwyn has written that 'if he was indeed Laurier's son, he reacted as the sons of famous men so often do – by fighting his father' and that by about 1905 he 'found his father-figure and hero' in Henri Bourassa.[2]

I had a number of long talks with Mitchell Hepburn, who had been a Liberal MP and was then leader of the Liberal party in Ontario. He told me that the source of his political strength in his rural constituency was that he knew half the people in the constituency by their first name; when I drove around the constituency with him I found that this was no exaggeration. He would talk to almost everyone we passed on the road, call them by their first name, and they would call him Mitch. He told me he had got the vote of the workers on the railway, though they were traditionally Conservative. I could see how he had done this; when we were in the town of Port Stanley a car came up with five railway men in it selling lottery tickets in aid of the unemployed, and he was hail-fellow-well-met with them. We later passed a group of seven men who looked like street loafers and he knew them all by their nicknames. We went to a bootlegger's to have a drink of beer. (Prohibition was still in force in Ontario.) He explained to me that he had to do things like that so that people would not think he had become stuck-up; it was that assertion which damned a member of Parliament in a rural constituency.

I went with him by train to the banquet and the annual meeting in Peterborough of the Central Ontario Liberal Federation. He had been taken to a party the night before in Toronto by the Liberal organizer for Ontario and had a hangover in the morning. After the banquet we gathered with a group of Liberal stalwarts in a hotel room and consumed whisky. After that we went to the house of a judge, a former leading Liberal. At about two in the morning Hepburn left to catch the train to Toronto. My comment in my diary was: 'Only a tremendously strong man could stand the strain of that, week in and week out. He apparently never reads anything but the newspapers and memoranda given him by others – cranks or friends or party organizers – but even if he had the capacity and desire to read he would find little time for it.'

In a letter to Ruth I wrote: 'Hepburn isn't a bad sort. He is sincere, with not much education and feels restive under the control of the party managers who put him into the leadership and want to dictate his policy. It is said that he won't be in the leadership many years longer but that he will be forced out and will join an independent party – probably farmer-labour.' I was mistaken. He won the provincial general election

2 Sandra Gwyn, *The Private Capital: Ambition and Love in the Age of Macdonald and Laurier* (Toronto: McClelland and Stewart 1984), 271

in 1934, bringing the Liberals into power after twenty-nine years in opposition, and he was premier of Ontario from 1934 to 1942.

I had a talk with James Gardiner in August 1931 at his home in Regina. He had been premier of Saskatchewan from 1926 to 1929 and later became one of the most powerful members of the Liberal cabinet in Ottawa. He told me that the difference in principles between Liberals and Conservatives extended to both federal and provincial affairs. I asked: 'What are the great Liberal principles which apply equally to federal and provincial politics?' He replied: 'The great principle of economy of administration' – a highly improbable assertion.

I was fortunate to be in Calgary at the end of August 1931 when the Ranchmen's Club gave a dinner in honour of R.B. Bennett on his accession to the prime ministership. Harry Nolan, a partner in Bennett's law firm, took me to the dinner. I wrote to Ruth: 'The dinner was very good and I had not had so many wines since my last big dinner in Christ Church ... R.B.'s speech was very good – informal and reminiscent. I liked him better that night than I have before. One reason is that he remembered my name when he was leaving. A little flattery goes a long way.'

One of the questions I asked retired politicians was the importance of patronage. How much value did a politician get out of his ability to find government jobs for his party workers? A member of the Ontario legislature told me that he would rather not have the patronage. A position of bailiff, worth about $2,000 a year, was vacant in his constituency; he had seventy-five applicants; he would make seventy-four enemies when he made the appointment. T.A. Crerar told me a story about a Conservative candidate in Nova Scotia in the election of 1911 who received 3,900 votes and was elected. He went away after the election for a fortnight's holiday during which he was appointed to the cabinet; when he returned he found 2,200 letters from his constituents asking for favours. A leading Liberal in Nova Scotia, in discussing patronage with me, said that it was not simply that party workers wanted jobs for themselves; they wanted the feeling of power which they got from their ability to find jobs for their supporters or to have an official fired. The motives which moved men to work for a political party were mixed; the motive might be money or prestige or power or the emotional relief which came to a man who could say to himself when some government official annoyed him, 'I'll get back at you, you bugger, when my party gets into power.'

I was told a story of the technique which Edward Farrer, one of the editors of the Toronto *Globe* in the early nineties, used to build up public support for some new departure in the policy of the Liberal party. After making a thorough study of the subject he would write an editorial covering the whole ground of his argument. This would be followed by an editorial on some aspect of the subject every four days or so for four weeks. Then he dropped it. Six weeks later an editorial would appear rehashing everything he had previously written about it. The readers would have forgotten the earlier editorials and after reading this one they would say to themselves, 'That's just what I've been thinking myself for a long time.'

I end these selections from my notes on my interviews with statements J.W. Dafoe made to me when I talked with him in his office at the *Winnipeg Free Press* in August 1930 and July 1931. Canadian prime ministers would never realize that they could be defeated in a general election. The office of prime minister went to their heads. Arthur Meighen in 1921 should have realized he would be defeated and should have planned his campaign with an eye to succeeding elections. A prime minister starts, as did Laurier in 1896, as being only *primus inter pares* in his cabinet but gradually he becomes a dictator, presenting his cabinet with accomplished facts and getting his way. This results in part from the turnover in cabinets. King was getting the power into his hands by the end of 1926; Bennett apparently took all the power into his hands from the very beginning. Bennett was not at all the man Dafoe had expected him to be when he took office as prime minister. He had thought Bennett was a simple person to understand; instead he was extraordinarily complex. He had thought he would never go back on anything he had said or done; instead he apparently had no fixed convictions. The nineteenth century liked hero-worship, the worship of the man who rose above the mass. The present generation asked, 'How did this fool do it?' Jaffray of the *Globe and Mail* claimed in 1925 that Mackenzie King had double-crossed him, which was probably true because no one became prime minister who had not double-crossed and was willing to continue to double-cross. A general election is a dirty business.

6

National Secretary of the Canadian Institute of International Affairs

1932–1938

To try in old age to discern the useful accomplishments of one's public life is a puzzling task. So many achievements which seemed important at the time look trivial or evanescent from a distance of decades. What does encourage me is that I played a part in moulding six institutions: the Canadian Institute of International Affairs, the Department of External Affairs, the International Civil Aviation Organization, the United Nations, the North Atlantic Alliance, and Glendon College. I like to think that because of my efforts these institutions have been a little less imperfect than they otherwise would have been.

In June 1932, when my fellowship from the Rockefeller Foundation was about to expire and I did not know what work I could get, I was offered the post of national secretary of the Canadian Institute of International Affairs. Vincent and Alice Massey had given the institute a grant from the Massey Foundation to finance the setting up of a national office and the appointment of a full-time secretary. I accepted the offer. I was instructed to open an office in Toronto, to assist the branches of the institute to secure speakers, to establish new branches, and to help in making arrangements for two unofficial international conferences which were to be held in Canada in 1933 – the Institute of Pacific Relations Conference in Banff and the British Commonwealth Relations Conference in Toronto. Shortly after I had accepted this appointment I received a letter from Magdalen College in Oxford asking if I would like to apply for a lectureship in the college in the political side of Modern Greats (philosophy, politics, and economics). I wrote to Ruth: 'But what the hell. Free rooms and dinner (but where would you live and eat) and £300–£350 per annum (but how could you eat). Let us praise the Massey Foundation and the Institute and Ferg.' It was George Ferguson of the

Winnipeg Free Press who had suggested my name to his editor, J.W. Dafoe, as a possible national secretary of the CIIA. In the spring of 1932 Dafoe told Ferguson that the institute was looking for a national secretary who would be a good organizer, good at research, and good at raising money. Ferguson replied: 'You're looking for some one who doesn't exist. No one can be good at all those three things. You'll be lucky if you find a man who is good at two of them.' He had then suggested me as national secretary. Dafoe agreed with the suggestion and proposed my name to Rowell and Massey.

I had no regrets that my appointment to the CIIA made it impossible for me to consider the offer from Magdalen College. I was, however, in two minds about the offer I received from Harvard two weeks after I had accepted the institute appointment, to join the Department of Government, where I had spent a few months in the winter of 1931–32. If the invitation had arrived earlier – and it might have if it had not been misdirected – I might have accepted it rather than the post in the CIIA. I often speculate on how this might have affected my life. Would I have made a career at Harvard as a political scientist or would I, after Roosevelt came to power, have jumped at an opportunity to leave Harvard to join a New Deal agency in Washington? If I had joined a New Deal agency might I have become a member of a left-wing discussion group used by the Soviet government as a recruiting ground for agents? Certainly I had by the mid-thirties decided, like most liberals and social democrats, that if, as then seemed possible, the choice before us became limited to fascism or communism I would choose communism as the lesser of the two evils. I remember my brother Lionel and I agreeing in the mid-thirties that the advantage of the evil of communism over the evil of fascism was that communism had the right slogans and, in time, the slogans might affect the nature of communist rule.

I was national secretary of the CIIA from the autumn of 1932 until the end of 1938 with the exception of seven months in 1937–38 when I was teaching at Dalhousie University. My work took me to four of the most influential unofficial conferences on international affairs held in the thirties: the first British Commonwealth Relations Conference in Toronto in 1933, the conferences of the Institute of Pacific Relations at Banff in 1933 and at Yosemite in 1936, and the International Studies Conference in London in 1935.

There were two great advantages to me of the posts I held in the thirties. The first was that they made it necessary for me to travel across Canada from coast to coast about half a dozen times visiting the principal cities; from 1930 to 1932 I was collecting material on the development of Canadian political parties; from 1932 to 1938 I was visiting the branches of the Canadian Institute. I talked to leading Canadians, especially in universities and newspapers, and made friends with many of them. In 1931, 1932, and 1933 I got to know officers of the Department of External Affairs in Ottawa. I had met O.D. Skelton, the head of the department, in Geneva in 1927. When I was in Ottawa in 1931 collecting material on the history of Canadian political parties Ruth and I had tea at his house on Easter Sunday and met there for the first time Norman Robertson and his wife Jetty. I wrote to my mother: 'There was a young man there from the Department of External Affairs and his Dutch wife. She had come to the States as a fellow of the old Laura Spellman Foundation which is now absorbed by the Rockefellers but she gave up research for marriage. Two weeks ago she gave birth to a daughter. Robertson told me a few days afterwards that she wished she had continued in academic research.' Robertson was then twenty-seven years old. Ten years later he became the under-secretary of the Department of External Affairs.

Just before the tea at Skelton's we had met Lester (Mike) and Maryon Pearson at dinner at the house of an Oxford friend Alan Plaunt, and a few days later we had tea at their house. Ruth had known Maryon Pearson in Winnipeg and had been at their wedding. In November 1932 I visited Ottawa as secretary of the CIIA to get assistance from the Department of External Affairs in preparing papers for the British Commonwealth Relations Conference. I called on Skelton, John Read, and Pearson. In May of the next year I again visited Ottawa on business relating to the Commonwealth Conference and again called on Skelton and Robertson. It was either at this time or a year later that Skelton considered inviting me to join the Department of External Affairs but decided it would not be fair to take me away from the Canadian Institute so soon after I had started working for it.

When I was in Ottawa in May 1933 I dropped in at the house of the former prime minister, Sir Robert Borden, the honorary president of the institute, to talk to his secretary. While I was waiting in the hall I could not help reading a note on the table in the hall in Borden's handwriting, 'Don't forget the blueing for my hair.' He was proud of his white locks.

The second advantage to me of my posts in the thirties was that I lived for almost all the time in Toronto, which was the centre of left-wing intellectual activity in Canada. I was a member of the small closely knit group of friends and acquaintances centred in the University of Toronto who worked together in some or all of six organizations: the Canadian Institute of International Affairs, the League of Nations Society, the Canadian Political Science Association, the *Canadian Forum*, the Co-operative Commonwealth Federation, and the League for Social Reconstruction. I was a member of the national council of the League of Nations Society, and a contributing editor of the *Canadian Forum*. I wrote articles on foreign affairs which were published in half a dozen Canadian publications and I had an article in the *Round Table* and one in *Pacific Affairs*.

In the thirties thinking about foreign affairs and Canadian foreign policy did not take place in closed compartments of the CIIA, or the League of Nations Society, or the League for Social Reconstruction. Most of my friends in the LSR who were especially concerned with Canadian foreign policy were active members of the CIIA and many of them were also active members of the League of Nations Society. There were also informal groups of friends who met together to help each other draft statements on Canadian foreign policy. One such group in the spring of 1934 consisted of Underhill, Larry MacKenzie, Hume Blake, and me. We met at Hume Blake's house to help him draft a statement on Canadian foreign policy in the form of a letter to Ramsay MacDonald, then British prime minister, and to help me write my speech to the League of Nations Society in May 1934. Thus my views on foreign affairs were influenced by discussions and correspondence with a wide spectrum, including such people as Brooke Claxton, Larry MacKenzie, Hume Blake, H.F. Angus, George Glazebrook, R.A. MacKay, and T.W.L. Mac-Dermot, as well as such LSR stalwarts as Frank Underhill, Frank Scott, Eugene Forsey, and Harry Cassidy.

What was it that this group had in common, apart from all being men and none being French Canadians, significant aspects of the thirties? They were all liberals (with a small l) or social democrats. And they were all young. Underhill was the elder statesman among us and in 1933 he was forty-four. I at twenty-eight was the youngest. All, or almost all the rest, were in their thirties. At that time it was the thirties who ran the LSR, the CIIA, and the League of Nations Society, though an older generation continued to fill the top positions in the CIIA and the League of Nations Society. I cherish the hope that by the middle of the nineties the thirties will once again be running the CIIA.

The Canadian Institute of International Affairs had a divided personality. The dominant group at its foundation in 1928 were the Canadian members of the Royal Institute of International Affairs, which had its headquarters at Chatham House in London. Some were elder statesmen like Sir Robert Borden, Newton Rowell, and Sir Arthur Currie; others, like Vincent Massey, were public-spirited, well-to-do, and influential in public affairs. This group was, in the terminology of the time, imperialist

– that is, they believed in close links between Canada and Britain and a closely knit empire. Another group came into the CIIA through the Institute of Pacific Relations, when the institute became the Canadian unit of the IPR. This group was on the whole younger and included more academics, most of whom did not believe in close links between Canada and Britain or a closely knit empire. Then there was a third group among the original members of the institute, members of the Canadian League, which had been established in 1924 to foster the national spirit as opposed to sectionalism, and to stimulate popular interest in public affairs. The members of the Canadian League were younger than the members of the other two groups and more nationalist. Brooke Claxton was a leading member of the league. Of course not all the early members of the CIIA could be fitted into one of these three compartments. J.W. Dafoe, editor of the *Winnipeg Free Press* and the leading newspaper editor of his time, was an internationalist, a nationalist, and no great admirer of the British governing classes or of the British Empire. Edgar Tarr of Winnipeg held much the same views as Dafoe. Rowell, in a letter in October 1933, said of Tarr, 'We do not see eye to eye on Empire problems.'

When I started working for the institute in 1932 it had only nine branches and fewer than four hundred members. Now it has twenty-four branches and twenty-seven hundred members. It attempted to be an elitist organization on the model of the Royal Institute of International Affairs. Membership was supposed to be confined to 'persons able to contribute to the knowledge or thought of the Institute in respect of international affairs.' An applicant for membership had to be proposed and seconded by members of the institute who from personal knowledge recommended him as a suitable candidate for election, and they were required to 'specify any special qualifications that the candidate, by reason of his experience or training, may have for membership.' Now the institute advertises for members.

The sole activity of the branches when I became national secretary was to hold evening meetings at which an off-the-record talk would be followed by informal discussion. The speaker would almost always be someone from out of town who happened to be passing through the city. Some branches were reluctant to expand their membership; perhaps they wanted to confine their membership to an elite, or they may have wanted their membership to be small enough to make informal discussion easier. In a letter to me in October 1934, T.W.L. MacDermot, then secretary of the League of Nations Society in Canada and a member of the Ottawa branch of the institute, said that it was a little exasperating that 'although Ross McLean and myself moved and seconded some eight or nine new members last year – people like Charlie Hébert and Don Buchanan and so forth – nothing has been done since.'

John Holmes, who was the senior officer of the institute in the sixties, declared in 1978, with his customary attractive blend of wit and wisdom spiced with exaggeration, that in the thirties 'the Institute, entirely male, attired in black ties, inhabiting the best clubs across the land, was composed of those who could, it was believed, affect decision-making [on Canadian foreign policy] by a well-placed phone call.' Five years later I asserted that there were no less than three errors in that one sentence: 'The ties at Institute meetings were seldom black; they usually had discreet stripes. People in the thirties who wanted to influence policy didn't make phone calls. Fortunately for the historian, they wrote letters. They also wrote editorials and articles. The third error is one of omission. In the thirties the Institute was not only male, it was almost entirely English-speaking and Protestant. It was composed of MASPS – male Anglo-Saxon Protestants.'

Inevitably I, as national secretary, was not satisfied with this. I encouraged the branches to broaden their membership and to establish study groups on some specific international problem, in addition to holding meetings to listen to an off-the-record talk. In the autumn of 1933 I urged that the institute should hold a national study conference every year at the same time and place as the meetings of the learned societies. In the governing bodies of the institute there was a good deal of scepticism about my proposal and some resistance to it, but it was accepted and the first conference was held in 1934. It proved to be a success and conferences have been held almost every year since.

By the time I left the institute at the end of 1938 the number of branches had increased from nine to seventeen, the number of members from 395 to 1,061, there were many branch study groups, the annual conference had become an established institution, the institute had started publishing books, and it was no longer exclusively male. Clearly this was only a beginning, and before I left I submitted to the governing body a series of memoranda on the future policy and problems of the institute. I advocated that the institute should strive to double by 1950 the number of its branches and of its members. What was more important was that the membership cease to be so unrepresentative: 'Today it is composed in the main of English-speaking upper-middle-class men who are Protestants, who are over forty, who live in the larger cities, who are of British racial origin, and who hold moderate views on public questions ... Eighty percent of the members of the Institute belong to a group to which less than one-quarter of one percent of the Canadian people belong.'

I said that by 1950 – that is, in twelve years – the institute should have published a five-foot shelf of research studies on matters impinging on Canada's external relations. It should publish every year an annual survey of Canada's external relations, two or three research monographs, one or two popular books, six popular pamphlets, twelve information department memoranda, a weekly foreign news letter, and the proceedings of its annual conference. It should have an Ottawa bureau to which senators and members of the House of Commons would turn for memoranda and documentary material. If this sort of program were carried out, the institute by 1950 would feel that there was tangible evidence that its efforts were meeting with success, that there had been laid in Canada firm foundations for a democracy which would have a sufficiently accurate knowledge and a sufficiently wise understanding of international affairs to be able to conduct its external relations on a higher plane than any nation had yet reached. By 1950 a few of my recommendations had been put into effect; by 1988 most have.

Some of the most influential members of the CIIA at that time doubted the wisdom of my emphasis on study groups, research, and the holding of an annual conference. Both Dafoe and Rowell believed that the changes for which I was pressing would make the institute, as Rowell put it, 'less acceptable to business and professional men interested in international affairs,' men who, according to Dafoe, 'are not keen about forming study groups or doing research work.' Dafoe realized that a change in the nature of the institute would make necessary a change in its membership. 'We shall have to some extent to make over our membership by getting in more men of the academic type.' It would also, he said, mean that it would be necessary to get a secretary for the Winnipeg branch, and presumably for other branches, 'who can give a good deal of time to the duties of the office.' What was needed was to find among the members of the Winnipeg branch 'two or three men' to be officers of the branch 'who would be prepared to make a hobby of the work of the Institute.' Dafoe was right on both these points. The institute was fortunate that it did find in most of its branches members who were prepared to make the CIIA one of their principal hobbies.

Dafoe and Rowell realized that what I was trying to do was to have the Canadian institute develop in a similar way to the parent organization in Britain, the Royal Institute of International Affairs, and the sister institution in the United States, the Council on Foreign Relations. Dafoe, in spite of his doubts, was prepared to consider the possibility that this might be desirable. 'Apparently there is developing a policy of adjusting the Canadian Institute so far as this is possible to the methods of the Royal Institute, and it may be desirable that new policies of this kind should be pursued.' Rowell was not prepared to go this far. He believed that 'any attempt to pattern our Institute upon Chatham House will not prove a success ... We must not permit Reid's energy and enthusiasm' to push the CIIA in this direction. The central office should give suggestions and help to the branches, but not press them to form study groups or hold conferences.

Vincent Massey's dissatisfaction with the developments in the institute was one reason, perhaps the main reason, the Massey Foundation did not renew its annual grant to the Institute in 1937. In explaining his decision to Dafoe, Massey wrote that he could not help feeling 'that there is some doubt as to the wisdom of embarking on the programme of development which has recently been under consideration,' a program I had put forward. There were, he felt, 'definite disadvantages in building up too much machinery at headquarters and emphasizing out of its relative position those various activities which come under the heading of Research.'

Because businessmen in the CIIA, such as Edgar Tarr, J.M. Macdonnell, and Ralegh Parkin, supported the kind of development for which I was pressing, the apprehensions of Dafoe, Rowell, and Massey turned out to be unfounded. The development of the institute from a small group of business and professional men who met to listen to off-the-record talks by visitors to a larger group containing more academics and professional men, and more younger men, which not only continued to hold this kind of meeting but also held meetings addressed by their own members, who met in study groups and at an annual study conference, and supported the publication of books, far from weakening the institute, strengthened it and did not make it less acceptable to business and professional men. When I now recall the criticism that as national secretary I alienated businessmen from the institute I turn with pleasure to two favourable assessments of my work by businessmen – one in 1938 by Edgar Tarr, head of the Monarch Life Assurance Company and at that time president of the institute, and the other in 1966 by Ralegh Parkin, an officer of the Sun Life Assurance Company and a leading member of the Montreal branch. Tarr, in his introduction to the institute's annual report for 1937–38, after listing the developments in the institute in the six years of my secretaryship, said:

It is difficult to over-estimate the part which Mr. Reid has played in the attaining of these results. He has in rare combination great administrative ability with a high standard of scholarship, and a mastery of detail with a sure sense of relative values. These qualities, together with an unusual capacity for work, have been devoted unsparingly to the service of the Institute, with results in which he may well take pride and for which we are certainly grateful.

Parkin wrote that I was

the second founder of the Institute after John Nelson. He presided not only over the real making of the Institute into a living thing, but also, in doing this, over the period when Canadian foreign policy began to be thought out and articulated, both within and without government ... It was he who had the ideas, who made life happily miserable for a lot of us all around Canada by needling the key people in the few branches to do this or that ... It was in those years between about 1930 and 1940 that the Institute made a national and international position for itself and without doubt both articulated and influenced Canadian foreign policy.

Rowell and Massey were devoted admirers of the British and of the Royal Institute of International Affairs. Why then were they opposed to the CIIA modelling itself on the British institution? Massey was indeed in favour of the Canadian institute following the example of the Royal Institute on small matters; for example, he wanted to have 'Royal' added to its name. I did nothing about this and this may have rankled. Massey used to speak to Burgon Bickersteth about his disappointment in my work as national secretary and Bickersteth would pass the information on to me. Thus he told me that Massey was annoyed by my choice of a cable address. The Royal Institute's cable address was 'Areopagus.' I should have chosen a similarly high-sounding word, not 'Canint,' which Massey said was appropriate for a business firm but not for the CIIA.

Perhaps the reason Rowell and Massey were opposed to the institute establishing study groups, holding conferences, and publishing books was that they had discovered at the British Commonwealth Relations Conference in 1933 that younger Canadians, particularly younger academics, did not share their devotion to the British Empire and their trust in the wisdom and good faith of National or Conservative governments in Britain. Even before the conference, Massey had had doubts about many of the people who were members of the institute – at least of its Montreal branch. On 20 April 1932, after addressing the Montreal branch on Canadian foreign policy, he described his audience in his diary as 'a rather unresponsive group.' On 5 May, after attending a meeting of the branch, he wrote in his diary that it was 'a rather frigid, over-intellectual body dominated by able but rather arrogant young men.' It may be that the arrogant young men had been unresponsive to his talk on Canadian foreign policy because they were reluctant to express openly their opposition to his views. Their arrogance was tempered by their courtesy. As long as the institute held only confidential branch meetings addressed by visitors, the dissident views of the younger members had limited opportunities for expression. Once the institute started study groups and held national study conferences and published books on Canadian foreign policy, the dissidents would have ample opportunity to air their views and to make converts. This is indeed what happened.

My memories of my years with the CIIA are not all of solemn discussions on the future of the institute or on Canadian foreign policy or world affairs. When I travelled across Canada visiting the branches I had many happy, relaxed evenings at the homes of members. I made friends across Canada, and at international conferences I met interesting people from many countries.

Owen Lattimore, the explorer of Mongolia, was at the Yosemite conference of the Institute of Pacific Relations in 1936. He explained to the conference the role of the sheep in the economy of Inner Mongolia: 'The Mongolian sheep is an all-round animal unlike the specialised Western type. Its wool is fairly coarse, but it is excellent for making felt tents. The skin makes a warm coat. The meat is of good quality, and supplies food. It supplies milk in the summer rather than meat. In the Steppes, which are treeless, sheep dung is used for fuel. From this one animal the Mongols get food, clothing, housing and fuel.' Many of us at the conference became convinced from the fumes emitted from Lattimore's pipe that the dung of the Mongolian sheep was used not only for fuel but also as a substitute for tobacco. Lattimore went on to say that because the Mongolian sheep economy was self-sufficient it provided no surplus for exploitation by the Japanese conqueror. A poet at the conference lauded this sheep.

> The Inner Mongolian sheep
> Makes ev'ry good Japanese weep;
> It leaves to its neighbour
> Division of labour,
> And insists that it live like a sheep.[1]

Hu Shih, the eminent Chinese scholar, was at the Banff conference of the IPR. He used to describe me at the time as 'the elegant young man

---

1 Sir Anthony Jenkinson, *Where Seldom a Gun Is Heard* (London: Arthur Barker 1937), 58, 60

in white pants.' When I went to Washington in January 1939 as second secretary at the Canadian Legation, Hu Shih was the Chinese ambassador. In December of that year President Roosevelt gave the customary annual White House reception for the diplomatic corps. In those days the corps was so small that every member from ambassador to third secretary and their wives, was invited and most of the diplomats came in resplendent diplomatic uniform with glittering decorations. Each was introduced to the president by his ambassador or minister. This was the last such diplomatic reception given at the White House. Before the outbreak of the war I had got to know some of the German diplomats. I asked my minister, Loring Christie, what I should do if I met one of them at the reception. He said: 'If they bow to you, you should bow at them.' Hu Shih and the Japanese ambassador set a better example. Their countries had been at war for years but when they met at the reception they sat down together and talked like civilized men. Their behaviour accorded with nineteenth-century diplomatic etiquette and served the national interest. The preservation of polite social relations between ambassadors of warring powers in a neutral capital meant that their governments could, when they so desired, instruct their ambassadors to talk informally, quietly, and without publicity about what might be done to limit or end hostilities.

At the conclusion of the Yosemite conference of the IPR in 1936 the younger members of the Japanese delegation gave a dinner to the younger members of other delegations. They had been told that westerners were accustomed to having cocktails before dinner, wine at dinner, brandy at the end of dinner, and then whisky. As good hosts they manfully followed this regime, with the result that two or three of them became so happy that they crawled under the dining table biting the ankles of the women guests. At the IPR conference in 1933 at the Banff Springs Hotel, I, as secretary of the Canadian delegation, gave a cocktail party. One of the guests, an English girl from Hong Kong, put herself in charge of mixing the martinis. In those days I was accustomed to martinis composed of one part gin, one part French vermouth, and one part Italian vermouth. She, unknown to me, was more up to date; her martinis were two parts gin to one of vermouth. It was too much for me. At dinner that night in the main dining room of the hotel I found myself reciting 'Horatius at the Bridge' from beginning to end, an accomplishment which I did not know I possessed. My friends kept feeding me bread in the hope that this would quieten me so that my state of inebriation would not become apparent to the president of the institute, Newton Rowell, who was at the next table; he was a foremost foe of alcohol.

7

Adviser to the Canadian Left and the League of Nations Society

1933–1934

The miseries of the great depression precipitated the formation in 1932 of the League for Social Reconstruction (LSR) and the social-democratic party, the Co-operative Commonwealth Federation (CCF), the precursor of the New Democratic Party. The LSR was the Canadian counterpart of the British Fabian Society but, as its historian Michiel Horn has written, 'much more important to the CCF than the Fabian Society ever was to the Labour Party.'[1] Frank Underhill was president of the LSR until 1935 and J.S. Woodsworth was honorary president until his death in 1942. Ruth and I joined the LSR and the CCF as soon as they were founded and we took part in the weekend meeting of the LSR at the Somerset farm at Burlington in April 1933, where two dozen of its members, including Woodsworth, discussed the nature of the book the LSR had decided to prepare. It was published two years later under the title *Social Planning for Canada*. One evening in early June 1933 I was at Frank Underhill's house, along with Harry Cassidy and Joe Parkinson, to go over the draft Underhill had prepared of what was to become the Regina Manifesto of the CCF. In June 1933 I wrote at Underhill's request the first draft of the chapter on foreign policy for the LSR book and a year later, again at Underhill's request, I wrote the first draft of a manifesto on foreign policy for the CCF.

The starting point of my argument in my draft chapter on foreign policy was that for Canada the establishment of a secure regime of peace was essential, since without it there could not be the free flow of inter-

---

1 Michiel Horn, *The League for Social Reconstruction: Intellectual Origins of the Democratic Left in Canada 1930–1942* (Toronto: University of Toronto Press 1980), 209

national trade required for Canadian prosperity and without it Canada might cease to exist as a nation, since in a great war involving Britain Canadians would be bitterly divided on whether Canada should enter the war at Britain's side. A socialist government in Canada would therefore support the League of Nations and strive to strengthen it, 'for the League can be used to lay the foundation of a socialist world state and it also provides our only hope for maintaining peace long enough for socialist governments to be established in the majority of the countries of the world.' (At that time socialists in many nations believed that the miseries of the depression would soon bring socialist parties to power.) Canadian support of the League of Nations meant that Canada should cease to be at Geneva 'a last ditch defender of national sovereignty' as it had been at the first League Assembly when its 'representatives vigorously opposed a plan for the distribution of the world's raw materials that had been raised by the Italian delegation ... in spite of the fact that, if one of the most fruitful causes of war is to be removed, raw materials must be subjected to international control.' In the next two years I was to refer again and again to this incident.

The sting of the draft chapter was in the tail, in the final three hundred words which dealt with what Canada should do if the League system weakened further or broke down and if imminent war threatened in Europe.

Canada should not allow herself to become a member of either of the two great camps into which Europe will probably divide ... If war should break out and one nation or group of nations be declared the aggressor by the League, Canada should loyally and effectively cooperate in enforcing financial and economic sanctions against that state or states but she should not intervene with armed forces. In the more likely event of the League being unable to decide which state was the aggressor Canada should refuse to take any part in the war [even if Britain became involved] and should declare an embargo upon the export of everything but foodstuffs to all countries engaged in hostilities.

I have found in my files comments on my draft chapter from Eugene Forsey, Frank Scott, and Harry Cassidy. Forsey thought the chapter admirable and Scott thought it excellent. But Forsey, Scott, and Cassidy all opposed my proposition that since 'wars arise in the main out of the rivalries of groups of capitalists seeking to exploit the raw materials and markets of the world,' what was required was a planned world order in which Canada would accept 'control by the world society of many matters which are now considered to be of purely domestic concern such as tariffs, immigration and raw materials.' Forsey favoured inviting the League to inquire into such matters and to prepare proposals for international control; but if we were to bind ourselves in advance to accept the dictation of League machinery, which was still controlled by capitalist governments, 'we may as well give up hope of socialist planning here ... Once you've got a League of Socialist Governments, the position changes!' Frank Scott agreed on the whole with Forsey's comments. Cassidy believed that we should make every effort to avoid measures which would exert harmful effects upon the economic life of other countries, since this would be 'a means of avoiding incidents that might lead to warfare ... which would, no doubt, wreck our own system of planning,' but 'I am inclined to think that the suggested international control of raw materials, immigration, tariffs, etc. ... is not exactly compatible with the economic planning scheme which is to be the central point in our programme ... We have to pin our hope in Canada mainly upon national rather than international economic planning for the proximate future.'

When I wrote the first draft of a manifesto on foreign policy for the CCF, Hitler had been in power for a year and five months and it seemed, as Underhill put it two months later, quoting Frank Simonds, 'that with the opening of 1934 the world passed from the post-war to the pre-war era.' This feeling was reflected in the opening sentences of my draft manifesto: 'The international situation is desperate. The danger of another great war or series of wars in the not distant future is grave. Though the international situation is desperate, it may not yet be hopeless.' If the situation were not hopeless, an intelligent Canadian foreign policy could diminish the danger of war breaking out. If the situation were hopeless, an intelligent Canadian foreign policy could make it possible for Canada to remain neutral. Every citizen had a duty to make a conscious and deliberate choice between alternative foreign policies. He could not perform this duty unless foreign affairs were freely and fully discussed in Parliament; but successive Liberal and Conservative governments had made this impossible by their failure to declare what their foreign policies were. The CCF was prepared to declare its foreign policy. It believed that never under any circumstances should Canada send armed forces overseas to take part in hostilities. Canada should do everything in its power to make possible the creation of a reformed and strengthened League of Nations, but so long as the League was unreformed Canada should not bind itself in advance to assist in applying the moral, economic, or financial sanctions of the League. If the attempt to create an effective system of world security met with failure and war broke out, Canada should preserve its neutrality even if this meant secession from the Empire.

My draft manifesto contained specific proposals on how a reformed and strengthened League might be created. The first step in the abolition of national armaments should be the destruction by all nations of the arms denied to Germany by the Treaty of Versailles. Treaties should be revised to satisfy the legitimate demands of Germany and other dissatisfied powers. The Soviet Union should be invited to join the League. Machinery should be set up to deal adequately with the fundamental causes of international disputes: the struggle for raw materials and markets, competitive exchange depreciation, conflicts over international investments, population problems, treatment of minorities. All colonies should become League mandates. The sanctions of a reformed League should be definite, certain, and automatic.

In my note to Underhill, sending him my draft manifesto, I wrote: 'No mention of capitalist wars in it, because there is as much danger now of Canada being dragged into a war in defence of communism as in defence of capitalism or the collective system. In fact if Russia goes into an "unreformed" and therefore anti-German or *status quo* League, the war will be in defence of capitalism, communism and the collective system.'

Underhill wrote me at the beginning of July to say that he thought my draft was good but that

I should like to emphasize more the sins of the present 'national' government in England and to say that we'd cooperate willingly with a Labour government which is genuinely seeking a peaceful world but not with the forces of imperialism as entrenched in the present government. I think also that mention should be made of the pressure for another imperial conference next year, which is the most sinister development in the immediate future. Also more emphasis is needed on the danger of the next war coming in the guise of a war for democracy, the League, etc.

A week later he sent me a new draft of the manifesto which he had written based on mine and asked me to send it on to Woodsworth with my comments. He said that he had changed and enlarged my introduction but had followed me pretty well in my concrete proposals. 'I am inclined to think something should be added about mass war resistance if a Canadian government does involve us in another war. What do you think?'

In a letter to me on 6 July Woodsworth said that he was 'a bit doubtful as to the wisdom of our Convention adopting anything like a detailed programme, even on as important a matter as foreign policy.' The convention agreed with him. It adopted the following brief manifesto:

We recognize that modern war arises primarily from the clash of interests in a world economy based on competition; therefore the establishment of permanent world peace depends on abolishing competition and on building the Cooperative Commonwealth. The CCF is unalterably opposed to war. If the great capitalist powers drift into another world war Canadian neutrality must be rigorously maintained whoever the belligerents may be. Canada must refuse to give military assistance to the League of Nations as at present constituted. We stand for the thorough reorganization of the League in order to make it an effective instrument for peace.

In the summer of 1935, a year after the adoption by the CCF of this statement, Underhill wrote the final version of the chapter on foreign policy for *Social Planning for Canada.* This bore little resemblance to my draft chapter or to my draft CCF manifesto. Underhill devoted almost the whole of his chapter to the necessity of Canada remaining neutral in the big war which 'is more than likely now.' But he too could not end on a negative note. In the final paragraph of his chapter, which is also the final paragraph of the book, he wrote:

While the immediate urgency is to concentrate on keeping out of the wars that threaten, we must work for a world which is genuinely based upon the collective organization of security. But security is not attainable without an equitable distribution of the opportunities for material well-being among all the peoples of the world. The way to bring this about is to begin to build up at Geneva the institutions of world economic planning. There is little hope of much immediate advance in this direction as long as national policies are in the control of private profit-seeking interests. It can only be a gradual process; and any honest facing of what is involved in it would compel us to modify many of our traditional Canadian policies on such matters as tariffs, control of raw materials and the treatment of Oriental settlers. Canadians who look forward to a League of socialist commonwealths should be doing their best now to educate public opinion in favour of such modifications. But the best contribution we can make in such a direction is to establish a socialist commonwealth within our own borders.[2]

2 The Research Committee of the League for Social Reconstruction, *Social Planning for Canada* (Toronto: Thomas Nelson 1935), 523–4

Now it is conventional wisdom in discussing North-South issues to assert that the preservation of peace requires 'an equitable distribution of the opportunities for material well-being among all the peoples of the world.' Then it was not and Underhill in this, as in much else, was in advance of his time.

In May 1934 the older members of the League of Nations Society in Canada used me to put forward at the annual meeting of the national council of the society views on Canadian foreign policy which they were reluctant to advance themselves. Here was I at the age of twenty-nine having the effrontery to advocate unorthodox proposals on Canadian foreign policy before a distinguished audience: the chairman of the luncheon meeting was the second-in-command of the Liberal party, Ernest Lapointe, and the guests of honour were the prime minister, R.B. Bennett, the leader of the opposition, Mackenzie King, and the leader of the CCF, J.S. Woodsworth.

Only a small part of the speech dealt with the reasons I gave for 'the collapse of the so-called collective system set up after the war to maintain peace,' but it was that part which aroused controversy – mainly because I blamed 'the victorious great powers' for the collapse of the League and the chief of these powers was Britain. The League, I said, had attempted to prevent war without dealing adequately with the causes of war: 'Such matters as access to the sea, trade routes, markets, raw materials, colonial opportunities, treatment of minorities and territorial boundaries ... Because the victorious great powers in control of the League refused to permit the League to deal adequately with these matters, the League became an instrument of the possessing powers against the dispossessed – the satiated powers against the proletarian powers ... Germany, Japan and Italy ... [This] has been a major cause of the ineffectiveness of League sanctions.'

I then asserted that there ought to be no effective machinery for enforcing League sanctions against an aggressor unless the League had established, under article 19 of its covenant, effective machinery for revising treaties and for changing international conditions whose continuance might endanger the peace of the world. To make this assertion in May 1934 when there was no proposal before the League to impose sanctions was one thing; to repeat it, as I did in October the following year, when sanctions were about to be imposed against Italy, was an entirely different thing. It was this which embroiled me in 1935 in serious trouble with Rowell, Dafoe, Brooke Claxton, and other influential members of the Canadian Institute of International Affairs.

My speech was followed by a speech by Bennett. He vigorously attacked me for my criticisms of the League of Nations. He said: 'I do not recall ever having heard as violent an indictment against an organization as that to which we have just listened.' After the meeting he said to me, 'That was a very extreme speech, Mr. Reid.' I said, 'It was intended to be extreme, Mr. Prime Minister.' He said, 'You succeeded in your intention.'

Mackenzie King came up to me after the speech to say that it was a very good speech. I thought he was just being polite but that night he wrote in his diary:

Escot Smith [sic] spoke on foreign policy – a very good address but revealing a want of understanding of the magnitude of the forces to which he was referring as in the following sentence as to what the League's members [he meant the members of the League of Nations Society] should do, 'bring pressure to bear on the Government to adopt perilous policies for peace.' That is the kind of thing for which Massey is responsible – 'live dangerously' etc. Why the need of this when the end to be achieved can better be achieved by the opposite course, taking safe and sane policies.

Poor Vincent Massey! He bore not the slightest responsibility for anything in my speech. King was apt at that time to blame Massey for developments in the discussion of public affairs in Canada which he did not like.

The phrase in my speech to which King took exception, 'a perilous policy for the organization of peace,' came from a letter in the *New Statesman and Nation* the previous December signed among others by Philip Noel-Baker, Charles Trevelyan, and Leonard Woolf.

A few days after I had given the speech R.B. Inch, the national secretary of the League of Nations Society, wrote me: 'I have heard a great many complimentary references to your courageous effort at the luncheon. I understand that the P.M. was really not as annoyed as he seemed and was inclined to regret his onslaught on you.' Donald Buchanan headed his weekly article in *Saturday Night* 'Demand foreign policy' and said of my speech, 'Youth at the head table. This was the remarkable, the hopeful, significance of [the League of Nations] Society's banquet held on Friday. Mr. Escott Reid, ... a man whose age is well within this century, gave an address that advocated principles of foreign policy in place of shiftlessness.' Le Rougetel of the British high commissioner's office in Ottawa was at the meeting and sent a report on it to London. He characterized me as 'rather a "bright" young man (both in the good and bad senses of the word)' and called some of my sallies 'pert' but said that my 'speech was in the main both interesting and constructive and was well received by a distinguished gathering.'[3]

In an article in *Interdependence* published the month before the society's lunch I had urged the Canadian government to put forward a bold, far-reaching program for strengthening the collective peace system. The first step would be to try to secure the adherence to this program of the governments of the Commonwealth and of the United States. 'The Canadian *démarche*, to be effective,' I wrote, 'would have to be accompanied by threats and promises.' Two threats would have to be made: the first that if steps were not taken immediately to make the collective system a reality Canada would with great regret be compelled to give notice of withdrawal from the League of Nations, since it would be obvious that it was no longer a real League but only one of the competing alliances of Europe; the second, that at the same time Canada would have to declare its intention of remaining neutral in all overseas wars. The promises would be that Canada, in order to co-operate loyally and effectively in the establishment of a real collective system, was prepared to make its full share of the necessary sacrifices of immediate national interests. The extent and nature of the Canadian sacrifices would have to be made very clear.

My proposals on how the collective system might become a reality were far-reaching. All colonies should become League mandates and be administered by the League. The covenant of the League should be amended to include the provision on racial equality which Japan had proposed at the peace conference in 1919. The Italian proposal of 1920 on the unequal distribution of raw materials among the nations of the world which Canada had successfully opposed should be resurrected, and there should be some sort of international control not only of raw materials but also of tariffs, currency, migration, and international investment. Forty-five years later John Holmes wrote in the first chapter of *The Shaping of Peace*: 'The troublesome propositions raised by the Japanese and Italians have become eventually the dominant issues of the United Nations.'[4]

The first trouble I got into because of my views on Canadian foreign policy was over my activities at the unofficial conference on British Com-

3 Public Record Office, FO 371/18SS1, XPA1.5033, letter of 31 May 1934 to Batterbee
4 John W. Holmes, *The Shaping of Peace: Canada and the Search for World Order, 1943–1957* (Toronto: University of Toronto Press 1979), 10

monwealth Relations held in Toronto in September 1933. I was not entitled to speak at the conference but I was able to make suggestions to some of the younger Canadian and British delegates about what they might say. This resulted in my being summoned a few weeks after the conference to call on Sir Joseph Flavelle in his office. He was one of the leading businessmen in Canada, a millionaire, one of the very few Canadian baronets, a strong supporter of close Canadian ties to the British Empire, a founder of the CIIA and one of its principal financial supporters. He said to me that he had been told that at the conference I had been one of the organizers of an anti-British group and that because of this he would no longer give financial support to the institute. I protested that I had not helped to organize an anti-British group. He blandly countered by saying that he had not said that I had done this but that he had been told that I had done it. I immediately sent J.M. Macdonnell, the chairman of the national executive committee of the institute, an account of this interview. In reply he said that he quite understood that I was somewhat disturbed by this conversation with Flavelle. 'He is,' I wrote to my wife, 'going to consult Massey on ways of persuading Sir J. to change his mind. In the meantime he urges me not to allow the matter to worry me or get on my mind. Nice man, Macdonnell.' When I told my friend George Ferguson of the *Winnipeg Free Press* of my interview with Flavelle, he was most amused. He said I had been privileged to participate in a demonstration of the way in which Flavelle must often have destroyed the careers of people who worked for him.

J.M. Macdonnell was much more than a 'nice man.' He was intelligent, well-informed, intellectually honest, public-spirited, compassionate. He was a leading businessman in Toronto in the thirties and early forties. In 1944 he entered politics and was a Conservative member of Parliament from 1945 to 1962. Unlike most of the other leading businessmen in Toronto at the time who professed devotion to British ideals but supported policies repugnant to them, Macdonnell's devotion to British ideals was real and consistent. He and his friend and fellow businessman, Stanley McLean of Canada Packers, came twice to the defence of Frank Underhill – and thereby to the defence of academic freedom, freedom of speech, and British ideals – when Underhill was threatened with dismissal from the University of Toronto for his views on public affairs. Macdonnell was one of the few leading Conservatives in the early sixties who understood the importance of rich countries giving economic aid to poor countries. He wrote to me in March 1962 that he had been 'ploughing rather a lonely furrow' in connection with aid to underdeveloped countries. 'I make myself believe that it is worth trying to get re-elected in the forthcoming election for this and one or two other purposes ... I have been carried away by the arguments of Hoffman, Black, Barbara Ward, etc., and I feel that if we do not take this much more seriously we may be asking ourselves ten years from now – "What were you doing in the early sixties?"' Macdonnell was what is now called a Red Tory. Diefenbaker when he came to power in 1957 should have made him foreign minister or minister of finance. He made him minister without portfolio and two years later dropped him from the cabinet.

The second time I got into trouble with influential members of the CIIA was over my speech to the League of Nations Society. This incident throws light on the views and the influence at that time of some of the more fervent Canadian advocates of 'loyalty' to Britain and the British Empire, and of how damaging in English Canada was a charge of disloyalty to Britain or the Empire. The account by the Canadian Press of my speech and of R.B. Bennett's rejoinder had identified me as secretary of the institute. The next day the principal editorial in the *Winnipeg Tribune*, entitled 'Busy with the Stiletto,' said that I had 'in the circuitous language common to those who share his views ... [conveyed] the impression that Great Britain has been the arch traitor within the gates of the League of Nations ... And so, according to the secretary of the Institute of International Affairs in Canada, this country must have a foreign policy separate and distinct from Great Britain and the Empire ... If Great Britain is such a dangerous and dishonourable partner, why not assail her in the British way and not with the stiletto?'

I had just been successful in establishing a branch of the institute in Calgary. C.B. (Bo) Clark, the manager of the Calgary branch of the Toronto General Trusts, was secretary of the branch. He wrote me that 'Honorary Colonel' J.H. Woods, 'quite a man in the eyes of numerous people across the country,' had, as soon as he read the *Tribune* editorial, handed in his resignation from the institute, saying that 'we right thinking people must not allow ourselves to be connected with an institution which in any way sponsors such ideas.'

When I visited Saint John, New Brunswick, to try to establish a branch of the institute there, I heard myself being discussed in the room adjoining mine at the hotel. The walls were very thin. One man, obviously interested in the proposal to establish the branch, said he had heard I was anti-British. The other man dismissed the possibility of this since I was descended from a United Empire Loyalist officer who had fought for the

British in the American Revolution and had settled in Fredericton. Perhaps if it had not been for this great-great-grandfather I would not have succeeded in establishing a branch at Saint John.

The trouble I got into because of my activities at the British Commonwealth Relations Conference in 1933 and my speech to the League of Nations Society in 1934 was not serious. What was very serious was the disturbance in the institute which I precipitated in 1935 and 1936 by opposing the imposition of sanctions against Italy.

8

No Sanctions against Italy
1935–1936

My opposition to League sanctions against Italy in October 1935 when Italy invaded Ethiopia plunged me into public controversy with such leading members of the CIIA as N.W. Rowell, J.W. Dafoe, and Brooke Claxton. My opposition was consistent with the contention I had advanced in my address to the League of Nations Society in 1934 that unless effective machinery was established under article 19 of the League covenant for revising treaties and for changing 'international conditions whose continuance might endanger the peace of the world,' there ought to be no effective machinery for enforcing sanctions.

A year later I stressed this argument in an article on international sanctions and world peace in the *University of Toronto Quarterly*. It appeared just six months before sanctions were applied against Italy. I said that to subject the French, British, Americans, Canadians, and Russians to the temptations of possessing unchallengeable sovereignty over their own comparatively rich natural resources – a sovereignty untempered by the fear that the discontented powers might defeat them in war – would most certainly put their elastic national consciences to too severe a strain. Japan, Germany, and the other proletarian powers would probably get in return for their petitions for the redress of grievances little more than a few kind words of advice on the necessity of lowering their standards of living and establishing government birth control clinics. (Half a century later this advice is being given to many poor third world countries.) If the proletarian powers were then to embark on a desperate war of revenge, the 'pious, satiated, democratic, and welfare states' would impose the economic sanctions of the League against 'the impious, proletarian, autocratic and power states.' To escape this nauseating spectacle the world 'can, by making a simultaneous and rapid advance along the three fronts of sanctions, disarmament, and international legislation, establish an effective League which can maintain peace on the secure foundation of international justice.'

The indivisible trinity of the twenties had been sanctions, disarmament, and arbitration. Now international legislation replaced arbitration as the third member of the trinity. This was a fundamental change, since arbitral tribunals make their decisions on the basis of existing rights, thus ruling out peaceful change, while through international legislation peaceful change would be accomplished.

I sent an offprint of this article to Skelton. He replied in a hand-written letter that he 'had been impressed by its vigour and lucidity.'

You are realistic in so far as facing the requirements of your thesis goes however distasteful they may be to public opinion, but I wouldn't say you were realistic in so far as you judge the possibility of public opinion going along with you to the bitter end of your road – at least in this generation. If it's automatic sanctions plus international legislation or chaos, the public will take its chance on chaos, in the trust that some other road will open up in the multitudinous shiftings of the next ten years – at least on this continent. However, alike on the many points on which I agree and those on which I disagree, I congratulate you on the way in which you avoid platitudes and fuzziness and make your meaning starkly clear.

The kind of argument which people like me were making in the second half of the thirties is now being made in the second half of the eighties though the terminology is different. Now the proletarian powers are not the poorer of the relatively wealthy countries, which is what Germany, Japan, and Italy were in the mid-thirties, but the very poor nations of the world – the nations whose populations consist to a great extent of the absolute poor, people who are constantly hungry, who are clothed in rags, and who live in hovels. Now we argue that if we are to have peace we must create a new international political and economic order where wealth and power are shared more equitably among nations and within nations and where the billion absolute poor of the world are enabled to support themselves in decency by productive work which gives them a reasonable income. Again, as in the mid-thirties, the slogan is peace with justice.

In June 1935 I went to London as the representative of the Canadian Institute of International Affairs at the International Studies Conference. After the conference I had talks with H.V. Hodson, the editor of the *Round Table*, Arnold Toynbee, the author of the annual survey of international affairs published by the Royal Institute of International Affairs, Lord Lothian, Vernon Bartlett, a well-known writer and broadcaster on foreign affairs, and Hugh Dalton, a leading member of the British Labour party. This was a time of soul-searching in Britain about the direction which British foreign policy should take after the collapse of the Stresa front and the threat of an Italian invasion of Ethiopia. At Stresa in April, Britain, Italy, and France had agreed to oppose 'any unilateral repudiation of treaties which may endanger the peace of Europe.'

Hodson said to me that the Stresa front was broken as soon as it was made; the British public had recoiled when it realized that its government had committed Britain to a common front with Italy and France to maintain the Treaty of Versailles. Hodson, Toynbee, Lothian, and Bartlett insisted that the only possible policy for Britain was to attempt to conciliate Hitler's Germany by remedying Germany's legitimate grievances against the Treaty of Versailles. Bartlett said that the long delay in making concessions to Germany would mean that the concessions would not have the full effect they would have had if made earlier, but they would nevertheless prevent war for a time. He feared that an Italian invasion of Ethiopia would greatly increase the difficulties of making the necessary concessions to Germany, since action by the League of Nations against Italy would be impossible without the concurrence of France, and France might demand as the price of agreeing to economic sanctions against Italy assurances from Britain that it would resist by force of arms German aggression against Czechoslovakia and Austria. This would result in making the League an effective defender of the status quo in Europe; it would postpone war for a while but the result would ultimately be disastrous.

Lothian and Toynbee dismissed the French contention that it was impossible to make an agreement with Germany. The French, Lothian said, were hopeless. Theirs was a 'No No policy' – a policy of refusing German offers whenever they were made. They wanted to put Germany into a cage; but if they believed in that policy, they should have attacked Germany long ago. Toynbee made the same point: the reply to the French 'No No' was, 'Why did you not make a preventive war in 1933?' It was, he added, to the credit of France that it had not made a preventive war then: it showed that France was truly pacific; its troops would not have marched.

Lothian was certain that he knew what Hitler wanted: it was peace with Britain and France, and a free hand in Eastern Europe. He wanted assurances that if there were a war between Russia and Germany, either on his provocation or Russia's, France and Britain would not interfere.

In Central Europe he wanted Austria but probably not the German part of Czechoslovakia. In Eastern Europe he did not want annexation – this was contrary to the whole teaching of Nazism – but he really did conceive of Germany as playing the historic role of the defender of Western Europe against the Slav. Lothian believed that Britain should retain a free hand in the whole of Europe except France. It should not say in advance whether or not it would participate in a German-Russian or a German-Czechoslovakian war. The price for Britain giving a military guarantee to France against Germany should be that France would not stab Germany in the back in the event of a German-Russian war. Lothian, Bartlett said, had influence on British foreign policy because of his influence on *The Times*. He was dangerous because of his advocacy of a free hand for Germany in Eastern Europe.

Dalton disagreed with the recent decision of the Labour party to vote against increased British expenditures on the air force. This failed to take into account the state of panic in Europe which demanded immediate assurances of help. The socialists in Czechoslovakia were counting the time it would take German airplanes to get to Prague from Germany; it was twelve minutes. The Belgian socialists favoured keeping their airplanes up twenty-four hours a day to repel a sudden German attack. The Danes every night heard German airplanes droning over their heads. Paris was panicky: no one went to sleep without thinking of a German attack.

This was the picture of British opinion on foreign policy which influenced my thinking when the crisis between Italy and Ethiopia came to a head in the first week of September 1935 and it looked as if the members of the League of Nations might soon have to decide whether to impose sanctions against Italy.

In my article on sanctions in the *University of Toronto Quarterly* I had written that in 1919 there had been some hope that the League might gradually assume increasing legislative power, in addition to its police and judicial powers. By 1921 the League had given up most of its pretensions to police powers, and one of the first and most promising attempts which certain of its members made to develop its legislative powers was vetoed by Canada when it insisted that the League should not investigate the question of access to raw materials. I now decided to develop this point and I sent a long article to the Toronto *Saturday Night* which was published in two parts, the first part in the issue for 28 September under the title 'Did Canada Cause Next War?' and the second part a week later under the title 'League Must Give Justice as Well as Peace.' The League of Nations Society in Canada printed the two articles as a pamphlet and this gave them a wide circulation and a special status.

I began the first article with the kind of defence an Italian might make for an Italian invasion of Ethiopia. Before the outbreak of the war in 1914 Italy had depended on emigration to ease its economic problems; the net emigration in the five years before the war was about 620,000 a year; in the past five years it had dropped to about 55,000 a year as countries put up barriers against immigrants. From 1929 to 1932 the depression had halved the value of the remittances which Italian emigrants sent home; it had more than halved income from tourists; Italy's commodity exports were less than 40 per cent of pre-depression levels. An Italian might say that as a result of all this:

We have not been able in recent years to get possession of enough foreign currency to pay for the raw materials which are essential to our existence. The inevitable result has been a lowering of the standard of living of our people and the prospect of a continued decline in the future if economic nationalism throughout the world forces even higher the barriers against the entry of our goods and our people. A continued decline in the standard of living of our people would bring many of them near to starvation. Even in 1929 the average income per head in our country was only about two-thirds of that in France; less than half that in Germany; less than one-quarter that in Great Britain. There is no sign that the nations which are better off than we are prepared to help us by changing their economic policies. Instead economic nationalism is on the increase. Consequently we are faced with virtual starvation if we keep the peace. War is our only way out.

I said in my article that the peaceful way out of Italy's difficulties was international economic co-operation and that Italy had, shortly after the war, made halting attempts to pursue this policy. On Italy's initiative the Council of the League of Nations had in 1920 recommended to the first Assembly of the League that the Assembly establish machinery to consider the question of the danger to world peace caused by the unequal distribution of raw materials among the nations of the world. The chief supporters of the resolution, in addition to Italy, were Belgium, Sweden, and Switzerland. The only states which openly opposed the resolution were four countries of the British Empire: Canada, Australia, New Zealand, and India. The firmest opposition had come from Canada. The Italian proposal, 'though not perhaps of particular importance in itself, would have pointed the way to a peaceful solution of the economic difficulties of the hungry states.' The Italian delegate, Tittoni, had appealed to the 'privileged states' to come before the bar of the Assembly and declare themselves ready to support the cause of international solidarity. Instead, under the leadership of Canada, they had sabotaged the proposal. By so doing they had dealt an effective blow at the conception of the League of Nations as a body which could provide a peaceful solution to international economic conflict. 'Thus the possibility of a peaceful solution to the difficulties faced by Japan, by Italy and by Germany faded into the far distance.'

The deliberately provocative conclusion of my first article was: 'It is possible to maintain therefore that the nation which is the real cause of the next war is Canada, since Canada vetoed at the first Assembly of the League an Italian proposal which would have blazed the way to a new world order in which Italy might have solved her economic difficulties without having recourse to war.'

I was criticized at the time for attaching so much importance to Canada's opposition to the Italian proposal. I was therefore relieved to read a year later Arnold Toynbee's statement at the beginning of his authoritative book on the Italo-Abyssinian war (the second volume of his *Survey of International Affairs for 1935*) that the guilt for that war was shared in some measure by the 'Canadians whose gentle spokesman [N.W. Rowell] had inflicted at Geneva, in 1920, a diplomatic defeat upon the Italian's timid spokesman, Signor Tittoni.'

In my second article in *Saturday Night* I turned to what Canadian policy should be in the Italo-Ethiopian crisis. Sir Samuel Hoare, the British foreign secretary, had recently declared that Great Britain would support an inquiry by the League into the distribution of raw materials produced from colonial areas, including protectorates and mandates. But this did not go far enough. Italy's difficulties in acquiring essential raw materials could not be intelligently discussed without considering the related questions of tariff and migration barriers. The Canadian government should therefore urge that a League commission be appointed immediately to report to a special meeting of the Assembly on measures which the members of the League might take to provide Italy with the possibility of a peaceful solution to its economic problems. If the states that dominated the League made no genuine attempt to help Italy find a peaceful solution of its economic difficulties, the Canadian government should oppose the imposition of sanctions against Italy if it attacked Ethiopia.

At the same time O.D. Skelton, while not going so far as to recommend that Canada oppose the imposition of sanctions against Italy, did on 10 October recommend to Prime Minister Bennett that the Canadian representative in Geneva should not commit Canada to imposing sanctions. Bennett rejected his advice. The general election in which King defeated Bennett took place four days later.

Having committed myself publicly to opposing Canadian participation in League sanctions against Italy, I could scarcely retreat from this position when Italy invaded Ethiopia a couple of days before the second of the two articles appeared. I could have remained silent. I was, however, a member of the national council of the League of Nations Society and when a special meeting of the council was held in Ottawa on 8 November to discuss the crisis over Ethiopia, I attended it and took a leading part in defending the thesis I had put forward in my *Saturday Night* articles. Then, at the beginning of December, the Riddell incident occurred. W.A. Riddell, the Canadian representative at Geneva, had proposed that the members of the League embargo the export to Italy of oil, coal, iron, and steel. This became known as the Canadian initiative. The Mackenzie King government which had taken office on 23 October considered that this misrepresented the position of the government and issued a statement on 2 December, the Lapointe statement, that Riddell's proposal 'represented only his personal opinion, and his views as a member of the [League] Committee [on sanctions] – and not the views of the Canadian Government.' A storm of controversy broke out in Canada. The *Toronto Star* interviewed me as a member of the national council of the League of Nations Society. I took the precaution of saying nothing orally but of giving the reporter a written statement together with a suggested headline, "Declares Lapointe checks Dominion's drift to war.' My statement appeared under this headline. What I said was provocative:

Before anyone gives an opinion on Mr. Lapointe's statement, I think he should ask himself whether he is in favour of Canada participating in the application of military sanctions against Italy today or Germany tomorrow. If he is opposed to Canada's participating in military sanctions or war overseas then he should give general support to Mr. Lapointe's statement.

I had given a preview of my *Saturday Night* articles in a talk to the clerical alumni of Trinity College, and the *Star* on 18 September published an inaccurate account of it. Rowell sent me the newspaper report and, in order to make clear what I had said, I sent him the text of the talk. In his reply on 26 September he said that he believed I was 'absolutely wrong in stating that Canada is in any way responsible for the present economic position of Italy or for Mussolini's attitude.' He defended the position which the Canadian delegation had taken in 1920 and added: 'I was asked by a member of the Institute if your address before the Trinity alumni represented the views of the Canadian Institute. Do you think it is possible for you to deliver public addresses of a propagandist nature without involving the Institute to some extent in your views?' In a postscript he put the strongest argument against the position I had taken: 'Even assuming that all you say about Canada and the Canadian delegation were true, how is Abyssinia in any way responsible, and why should she be made to suffer? Why is she not entitled to the full protection of the Covenant?' He sent a copy of his letter to Vincent Massey, the president of the institute.

Not everyone criticized me for my views. Loring Christie, by this time the second-in-command of the Department of External Affairs, wrote me on 7 October, 'I read your article in *Saturday Night* the other day with much interest and a good deal of sympathy. I don't think any one can find a really good answer to your thesis.' B.K. Sandwell, the editor of *Saturday Night,* came to my defence in an editorial on 19 October:

As we understand Mr. Reid, he was merely trying to establish that certain acts and attitudes have certain consequences and that it is no use pretending that they haven't; and that a rigid what-we-have-we-hold attitude in regard to certain natural resources of which the world has only a limited supply is bound to result in a what-we-don't-hold-we've-got-to-get attitude on the part of nations with an increasing population and only a small share of these resources. This is an unpleasant idea, but it is probably a true one.

My old friend from Oxford days, James MacColl, who was in 1945 to become a Labour MP at Westminster, wrote me at the beginning of February 1936 a criticism of my views which was also a defence of the Labour party against those of its members who had attacked it for supporting sanctions against Italy. They included Stafford Cripps, Nye Bevan, George Lansbury, Lord Ponsonby (the leader of the Labour party in the House of Lords), and George Catlin. They had taken much the same line as I. MacColl wrote:

I do not agree with your isolationist attitude ... I concede to you at once a. that the motives behind the intervention of the League Powers are primarily corrupt, b. that the complaints of the dynamic powers against the static are well founded in terms of economics, c. that in particular our own record in India, in Egypt, perhaps peculiarly in Ireland, has dyed with hypocrisy any attitude we may take. But if the only permanent basis for peace is an international order with both judicial and legislative foundations, we must meet this challenge. Dangerous as are the analogies from national to international society, this much I think can be said ... If the League asserts its authority there is a danger as you say that the static powers may say, 'We need not make concessions.' But equally if it does not they, great and small, are going to say we cannot give because we have no guarantee that our giving will be the limit of our fellow countries' taking.

I discovered many years later that while J.W. Dafoe strongly disagreed with my opposition to sanctions against Italy he had much the same views as I on what should be done to make the League effective. On 27 January 1936 N.E. Archer of the British High Commissioner's office in Ottawa reported to London on a talk with Dafoe which he had had the previous day.[1] He described Dafoe as 'the Editor of the influential Liberal *Winnipeg Free Press*, who, as you know, recently refused the Prime Minister's offer of the post of Canadian Minister at Washington ... [and] certainly one of the strongest forces in the Liberal Party here and *persona grata* with Mackenzie King.' The League, he reported Dafoe as saying, must 'maintain the view that fighting, whatever the reason, was criminal [but] that this aim and attitude could not be achieved if the League were allowed to remain merely a machine for the maintenance of the *status quo*, (territorial, financial, tariff or migration). War had hitherto been the only method of adjusting the *status quo*, and as the world was not static, war could not be prevented unless some alternative method of adjustment were provided.' The open door in colonies was essential. Sacrifices might well be required of Canada in respect of tariffs and migration. In the event of the disruption of the League of Nations, Canadian public opinion would be eight to one in favour of isolation from Europe and in such circumstances Canada's absorption by the United States would certainly follow.

The national council of the CIIA at its annual meeting in Montreal in February 1936 discussed whether my appointment as national secretary should be renewed when it expired in August. Rowell had suggested to Dafoe that the council and I 'should come to some understanding about propaganda.' Dafoe agreed but counselled caution; the best solution was for the council to convince me to use some discretion. My defence came from an unexpected source: J.T. Thorson, dean of the Manitoba Law School, later a Liberal cabinet minister, and afterwards president

---

1 Public Record Office, FO 372/3006, XP 5033, letter of 27 January 1936 from N.E. Archer to G.W. Dixon

of the Exchequer Court of Canada. I did not know this until a few years ago when I read Brooke Claxton's letter of 20 February 1936 to T.W.L. MacDermot giving an account of the meeting:

I think that but for Thorson, Escott would not have been hired without an undertaking to be good, or at least better ... I made the suggestion that the secretary of the Institute should not express his views sharply on any matter of acute controversy and that Escott should be hired on that understanding. Everyone thought the formula good, but Thorson took an extreme liberal view on principle only. He did not know Escott and did not know anything about what we were talking. Everyone leaned backwards to say how liberal they were, too, and the result was that Escott was hired without any understanding. Dafoe talked to him that night but what the result was I don't know.

I made my own report in a letter to Ruth immediately after the meeting: 'I guess the battle was a draw. The main gain I made was that I secured reappointment without any strings being attached to it. Dafoe conveyed to me after the meeting the general sense of the Council that I should at all times keep in mind the effect on the Institute of anything I say or write. The point they gained was the rebuff they gave me by not raising my salary and by appointing me for only a year.'

In spite of Dafoe's advice, I continued to write articles which, in the opinion of my critics, damaged the institute. There were two articles in the *Canadian Forum*, one in February and one in April, and a long article in *Maclean's* magazine in May. The first article in the *Forum*, 'Did Mr. King Flout Parliament?' argued that King on 29 October 1935 had, by accepting League proposals on sanctions against Italy, violated the promise he had made on 21 June 1926 that before the Canadian government signified acceptance of any agreement involving economic sanctions the approval of the Canadian Parliament would be secured. The second article, 'Canada and League Sanctions,' put the argument that the sanctions provisions of the League covenant did not involve Canada in any obligation to co-operate in imposing sanctions. These two conclusions were repugnant at the time to many Canadian supporters of the League of Nations but a year later they became the policy of the Mackenzie King government.

My contention in my second article in the *Forum* that the sanctions articles in the League covenant were no longer binding was supported two years later by the leading British authority on the interpretation of the covenant, Sir John Fischer Williams, in an article in the March-April 1938 issue of *International Affairs*, the journal of the Royal Institute of

International Affairs. I wrote to Underhill in March 1938 that I derived a malicious pleasure from reading it since it was exactly what I wrote in 1935-36 on the Abyssinian crisis and Percy Corbett, Norman Mac-Kenzie, Rowell, and Alfred Zimmern had poured scorn on my argument. I suggested that Underhill should draw all the attention he could to Fischer Williams's article. 'It will be bad enough in the next war having Dafoe, Rowell, Zimmern, et al, preaching "that clear *moral* issue". Let us try to make it impossible for them to preach a clear *legal* issue.'

In 1932 Brooke Claxton had thought so much of me that he had suggested I might become national secretary of the Association of Canadian Clubs as well as of the CIIA; four years later he thought the institute would be better off without me. In a letter to T.W.L. MacDermot he said that in a discussion with me the evening before the meeting of the council of the institute he had found me 'obdurate, obstinate and obtuse.'

As he is also a fanatic and completely spoiled and undisciplined, it makes ordinary human relations, not to speak of business relations, rather difficult ... He refused to admit that anything he had done had injured or could injure the Institute. He said that he was serving the purpose for which he was hired. Alternatively he was free to use his spare time as he liked ... I am not going to talk to Escott any more about this. If he insists on hanging himself, that is his own lookout, but it will be hard on his family as he will find it very difficult to get a similar job in Canada.[2]

Though Claxton had decided not to talk to me any more about my behaviour he did, a fortnight later, write me a long, closely argued, stern letter in reply to a letter I had written him enclosing a draft of my article for *Maclean's*. He said that my articles in the *Forum* irritated 'like a barbed arrow.' As for the *Maclean's* article, while it went through the motion of holding a balance between opposing points of view, 'it is in fact strongly tendential throughout and is I think misleading propaganda in favour of a policy of isolation for Canada ... Consequently I am convinced that its publication would do the Institute harm in Canada because of your inevitable association with the Institute.' He urged that I should recognize the principle that so long as I was employed by an organization such as the CIIA, which depended for its existence and support on having no views of its own, I as its only paid official should not sharply express my views in public on a matter of acute controversy. Everyone 'in our

2 J.L. Granatstein, *The Ottawa Men* (Toronto: Oxford University Press 1982), 240

various walks of life, would like to say things which, by reason of our associations, we feel we cannot freely say. It is sometimes merely a question of tact, on others a question of right-dealing and loyalty.'

Would it not be well for you if you wish to continue as Secretary of the Institute to try to come closer to conforming to the standard of personal conduct which those who are closest to the Institute's work and most friendly with you feel you should follow. In business you would have been fired long ago, out of hand. As it happens, you have been far more fortunate than you think in having a number of really terrific liberals to deal with. In conversation with me you blamed Rowell and Dafoe for trying to knife you. I tell you frankly that you should thank them that you still have a job.

I have no recollection of using this language about Rowell and Dafoe and I am humiliated to learn from Claxton's letter that I did. My only excuse is that I said it in the heat of an argument with Claxton and it was easy to get overheated when arguing with Claxton.

My article in *Maclean's* to which Claxton took such exception was, I believe, an accurate account of the thinking of many Canadians interested in and informed about public affairs on the dilemmas in foreign policy which then confronted Canada. And how they viewed those problems was not very different from the way many of their contemporaries in the western world viewed them.

One group of Canadians, I said, contended that Canada could not remain neutral in another great war; the United States had found it impossible to keep out of the last war; the next great war would inevitably drag in both Canada and the United States. To this the isolationist replied that he could with equal force maintain that the non-participation of Spain, the Netherlands, and the Scandinavian countries in the last great war demonstrated the possibility of Canada remaining neutral. 'Fifty million Europeans took a cool view of the last disturbance and remained neutral. Why should not eleven million Canadians take a cool view of the next disturbance and remain neutral? And even if Canada succeeded, like the United States, in remaining neutral for only the first half of the next great war, it would be worth while, for her losses of men and money would be less than half as great as if she had recklessly plunged in at the outset.'

The isolationist argued that Canadian participation in the last war strained Canadian confederation almost to the breaking point; that entry into another war would be bitterly opposed not only by the French Canadians who constituted 30 per cent of the population but also by a considerable proportion of the other non-British races in Canada who together made up 18 per cent of the population, and even by a large section of Canadians of British stock. Entry into an overseas war would find Canadian opinion so evenly divided that 'either internal revolution or a break-up of the Dominion as we have it would take place.' But it could equally well be argued that these results would be likely to flow from refusal by a Canadian government to come to the assistance of Great Britain in a first-class war.

How could Canada most effectively help to postpone indefinitely the outbreak of another great war and thus postpone indefinitely the un-pleasant choice between participation and non-participation. I quoted Anthony Eden, the British foreign minister, in a speech to his constituents a few months before: 'If a collective peace system is to be effective it must possess two characteristics – strength and elasticity: strength, in order that aggression may be effectively discouraged; elasticity in order that some of the causes of war may be removed through the promotion, by consent, of necessary changes when the time is ripe for them to take place.' If Mr Eden were correct in his analysis of the requirements of an effective peace system, the Canadian government would have to be pre-pared to support sanctions against a state which committed aggression and to support measures to remove the causes of war.

I listed some of the proposals which were being made for international action to remove the causes of war: the lowering of barriers against trade and migration, and the restoration of monetary stability; the bringing of all clearly non-self-governing colonies under the mandate system of the League; the making of a number of comparatively minor revisions in the frontiers of Europe; the restoration to Austria of the right of self-deter-mination; and agreement on a convention for the drastic reduction of national armaments.

Such a program of international action to remove some of the eco-nomic and psychological causes of war would constitute a recognition by the nations of the world that a nation's tariffs, its monetary policy, and its migration policy had ceased to be purely its own affair; from this it would follow that no nation could make a change in its policy on one of these matters without first consulting the other nations affected by it. Before very long, if this program were successful in averting war, the nations of the world would find that they had by slow degrees become members of an international federal system under which no nation had the right to determine for itself its own policy on tariffs, currency, or migration. The Canadian government might be prepared to take the first faltering steps toward this ultimate goal of an international federal state, but it might be afraid of the Canadian people discovering where they were headed and then protesting violently. One of the wisest of Canadian thinkers on this subject had said recently to me in private: 'If it is automatic sanctions plus international legislation or chaos, the Canadian public will take its chance on chaos, trusting that some other road will open up in the multitudinous shiftings of the next ten years.'

Any Canadian foreign policy had its costs. The price of participation in another overseas war might be some sixty thousand dead and perhaps the break-up of Canada. (In the Second World War about forty thousand members of the Canadian armed forces were killed in action or died of wounds.) One possible component of the price of neutrality was also the break-up of Canada; neutrality would probably cost us our membership in the Empire; it might result in our becoming a junior partner in a North American alliance armed to the teeth. The price of peace might be an invasion of Canada's national sovereignty, of Canada's right to determine its own policies on tariffs, currency, and migration. The costs of all three policies were so great that few Canadians would ever persuade themselves that they had to choose among them. And, of course, if matters were allowed to drift too far we would not need to make a choice – it would be made for us; we would have drifted into a current from which we could not escape.

9

Mackenzie King's Foreign Policy 1937–1938

The high point in my career in the thirties as a writer on Canadian foreign policy was on 7 February 1937 when the prime minister, Mackenzie King, wrote in his diary: 'After breakfast ... read some excellent articles by Escott Reid on Canada's Foreign Policy – also splendid article by Gibbs on Spain – cleared my mind on many points.'

Twelve days later in a debate on foreign affairs in the House of Commons he quoted the seven-point summary of his foreign policy which I had set forth in the first of the two articles he had referred to and said: 'That, I think, is a very good statement of some of the features of Canada's foreign policy. Possibly it stresses too much what has to do with possible wars and participation in war, and it does not emphasize enough, in my opinion, what has been done in the way of trade policies and removal of causes of friction between this and other countries.' This passage was probably written by O.D. Skelton or Loring Christie.

Some friends of mine suggested at the time that King, when he read my articles, discovered for the first time that he had a foreign policy, and they made the inevitable reference to Jourdain's exclamation in Molière's play, 'For more than forty years I have been speaking prose without knowing it.'

The seven points of King's foreign policy which I had deduced from his public statements and which he quoted in his speech in Parliament were:

1 The guiding principle in the formulation of Canada's foreign policy should be the maintenance of the unity of Canada as a nation.
2 Canada's foreign policy is, in the main, not a matter of Canada's relations to the League, but of Canada's relations to the United Kingdom and the United States.

3 Canada should, as a general rule, occupy a back seat at Geneva or elsewhere when European or Asiatic problems are being discussed.
4 Canada is under no *obligation* to participate in the military sanctions of the League or in the defence of any other part of the Commonwealth.
5 Canada is under no *obligation* to participate in the economic sanctions of the League.
6 Before the Canadian government agrees in future to participate in military or economic sanctions or in war, the approval of the Parliament or people of Canada will be secured.
7 Canada is willing to participate in international inquiries into international economic grievances.

In the second of my two articles I revised the seventh point in the light of comments I had received from Skelton and Christie. The revised version was:

Canada should pursue within the measure of its power 'the attempt to bring international trade gradually back to a sane basis, to lessen the throttling controls and barriers' ... Coupled with this desire ... is a desire to see the League used as 'a forum for the discussion of economic grievances' and a willingness to have Canada participate in international inquiries 'into any question, raw materials, population movements, labour conditions, that is felt as a grievance.'

The passages in quotation marks are from a speech by King in the House of Commons on 18 June 1936.

I gave the seven points of King's foreign policy a qualified blessing. I said that they demonstrated '(to one critic at least) how well each point, taken by itself, is suited to present conditions,' a commendation which was, no doubt, one reason King considered the articles were excellent. But I wonder if he was pleased with what I wrote immediately after that commendation: 'But the adequacy of the policy as a whole is a different matter. Mr. King has certainly not provided an answer to many pressing questions about Canada's foreign policy.' I listed seven such questions. In what circumstances and to what extent did King favour Canada participating in war or other forms of force? Before such participation was the consultation he had promised to be with Parliament or by general election or by plebiscite? If Canada were neutral in a great war not involving Great Britain, was it to be the old-fashioned neutrality of selling as much as possible at as high a price as possible to all belligerents, or the new-fashioned neutrality of no export of arms and munitions and no public floating of loans to belligerents? If Canada were to take no active part in a great war involving Great Britain, was Canada to be a passive belligerent or a neutral and if a neutral an old-fashioned neutral or a new-fashioned neutral? In a great war in which the United States was neutral, would Canada co-operate with the United States in an effort to ensure that the purpose of its neutrality legislation was not frustrated? What would Canada do in a war between the United States and Japan? How far should Canada be willing to modify its policies in the light of the recommendations of international inquiries into international economic grievances?

I went on to say:

Mr. King has put forward a seven-point foreign policy. If he wants to give the Canadian people a fairly complete picture of his foreign policy, he will have to emulate President Wilson and give us a fourteen-point programme. But if Mr. King were to give unambiguous answers to the seven questions he has left unanswered, he would raise a tremendous political storm in Canada. Parties would split. Passions would be aroused. The national unity of Canada would be subjected to severe strains. If war should break out, such a crisis will probably be inevitable. It is human not to wish to hasten the arrival of the inevitable, if the inevitable is unpleasant – and perhaps dangerous. The argument in favour of provoking the crisis now instead of waiting, is much the same as the argument for a 'preventive' war. A crisis now would settle the question, and as a result there would be no crisis of any importance when war did break out. A crisis today would not be as severe as a crisis during a war. In other words, a crisis today would be a 'preventive' crisis. But democracies and democratic statesmen hate both preventive wars and preventive crises.

In October 1936, three months before my articles on King's foreign policy were published, I sent J.W. Dafoe and Loring Christie a draft of the articles. Dafoe in a letter on 10 November congratulated me on the draft. 'It is much the best analysis of this tangled problem I have read. I have myself learned much from it.' He believed that I had 'well sized up' King's views on the Empire. King's inclinations were 'for one hundred percent isolationism though he probably will never get to the point of saying so in words so explicit as to leave no doubt in the minds of his hearers.'

I am satisfied in my own mind that Mr. King's private hope is that it will be possible for Canada to keep out of external wars whether League or imperial without thereby setting up reactions in Canada which would lead to internal strife. I myself am far less hopeful that this could be accomplished ... We are encouraging the discussion of this question [in the *Winnipeg Free Press*] because it is high time the individual citizen of Canada began to determine for himself where he stands on an issue which I very much fear he will have to face within the next three years.

Dafoe's prophecy was accurate. The issue had to be faced in two years and ten months. I wonder, however, if he was right in believing that King in 1936 hoped Canada could stay out of the coming war. My impression now is that he may have decided by then that that hope was illusory.

Loring Christie sent me a long comment on my draft. He emphasized the personal and unofficial character of his reply by dating it from the Rideau Club, not from the Department of External Affairs, and by marking it 'personal, private, confidential.' The idea of the foreign policy of a foreign minister or of a country, he said, had to be approached with many reservations.

I suppose the act of state itself is best worth looking at; the explanatory statement accompanying it comes next; while general debate in the air, whether in Parliament or [League of Nations] Assembly, becomes somewhat doubtful ... This is far from saying that a review like yours of one statesman's way of recording his calculations and guesses [about foreign policy] is of no use. On the contrary it may be of great use to him and others to try to confront him and them with a picture of what he has seemed to disclose.

He criticized my constant use of the word isolation as an antithesis apparently to internationalism:

This particular word seems to derive from the typically Wilsonian conception that was imbedded in Article 11 of the Covenant. 'Any war or threat of war, whether immediately affecting any of the members of the League or not, is *hereby declared* a matter of concern to the whole League', etc. ... Wilson, the man and moralist, was 'concerned' about wars and threats of war; they distressed him; and most of us are 'concerned' in that way. But to a State a matter of 'concern' is, technically and diplomatically, a matter which immediately affects its interests. This is inherent in the nature of the State and has always been recognized – and all experience since the enactment of Article 11 has shown States acting according to their nature and not according to this dictum.

Shortly after my two articles were published Christie wrote me, 'I have heard several people speak favourably of the articles, none unfavourably and I congratulate you upon doing them.'

In December 1937 Skelton sent a memorandum to Frank Scott commenting on a draft paper on Canada and the Commonwealth which Scott was preparing for the Canadian Institute of International Affairs to present to the second unofficial British Commonwealth Relations Conference. This paper, after many revisions, became the book by Scott, *Canada Today*. In his memorandum Scott had said that my seven-point summary of King's foreign policy in my articles published in January and February 1937 meant very little. 'Not so,' said Skelton. The first principle, the necessity of preserving national unity, was important because Empire unity or League unity were more talked about than national unity. Scott had stated that the second principle, that Canada's foreign policy was in the main a matter of relations to the United Kingdom and the United States, was 'not a statement of policy' but a fact but, wrote Skelton, 'When did the realization of a fact become unimportant? The significant trend in Canada is the willingness to face facts, our facts not traditions or other peoples' facts or aspirations.' As for the sixth principle, reference to Parliament or the people before the government agreed to participate in military or economic sanctions or war, this was indeed

not a final settlement – the vital question remains what will parliament decide and what will the Government recommend to parliament, but surely the stand that parliament must decide, that action in any special direction cannot be taken as certain or predestined, does secure and preserve some measure of free decision. 'It only postpones the evil day' – but as someone has said, 'Isn't that the best thing to do with evil days.' They may never come – most don't – and if they do, the balance of forces will be different from today.

When Frank Scott wrote the second edition of *Canada Today* at the end of 1938 he accepted Skelton's arguments and gave his blessing to my analysis of King's foreign policy. He also said, quoting without attribution Skelton's reference to the evil day: 'The "wait-and-see" policy enables politicians to put off the evil day of decision; this may seem a good thing to do with evil days, but it is the negation of the democratic method; it means that when the decision must be made a foreign policy dictated by blind forces instead of conscious purposes will prevail.'

Skelton in his memorandum of December 1937 to Scott spoke of the evil day when Canada would have to decide whether to enter another great war. The evil day came less than two years later, and on 10 September 1939 Skelton wrote a memorandum pouring forth his anguish:

... There is a widespread feeling that this is not our war, that the British Government which blundered into it, should have been allowed to blunder out, that it is fantastic and insane for Canadians to allow themselves to be maneuvered and cajoled every quarter century into bleeding and bankrupting this young country because of the age-long quarrels of European hotheads and the futility of British statesmen.

The British government had, he wrote, announced that it was preparing for a three-year war. Skelton's comment on this was wise and far-seeing. The only thing certain was that the effects of a three-year war

will be as tremendous as they are incalculable and that the results of the war will be something entirely different from the professed or even the real objectives of either side when it began ... [W]hat social revolutions, what changes of boundaries, what new alignments of powers, what new dictators, what new memories of hate and hopes of revenge, who can say? After all, the human race can stand a lot of punishment, and it is possible that even after three years of destruction the survivors, after this second lesson, will achieve a juster peace and build a more adequate world order than the past generation. I fervently hope so.[1]

Skelton died in January 1941, sixteen months later. The Department of External Affairs was his creation. He would have been proud of the efforts the department made after the war to build a more adequate world order.

1 Papers of the Under-Secretary of State, vol. 13, memorandum of 10 September 1939

10

*R*eflections on the Thirties

Ruth and I started off our married life in September 1930 in a basement apartment in Toronto in a new apartment house on Wellesley Street near Jarvis. As my salary increased we moved north – first to Gloucester Street, then to Summerhill Gardens, and finally to Farnham Avenue. We had three children: Patrick born in 1931, Morna in 1934, and Timothy in 1936. Ruth bore children easily but I found the birthing of babies exhausting. A week before Patrick was born I had an emergency appendix operation. A few days after Ruth came home from hospital after giving birth to Timothy I went to hospital with what was then called low-grade pneumonia. In the thirties I suffered from painful bouts of lumbago and arthritis.

On Farnham Avenue we lived in a nest of CCF supporters. In those days the party had local clubs which met to discuss public affairs. Ruth and I soon ceased attending our local club because the discussions on questions of substance were constantly interrupted by tedious discussions about procedure and organization. I later realized that the hidden communists in the CCF deliberately provoked these discussions in order to make the meetings boring so that non-communists would stop attending and they could take the clubs over and so increase their influence in the CCF.

Our closest friends were Larry and Margie MacKenzie and Frank and Ruth Underhill. We occasionally went skiing with Larry and Margie and we twice rented a summer cottage near theirs at Bayfield on Lake Huron. But from 1932 on – indeed until 1969 when I retired as principal of Glendon College – I did not play enough and I worked too hard. My work in the CIIA was heavy, since I was the only officer in the organization and I had large ideas about the need to expand its work. Then from

1933 on I was obsessed with the danger of war. All I could do in the face of this threat was to give speeches and write articles and this was a drain on my strength. The result was that I sacrificed Ruth and our children to my work. Ruth bore much more of the responsibility for bringing up our children than was fair.

The most enduring effect on me of my work in the thirties was that I learned a good deal about Canada from my travels in Canada and my talks with makers of public opinion in business, politics, universities, and newspapers. This was good training for the many talks, formal and informal, which a diplomat has to have to do his job. Another enduring effect was that I discovered I could write publishable articles quickly and clearly, not just for the journals of learned societies and university quarterlies but also for more popular periodicals such as *Saturday Night* and *Maclean's*. When I joined the External Affairs Department I found it relatively easy to write official memoranda, despatches, and telegrams and, later, speeches for the foreign minister. Indeed, my facility in writing and the pleasure I took in it resulted in my writing too many – and too lengthy – memoranda, despatches, and telegrams.

My three heroes of the thirties were Frank Underhill, Edgar Tarr, and J.W. Dafoe. When Frank and Ruth Underhill came to our house and we to theirs we used to joke about the possibility that members of the security service of the Royal Canadian Mounted Police were hiding in the bushes spying on us. (Years later I learned that in the mid-thirties Underhill was indeed under surveillance by the RCMP who reported at least once to the president of the University of Toronto about his 'subversive activities.' And in 1940 the attorney general of Ontario had him investigated by the head of Ontario's 'anti-sabotage-subversive squad.')[1] To show our affection for Underhill we asked him to be a godfather at the christening of our son, Timothy. He had long ceased to go to church and he must have been an agnostic, but he showed his affection for us by agreeing. He was not, however, enthusiastic over giving the responses a godparent gives in the Anglican christening service. In fact I think he did not respond at all. Fortunately the other godfather gave the responses loudly and firmly.

Underhill was more than a distinguished historian and an outstanding writer on public affairs. He had a genius for friendship and he was a brilliant teacher, as thousands of his former students at the universities of Saskatchewan, Toronto, and Carleton can attest. There is one state-

1 R. Douglas Francis, *Frank H. Underhill: Intellectual Provocateur* (Toronto: University of Toronto Press, n.d.), 97, 117

ment of his I especially cherish: 'A nation is a body of people who have done great things together in the past and who hope to do great things together in the future.' He once insisted that I should not in an article of which I had sent him a draft give him credit for this statement, since he had been quoting Ernest Renan; he said that he had indeed been quoting this passage from Renan for years without looking it up. I looked up the passage in Renan and told Underhill that he had said better in twenty-seven words what Renan had taken seventy-five words to say. This demonstrates the wisdom of intelligent people not checking their unattributed or hidden quotations, since by not checking them they may improve them.

At the beginning of November 1937 I wrote to Underhill, 'I hope you don't get into any trouble this year with the oligarchs of Ontario or, as John Stevenson calls them, the inflated gold bugs.' (Some of the most influential oligarchs had made their fortunes out of gold mines.) Two years later Underhill did get into trouble with the oligarchs and from 1939 to 1941 he was repeatedly threatened with dismissal from the University of Toronto. His friends and admirers successfully rallied to his defence. Three of his colleagues in the LSR and the CCF were less fortunate. They were penalized for their left-wing views. King Gordon was dismissed in 1934 from his professorship at the United Theological College in Montreal, and Eugene Forsey and Leonard Marsh in 1941 from their lectureships at McGill University. Frank Scott was not dismissed in 1947 from the law faculty of McGill but he was denied appointment as dean of the faculty, an appointment he richly deserved. He was not made dean until 1961. We had McCarthyism in Canada before McCarthy.

One of the greatest good fortunes of my life is that I had the privilege of working with Edgar Tarr in the Institute of International Affairs and that he granted me his friendship. In 1935 I was thirty and he fifty-four but I never felt that we belonged to different generations. Tarr, like Underhill and J.W. Dafoe, was one of the most outstanding participants in the public affairs of Canada in the twenty-seven years from the end of the First World War to the end of the second. He could in 1942 have been the first Canadian minister to China but he turned the offer down – an offer which demonstrated the Canadian government's confidence in him. But this confidence did not extend to his correspondence. In 1941 and 1942 when I was in the Department of External Affairs in Ottawa I was on the circulation list for extracts which the Canadian censors had made from mail coming into and going out of Canada. I was angered to find in my in-basket one day extracts from a letter by Tarr.

I tried in November 1950 to express my feelings about Tarr in a letter to Mrs Tarr on his death: 'He taught me by his example that a man may so discipline himself that he can practise virtues which are rarely found together. Joyous devotion to duty and patience with fools but not with folly. Selflessness and a holy obstinacy in pressing with all his energy for the realization of the ideals he believes in. A wide-ranging mind, intellectual integrity, and a compassionate concern for the welfare of his country and his neighbours throughout the world. Of such are the Kingdom of Heaven.'

I first met Dafoe in August 1930 when I came to Winnipeg to be married. George Ferguson of the *Winnipeg Free Press* was a friend of Ruth's. He arranged an interview for me with Dafoe in his office at the *Free Press* to discuss my research project on Canadian political parties. I had a long, helpful talk with him then and other talks on Canadian politics a year later. I knew in 1932 that it was he who had proposed to Rowell and Massey that I be appointed national secretary of the CIIA, but I did not learn until recently of the trouble I had put him to in his efforts to protect me from my critics in the institute. In his book *The Ottawa Men*, J.L. Granatstein quotes a letter of January 1937 from Dafoe to Grant Dexter, the correspondent in Ottawa of the *Winnipeg Free Press*. Dafoe was explaining to Dexter that he had had to make a visit east: 'the business of the Canadian Institute of International Affairs required my presence in Toronto at the end of January. I stepped into a bit of trouble in the Institute which Escott Reid has precipitated – he is not a judicious young man' (p. 240).

Excess of zeal exacerbated by an addiction to working too hard has too often led me, before and after joining External Affairs, to being impatient and provocative on issues I have felt deeply about. This explains but does not excuse my belief early in 1936 that Dafoe was hostile to me because of my views on the Italo-Ethiopian crisis, when his hostility was not to me but to my views. Fortunately for me I soon realized this. But it shames me now to remember my stupidity and it hurts me to realize how much trouble I caused Dafoe when I was secretary of the institute. Then I comfort myself by rereading the handwritten letter he wrote me on 1 January 1939, the day I joined the Department of External Affairs: 'This is my first letter of 1939: I send you my regards and best wishes. I expect nothing from 1939 in world affairs but some more of 1938. But fortunately there can be individual happiness in a disordered world.'

The intellectual I knew in the thirties who influenced me most was Arnold Toynbee. I met him first at the unofficial British Commonwealth Relations Conference in Toronto in 1933 when he was forty-four years old and I immediately became his disciple. He impressed me at the conference not just by what he said, which was impressive enough, but by the way in which he said it. I was once responsible for persuading him to intervene at one point in the conference's deliberations, so I know that he had had no chance to prepare in advance what he was going to say. Yet if the speech had been taken down verbatim by a stenographer it could have been published without change as a polished essay.

An example of his perspicacity about trends in international affairs was his forecast in a letter to me in May 1933: 'If Australia found that she could not get the British Fleet to protect her, would not she be inclined to turn to the United States and represent to her that the protection of Australia was an American interest? This position might easily arise if a Hitlerite Germany and a militarist Japan were to make common cause – a possibility which does not seem to me to be at all fantastic.'

When the first three volumes of Toynbee's *A Study of History* came out in the mid-thirties I immersed myself in them. When the second batch of three came out in 1939 I immediately read them. The influence of these six volumes by Toynbee permeates many of the memoranda I wrote while an officer in the Department of External Affairs.

When I try half a century later to recall what chiefly influenced my views on foreign affairs in the apocalyptic thirties, I think first of the pamphlets and books I devoured written by members of the British Labour party. The two pamphlets which influenced me most were *The Dying Peace* by Vigilantes, published in September 1933 by the *New Statesman and Nation*, and *Labour's Foreign Policy* by Arthur Henderson, the former Labour foreign minister, published in July 1933 by the British Labour party. The main author of Henderson's pamphlet may have been Philip Noel-Baker. The book that influenced me most was *The Intelligent Man's Way to Prevent War* edited by Leonard Woolf; it too was published in 1933. Then there were the books of the Left Book Club, especially those by H.N. Brailsford, G.D.H. Cole, Harold Laski, Arthur Koestler, John Strachey, and Vigilantes.

I was also greatly influenced by the mass of articles and books written since 1918 by liberals in the United States. In the period between the two world wars almost all American liberals were determined that the United States should keep out of a second world war. This determination was rooted in their belief – a belief which I shared then and continue to hold – that the world would have been a better place if the United States had not entered the First World War, since its intervention aborted the possibility of a sensible compromise peace. In their opinion, the essential contribution the United States could make to world civilization was to keep out of the next war and so preserve civilization in at least one great country. These beliefs led to the passage of the American neutrality legislation. Charles Beard, the eminent American historian, was one of the most eloquent and persuasive apostles of what most people called isolationism but which he insisted should be called 'continentalism': 'American democracy should not ... assume that it had the capacity, even with the best of good will, to settle the difficult problems of European nations encrusted in the heritage of their long and sanguinary history.' Loring Christie, one of Canada's leading continentalists, said much the same thing in a private letter to me in October 1935: Canada 'cannot practically contribute to what is a problem, first, of European political invention. There are strict limits to what outsiders can do for insiders in any show.'

I can distil from two of my writings in the first half of the thirties most of my hopes and fears, predilections and prejudices about foreign affairs: one is a speech I gave at my former high school in mid-April 1933, and the other an outburst published in *Saturday Night* in May 1935, occasioned by my anger at a film, 'Lest We Forget,' produced by a committee of the Canadian Department of National Defence. I said the film should have been called 'Lest we forget our simple faith in the simple war-time fables.' I find in these two documents four influences on my thinking.

I was revolted by the senseless slaughter of Allied soldiers on the western front in the First World War, caused in my opinion by stupid western generals who wasted the lives of their men and by equally stupid western politicians who insisted on fighting the war to a knock-out blow instead of doing their utmost to make a compromise peace. I had been moved by the great British classics of disenchantment: by Siegfried Sassoon, Edmund Blunden, Robert Graves, and C.E. Montague, and by Erich Remarque's *All Quiet on the Western Front*. In my article in *Saturday Night* I urged that we should not forget what western troops felt about the stupidity of their generals and I quoted Sassoon's poem:

'Good morning; good morning!' the General said
When we met him last week on our way to the Line.
Now the soldiers he smiled at are most of 'em dead,
And we're cursing his staff for incompetent swine.

'He's a cheery old card', grunted Harry to Jack
As they slogged up to Arras with rifle and pack.
But he did for them both by his plan of attack.

(In the late sixties I said to a small group of American academics that it was perhaps a pity that the United States had not entered the First World War in time to have its troops slaughtered at Passchendaele in July 1917, since that might have taught the people of the United States not to trust their generals. I suggested that the greater their distrust of their generals the sooner they might extricate themselves from the Vietnam quagmire.)

A second influence was also a revulsion – a revulsion from the wartime propaganda we had swallowed: the tales of German atrocities, the war in defence of the rights of small nations, the war to end war, the war to make the world safe for democracy. We were resolved that we were not going to be so naive as to swallow that kind of propaganda the next time it was fed to us. (After the Second World War there was no revulsion against wartime propaganda on Germany. Rather we discovered that Germany, by its slaughter of the Jews, had behaved more criminally than we had thought possible. If there was a revulsion against propaganda it was against the depiction after the Soviet Union entered the war of a benevolent 'Uncle Joe' Stalin. As we became more conscious after the war of the mass slaughter by our own side of civilians in Hamburg, Dresden, Hiroshima, and Nagasaki we were revolted by our own behaviour.)

Another influence on us in the first half of the thirties was the generally held belief that a second world war would destroy civilization. Stanley Baldwin had said, 'Who does not know that one more war in the West and the civilization of the ages will fall with as great a crash as that of Rome?' It is unlikely that Baldwin was thinking of the civilizations of India or China or the Muslim world when he spoke of the civilization of the ages; he was probably thinking of the civilization of which Britain is a part, the civilization of Western Europe, descended from western Christendom. (Today Western European civilization seems secure against collapse, provided there is no third world war, but seventeen years ago it was possible for a wise Western European to echo Baldwin's prophecy of doom. One of my best friends when I was ambassador to Germany in the late fifties and early sixties was G.F. Duckwitz of the German foreign office. He later became head of the office. He wrote to me in 1971: 'I have the strong feeling that Europe's stage is that of the last fifty years of the Roman Empire. And that is, I am afraid, the fate we deserve.')

A fourth influence was the belief taught us by Maynard Keynes in his *Economic Consequences of the Peace* that the peace treaty imposed on Germany in 1919 was iniquitous and that we were reaping the bitter, bitter fruits of that Carthaginian peace. This influence permeates my speech to my former high school in April 1933, two and a half months after Hitler had come to power. I said that the Allies, instead of welcoming the democratic German government which had taken power after the war, had burdened it with reparations it could not possibly pay. When it was clear it could not pay, France had invaded German soil and sowed on that soil the seeds of bitterness which were now being harvested. The former allied governments had for fourteen years refused to give Germany and the other former enemy countries the justice they had been demanding. Largely as a result of that refusal, democratic Germany had collapsed before a tide of national bitterness. If that tide were not to result in a European war in about five years (it turned out to be six years), 'the justice which was refused to democratic Germany must now be given to Hitlerite Germany. That will be unpleasant. It will also be risky, for justice may not satisfy Hitler. Having received justice Hitler may demand more, and more, and more, and finally resort to war. Revision of the treaties may not bring peace. On the other hand, refusal to revise will eventually bring war.'

Ever since the Soviet Union imposed its control over Eastern Europe after the Second World War many people in the West have wondered whether the western powers could not have done more to prevent that takeover, but so far as I am aware there is today in the West no feeling of guilt about the post-1945 peace settlement comparable to the feeling of guilt in the thirties about the post-1918 settlement. Many of us in the West today who live in comfort do have feelings of guilt, but it is not guilt about the post-war settlement but about the inequitable distribution of wealth and power among nations and within nations.

To these four principal influences on my thinking in the first half of the thirties were added other influences in the second half of the decade. In my 1933 speech I said that 'by 1929 the world was well above pre-war standards [of wealth] and seemed to be advancing at an unprecedented pace to levels of prosperity never before thought possible.' The sudden descent from these visions into the miseries of the great depression, the incompetence of western governments in dealing with it, the coming of Hitler to power, the refusal of Britain and France, the two powers that dominated the League of Nations, to work through the League in an effort to deal with the underlying causes of world tension, their refusal to help the democratic government of Spain in its civil war against rebels supported by Nazi Germany and fascist Italy contrasted with the support the Soviet Union gave the Spanish government, and what seemed to us to be a movement in the Soviet Union towards sensible long-term economic planning (the first Soviet five-year plan of economic development had been inaugurated in 1928) and the adoption by the Soviet Union in 1936 of a new ostensibly democratic constitution led us to question the conventional wisdom that there was more hope for the world in western civilization than in Soviet civilization.

I wish I could recall how far my relative optimism about the long-run development of Soviet civilization was affected by the Soviet treason trials and purges of 1936, 1937, and 1938. Perhaps like my contemporary at Oxford, the poet Stephen Spender, I at first believed in the guilt of the accused. Spender has written: 'To the reader today the very idea that anyone could have thought them to be guilty is shocking as it is to me myself [but] ... to understand the Thirties one ought to realize that at the time it was not at all certain that they were innocent.'[2] Or did I, like Louis Fischer, balance in the scales Soviet support for the Loyalists in Spain against Soviet domestic policy?[3]

The Spanish civil war influenced my generation profoundly. Hugh Thomas put it well when he wrote that it looked to western intellectuals 'at least at first, when all the parties of the Left seemed to be cooperating, the great moment of hope for an entire generation angry at the apparent cynicism, indolence and hypocrisy of an older generation with whom they were out of sympathy ... For intensity of emotion, the Second World War seemed less of an event than the Spanish War.'[4]

We were also influenced by our suspicion of the Great Britain of Stanley Baldwin and Neville Chamberlain, a suspicion shared by a moderate liberal such as J.W. Dafoe, who in a letter of 21 July 1936 to N.W. Rowell condemned 'the obvious sympathy for Nazi-ism and Fascism that has taken possession of a very large section of what might be called the governing group of England which is growing daily now that France is swinging left and thus getting closer to Moscow.' Frank Scott in his brilliant *Canada Today* published in January 1939 by the Canadian Institute of International Affairs wrote that Canadian supporters of the

2 Stephen Spender, *The Thirties and After: Poetry, Politics, People, 1933–1970* (New York: Random House 1977), 15

3 Arthur Koestler, et al., *The God That Failed* (London: Hamish Hamilton 1950), 222

4 Hugh Thomas, *The Spanish Civil War* (London: Eyre & Spottiswoode 1961), 616

League of Nations believed that the British government should cease 'to make avoidance of social revolution in European countries one of the objectives of its foreign policy.'[5]

I had in October 1935 expounded my own views on the untrustworthiness of the British National Government in a letter to Philip Noel-Baker, one of the leading spokesmen on foreign affairs of the British Labour party:

The enforcement of sanctions against Italy by a left-wing U.K. government in which you were foreign secretary is to me an entirely different thing from the enforcement of sanctions against Italy by a right-wing U.K. government which contains enemies of the League. Your purpose in enforcing sanctions would be to defend the collective system; their purpose to defend immediate British interests, such as the route to India. The peace which you would make would be actuated by a desire to remove the causes of war and by a belief that the fundamental causes of war are economic in character. The peace they would make would be one which would safeguard immediate imperial interests and which would sow the seed of future wars.

Another influence on my thinking in the late thirties and on the thinking of many, perhaps a majority of, persons in Britain, the rest of the Commonwealth, and the United States interested in and informed about foreign affairs was our belief that there was a balance of forces in Europe. One reason for this belief was the contention of the then leading western writer on defence, Liddell Hart, that the offensive had to have a two-to-one or three-to-one superiority to break through. O.D. Skelton, the under-secretary of state for external affairs, wrote in a memorandum to the prime minister on 25 August 1939: '... an overwhelming victory over Germany ... could only be secured by smashing the Siegfried line. There is as little chance of that as there is of Germany's smashing the Maginot line. In other words, the defense has a tremendous advantage – Hart says two or three to one.'[6]

In 1950 Frank Underhill in an article in the *Canadian Forum* wrote: 'We ought not to have been so foolish [in the thirties as to believe] that the power of the British navy and the French army was so overwhelming that the Nazi challenge could be handled within Europe without outside intervention from North America.' Loring Christie, who along with Skel-

5 F.R. Scott, *Canada Today*, 2nd ed. (Toronto: Oxford University Press 1939), 114
6 *Documents on Canadian External Relations* (DCER), vol. 6, memorandum of 25 August 1939: 1251

ton was one of the leading neutralists in the Department of External Affairs from 1935 till the outbreak of the war, said the same thing to me in June 1940 after France had collapsed. He was then Canadian minister in Washington and I was second secretary at the legation. He was ill in hospital in Baltimore and Ruth and I drove out to see him one lovely June day. He said that the mistake he had made was that he had thought there was a balance of forces in Europe; he had overestimated the strength of the French armed forces and underestimated the strength of the German.

As the result of all these influences it is likely that by the beginning of 1939 a majority of Canadians – not just a majority of the younger intellectuals – were opposed to Canada participating in the coming war. This was Skelton's opinion. Early in 1939 he wrote that it was probable that a majority of the people of Canada were 'opposed to participation in British wars,'[7] and since the only wars likely to involve Canada were wars in which Britain was a belligerent, he was stating that a majority of Canadians had become neutralist.

One evening in 1943 when my friend Graham Spry and I were walking in Hyde Park in London and bombs started dropping Spry accused me of having made war more likely by opposing sanctions against Italy in 1935. He argued that if the League of Nations had compelled Italy to cease its aggression against Ethiopia by imposing economic and financial and, if necessary, military sanctions, Hitler would have realized that if he committed aggression the League would likewise compel Germany to cease its aggression and there would have been no second world war. R.B. Inch was national secretary of the League of Nations Society when its council debated the issue of sanctions against Italy in November 1935. He had supported me in my opposition to sanctions. When war broke out this weighed on his conscience. He was in the Canadian army in the invasion of France and Belgium. In September 1967 he wrote me: 'I have had a sense of guilt from those days. One of my letters to E [his wife] when we had gone up through Normandy and into Belgium: "I have paid the bill or most of it." '

Most of the historians who have studied the question have concluded that the imposition by the League of economic and financial sanctions against Italy would have resulted in Italy giving up its attack on Ethiopia only if Mussolini had been convinced that, if economic and financial sanctions proved ineffective, Britain and France were prepared to impose military sanctions, and there is little evidence that they were so prepared. Mussolini would have known this or at least guessed it and therefore it

7 NAC, Hume Wrong Papers, vol. 3, 'Automatic Belligerency,' n.d., 1939

is highly unlikely that League sanctions against Italy could have been effective. But if we assume, for the sake of argument, that League economic and financial sanctions, accompanied by a bluff that military sanctions would, if necessary, be imposed, would have stopped the Italian aggression, and if we further assume that stopping the Italian aggression would have made German aggression less likely, then I am left with the possibility that my opposition to sanctions against Italy contributed, however slightly, to making the outbreak of the Second World War more likely. My contention at the time was that a League which was effective in imposing sanctions but ineffective in dealing with the causes of international tension was not a League which was worth supporting because peace had to be founded on justice between nations. Arnold Toynbee, of whose wisdom I stood in awe, likewise believed that peace had to be founded on justice and that the twin pillars of justice were peaceful change and collective security; he attacked the western world for not giving Italy justice through peaceful change in the seventeen years from 1918 to 1935; nevertheless he supported sanctions against Italy in 1935. If I committed an error in 1935, it was that I had, in my writings on the League from April 1934 on, made the better the enemy of the good, an error to which perfectionists like me are prone.

Did I commit an error in the second half of the thirties in contending that Canada should be neutral in the impending world war? If so I was wrong in good company. Neutralism was the policy of seven of the most highly respected democratic nations in Western Europe: Norway, Sweden, Denmark, Finland, Belgium, the Netherlands, and Switzerland. In the United States the overwhelming majority of those who were interested in and informed about international affairs, on the right, in the centre, on the left, were neutralist. Neutralism was the belief of five of the seven senior officers in the Department of External Affairs in Ottawa: Skelton, Christie, Laurent Beaudry, Hugh Keenleyside, and Scott Macdonald. The only senior officers of the department who were not neutralist were Norman Robertson and John Read; they had allies in two of the most senior officers of the foreign service abroad: Hume Wrong in Geneva and L.B. Pearson in London. Of the five neutralists only one, Beaudry, had been to Oxford. All four non-neutralists had been to Oxford.

To be wrong in good company is not a sufficient excuse for being wrong. Perhaps, however, we Canadian neutralists of the second half of the thirties can comfort ourselves with the argument that if we had successfully advocated the opposite course – that Canada should declare publicly that it would ally itself with Britain if Britain became involved in war against Germany – this would have made no difference to the course of events. The main argument for the North Atlantic treaty which its advocates advanced in 1948 and 1949 when it was being negotiated was that the two world wars might have been aborted if the Kaiser and Hitler had known that if war broke out Germany would face a coalition of the United States, Britain, Russia, and France and that, to avert a third world war, a grand alliance against the Soviet Union should be created in peace-time. There was, however, no possibility in the late thirties of the United States, Britain, the Soviet Union, and France agreeing to form an alliance against Germany, and a declaration by Canada that it was prepared to join such an alliance if it were created would not have affected the outcome.

Perhaps a persistent uneasy feeling that I might have been remiss in pressing for a policy of neutrality in the second half of the thirties contributed to making me a fervent advocate in the second half of the forties of a strong United Nations and a powerful North Atlantic alliance.

11

*T*he Legation in Washington
1939–1941

Early in 1936, when I was calling on Skelton in his office in Ottawa to discuss CIIA affairs, he told me that he had thought some years before of sounding me out on the possibility of my joining the Department of External Affairs but had decided against it because he did not think it fair to deprive the institute of my services so soon after I had become its national secretary. I did not commit myself then, but in November I told him I was interested in joining the department. He told me he had already talked the matter of my appointment over with some of the senior officers of the department. My appointment, Skelton said, was tied up with the whole question of the opening of new legations, a concomitant increase in the staff in Ottawa, and the transfer of senior officers – Hume Wrong from Washington, Georges Vanier from London, Walter Riddell from Geneva, and Jean Désy from Paris. Because of this my appointment did not take place until January 1939.

My first post in the External Affairs service was as second secretary at the legation in Washington. When there was no minister or when the minister was not well enough to discharge his duties – which was two-thirds of the time I was in Washington – I was the senior political officer. This was excellent training for a neophyte in diplomacy.

I knew only two people in Washington when I arrived there: Hu Shih, the Chinese ambassador, whom I had met at conferences of the Institute of Pacific Relations, and Angus Malcolm, who was second secretary at the British embassy. He generously invited me to stay with him in his pleasant house near the Episcopalian cathedral until my wife and our three children could join me.

In those days the legation was small; it had only five officers in addition to the minister, Sir Herbert Marler. Walter Riddell, formerly head of the Canadian mission to the League of Nations, was counsellor and Merchant Mahoney was commercial counsellor. I ranked next as second secretary, and there were two third secretaries, Ronald Macdonnell and Hector Allard. The only other Canadian office in the United States was the trade commissioner's office in New York. The diplomatic corps in Washington was so small that all its members from ambassadors to third secretaries and their wives were invited to the president's annual reception for the diplomatic corps at the White House in December 1939. This was the last of such receptions. The city was so small that there was still a farm opposite the house we rented on Massachusetts Avenue just beyond the border between the District of Columbia and Maryland. Our children and the farmer's children became friends. The farmer raised turkeys and our five-year-old daughter became so fond of them that when we had one of the turkeys for Christmas dinner she would not eat it.

I arrived on a Friday. I started work at the legation the next morning. I wrote that afternoon to Ruth: 'My immediate file is concerned with unfortunate German Jews in the States who want to get their relatives out of Germany immediately and offer to support them in Canada until they can enter the U.S. Unfortunately I am afraid there is nothing we can do except turn them down. If I could find a loop-hole I'd feel I'd justified my existence before I became a machine-like cold-blooded bureaucrat.'

The following Monday I spent a couple of hours studying the file. I told Ruth that some of the cases reduced me to the edge of tears: 'Wealthy Jews in this country cannot get starving relations out of Germany because the U.S. quota is exhausted for two years or so and we won't take people who are *en route* to the U.S.A. I think Cuba is more humane and if so I can in the final paragraph of my letters tomorrow tell them to inquire at the Cuban Embassy.'

Even worse than telling American Jews that Canada would do nothing for them was to see them when they called at the legation. At the beginning of March I wrote:

A terribly sad, good-looking and charming Jew came in to see me this morning about getting his parents out of Vienna. They are too frightened even to go to the U.S. consulate. His father has already been attacked on the street by some young hooligans. Every time one of them comes in it leaves me shaken and ashamed of Canada. I can't see any reason why we can't let these old people in when they are not going to work and their children in the States are willing and able to support them. It's like being a bystander at an especially cruel and long-drawn-out murder.

There was no reason except anti-semitism for the Canadian refusal to admit these old people. I learned from dealing with these cases early in 1939 that within the Canadian government humanitarian considerations were not strong enough to overcome the pressure on the government from anti-semites, especially those in Quebec. After the war broke out I hoped that economic considerations might overcome the anti-semitism. Our entry into the war meant that we needed all the American dollars we could get to finance our purchases of munitions and war materials in the United States and the financing by American Jews of their relatives in Canada would provide us with American dollars. But economic considerations were no more effective than humanitarian in overcoming our anti-semitic immigration policy.

The case of an aunt of Felix Frankfurter demonstrates that the Canadian immigration authorities were adamant even when to economic and humanitarian considerations was added the desirability of meeting the wishes of a distinguished justice of the Supreme Court who had considerable influence in the White House and the State Department and was a friend of the Canadian minister in Washington. In April 1940 Frankfurter spoke to the minister, Loring Christie, of his desire to get his aunt out of Czechoslovakia; her son in the United States was willing and able to 'provide ample means for her' to live in Canada; she could not get into the United States because the quota was overloaded; if 'it ever became possible' her son would wish her to join him in the United States. Christie wrote a personal letter to Skelton urging that Frankfurter's request be granted, adding: 'I feel you will realize that for a number of reasons it would be desirable and useful to facilitate the carrying out of this idea if it is at all possible under our immigration laws and policies. Of course, I have to add that I have a strong personal sympathy in the matter.' Skelton took the matter up by letter and also personally with the director of immigration, 'emphasizing the desirability of meeting the situation in any way that could be done.' The director replied that the aunt could be admitted to Canada only if she was coming to Canada for permanent residence and was 'not making Canada a back door to the United States.'

It was this formula of 'not making Canada a back door to the United States' which was used to justify excluding Jews whose relatives in the United States were prepared to support them in Canada until they could gain entry to the United States, even though serving as a back door would have provided Canada with American dollars and have saved some Jews from being murdered by the Nazis. This was the first of two problems I had to deal with as a diplomat that aroused my contempt for the policy of my government. The other was the internment of Japanese Canadians after Japan entered the war.

My host in Washington, Angus Malcolm, intelligent, good-looking, charming, a grandson of Lillie Langtry, moved in the upper circles of society in Washington. Some of his social prestige rubbed off on me and I attained the heights of lunching with Mr and Mrs Robert Woods Bliss at their house, Dumbarton Oaks. Sir Herbert Marler, when I met him at the entrance of the legation on returning from this lunch, was greatly impressed by my achievement. Not all the meals I owed to my sponsorship by Malcolm were as pleasant as that lunch. At one dinner given by an acquaintance of his at the beginning of February the guest of honour was Hector Bolitho. I described him to Ruth as the press agent for the royal family and 'the most poisonous man ... I had with difficulty restrained myself from being very rude. I was merely rude.' Bolitho said that the extraordinary thing about the British royal family was that they were related to almost all the royal houses of Europe. I could not restrain myself. I said, 'The most extraordinary thing about the royal family is that they do not have a drop of British blood.' I was wrong. George VI had a drop of British blood derived from James I who had reigned three hundred years before. George VI was the first Hanoverian king to marry a British subject. A State Department officer at the dinner told me that he very much enjoyed my remark; he had wanted to be rude but did not dare.

After eleven days in Washington I wrote Ruth:

If I don't meet a good middle-westerner soon who believes no Americans should ever again fight in Europe I'll wake up in the middle of the night and scream. So far the Americans I've met are more loyal than the King. I sit in my chair bursting with a suppressed desire to tell them I think they're crazy to advocate that their country fight in the next war, but I'm not supposed to say such things.

In order to meet 'real Americans instead of the bastard Anglicized type,' I wrote to the head of the Foreign Policy Association in Washington, William Stone, with whom I had corresponded when I was national secretary of the Canadian Institute of International Affairs. He immediately invited me to a small confidential meeting of about thirty Americans to discuss pan-Americanism. Bill Stone and his wife Grace became great friends of ours. At the swimming-pool at the Kenwood country club we met Marquis Childs, the distinguished columnist, and his wife Biddy. We became close friends. It may have been through them that we met and became friends with Erwin Canham of the *Christian Science Monitor* and Barnet Nover of the *Washington Post*. Stone and Childs, Canham and Nover gave me wise guidance in my efforts to understand how the United States was reacting to the tumultuous developments in Europe. In my diplomatic postings I have found the best newspapermen to be shrewd interpreters of government policy and public opinion.

After three weeks in the legation learning how to do the consular work which was part of my duties I embarked on the other part of my work, which was to write despatches on American foreign policy. The conclusions I advanced in my first despatch written on 17 February 1939, seven months before the war broke out, were to remain valid until the collapse of France in June 1940:

There is general agreement [in the United States] that if Germany and Italy made a successful, sudden, smashing attack on Great Britain and France and thus won a war without much cost to themselves, the defensive position of the United States would be greatly weakened. But there is disagreement over the extent of the weakening, and over the probability of a sudden smashing attack and the probability of its success were it to occur. There is consequently disagreement over the extent of the aid which the United States should give Great Britain and France in order to avert an attack by Germany or in order to make it unsuccessful and over the necessity of doing anything immediately. And while there is a measure of agreement over the danger to the United States of a successful short war waged by Germany and Italy against Great Britain and France, there is little agreement over how greatly the security of the United States would be endangered by a German-Italian victory which followed a long-drawn-out war of attrition, since it can be argued that the United States would have little to fear from the impoverished victors.[1]

In the middle of March Germany occupied Czechoslovakia. On 31 March Britain guaranteed Poland against attack, thus reversing its foreign policy. On 7 April Italy invaded Albania. Roosevelt responded by making unprecedented threats against Germany. He couched his first threats on 31 March and 8 April in the form of statements by 'the White House spokesman.' It was obvious that the spokesman was Roosevelt. He declared that unless Germany's policy was checked it 'could mean German domination not only of the small nations of Europe but its extension to other continents'; if war broke out Germany would be responsible. On 11 April Roosevelt went further; at a press conference he embraced without reservation an editorial in the *Washington Post* that morning which spoke of 'the virtual certainty of American involvement'

---

1 This and other despatches I quote from in this chapter are in the Escott Reid papers in the National Archives of Canada.

in another world war. On 14 April he sent a peace message to Hitler and Mussolini to which Hitler replied on 28 April. In a despatch at the beginning of May I wrote: 'It is possible that the net effect of the threats, the peace message, and Herr Hitler's reply has been at least a temporary increase in non-interventionist feeling in this country. But the President may well feel that this is a small price to pay for the international results of his participation in the European crisis of the first two weeks of April 1939.'

Events of the next three months demonstrated that the price the president had to pay was far from small. Congress rejected his proposal of 14 July to delete from the neutrality act the provision for an embargo on the export of arms to belligerents so that war materials could be sold to Britain and France if they became involved in war. This, I said, constituted a vote of no confidence by the Congress in the European foreign policy pursued by Roosevelt since the beginning of the year; the administration had met with a stunning defeat, and until the vote of no confidence was reversed, either by a vote in Congress or by an upsurge of public opinion, the president, in the event of another crisis in Europe similar to those in September 1938 and April 1939, would not be able to intervene with nearly as much force as in the last two crises.

I was nervous when, after two months in Washington, I paid my first official call as a diplomat on a foreign office. I had been instructed by Ottawa to discuss with 'a high official confidentially and informally' a problem on which the Canadian government wanted the views of the United States government. I was fortunate that the appropriate high official was J.D. (Jack) Hickerson who had a specially friendly feeling towards Canadians and was kind to juniors like myself. After the interview I wrote that I had talked with him for an hour. 'He was agreeable and when he said anything indiscreet he would preface it by saying, "As your former minister, Bill Herridge, used to say under similar circumstances, 'If anyone ever says I said this, I'll deny it like hell.' " A variant of this which I later heard him use many times was, "I'll deny it on a stack of bibles ten feet high." '

Herbert Marler became ill in June, and until Loring Christie succeeded him in September we were in fact, though not in form, without a minister. By the middle of July, with Riddell and Macdonnell on holiday, the officers at the legation were reduced to three – Mahoney, Allard, and I. On 12 July I wrote:

The result is that my phone is all the time ringing. Today I was asked: (1) How many pounds of tobacco an American tourist could take to Canada? (2) What special regulations applied to the sending of the ashes of a deceased Canadian from the U.S. to Canada? (3) Who corresponded in Canada to J. Edgar Hoover, chief of the Federal Bureau of Investigation? (4) Who was the premier of Prince Edward Island and where was he born? (5) Was there a city in Nova Scotia which elected a Roman Catholic as mayor one year and then a Protestant for two years? (6) How was Sir Herbert Marler getting along? (7) How long could a naturalized Canadian stay in the United States and keep his Canadian citizenship? (8) Could a car with dealer's tags be brought to Canada by a tourist?

On 4 September, the day after war broke out, I wrote to my mother:

It's hard to write letters now. That's why I've put off writing you. The important things don't bear thinking of and the trivialities are not worth mentioning ... Tell Bo [my brother] that my views on Canadian participation in the war remain as they were twelve months ago ... I wrote today to a friend who asked me for advice on war work that the only thing worth doing today was studying the problems of post-war reconstruction but the trouble was we had not the foggiest idea of the nature of the post-war world except that compared with that which existed last month it will be more brutal and less civilized as well as less wealthy and less well-populated.

About a week later I wrote 'that if the war lasted for more than a short time Russia would be the only victor, and she'd probably rule from the Rhine to the Pacific.' I was not far out. East Germany is at one point only eighty miles from the Rhine.

In the debate in Parliament preceding Canada's entry into the war on 10 September the CCF supported Canada's entry into the war but insisted that 'her assistance overseas should be limited to economic aid and must not include conscription of manpower or the sending of any expeditionary force.' J.S. Woodsworth, the leader of the party, took a more extreme position. He opposed Canada's entry into the war. As soon as I read his speech in Parliament defending his position I wrote him a personal letter:

I have read with the greatest admiration your most moving speech in the House of Commons. That is a speech of which you and your friends will always be proud. Their pride will increase as time goes on and we can see the events of these days in better perspective. These days are bitter and the future is terrifying. You must often be tempted to feel your task is hopeless. But I know you will continue to fight for sanity and toleration and reason – because you are too intelligent and courageous to do otherwise. Here I feel a shirker on the edge of the battle. But I do not know what else I can do.

At that time I did not believe it possible that Germany could succeed in an attack on Western Europe and I agreed with the position the CCF had taken. When it became clear in the spring of 1940 that Germany might succeed and that German success would gravely endanger Canada's direct and immediate national interests I became a supporter of all-out Canadian participation in the war.

Loring Christie arrived at the legation at the end of September 1939 to take up his post as minister. He was a most welcome change from his predecessor. Paul, the principal black member of the staff, told me that he was very honoured that Christie shook hands with him. Christie asked that he not be called 'Mr Minister.' Marler's revisions of my draft despatches had invariably been changes for the worse. I wrote after Christie had been at the legation for a fortnight, 'It's a relief to know that your despatch will be improved after Christie sees it instead of being mangled. I'm willing to bet that he'll succeed Skelton when Skelton retires.' Alas, it was not to be. He was taken ill in the middle of May 1940. He returned to the legation in the middle of July but was again taken ill at the end of November and died in April 1941 shortly after Skelton's death.

The foreign policy elite in Canada knew that Christie, like Skelton, had believed from at least the mid-thirties that Canada should stay out of the coming war. Those who shared his beliefs welcomed his appointment to Washington. Thus Edgar Tarr wrote me on 5 October 1939: 'Christie's appointment is splendid. I was particularly anxious that whoever went to Washington to represent us would be one who is genuinely sympathetic to the United States' desire to keep out of war, if they can do so in their own national interests. Whatever may be our national policy in Washington, a man of that type will certainly be the best to get it across.'

J.W. Dafoe, who had favoured Christie's appointment to Washington, had by September 1940 become doubtful. In a letter to J.M. Macdonnell he wrote:

If he is showing no initiative and is merely ... carrying out instructions from Ottawa, it is either that he has been instructed to act in this way or that he is keeping his activities to a minimum on account of a continuing mental attitude towards the question of the war ... The association of Escott Reid with Christie in the direction of the office is somewhat unfortunate because their private views are closely akin to one another, and they both held attitudes in the period preceding the war which were exasperating to me. Reid, in theory, is only a subordinate member of the staff, but I can understand that he may be wielding an influence greater than his position would seem to suggest.[2]

On 29 September I wrote a despatch on developments in United States policy and opinion since the outbreak of the war. I began by saying that as soon as Great Britain entered the war the tone of the United States press and radio had changed. Before Great Britain entered, the almost hysterical emphasis had been on the necessity of stopping Germany from further aggression. After the outbreak the emphasis was on the necessity of the United States remaining calm, collected, and united. Most papers, while freely admitting that the United States desired the victory of the Allies, urged that the United States 'stay out of Europe's war.' The great majority of the public 'are opposed to the United States becoming a belligerent; [but] they fatalistically expect that if the war is not speedily concluded the United States will nevertheless become a belligerent.' The administration had so far been afraid to use openly the most effective argument for repeal of the arms embargo: if the Allies were unable to defeat Germany by their own efforts the United States might have to take part in the war; repeal would assist the Allies to defeat Germany and therefore repeal would make less likely eventual United States' participation in hostilities. The administration did not use this argument in the autumn of 1939 because it called in question the general belief in the United States that the Allies would be able to defeat Germany by their own efforts. In the two months between the German invasion of Norway and Denmark on 9 April 1940 and the German entry into Paris on 10 June, this belief was shattered. Our world crashed about our ears.

Because I went to the Mayflower Hotel on 24 May 1940 for a haircut I was the first to give Ottawa news of the possibility of a deal between Britain and the United States under which the United States would receive naval and air bases in the West Indies and Newfoundland. The destroyers–naval bases agreement was concluded on 2 September about three months later. In the next chair to mine at the barber shop was Professor W.Y. Elliott of the Department of Government at Harvard, whom I had known for many years. He said he wanted to have a talk with me as soon as we left the shop. I immediately reported the talk to Ottawa in a letter which Skelton sent on to the prime minister, drawing

2 NAC, J.W. Dafoe Papers, Dafoe to Macdonnell, 16 September 1940

his particular attention to Elliott's report of a conversation with Cordell Hull, the secretary of state.

Mr. Elliott is a member of the Business Advisory Council, which has just been meeting here. He states that the Council unanimously passed a resolution, which is not being given to the press, that the United States Government should immediately open negotiations with the United Kingdom and France concerning their possessions in this hemisphere. The Council proposes that the United States should secure from the United Kingdom and France long-term or permanent leases of certain areas in their possessions in this hemisphere, on which the United States could construct naval and air bases. In return for these leases, the United Kingdom and France would secure a credit on their war debts. The leases should be accompanied by the provision that the United States would have the right to take over the possessions completely, if the situation of the United Kingdom and France becomes desperate.

Elliott believed that it would be best if negotiations over the British possessions were initiated by Britain rather than by the United States. Perhaps the Canadian government might indicate its interest in this matter to the British government. Cordell Hull had told him that 'the people here are considering seriously what would happen to the British fleet in the event of a British debacle.' The fleet would probably be surrendered to Germany, but in the unlikely event that a part of the fleet got away to this side of the Atlantic, Canada and the United States would face difficult problems. How, in such circumstances, could Canada be expected to support any considerable part of the fleet? The United States might have to work out some arrangement with Canada. Elliott said that the president had indicated to him a willingness to begin discussions with Canada on post-war defence arrangements, but he was so pressed at the moment that it was unlikely he would himself initiate such conversations. He thought that the same was true of Cordell Hull but that Hull would welcome an initiative from Canada. (On 18 August, a little less than three months later, Roosevelt and King established the Permanent Joint Board on Defence to consider immediate defence problems.)

At the end of our talk Elliott said to me that he had hoped to see Lord Lothian, the British ambassador, before returning to Harvard but was unable to do so. Could I pass on to Lothian what he had told me about the resolution of the Business Advisory Council? I did this three days later in a private talk at the British embassy. My report to Ottawa on our talk did not reflect the passion with which Lothian denounced the blindness of the United States in not recognizing that one by one the keys to its security were falling into the hands of Germany. He paced up and down his office when he said this.

J.T. Trippe of Pan American Airways had given Lothian the same information that Elliott had given me. Lothian's personal and private view was that the British government should inform the United States government that it would be willing to give the United States long-term leases of land in its possessions in this hemisphere for the construction of such air and naval bases by the United States as that country thought necessary for its defence. No charge would be made for these bases and the question of war debts would not be mentioned, nor would any mention be made of any contingent transfer of sovereignty. (Lothian said that obviously if the worst came to the worst the United States would take possession of the British colonial possessions in this hemisphere.) On 25 May, Lothian had cabled the Foreign Office, suggesting that the United Kingdom consider this question.

Lothian's own view was that the United States would be content with establishing bases in Newfoundland and either Trinidad or Georgetown. He

feels strongly that the question of the transfer of the British Fleet to the United States or to waters surrounding the United States, where it would serve to protect this country, would not even be considered by the United Kingdom Government so long as the United States remains out of the war. He feels the same way about any question of transfer of sovereignty over British possessions in this hemisphere. The purpose of the transfer of the Fleet or of the transfer of possessions would be to protect the United States, and the British public would not consider such proposals so long as the United States maintains its neutrality.

Mackenzie King's marginal comment on this passage was 'I think this would be true of Britain.'

I asked Lothian what he meant by United States' entry into the war. He said he did not mean that the United States should send an army to Europe. He meant that, 'if the worst came to the worst, the United States should declare that its immediate policy is to defend this whole hemisphere and that its long-term policy is, when it becomes strong enough, to seek to re-establish the independence of France and Great Britain, even if this should take twenty years.'

He is convinced that, should Germany smash Great Britain and France this summer and seize or destroy the British Fleet, it will by August of this year have fomented an uprising in Brazil, where the large German and Italian colonies provide the strongest fifth column in the world. Having established a German-dominated government in Brazil, Germany will then have air bases constructed in Brazil. Faced with this threat, the United States will probably, he thinks, have to transfer the bulk of its fleet to the Atlantic, though even this would not make impossible the establishment of German bases in Brazil. Japan, in such circumstances, will make an alliance with Germany and will seize Alaska and Hawaii. He dismisses the possibility of Germany and Japan invading this country. He does, however, believe that they would conceive that their interests would be served by taking away from the United States possible outposts for offensive operations against them. Having seized Brazil, Alaska and Hawaii, Germany and Japan would be able to force the United States to come to terms. He did not elaborate on this, but spoke of international economic arrangements. He did, however, go on to say that in such a situation there was no possibility of the United States maintaining a democratic form of government.

The fear at the time that the United States would cease to be a democracy if it had to face a Germany which had been victorious in Europe was common. I said in a letter to my mother that the price might be 'establishing on this continent a system just about as bad as that of Hitler's.' But I went on to say, 'We don't need to if we are wise and courageous.' When I wrote this I did not know that on 25 May Roosevelt and Cordell Hull had said to Hugh Keenleyside, who was on a special mission to them from Mackenzie King, that they believed that if the Nazis got control of the British and French fleets, Germany and Italy would seize all British and French possessions except those in the Americas and that the 'United States itself will probably become totalitarianized as a result of the necessity of arming and organizing on a colossal scale against the imminent dangers on both the Atlantic and the Pacific.'[3]

On 1 June when the evacuation from Dunkirk was taking place I reported that 'the people I meet talk no longer of the possibility of an ultimate Allied defeat; instead they talk of the probability – almost a certainty barring a miracle – of a smashing German victory this summer.'

I sense a feeling not merely of defeatism, but of frustration and impotence ... Gradually ... informed and articulate opinion seems to have become convinced – rightly or wrongly – ... that, given the state of the defence forces and the

3 *Documents on Canadian External Relations* (DCER), vol. 8, contains on pp. 72–3 my letter of 24 May and on pages 84–7 my letter of 27 May. Keenleyside's account of his interview with Roosevelt and Hull on 25 May is on pp. 67–71.

armament industry of the United States, even an immediate declaration of war would not result in any substantial measure of effective assistance being given the Allies within the next few months, and they fear that it is within the next few months that the outcome of the war will have been decided ... To the prevalent feeling of defeatism, of frustration and impotence there was added for a time a feeling of almost panic hysteria at the defencelessness of the United States if faced this summer by a victorious Germany.

For about a fortnight after the successful evacuation from Dunkirk the feeling of impotence and hysteria lessened and Roosevelt was able to authorize the sale to the Allies of airplanes and other arms and munitions which he had declared to be surplus supplies of the United States army and navy. But when France collapsed in the middle of June the sentiment in favour of effective assistance to the Allies declined rapidly. The explanation, I reported to Ottawa,

is the increasing belief that 'the probability of a German victory in the European war is changing towards virtual certainty' (Felix Morley, *Washington Post*, 22 June). The United States [it is argued] may itself have to face a victorious Germany within a few weeks or months. It cannot therefore afford to throw away any of its so-called surplus aeroplanes, ships or other munitions on what is considered to be a virtually hopeless effort by Great Britain to withstand the German attack.

I was, at this time, trying to find out what the United States was planning to do if Germany was victorious in Europe. My conclusion at the end of June was that the United States would 'organize North America and at least half of South America into an economic and military alliance capable of standing Hitler off and perhaps ultimately capable of bringing him to terms.' In a letter to my mother I said: 'What is going to happen in the next few weeks and months does not bear thinking of unless one can look beyond to the creation first in this hemisphere and later in the world of a civilization in which men will cultivate the gift of pity and not strive to make themselves pityless, where men will think courageously instead of fighting courageously, where men will be wise and not clever.'

In July and August, as the British successfully fought the Battle of Britain, American belief in the certainty of a German victory began to change. At the end of August I wrote: 'The people here are a little more cheerful about the prospects of stopping a German victory than they were a month ago. They are even beginning to believe the British claims about the losses to German aircraft.' And a month later, 'I have a curious feeling these days – I feel that the world is standing still as long as the Battle of Britain is unresolved. At the same time I know it is not standing still but moving rapidly – especially in the Far East.' On 10 October I wrote, 'It looks increasingly as if the United States will be in this war. I am told that people throughout the country are becoming fatalistic about it. The Far East may provide the spark.' Fourteen months were to elapse before Pearl Harbor.

In a letter at the end of September I tried to describe my own feeling during these months of bated breath, a feeling I said was probably baseless. It was that 'one's friends and acquaintances are more sincere now when you meet them – less surfacy, more human. People seem to be reaching out for kindness and friendliness and sincerity. I think we all want to hold hands because we are afraid of the dark.'

While the presidential election campaign was on in the autumn of 1940 Roosevelt felt precluded from initiating any move to help the Allies which might increase apprehensions among the voters that he intended to drag the country into war. It was not until the middle of December that he launched his campaign for lend-lease. Loring Christie was ill and the task of reporting to Ottawa on the lend-lease bill fell on me. I read the debates in Congress so solidly night after night that I would dream about them.

The best exposition of my views was not in my despatches to Ottawa, but in a personal letter to Loring Christie at the beginning of March 1941. He was in hospital in New York. His wife told me that he had decided to take a holiday for three to six months before returning to Washington. He died a month later. In my letter I wrote:

My guess is that the President's policy so long as he and the people do not become convinced that further defence of the British Isles is hopeless is to intervene with just that minimum amount of aid which the march of events demonstrates is necessary to prevent a defeat of Great Britain. I think that this means convoying within two months. Guns will probably go off, but I still believe that the President does not want the United States to declare war. The acts of armed force by the United States will be called legitimate measures of self defence and the President will try to damp down agitation in the country for a declaration, because if the country gets into war, public opinion may in time demand all out participation which I do not think he wants. Perhaps, however, I am giving him credit for being more cold-blooded and calculating than he actually is. As a *quid pro quo* for aid to Great Britain, I think he will ask for assurances on post war policy. Whether he will also want to make himself Director General of War

Strategy, I don't know. He is supposed to like playing about with boats, and perhaps he will not be able to resist the temptation to play about with the boats of the United States and British navies.

The way things are going at present it seems probable that after the war the people of this country will be fairly well agreed that they have a 'national mission' to organize this hemisphere politically and economically. Adolf Berle will say that this does not mean imperialism or dictation, but a 'cooperative peace'; but if the hard-faced businessmen who have done well out of the war get into power in the election of 1944, I should imagine the imperialism is likely to be pretty tough and not very intelligent.

I don't know what the people in Ottawa think about it, but my guess is that Canada's best chance of maintaining a fair degree of real autonomy after the war is to push as hard as possible for a federalization of matters which are of joint concern to Canada and the United States. We might also, though this is less important, push for a federalization of matters which are of concern to all the American nations. The more joint organs for the administration of common interests, the better are our chances of having some influence over United States policies which affect us.

For the rest of my life I would search for ways by which we might influence United States' policies which affect us.

A week after I wrote this letter I was told that I would be transferred to the Department of External Affairs in Ottawa and we moved to Ottawa at the end of April 1941. So this letter to Christie constitutes a summing up of my views on the United States and the war at the end of my first tour of duty in Washington.

At the beginning of November 1940, Jack Hickerson, acting on instructions from Berle, told Christie that the State Department found 'themselves in a somewhat embarrassing position' because of the operations of Clayton Knight and Homer Smith who had their headquarters in the Waldorf Astoria Hotel in New York since in their efforts to assist U.S. citizens to enlist in the Royal Canadian Air Force, they might be violating United States law. Later in the month, on Ottawa's instructions, I had a long talk with Hickerson on the subject. These talks demonstrate the way in which, in the period of American neutrality, the American administration tried to be helpful to Canada. The administration did not ask that the Clayton Knight committee be terminated, but that they 'pull in their horns,' that they not be so 'unnecessarily careless' in the way they had gone about 'loaning' money to possible recruits; and that they should get rid of a certain amount of their incriminating correspondence in case their files were investigated by the FBI. The Canadian government should, he added, get the advice of a friendly United States lawyer with the 'instinct of an ambulance chaser,' a lawyer who would be able to stretch the law a little. He recommended Dean Acheson – who would not have relished being described as having the instinct of an ambulance chaser. Acheson was consulted and gave the required advice: recruiting in the United States for the Canadian armed forces was unquestionably against the law but there would be no objection to men being engaged in the United States for a civil task; if later, when in Canada, some of them wished to join the RCAF and were accepted, no objection could be taken, provided it was not done in such a way as to make it appear a colourable evasion. Acheson's advice, for which he refused to accept a fee, was taken.

The State Department also helped us to recapture German prisoners who escaped from prisoner-of-war camps in Canada. Ottawa would tell me immediately they learned of an escape. I would tell the State Department. The State Department would tell the U.S. immigration service. Then when the escaped prisoner tried to enter the United States he would be refused entry and be delivered into the hands of the RCMP.

One day in the spring of 1941 Hickerson asked me to drop in to see him. He said, 'Have you any naval ships in the Pacific?' I said we had one, an armed merchant cruiser, the *Prince Robert*. He said, 'Could you have it near Honolulu at the end of May? We know that four German spies who know too much about the Panama Canal will be sailing in mid-May from San Francisco on the *President Garfield* on their way back to Germany. We will give you their cabin numbers. Could your ship board the *President Garfield* and arrest the spies?' The official report of the Department of National Defence states that the *Prince Robert* sighted the *President Garfield* at 14:05 on 29 May and stopped it by loud hailer. 'A boarding party went across to the American ship, whose captain seemed to know exactly what was required of him,' and the men were 'seized with despatch in spite of their efforts to look inconspicuous among the passengers.'

I naively thought at the time that the United States was doing Canada a favour by giving us an opportunity to take German spies into custody, whereas in fact we were doing the United States a favour by taking into custody men who constituted a danger to United States security, but who under their law they could not in peace-time take into custody.

In January 1940 I had an opportunity to study how an expert conducted negotiations on a treaty. The expert was O.D. Skelton and the treaty was on the development of the Great Lakes–St Lawrence basin for power and navigation. Loring Christie told me after the negotiations that Skelton's handling of the negotiations was a beautiful piece of work. 'Skelton was,' I wrote my mother, 'firm as a rock on the important points, conciliatory on the others and always good-humoured.' In my time, and presumably today, United States' negotiators would often attempt to strengthen their bargaining position in international negotiations by saying, 'Of course, we agree entirely with your proposal but we could never get the Senate to accept it.' Skelton used a similar ploy, substituting the Canadian cabinet for the United States Senate. He refused to discuss the merits of the proposal the Americans put forward for the division of the costs of the project between the two countries. Instead he 'stated that the Canadian Cabinet would not agree to any scheme which would cost the Dominion Government more than the 1932 scheme [negotiated by the previous Conservative government] would have cost them'4 and the American proposal would have cost Canada more. When the Americans gave in to his ultimatum I thought he would thank them. He did not. If he had thanked them the Americans might consider that they could expect a *quid pro quo* on some other aspect of the negotiation. Skelton was determined to leave the impression that the Americans had not been generous but had merely accepted a fact of life.

A few months later Skelton sent me copies of his correspondence about me with S.T. Wood, the commissioner of the Royal Canadian Mounted Police. This correspondence further increased my admiration for him. At a time when the possibility of a successful German invasion of Britain increased his worries and burdens as principal adviser to the prime minister, he took it upon himself to reply to a suggestion from the RCMP that he should 'cause inquiries to be made respecting [my] bona fides.' Commissioner Wood in his letter to Skelton of 10 August 1940 said that postal censorship had intercepted a communication addressed to me at my former office in Toronto, 43 St George Street, from a publishing house in Moscow containing 'a bulletin describing publications available on communistic propaganda material.'

Investigation through our Divisional Headquarters in Toronto discloses that 43 St. George St. is one of the student buildings of the University of Toronto. Subsequent inquiries reflect that Escott Meridith [sic] Reid was a former student of the University of Toronto, and was graduated in 1927. This subject was born in Campbellford, Ont., and for some time resided in Toronto where he was associated with the League of Nations Society of Canada. It is reported that

4 Minutes of the meeting of 23 January 1940

Escott Reid is presently employed as second secretary in the Canadian Legation in Washington, D.C. It has been ascertained that during his studies at the University of Toronto, Reid was a brilliant student and employed with the League of Nations Society in Canada, although investigation does not disclose that he was in any way associated with radical groups in this country. These particulars are respectfully submitted in the event you may wish to cause inquiries to be made respecting the bona fides of Escott Reid.

The incompetence of the RCMP was demonstrated by their undertaking investigations and inquiries to find out information about me printed in the *Canadian Who's Who*. If they had consulted *Who's Who* they would not have committed the error of stating that I had been employed in the thirties by the League of Nations Society. They incorrectly stated that 43 St George Street was a student building. Their 'investigation [did] not disclose that [I] was in any way associated with radical groups in this country' when I had been a member of groups the RCMP would have considered radical: the League for Industrial Democracy, the Student Christian Movement, the League for Social Reconstruction, the CCF, and the *Canadian Forum*. As for their English, Gowers of *Plain Words* would have been outraged by all the intransitive verbs, by the 'subsequent inquiries reflect,' and by the rest of the bureaucratic jargon.

Skelton's reply was a masterly put-down. The enclosure in the communication to me from Moscow

appears to be merely a bulletin advertising books, sent to Mr. Reid, as an officer, before his appointment to our service some years ago, of the chief organization for the objective study of international affairs in Canada ... Receipt of a book publisher's circulars could hardly be considered to indicate an intention to buy, much less an indication of sympathy with the doctrines, though as a matter of fact several of the books listed in this case are well-known writings with which any one desiring a thorough knowledge of European forces and trends would have to be familiar. Mr. Reid is one of the most valuable members of our Service and a man in whom we have complete confidence.

So far as I know the RCMP never again doubted my bona fides; if they did, their suspicions were overridden because in the late 1940s I was given the highest possible security clearance, 'cosmic top secret.'

When Skelton died in January 1941 I wrote my mother: 'Dr. Skelton's death was a terrible shock. We [at the legation] were entirely unprepared for it. In the Department in Ottawa some of them had known for two years or more that he knew he was in constant danger of death unless he gave up working so hard. It was the war that killed him. He was one of the best – wise and whimsical and kind. I used to talk to him quite often over the telephone from Washington and he almost invariably had some witty aside to make. He was always courteous, never hurried.'

The correspondence between the RCMP and Skelton gave me an indication of the incompetence of the Canadian security service. The case of our cook gave me an insight into the operations of the United States' security service. She was an Austrian and had been cook at the Austrian legation in Washington. When Austria was annexed by Germany the legation was closed; she lost her job and we hired her. In the autumn of 1940 Christie asked me to come to see him in his office. He said: 'I am embarrassed. I dislike doing this. The FBI tells me that your cook often goes to a restaurant where she meets people the FBI suspects are German spies. I have to ask you to let her go.'

Security considerations in the early years of the war not only resulted in our having to part with an excellent cook, they also resulted in my not going to an excellent international conference, the conference of the Institute of Pacific Relations at Virginia Beach in November 1939. I had been to two previous IPR conferences in 1933 and 1936, and the CIIA had invited me to go to this one. Again Loring Christie had the kind of task which he cordially disliked. He told me that the Department of External Affairs had decided that I was not to attend the conference. Adam von Trott was to be there. As fellow Rhodes scholars we were bound to meet, and the department did not want me to talk to him. I later learned that at this time British Intelligence believed that Trott was a dubious character who pretended to be an anti-Nazi and the FBI was convinced that he 'was not only a Nazi agent but Hitler's master spy.'[5] I think it was Edgar Tarr who said to me some years later with a bitterness unusual for him that it was only when Trott was executed by the Nazis for his involvement in the July 1944 plot to kill Hitler that the western countries were persuaded that he was an anti-Nazi. I regret that I was deprived of an opportunity to meet this brilliant, courageous man.

Christie's illness resulted in my seeing a good deal of another brilliant but very different kind of man, Adolf Berle, an assistant secretary of state, who had been described as 'the most able and the most ambitious man in Washington.' If Christie had been well he would have been the channel of communication between Ottawa and Berle on Greenland in 1940 and 1941; for a second secretary of legation to deal with an assistant

5 Christopher Sykes, *Tormented Loyalty: The Story of a German Aristocrat Who Defied Hitler* (New York: Harper and Row 1969), 104

secretary of state was unusual. It contributed to my education as a diplomat.

After the Germans occupied Denmark in the spring of 1940 Greenland, as a Danish dependency, became a focus of concern to the United States, Britain, and Canada. There were three reasons for this. Aircraft were being built in great quantities in the United States and Canada for the British air force. They had to be flown across the Atlantic and because they were short-range aircraft they needed landing fields en route. If a landing field could be built in Greenland the task of ferrying the aircraft across the Atlantic would be easier and safer. The Germans would want to establish weather stations in Greenland because, since weather moves east across the Atlantic, weather stations in Greenland would enable them to make more accurate forecasts of weather in Britain, and the more accurate their forecasts the better they could plan their bombing raids on Britain. The mineral cryolite was required for producing aluminum, and aluminum was essential for the production of aircraft. Since the aluminum industry in the United States and Canada was dependent on Greenland cryolite, German sabotage of the cryolite mine would seriously weaken the West.

I liked Berle partly, I am sure, because though I was only a lowly second secretary of legation he treated me as if I were a senior counsellor. I admired the clarity of his exposition. He was fertile in inventing formulas to justify actions necessary for political reasons. After Germany had occupied Denmark it was necessary for the United States to secure rights in Greenland to enable them to defend it. But who was competent to grant these rights? Berle told me that sovereignty was like a lot of bugs on a blanket. If one part of the blanket were submerged in water all the bugs would go to the part which remained above water. Since Denmark was under German occupation all the sovereignty of Denmark had passed to Greenland and the authorities in Greenland, acting through the Danish minister in Washington, were therefore competent to enter into a valid international agreement with the United States.

He was intellectually arrogant but he had a good deal to be arrogant about intellectually. His arrogance gave him a healthy suspicion that experts could be wrong. I remember him saying that all the experts, including Colonel Lindbergh, had reported that there was no place in Greenland on which it was possible to build an airfield; but that he did not believe they were right and had insisted that further investigations be made. The turning point came, he said, when a bearded professor, an expert on the Icelandic sagas, came into his office in the State Department and announced that he had discovered from one of the sagas that Leif Ericson had pastured many hundreds of reindeer on a certain spot in Greenland and that this must mean that there was a sizeable meadow there. There was indeed, and that was where the airfield was built.

Like many academics who move from a university to a position of power in a powerful country, he gloried in exercising that power. We told him in April 1940 that the Canadian coastguard cutter *Nascopie* would visit Greenland with an artillery officer in mufti and mining engineers who would look over conditions at the Ivigtut cryolite mine. At the beginning of June we were summoned to a meeting in his office and he delivered a stern lecture. The State Department, he said, had been informed that the *Nascopie* had arrived at Ivigtut with not only an artillery officer and mining engineers but also with officers of the Royal Canadian Mounted Police and some soldiers. This, and the presence in Greenland of three British naval officers, might be interpreted as meaning that the Canadian government intended to assume control of Greenland. 'I am being very blunt about this, and I could put our feelings in more diplomatic language, but I feel that I should report to you that I have discussed the matter with the President and he said that he would be "very angry" if the Canadian Government attempted to occupy Greenland. This is not the time for this type of 1890 imperialism. Cecil Rhodes has been dead a long time and, even if alive, Greenland is hardly a place for his talents.' In his diary for that day Berle described this interview as 'a knock-down and drag-out fight.'[6]

The next day, on instructions from Ottawa, we informed Berle that the reports he had received were erroneous and that even if they were true it was difficult to see how they could be interpreted as a Canadian attempt 'to occupy Greenland.' We had informed the United States that we had no intention of occupying Greenland and we felt justified in asking that our statement be accepted by the State Department.

I became involved in January 1941 in efforts to prevent the University of Toronto from dismissing Frank Underhill from his professorship of history. The campaign to fire him was led by Arthur Meighen, a former Conservative prime minister, Mitchell Hepburn, the Liberal premier of Ontario, and George Drew, leader of the Conservative opposition in the Ontario legislature. It had been launched in April 1939 by Hepburn and Drew. In August 1940 Meighen wrote to the government in Ottawa

---

6 My report on the interview is on pages 1016–18 of *Documents on Canadian External Affairs*, vol. 7. See Berle's account in *Navigating the Rapids 1918–1971*, edited by B.B. Berle and T.B. Jacobs (New York: Harcourt Brace Jovanovich 1973), 321.

demanding that Underhill be interned. During the next four months the board of governors of the university discussed whether Underhill should be dismissed and on 2 January 1941 he was summoned to a meeting with three members of the board who offered him a choice between resignation and dismissal. Underhill's offences went back to his demand in the four years preceding the outbreak of the war that Canada stay out of the war. Thus in 1935 he wrote: 'We must ... make it clear ... that the poppies blooming in Flanders fields have no further interest for us ... All these European troubles are not worth the bones of a Toronto grenadier.' In August 1940, five days after the Ogdensburg declaration of Roosevelt and King establishing the Permanent Joint Board on Defence, Underhill gave a speech at a conference at Couchiching in which he said: 'In defence matters ... we in Canada are now committed to two loyalties, the old one to the British connection involving our backing up of Britain, and the new one to North America, involving common action with the States to protect our geographical security in our North American home ... If the British cause suffers seriously in Europe these arrangements [with the United States] will bulk larger and larger in our policy.'

I happened to be in Toronto on 5 January, three days after Underhill had received the ultimatum that he would be dismissed if he did not resign, and I heard the story from him. I advised him to write Hugh Keenleyside of the Department of External Affairs giving him a full account of the story, which he did the next day, and I said I would also write Keenleyside. In my letter to Keenleyside on 6 January I said:

Canada is not trying to push the United States into war. Canada is, however, interested in the United States giving all possible assistance short of war, even though this involves the United States in a risk of war. The opponents in the United States of the President's policy contend that it is leading the United States to war and that the involvement of the United States in war will mean that democracy in the United States will commit suicide, and that therefore the United States must, in the interests of democracy, remain at peace ... We do not want Canada to give the United States isolationists concrete evidence that when a North American democracy enters the war it loses its democracy and goes in for witch-hunting ... Regardless of what the Board of Governors will say, Underhill is being dismissed ... because he advocated the general principle which lies behind the establishment of the Permanent Joint Board on Defence ... Walter Lippmann wrote about two weeks ago that if Great Britain is defeated and a pro-Nazi or Pétain regime is established in the United Kingdom all Canadians in the United States will be open to the suspicion of being Fifth Columnists. The danger which Lippmann foresees will be greatly increased if the provincial university of Ontario declares that it is improper for a Canadian to say that Canada has a loyalty to North America. The inevitable conclusion is that the Board of Governors of that university, supported by the Provincial Government, and by public opinion in Ontario, believe that Canada's only loyalty is to Great Britain.

Hugh Keenleyside successfully intervened. On 11 January Underhill wrote me that he guessed 'the storm is over.' In my reply I said: 'I am hoping that the unpleasant experience you went through may have a good effect on the university. It must surely have convinced the reactionary members of the Board of Governors that they are completely out of touch with intelligent opinion in Canada.'

At the end of my two years in Washington I thought that the legation, in spite of its small staff and the illness of its minister, had been doing a creditable job. Years later I found out that my opinion was not shared by some intelligent outside observers. Ken Wilson of the *Financial Post* was one of the best newspapermen of his time. After visiting Washington in January 1941 he informed his superior, Floyd Chalmers, that when he discussed with friends in Washington the present position and influence of the legation he 'got a very negative answer.' One friend

thinks our crowd are definitely high-hat and asleep on the job compared to what other legations are doing for their countries and nationals. His one criticism is that there is too much of the English accent around our Legation, and unless you are that sort they don't pay much attention to you ... Obviously there is a tremendous opportunity here and one which it is almost unbelievable to be missing. At the moment our 'career men' seem to be of the Christie-Reid type. Probably this will always be so as long as King is Prime Minister. He essentially is a man of principles rather than of action and salesmanship.[7]

Fortunately for me the Department of External Affairs did not share Ken Wilson's low opinion of my work. When Norman Robertson, the under-secretary, telephoned me in the middle of March 1941 to tell me that I was being transferred to the department in Ottawa, he said that they had intended to keep Hume Wrong in Ottawa but they had had to send him to Washington and that I could do the work that Wrong would

7 Queen's University, Grant Dexter Papers, K.P. Wilson to F.S. Chalmers, 3 February 1941

have done better than anyone else. This was immensely flattering since Wrong was one of the top five mandarins in the department, the others being Robertson, Pearson, Keenleyside, and John Read. I had become a mandarin.

12

*D*epartment of External Affairs
1941–1944

In the spring of 1941 when I was transferred to the Department of External Affairs in Ottawa the British Commonwealth stood alone in the war against Germany. France had collapsed. Germany was in occupation of Norway, Denmark, Belgium, the Netherlands, Luxembourg, and half of France and was poised to invade Britain. The United States, the Soviet Union, and Japan were neutral. Canada was Britain's most important ally.

I would not be able now after a lapse of forty-seven years to recollect clearly the uncertainties and fears and hopes which weighed upon me at that time if I had not put them in writing in a confidential memorandum soon after my arrival in Ottawa. In this memorandum I listed the possible developments I foresaw in world affairs.

Alliance between France and Germany; entry of the United States into the war; capitulation of the British Isles; entry of Japan or the u.s.s.r. into the war; a stalemate peace made by a Vichy government in the United Kingdom; a peace offensive by Germany; a sudden collapse of Germany; a long-drawn-out war followed by anarchy in most of Europe; a speeding up of the present trend towards political and economic unification of this hemisphere under the leadership of the United States ... [We are at] the beginning of a long period of war, anarchy and reconstruction, a period which will probably last for at least six to ten more years – at least three years of war, at least three years of anarchy and of early attempts at reconstruction.

Two months later Hitler invaded the Soviet Union and the nature of the war changed profoundly. Our immediate reaction in the department was undiluted joy that the Soviet Union had been forced into the war on our side. Then we learned that most of the experts in Washington believed that Soviet resistance would collapse within two or three weeks. This prompted me to write a memorandum[1] two days after the invasion urging the government to consider the problem which would face the Allies if Germany succeeded in occupying Ukraine and the Caucasus and so depriving the rest of the Soviet Union of grain and oil and putting it at the mercy of Germany. In such circumstances Germany would probably be able to establish a Vichy-type regime over the whole of the Soviet Union. In order to prevent this the Allies would have to supply the Soviet Union with grain and oil.

I quote most of the rest of the memorandum because it demonstrates the depth of the fears I had in the middle of 1941 – fears which I shared with many other people – and how I, who prided myself on being a liberal, advocated a smashing unprovoked armed attack on a neutral Japan if this was necessary to ensure access to the Soviet Union through Vladivostock, not realizing that access could be had through Archangel.

Our access to Russia would be via Vladivostock; this would be safe only if we had persuaded Japan to throw her lot in with the allies or if we had knocked Japan out. Japan might be amenable to persuasion on the ground that a German-controlled Russia would be an immediate and direct threat to Japan. It would eventually mean a German-controlled China and German control of the Netherlands Indies. Japan would be at Germany's mercy. If Japan is not open to persuasion perhaps the only thing for the allies to do is to gamble on a quick knockout blow to Japan by the combined forces in the Far East of the United States, Great Britain, China and the U.S.S.R.

The rest of my analysis and prescription in this memorandum stands up better to the test of time.

If we can keep Russia in the war and even if Russia loses the Ukraine and the Caucasus the war will be long but not hopeless. If we cannot keep Russia in the war the war becomes almost hopeless. Germany will be virtually self-sufficient and thus immune from the blockade. It can transfer much of its armament industry beyond the reach of effective bombing attack. It can settle down to resist a siege of which the most favourable outcome – barring a miracle – can be little more than the liberation of France and perhaps the Low Countries. If Russia can be kept in the war we can make Germany's eastern front a constant drain

1 *Documents on Canadian External Relations* (DCER), vol. 8: 1939–1941, part II (Ottawa, 1976), 1102–3

on her men and resources. In a year or two we could launch an offensive against Germany from Russia using Russia's vast armies equipped with the armaments of the United States.

As soon as the Soviet Union was forced by the German invasion to become our ally we and the British and the Americans stopped calling it the Soviet Union and called it Russia.

On 24 and 25 June, just after I had dictated this memorandum, I had talks with Adolf Berle, who was then visiting Ottawa. Berle 'was surprised at the undiluted cheerfulness with which Ottawa had greeted Russian entry into the war. He, himself, saw all sorts of difficulties which might arise.' He feared that Britain, in order to keep Russia in the war, might make immoral promises to Russia of what Russia would get if it stayed in the war and Germany were defeated. Britain might, for example, sign away the independence of the three Baltic states and Finland. ' For centuries, a struggle has been going on to keep Asia from extending into Europe. If the allies embrace Russia too enthusiastically the result may be a further advance of Russia into Europe. Russia should certainly be provided with arms but she should be given no political commitments ... He hoped that after the initial Russian defeats a new government might arise in Russia with which we could deal – perhaps under some general.'[2]

Berle was not certain that we benefited in a military way from the entry of Russia into the war, even if the alternative had been an unopposed German occupation of Ukraine and the Caucasus. Such an occupation would have meant that an undefeated Russian army would have remained as a continued threat to Hitler, whereas it was possible that by going to war Hitler might destroy the Russian army just as he had destroyed the French army.

The division to which I was assigned in the department was the American –Far Eastern under Hugh Keenleyside. This division dealt with the United States and the rest of the Americas, and with Japan and the rest of the Far East. I soon became the principal officer in the department concerned with Latin America. I wrote memoranda on possible Canadian entry into the Pan-American Union, I went on a trade mission to South America from mid-August 1941 to the end of October, and my wife and I were invited after that to the dinners at Government House in honour of visiting Latin American heads of state and foreign ministers.

2 E.R. to under-secretary, 28 June 1941, ibid., 1103–4

One of these dinners was in honour of the president of Colombia and his beautiful wife. When the time came for the governor general, the Earl of Athlone, to propose the toast he said, 'Ladies and gentlemen, the president of the republic of Venezuela.' In a high clear voice from the opposite end of the dining table his wife, Princess Alice, called out, 'Colombia, my deah.' From then on the menu at Government House dinners for visiting dignitaries contained a reminder to the governor general of who the principal guest was. Thus if it were the president of Argentina, the soup would be potage Argentine.

In July 1941 I was asked by Keenleyside to do a memorandum on possible Canadian participation in the Pan-American system in view of the probability of a Pan-American conference of foreign ministers later that year. This memorandum[3] is, I think, the first memorandum prepared in the department setting forth the pros and cons of membership in the Pan-American system. Before the war I had been opposed to Canadian membership; now I recommended that we join. One of my arguments in favour was that it would be an insurance policy for Canada against some of the losses and dangers which would result from the occupation of the British Isles by Germany. In that event Canada would be suspected by many citizens of the United States of being in favour of giving up the struggle against Germany even if the United States were willing to fight on to the bitter end. The more Canada emphasized its independent American nationhood, as it would by entering the Pan-American system, the weaker those suspicions would be likely to be.

The trade mission which visited South America in the autumn of 1941 was headed by James MacKinnon, the minister of trade and commerce, and the second-in-command was his deputy minister, Dana Wilgress. I became on this mission a friend and devoted admirer of Wilgress.

There was no nonsense in those days of flying from Ottawa to South America. We took a delightful nine-day voyage from New York to Ecuador on a ship brightly lit at night to show the large American flags painted on its sides so that German submarines would know not to attack a neutral ship. I had been studying a little Spanish before leaving Ottawa. On board ship a lovely young Chilean on her honeymoon taught me to memorize three sentences in Spanish. The first to use when I was introduced to a welcoming cabinet minister was the Spanish for 'Your Excellency is very kind to come to meet us.' When my impeccable accent led the excellency to believe I spoke Spanish (when none of the other members of the mission did) he would be sure to burst forth with a

3 Ibid., vol. 7, 1939–1941, part I (Ottawa 1974), 1105–8

torrent of Spanish. I was then to say, 'Unfortunately I can speak Spanish only a little, Your Excellency,' and I would gesture the little. The third sentence was for use on leaving a country: 'Your Excellency is very kind to come to say good-bye to us.' These three sentences I used with effect in Ecuador, Peru, Chile, Argentina, and Uruguay.

Though we were a trade mission we did not expect to sign any formal intergovernmental agreements. I did, however, take the precaution of asking the department's legal adviser what I should do if I had to affix a seal to an agreement. He said, 'Take a Canadian fifty-cent piece or twenty-five cent piece with you and use it.' I took both. It was in Chile that we signed our first most-favoured-nation trade agreement. The signing took place with pomp and ceremony in the Red Room at the foreign office. The signatures were affixed on the two copies. The red ribbon was laid. The wax was dropped on. I pressed the twenty-five cent piece down and then could not get it off. So I fished the fifty-cent piece out of my pocket, licked it, put it over the wax on the second copy of the agreement, and the same thing happened. Chile immediately received a benefit from entering into the agreement – my fifty-cent piece on its copy of the agreement.

Word of my incapacity as a sealer of documents must have gone ahead to other capitals, for when we signed an agreement in Rio de Janeiro the chief of protocol suggested that we affix our seals privately in his office before the formal signing ceremony. By then Wilgress had had a seal made.

The government of Brazil insisted we produce full powers for MacKinnon and Jean Désy, our minister in Brazil, to sign the agreement with them. We wired for them but they did not arrive in time. I therefore with a blank piece of paper in my hand got up and recited 'I, William Lyon Mackenzie King, prime minister and secretary of state for external affairs of Canada, do hereby grant full powers to the Honourable James Angus MacKinnon, Minister of Trade and Commerce, and Mr. Jean Désy, minister of Canada to Brazil' and so on.

In Ecuador, Peru, Chile, Uruguay, and Argentina our calls on the president were informal. Not so in Rio de Janeiro. The chief of protocol gave us precise instructions for our call on Getulio Vargas. We were to dress in morning coats. As soon as we entered the audience chamber we were to bow. We were to bow again half-way down the room and when we stood in front of the president. Leaving we were to walk backwards making the same three bows. We performed the first part of the ceremony quite well but we backed out in disgraceful disorganization since we constantly stepped on each other's feet and never bowed in unison. Presumably the explanation of this imperial protocol was that it had been inherited from the days before 1889 when Brazil had been an empire.

I constantly complained in my letters home of the ungodly hours at which I often had to get up. In those days airplanes did not fly at night and they almost always left at some such hour as 5:30 in the morning. When I wasn't grumbling about having to get up early I complained about not being able to get to bed till one since official dinners did not start until 9:30 and usually lasted until after midnight. My other complaint was about the number of official lunches, cocktail parties, and dinners we had to attend and the factories, abattoirs, schools, and industrial exhibitions we had to visit. I wrote to Ruth: 'I feel like the Prince of Wales inspecting schools and factories and am not at all surprised he resigned to marry Wallie Simpson ... Occasionally I have a moment of clarity of vision and ask myself when I am tramping my way through an industrial exhibition why anyone when civilizations are crashing about our ears should get paid for doing that sort of thing.'

In Chile I met Salvador Allende at dinner at the British embassy. He was then the socialist minister of health in the popular front government. He and the other socialist cabinet minister at the dinner were open in their support of the Allied cause. Allende toasted 'further bombardments of Germany like that of last night' (the previous night had seen the heaviest bombardment of Berlin since the outbreak of the war). He said that at present every cabinet minister could go his own way on his attitude to the war and that he might soon provoke a show-down in the cabinet in order to get the cabinet to agree on a pro-Allied line. In my report to Ottawa I said:

Both the British and the American ambassadors agree that German influence in Chile constitutes a greater danger than in any other South American country ... One reason for the peculiarly dangerous situation in Chile is the bitterness of the Right over their expulsion from power by the Frente Popular two years ago. The Right is struggling to get back into power; it is beginning to believe that it cannot get back into power by a free vote; it is honestly frightened of Communism and considers the mild measures of the Popular Front Government as being socialistic if not communistic. The Right might therefore make a temporary alliance with the Nazis in order to get into power by a coup d'état thinking that they could dish the Nazis afterwards ... One official in the Chilean Foreign Office is reported to have explained Chile's middle of the road policy in international affairs by saying that if the Government went too far in the Allied direction the right wing would revolt, and if it went too far in the opposite direction the communists would revolt.

When I called on the very intelligent American ambassador to Argentina, Norman Armour, I said to him that my impression was that in the four other Latin American countries I had visited, the greatest proportion of pro-Germans was to be found among devout Roman Catholics. He said: 'The reason is that the Church in Spain falls like a curtain between the Church in South America and the Vatican. The policy of the Vatican is as satisfactory as we could hope for. It is as pro-Allied as it can be. But the Church here is not influenced by that. It is influenced by the Church in Spain. This dates only from the civil war in Spain. The Roman Catholics here believe that Germany and Italy saved the Church in Spain from communism.'

In my despatch to Ottawa on my impressions of Argentina I said that a Canadian minister to Argentina 'by merely telling the story of the support which Roman Catholic French-speaking Canada is giving to Canada's all-out war effort can prove to the Catholics of Argentina that Catholics who are every bit as devout as they are (and are not tinged with protestantism as many of them consider the Roman Catholics in the United States to be) nevertheless heartily support the Anglo-American cause.'

I prefaced this despatch to Ottawa on Argentina by saying that it would be stupid for me to believe that after less than a fortnight's stay during which most of my time was taken up with formal receptions I had been able to penetrate beneath the surface of Argentina life, that to save time I would make flat statements but that these unqualified statements were all subject to the implicit qualification that 'I am not really certain about the truth of any statement about Argentina.' I then went on to say:

Argentina is rather like the England of the late eighteenth century. It is governed by a small landed aristocracy, the estancieros. The governing classes are, on the whole, not as charming as the Chileans, not as cultured as the Peruvians. They know ... that the upper classes on the West Coast look down on them as wealthy but rather raw and uncultured ... [T]he Argentinos claim that Argentina is the natural leader of Latin-America and they tend almost to despise the other Latin-American countries. Brazil is a 'nigger republic'; Peru and Mexico are Indian countries; the mass of the Chilean population is partly Indian and besides

Chile is a poverty-stricken country; the other countries of Latin-America are all small or are not 'white.' Argentina is the only white power of importance south of the Rio Grande. Argentina has a national mission – to be the leader of Latin-America against the Anglo-Saxon United States ...

The feelings of dislike, contempt and fear which the governing classes in Argentina seem, on the whole, to have for the United States ... do not by themselves explain the failure of the Argentine Government to cooperate with the United States today. The Argentino is intelligent and once he was convinced that the national interest of Argentina (which he would probably equate with the interest of the large land owners) demanded a policy of cooperation with the United States, he would cooperate, even though reluctantly. Argentina does not cooperate today because a sufficiently large number of men in important positions still believe that Germany is going to win the war, and that after the war Germany will reward its friends and punish its enemies.

A month after the return of the trade mission to Canada, Keenleyside wrote a memorandum to the under-secretary, Norman Robertson, recommending that he advise the government to accept the proposal which MacKinnon in his report on the mission was making that Canada should join the Pan-American union.[4] About a fortnight later the Japanese attacked Pearl Harbor and four days after that Robertson recommended to the prime minister that Canada should be represented at the meeting of the foreign ministers of the Pan-American countries to be held in Rio de Janeiro in the first week in January. The prime minister agreed not only to this but also that Canada should join the Pan-American Union.[5] Much to our surprise and chagrin the United States blocked Canadian participation in the Rio conference and Canadian membership in the Pan-American Union. Sumner Welles, the second-in-command of the State Department, justified the U.S. action by arguments which Robertson in a memorandum to the prime minister which Keenleyside had written said 'are known to be unsound and which he himself does not use when describing the situation to third parties':

When this fact is combined with the other evidences that have been accumulating lately of a growing American tendency to take action affecting Canadian interests, and even in some cases involving the use of Canadian soil without prior notification to the Canadian Government, we are justified in feeling that our relations

4 Ibid., 1108–10, memorandum of 21 November 1941
5 Ibid., vol. 9, 1942–43: 896–8

with the United States have entered an unsatisfactory phase, and one which should be ended just as quickly as possible.[6]

I had myself three months before discussed what Canada should do, assuming 'that there was a growing tendency on the part of the government of the United States to order Canada around.'[7] No useful purpose, I wrote, would be served by 'being indignant about what the United States is doing. We are being treated as children because we have refused to behave as adults. An adult makes his own decisions; he accepts responsibility for his own decisions. On matters of high policy in the realm of foreign affairs Canada does not make decisions; it has decisions forced on it.'

We had refused to take an adult part in the negotiations which preceded the attack of Japan on the United States because to have done so would have made us partly responsible for the outcome of the negotiations. Our refusal to accept adult responsibilities had been reflected in the nature of the Canadian legation in Washington and in the nature of two out of three of the recent ministers in Washington, Herbert Marler and Leighton McCarthy. 'Except for a period of a few months after Loring Christie had settled down as minister and before he fell ill, the State Department would be justified in concluding that Canada's foreign office was not interested in Europe, Asia, Africa, Australasia or Latin America, that it was interested only in problems arising out of the "line fence" between Canada and the United States.' We should appoint a minister to the United States competent to discuss general issues of foreign policy with the secretary of state and his principal assistants. We should encourage him to enter into such discussions. We should give him information about the general line of Canadian policy in various fields so that he could consult with the State Department and not merely, as at present, ask the State Department questions. Exactly three years were to elapse before Pearson was appointed ambassador to Washington.

In this memorandum of January 1942 I made what I think was my first plea as a foreign service officer that Canada should 'make the construction of an effective collective system the main goal of our policy':

The present trend towards the domination of Canada's external policy by the United States is the sort of thing which is to be expected under present conditions. Under a collective system a small state like Canada would have an opportunity

6 Ibid., 904–9
7 NAC, E. Reid Papers, memorandum of 12 January 1942

to exert a reasonable amount of influence in international politics at the cost of putting various aspects of its sovereignty into an international pool. But under the conditions of international anarchy which exist today the number of big states is likely to decrease and the few that are left are likely to run the small states which come within their respective spheres of influence.

A year later I wrote a lengthy memorandum on Canada-U.S. relations and circulated it for comments to Keenleyside, Wrong, Pearson, Arnold Heeney, and Jack Pickersgill. I said it was largely a scissors and paste job in which I had brought together material from various departmental files.[8] I intended to revise the memorandum in the light of the comments it elicited but by the time the comments came in I was about to leave on a four-week visit to England as a member of a mission to discuss air transport matters with the British. One point I made was that it might 'often be in the general world interest that medium and small powers should play a large part in determining the lines of the post-war settlement ... [because they] are not subject to the same temptations as great powers to pursue a nationalist line ... It may be easier for a camel to go through the eye of a needle than for a great power to support the establishment of an effective world order.' Nations, for example – and I was thinking of the United States – that thought that domination of the airways of the world was within their grasp would find it difficult to consider objectively proposals for the necessary amount of effective world control over international air transport.

The most difficult problem in Canada-U.S. relations after the war would be the problem of defence co-operation. Did the United States expect that if it got into a war with the Soviet Union Canada would automatically, regardless of the causes and occasions of the war, be at least a non-belligerent ally by granting the United States the right to use the Alaska highway for military traffic and to fly military aircraft over Canada?

It is hard to imagine that any self-respecting country would be willing, in the vital matter of peace and war, so completely to give up its right of independent judgment. My country, right or wrong, is a questionable and disreputable doctrine. Somebody else's country, right or wrong, is an impossible doctrine. We have not won from London complete freedom to make our own decisions on every issue – including that of peace and war – in order to become a colony of Washington.

8 Ibid., memorandum of 16 April 1943

This line of argument led me to reiterate my plea that Canada should press for the creation of an effective collective system. It seemed probable, I wrote, that effective military co-operation between Canada and the United States was possible 'only within the framework of an effective world order of which both Canada and the United States are loyal members.'

When I went to England in May 1943 to discuss air transport matters with the British I had a talk with Vincent Massey, then our high commissioner to London. He wrote in his diary that he was interested to see how alive I 'had become to the danger of American high pressure methods in Canada in connection with the war effort and the implications of this as regards our post-war relations ... This is a danger which External Affairs took a long time to discover, being preoccupied as they were with flogging the dead horse of "Downing Street domination".'

This was one of the rare occasions when Vincent Massey found my views satisfactory.

Norman Robertson telephoned me on Sunday morning, 7 December 1941, to ask me to come immediately to my office in the East Block. He said that we might be at war with Japan within a week and I was to draft a speech for the prime minister to give in Parliament on the occasion of the outbreak of the war. I had not got very far in drafting the speech – indeed the only idea which had occurred to me was to get the prime minister to quote poetry written in the last quarter-century and not, as he usually did, nineteenth-century poetry – when I was interrupted by a summons to go to the under-secretary's office. There I found that a meeting had been called to discuss a warning which the governments of the British Commonwealth were about to present to Japan that a Japanese attack on Thailand, Malaya, or the Netherlands East Indies would mean war with the nations of the Commonwealth. We were not discussing the merits of the warning, with which we agreed, but whether, as the British government had proposed, the British ambassador in Tokyo should present the warning on behalf of all the nations of the Commonwealth. We agreed that the Canadian chargé d'affaires in Tokyo should deliver a separate note to the Japanese foreign office associating Canada with the British representations. The only question that remained was whether he should accompany the British ambassador to the Foreign Office or make a call immediately after him. In the midst of our deliberations we were interrupted by a telephone call from an officer of the department who was at home. He said that he had just heard over the radio that the Japanese had attacked Pearl Harbor. My recollection is that the under-secretary and the rest of us were incredulous and that we continued our discussion of the nice point of diplomatic protocol until about 3:30, when we got confirmation of the attack from our legation in Washington.

I did not write the speech for Mackenzie King on the outbreak of the war with Japan. Pearson did and wrote a much better speech than I could have written.

I remember our profound relief when we learned that the Japanese had attacked U.S. territory, thus forcing the United States into the war. We had known for a week that a Japanese expeditionary force of fifty to seventy ships and about 30,000 men was moving south but, in spite of assurances from President Roosevelt, we feared that the United States might not declare war if the Japanese attack were on Thailand, Malaya, or the Netherlands East Indies. The nations of the British Commonwealth would be at war with Japan and the United States would still be neutral.

Our elation when the Soviet Union was forced into the war had been short-lived; it did not survive the smashing victories of the Germans over the Soviet armed forces in the first few weeks of fighting and the opinion of 'informed sources' in Washington that Soviet resistance would soon collapse. Our elation when the United States was forced into the war was tempered within a day when we learned from Washington the extent of the U.S. losses at Pearl Harbor.

A month after Japan entered the war I was asked by Keenleyside to be one of the External Affairs representatives at the conference he was organizing to discuss what should be done about the 22,000 people of Japanese origin in British Columbia. About 12,500 of them were Canadian citizens by birth or naturalization, the rest Japanese citizens who had become permanent residents of Canada.[9]

Immediately after Japan entered the war the government impounded the twelve hundred fishing vessels operated by Japanese Canadians. Thirty-eight Japanese considered by the RCMP to be potential dangers to national security were interned; the RCMP suggested to the Japanese-Canadians that the fifty-nine Japanese-language schools in British Columbia and the three Japanese-language newspapers in Vancouver be closed and they agreed.

9 The account which follows is based on the official documents on the conference which are referred to in Doc. 512 on pages 550–1 of DCER, vol. 9. Quotations and statistics are from these documents unless otherwise identified.

The conference took place on 8 and 9 of January 1942. F.J. Mead, the assistant commissioner of the RCMP reported that the police had received excellent co-operation from the leaders of the Japanese population in British Columbia. They had pointed out to the RCMP Japanese who should be interned as dangerous. As evidence of the excellent attitude of the Japanese population, Mead read three paragraphs from an operative's report of a secret meeting of Japanese fishermen in Vancouver which had taken place recently. The fishermen had stated that they realized that the seizure of the Japanese fishing fleet was inevitable under war conditions. Mead added that the Federal Bureau of Investigation had informed the RCMP that it 'had received no evidence of disloyalty by the Japanese in the United States; espionage had been committed only by persons attached to the [Japanese] consulates.' The RCMP considered that no further action needed to be taken. The representative of the navy said his service had no problem, as all Japanese-Canadian fishermen had already been cleared off the sea. General Maurice Pope said the army, too, considered no further action was necessary. The Department of Labour urged that because of the impending labour shortage in Canada nothing should be done which would interfere with making the most effective use of the abilities of persons of Japanese origin. The legal adviser of the Department of External Affairs warned that if Japan believed that Canada was mistreating Japanese nationals it would probably retaliate not only against Canadians but against other British subjects and nationals of other Allied nations.

Then, as Pope has put it in his memoirs, 'All hell broke loose.'[10] The minutes of the conference used less colourful language.

The members of the conference who had just arrived from British Columbia found it difficult to accept the assurances of the representatives of the Armed Services and of the Royal Canadian Mounted Police that the measures which had already been taken in British Columbia or which were recommended by a majority of the members of the Conference would be sufficient to meet the requirements of national defence and security. Most of them stated that they did not trust persons of Japanese racial origin and that they considered the continued presence of these persons in British Columbia a menace to public safety ... The people of British Columbia were definitely alarmed by the Japanese menace. There is grave danger that anti-Japanese riots may break out and that

10 Maurice Pope, *Soldiers and Politicians* (Toronto: University of Toronto Press 1962), 177

it will be necessary to call out the troops to defend Japanese residents from attack by other Canadians.

When I listened to what these British Columbians said about the Japanese-Canadians I thought that this was surely just the way the Nazis talked about Jewish Germans. It seemed to me also that the way in which they thrust aside the considerations of national interest advanced by the Department of Labour and the legal adviser of External Affairs indicated that they were motivated not by considerations of the national interest but by a desire to rid white British Columbians of the economic competition of efficient Japanese-Canadian market gardeners and fishermen. Pope confirms my impression. In his account of the conference he says that after the adjournment of the conference 'but before we separated I had an interesting conversation with one of the [British Columbia] delegation's political members. Sadly he said that for years his people had been telling themselves that war with Japan would afford them a Heaven-sent opportunity to rid themselves of the Japanese *economic* menace for ever more. And now after a period of some weeks nothing had been done. Not a word did he say about national security. This was enough for me.'[11] Four years later Pope said to me, 'I came away from that conference feeling dirty all over.' My own contribution to the discussion was so blunt that I stung one of the politicians from British Columbia into an outburst of anger.

All the members of the conference other than the British Columbia politicians were united in recommending to the government that persons of Japanese racial origin in British Columbia not be interned or moved inland. The only steps they recommended in addition to those already taken were to control strictly the sale of gasoline and of blasting powder to these persons and to prohibit the possession or use by Japanese nationals (but not by Japanese Canadians who were Canadian citizens) of short-wave radio receiving sets, radio transmitters, and cameras. The government on 14 January announced that it had accepted these recommendations and that it had also decided on another step not recommended by the conference: that all enemy aliens (German, Italian, and Japanese) except those possessing permits from the RCMP should be moved out of 'such Protected Areas on the Pacific Coast as may be defined.' This provision applied only to the 9,500 Japanese citizens, not to the 12,500 persons of Japanese racial origin who were Canadian

11 Ibid.

citizens. The politicians from British Columbia were not satisfied; they successfully appealed to Mackenzie King and at the end of February the government decided that every 'person of Japanese race' living within a hundred miles of the Pacific coast would be moved inland. Canada committed an evil act.

Eighteen years after the conference on Japanese-Canadians when I was reminiscing with Norman Robertson, I said to him that at that meeting I had felt the physical presence of evil. He was exasperated by that remark. He had not been revolted as Keenleyside, Henry Angus, Maurice Pope, and I had been by the demands of British Columbia politicians for the deportation of persons of Japanese racial origin. Two years after their deportation he said in a memorandum to the prime minister: 'On the whole, I think our treatment of the Japanese in Canada has not been unduly harsh and can be defended as reasonable in the circumstances.'[12] I find this hard to understand, for Robertson was a liberal. In a toast to him just before he left for London in the autumn of 1946 to be high commissioner, I applied to him the statement of Cyril Connolly: 'As we relive the horrors of the Dark Ages, of absolute states and ideological wars, the old platitudes of liberalism loom up in all their glory, familiar streets as we reel home furious in the dawn.'

It was not until 1988 that the Canadian government apologized to the Japanese Canadians for their treatment in 1942 and gave them compensation.

By May 1943 I was beginning to hope that the end of the war was in sight. I wrote to my mother: 'The war news is so good that even I, who am an almost uncurable pessimist, am beginning to believe that the war in Europe may be over in 18 months.' I was out by six months. The war in Europe ended on 7 May 1945, twenty-four months later.

But the way in which the war in Europe was ending appalled me. When I read of the bombing of Hamburg at the beginning of August 1943 I wrote: 'Hamburg is the culminating horror. My hands feel unclean simply because I am a citizen of an allied government. War is the dirtiest of all businesses and perhaps the misery of Hamburg will curtail the misery of the more innocent women and children of France, the Netherlands, Norway and the Jews. I hope we can lay that flattering unction to our souls. It looks as if the war will end in a nightmare of aerial

---

12 DCER, vol. 10, 1944–1945, part I (Ottawa 1987), 1132, memorandum of 27 March 1944

devastation of Germany. But it also looks as if the war will end sooner than we had dared hope.'

I was concerned at that time by what seemed to me in some departmental analyses of the problem of the treatment of Germany after the war a tendency to exaggerate the difficulties of creating and maintaining an anti-Nazi regime in Germany. My interpretation of the forces in Germany which had led to the triumph of Naziism was one which was generally accepted by liberals in the middle and late thirties: the Nazi movement had been supported by the owners of big landed estates in Prussia and the owners of heavy industries; and the Protestant church in Germany had failed to be the conscience of the state. I therefore proposed in a memorandum in September 1943[13] that the big landed estates and the heavy industries, including coal and steel, chemicals, and power, should be expropriated. The land of the big estates should be given to the peasants. The Protestant church should be separated from the state. Heavy industry might be controlled, at least during a probationary period of ten or twenty years, by an agency of the European community or of the United Nations. A high capital levy should be imposed and used 'to indemnify those in Germany and abroad who have suffered in mind, body or estate because of their opposition to Hitlerite Germany.' The principal officials in the Nazi administration should serve for five years or more in labour corps, which would do reconstruction work in devastated areas outside Germany. Germany might be required to include in a new constitution 'an immutable bill of rights of the citizen which would make illegal all the principal crimes which the nazi regime has perpetrated against the non-nazi element in the German community – for example, torture, beating, and other barbarous punishments, imprisonment and execution without trial, racial and religious discrimination and defamation.' The terms of the armistice, which should be signed by the Nazi leaders and the army leaders, 'should be as harsh as possible so that the post-Hitler regime may get credit for securing better terms.'

The Russians put an end to the big landed estates in East Prussia. The western powers did not expropriate heavy industry in their zones of occupation. What I in my memorandum proposed for Germany bore little resemblance to the terms the western powers imposed in their zones of occupation. It bore a marked resemblance to the terms the United States imposed on Japan.

13 NAC, E. Reid Papers, memorandum of 14 September 1943

One topic which my friends and I in the department used to discuss from time to time in those days was the failure of Canada to create the usual symbols of nationhood and to remove the remaining symbols of colonial subordination. In one of those discussions I was challenged when I said I could list at least twenty changes which should be made. In response to this challenge I wrote a memorandum with the resounding title 'Twenty-four point draft programme for the abolition of the vestigial remnants of colonial subordination and for the creation of appropriate symbols of Canadian nationhood.'[14] When I look at that memorandum now I am struck by how few of the normal symbols of nationhood we possessed in the mid-forties and how many remnants of colonial subordination still remained.

Five of the symbols of nationhood I recommended have been adopted: the recognition of a Canadian flag and a Canadian national anthem; the change of the royal title to King or Queen of Canada; the creation of a national library; and a 'national capital of which the whole of Canada can be proud.' Two have not: membership in the Pan-American Union, and the creation of a national university. Membership in the Pan-American Union would in those days have constituted a symbolic assertion of independent nationhood; now that argument for membership no longer has weight. As for a national university, it too is no longer needed as a symbol of nationhood but it is still very much needed, for a bilingual national university whose students came from all parts of Canada and who had passed a tough scholarship examination would strengthen the forces making for Canadian unity. Potential leaders of Canada in politics, the professions, the arts, and business would have got to know each other and would have learned from each other. A weakness of almost all Canadian universities is that they are parochial; few of their undergraduates come from other provinces.

Among the remnants of colonial subordination which I recommended be removed and which have been removed are appeals to the Judicial Committee of the Privy Council in London, going to the British Parliament to get the constitution amended, and acceptance by Canadians of United Kingdom orders of chivalry such as CBE and CMG. I made two other recommendations which have not been implemented: that diplomatic representatives exchanged between Commonwealth countries be called ambassadors not high commissioners, and that we use the terms 'Foreign Office' and 'foreign minister,' not 'Department of External Affairs' and 'secretary of state for external affairs.'

I disliked the term 'Dominion.' It seemed to me to denote something

14 Ibid., memorandum of 21 Mar. 1944

inferior in status to nation or national. I proposed that in official Canadian government documents the words Canada and Canadian government be used, not Dominion of Canada and Dominion government; that the term 'nations of the British Commonwealth' be used, not Dominions; and that the functions of the Dominions Office in London be taken over by the Foreign Office. These changes have been made. I disliked, and continue to dislike, the term governor general and I suggested that the office be abolished and that instead of a governor general we have an administrator as provided in the British North America Act, or counsellors of state. Two years earlier I had suggested that the term regent replace governor general. Unhappily, the absurd expression governor general, which puzzles and misleads many foreigners, is still in use. It is probably one of the reasons many Americans still believe that Canada has not yet become a fully independent country.

In 1952 the nations of the Commonwealth agreed that the time had come to change the royal title with its anachronistic 'British Dominions beyond the seas' and that each Commonwealth nation could choose a form suitable to its circumstances but with a common element. I assumed that the form for Canada would be 'Elizabeth the Second, by the Grace of God Queen of Canada and of Her other Realms and Territories,' et cetera. But when I saw Pickersgill at an official dinner he said that it would be 'by the Grace of God of the United Kingdom, Canada and Her other Realms and Territories Queen,' et cetera. I said this inclusion of the United Kingdom in the Canadian title was absurd. Pickersgill said that St Laurent was responsible for the formula. It was not until 1977 that the queen was designated by statute as Queen of Canada and this not by an amendment to the Royal Style and Titles Act of 1953 but by an amendment to the Oaths of Allegiance Act of 1952. This act had referred to the queen as 'Her Majesty Elizabeth the Second.' The 1977 act added after 'Elizabeth the Second' the words 'Queen of Canada.'

A friend in the British Foreign Office told me at the beginning of 1939 of an outburst from an overworked officer in the Foreign Office when he was told to produce a memorandum for the prime minister of a Dominion on the fluctuations in the pre-1914 boundary between the Turkish vilayets of Jerusalem and Medina:

Lord in thy mercy educate us
To love those with Dominion status
And tell them everything or nearly
On points which don't concern them really.

I found in my time in the Department of External Affairs in the mid-1940s that on points which did concern us really the British Foreign Office gave us enormous help in understanding what was happening in the world. We had at that time diplomatic missions in only sixteen countries. The British had a world-wide network of diplomatic missions and a large, skilled, and experienced staff in the Foreign Office. The principal way the British helped us was by sending us copies of their Foreign Office prints which contained a selection of the more important telegrams and despatches between the Foreign Office and its diplomatic missions and, when international relations were moving especially quickly from crisis to crisis, they would cable copies of telegrams to us. This information was supplemented by the briefings which the Foreign Office constantly gave officers of our high commission in London.

When I was at the San Francisco conference in 1945 I realized even more clearly the value to Canada of the information the British gave us. Ottawa passed on to us telegrams from the British on the breaking down of relations in Europe between the Soviet Union and the western powers, with the result that we, unlike most all the other delegations from middle or small powers, could look at what was happening at San Francisco against the background of what was happening in Europe.

In the two years after the San Francisco conference, I was again impressed with the value to us of this flow of information from the British. We had in those years no diplomatic missions in Poland, Czechoslovakia, Hungary, and Romania. If it had not been for the British Foreign Office we would have had no well-informed first-hand accounts from those countries to supplement newspaper reports on how the Soviet Union was imprisoning, torturing, and killing leaders of social democratic and agrarian parties in order to put in power puppet communist governments. Because Knox Helm, the British political representative and later minister in Hungary, was a friend from our time together in Washington, I read his reports with special interest and I remember how moved I was by them. It is not therefore surprising that our reaction of fear and hostility to Soviet behaviour in Eastern Europe was much the same as that of the British and that we therefore warmly welcomed their proposal early in 1948 for a North Atlantic treaty.

When Britain shared information with us it did not do so out of the kindness of its heart; it knew it served the British national interest. The British establishment, apart from a few relics of the past, had by the early forties given up hope of the member nations of the Commonwealth agreeing to establish a common foreign policy, but it realized that the chances of the other Commonwealth nations looking at international problems in much the same way as Britain were increased if they were given access to British diplomatic correspondence; the more they shared a common outlook, the more likely would their reactions to an international crisis be much the same. The Commonwealth would not have the nature of an alliance; it would have the nature of an alliance potential.

In my three years in the Department of External Affairs from 1941 to 1944 I served under Hugh Keenleyside. In his memoirs he made a shrewd assessment of my strengths and weaknesses as a foreign service officer in those years.

Intelligent and widely read, he had a notable command of the language and excellent judgement in the selection and marshalling of facts ... Not that he was always the easiest of associates; he wasn't. He was unusually confident of his own judgements and was far from flexible in both the positions he adopted and the determination, not to say obstinacy, with which he maintained his views. Some people found him a bit intolerant, and he was not always careful to conceal his low opinion of his opponents' intellectual capacity or moral rectitude. Even though his scorn was often justified, it was not always advisable to make it so apparent.[15]

15 Hugh Keenleyside, *Memoirs*, vol. 2 (Toronto: McClelland and Stewart 1982), 461–2

13

Creating the International Civil Aviation Organization

1944

The first official multilateral international conference I attended was the fifty-four-nation conference on international civil aviation held in Chicago at the end of 1944. This conference laid the foundation of a new law of the air and established the International Civil Aviation Organization.

My introduction to the problems of international air transport was through the interdepartmental committee on air transport policy set up in 1942. This was a distinguished committee. Its three most important members were the two leading civil servants of the time – Norman Robertson, the under-secretary of state for external affairs, and Clifford Clark, the deputy minister of finance – and H.J. Symington. Symington, a leading corporation lawyer and businessman in Winnipeg, had been persuaded in 1941 by C.D. Howe, the cabinet minister in charge of civil aviation, to become president of Trans-Canada Airlines, now Air Canada. He spent at least half his time on this task and accepted no salary. John Baldwin of the Privy Council Office and I, as junior members of the interdepartmental committee, drafted and redrafted the reports of the committee and wrote the speeches on air transport policy to be delivered by the prime minister and C.D. Howe. This was one of the happiest partnerships of my time in government service. I was delighted to be assigned responsibility in the Department of External Affairs for air transport policy. I wrote in December 1942: 'Air transport is going to bring us all so close together that we will have to either love our neighbours or kill them. I am optimistic enough to believe that after the war we will be tired with killing.'

The interdepartmental committee was the first to be served by the cabinet secretariat in the Privy Council Office, and its success had a good deal to do with the acceptance by the prime minister and leading cabinet ministers of the role of the cabinet secretariat within the Privy Council Office.

The committee's approach to the problems of international air transport was based on the belief that the pre-war system had to be radically changed. Under that system international air routes were established as a result either of bilateral agreements between governments or of concessions which airlines secured from foreign governments. Since every state had complete and exclusive sovereignty in the air space over its territory, a state could refuse to another state, or to the airlines of another state, the right to fly over its territory, or to land in it to refuel, or to pick up or put down traffic. Such a refusal might necessitate costly and even dangerous detours, or bar the establishment of the service. The making of bilateral agreements was often accompanied by hard bargaining. A government might refuse to grant air rights unless a number of outstanding political questions, unconnected with aviation, were settled in its favour. Concessions of air rights to one country might be refused at the instigation of a third country. This might be done by direct diplomatic pressure or by a great power forming a dummy local company in a smaller power which controlled the site of an essential air base and then securing a monopoly of air services for that company in all the national territory. The penetration of Latin America by the air transport systems of Germany and Italy immediately preceding the Second World War demonstrated how nations planning aggression were able to use air transport as a cloak for economic and military penetration into other countries. The granting of air rights was thus before the war a potent cause of friction and dispute between nations. The refusal of rights or the driving of a hard bargain held back the development of efficient and economical air services. It was clear that we would go a long way toward promoting the most rapid possible development of air transport and toward removing causes of international friction if air rights were no longer granted by bilateral agreements.

At the end of September 1943 the interdepartmental committee submitted its report to the Cabinet War Committee. Robertson's memorandum to the prime minister on the report demonstrates that at that time senior civil servants, not noted for starry-eyed, unrealistic idealism, supported proposals on international organization which less than twenty years later would be dismissed with such pejoratives as unrealistic, idealistic, doctrinaire, grandiose, and rhetorical. The fourteen years from 1929 to 1943 had been apocalyptic for those who lived through them and it is not surprising that many of us became apocalyptic in our dreams and visions. We had learned that civilization was fragile. We believed that the war had made international relations malleable. We believed that the times demanded and made possible revolutionary changes in the relations between nations.

Robertson in his memorandum told the prime minister that the majority of the members of the interdepartmental committee, including Clark and himself, felt that Canada should:

be prepared to support or, if necessary, to initiate proposals for the international operation of the main international [air] routes. They feel very strongly that such a policy would help to lessen the risks of new rivalries between countries which in their turn might involve the risks of new wars ... The importance of the decision which will have to be made during the next year or so on the post-war organization of air transport may be a key one. If we can settle this problem right we shall have gone a long way to establishing a new world order of security. If we don't settle it right our chances of another world war in the foreseeable future are greatly increased ... It may be that due to the opposition of the United States and other powers proposals for international operation may not get very far. But if the job is to be attempted now is surely the time to do it.[1]

The majority of the committee were not alone in advocating the international operation of the main international air routes. The first two advisory committees set up by the British government, the Shelmerdine and Finlay committees, had advocated it, and the third committee, the Barlow committee, had given it general support. Australia and New Zealand supported it.

Churchill brusquely dismissed the advice given by the Shelmerdine and Finlay committees. He wrote in June 1943 that if complete internationalization 'meant a kind of VOLAPUK ESPERANTO cosmopolitan organization managed and staffed by committees of all peoples great and small, with pilots of every country from Peru to China (especially China), flying every kind of machine in every direction many people will feel that this is at present an unattainable ideal ... We must agree upon some less high-spirited line of approach to guide us in the forthcoming international discussions.'[2]

The report of the interdepartmental committee, though not going as far in the direction of recommending the international operation of the main international air routes as the majority of the committee wished, went a considerable distance in that direction. It recommended that

1 *Documents on Canadian External Relations* (DCER), vol. 9, 1942–1943: 731–2
2 Ibid., 724

Canada 'should be prepared to discuss or, if the War Committee believes it desirable, to raise' this proposal. The report went on to state that whatever was done about the setting up of international operating companies, it would be necessary to establish an international air transport authority 'with effective regulatory powers over such matters as rates, schedules, subsidies, safety regulations and standards of operation.' This authority might be given power to license the air transport companies of the signatories of the civil aviation convention to operate air transport routes other than trans-frontier services between two contiguous countries.[3]

Mackenzie King was so impressed by Norman Robertson's arguments that when the interdepartmental committee's report came before the Cabinet War Committee he read to the committee the four paragraphs in the report on international operation and declared that this proposal 'was supported by strong military and political considerations of great importance to Canada and to the maintenance of world peace.' Howe, however, stated that while he approved the report, he believed that Canada would have little to gain by initiating proposals for internationalization. In his opinion a preferable solution was 'the establishment of an international licensing authority, which would divide and allocate routes and services between the various nations.' Cabinet War Committee approved the report.

The interdepartmental committee then drafted a detailed international convention for the establishment of an international licensing authority which would have jurisdiction over international air transport analogous to that which the Civil Aeronautics Board of the United States had over United States airline companies. This convention was presented by Howe to the House of Commons in March 1944. An outline of its provisions had been given to the State Department in February. A revised version was published in October and submitted to the Chicago conference.[4]

One valuable result for me of my membership in the interdepartmental committee was a lesson from Norman Robertson on diplomatic language. I wrote for his signature a letter to a deputy minister who was a member of the committee which betrayed irritation at his failure to understand a previous communication to him about the work of the committee. Robertson sent the letter back to me for redrafting. He said that he had constantly to work with this deputy minister and it was essential he not hurt his feelings. I then used a formula which I have used many times

3 Ibid., 732–8
4 Revised preliminary draft of an international air convention (Ottawa: King's Printer 1944)

since to a correspondent who has stupidly misunderstood a previous communication to him: 'I am sorry that in my letter to you of —— I did not make myself clear' – even though the letter had been crystal clear.

In those days the Canadian government was determined to resist efforts by the British to strengthen their bargaining position in discussions with the United States by lining up the other members of the Commonwealth behind them. We called this refusing to gang up against the United States. So when the British in May 1943 proposed a meeting in London of officials of the Commonwealth countries to work out ideas on post-war civil aviation 'which could afford the basis for useful informal discussions with United States representatives,' we informed them that we believed 'the chances of getting substantial international agreement on a desirable [air transport] policy would be lessened by the holding of prior Commonwealth discussions.' Churchill called our bluff. At a meeting of the Canadian Cabinet War Committee which he attended in Quebec on 11 August he said that Britain intended to go ahead with this meeting 'whether or not Canada felt able to participate.' The Canadian government capitulated. It knew that the publicity the British would give to Canada's absence from the Commonwealth meeting in London would precipitate adverse criticism of the government in Canada.[5]

Lord Beaverbrook was then the British cabinet minister responsible for civil aviation. The Commonwealth meeting in London confirmed him in his belief that he would be able to get a common Commonwealth policy on international civil aviation. After the meeting he wrote Harry Hopkins, then one of Roosevelt's principal advisers, that he now hoped to get agreement with the United States on a joint policy to be put before an international conference. 'After we get to know what U.S.A. and Britain will present our Dominions will be asked to give approval ... Howe would join us [in a conference with the United States in Washington] to keep the Dominions in line with our decisions.'[6] The terms 'our Dominions' and keeping 'the Dominions in line' indicate how far Beaverbrook was ignorant of the way the Canadian government regarded its relations with Britain. When in February 1944 we gave the British a twenty-page document setting forth our views, a member of Beaverbrook's office informed a member of the United States embassy in London that they

---

5 DCER, vol. 9, 700–22
6 *Foreign Relations of the United States Government* (FRUS), Department of State Publications, 1944; vol. 2: Geneva: Economic and Social Matters (Washington: U.S. Government Printing Office), 357

considered it 'impertinent' for Canada 'to present such a detailed plan particularly in view of the likelihood of offending the other Dominions and India.'[7]

In March 1944 I was transferred from Ottawa to the embassy in Washington and promoted from second secretary to first secretary. My son Timothy, then seven years old, asked me what was meant by my promotion. I said it was like him being promoted at school from grade 3 to grade 4. He said he thought it would also mean that I would be allowed to have a revolver to use against burglars.

In October I was told that I was to attend the Chicago conference on international civil aviation as an adviser to the Canadian delegation for the first two weeks of the conference. The delegates were Howe, Symington, and J.A. Wilson, the director of air services in the Department of Transport, and there were four advisers on general policy and twenty technical advisers. Howe had intended to be the active head of the delegation but the conference coincided with a first-class political crisis in Ottawa over conscription for overseas service and Howe, as a senior member of the cabinet, had to be in Ottawa for all but a few days of the conference. Thus Symington became the *de facto* head of the delegation, John Baldwin and I became his advisers on air transport policy, and I remained for the whole conference, which lasted from 1 November to 7 December.

In the report to Ottawa which I wrote after the conference I said that Canada became one of the three leading powers at the conference because we were the only delegation to come to the conference with a carefully worked out comprehensive draft convention. On 6 November, after the conference had been in session for only five days, it decided to take our convention as the basis of discussion in the key conference committee on the regulation of international air transport and the structure of the proposed international aviation organization. (The United States draft convention was taken as the basis of discussion in the committee on air navigation.) Once it was realized that the main struggle at the conference over the regulation of international air transport was between Britain and the United States with Canada in between, our role as mediator between Britain and the United States became obvious. Adolf Berle, the head of the American delegation and of the conference, wrote in his diary for the second day of the conference that the 'important

7 Ibid., 375

fact was that the Canadian delegation attempted to find middle ground between the British and the United States.'[8]

In my report to Ottawa I went on to say:

The acceptance by the United Kingdom and the United States of Canada as a mediator, and the concurrence of the conference in the consequent decision that Canada should be elevated to the rank of the big three would not have been so freely given had not other factors come into play. The most important of these was the ring of sincerity, idealism and hard common sense in Mr. Howe's opening speech of November 2. This was followed up by Mr. Symington's masterly exposition of the Canadian convention – article by article – in subcommittee on November 7, 8 and 10, and by Mr. Symington's explanation of the genesis of the Canadian proposals at his press conference on November 9, when he made it clear that the proposals were of Canadian birth and origin and that Canada was not a foster-parent of a child conceived and born in the United Kingdom.

Mr. Howe and Mr. Symington were in peculiarly strong positions from which to launch an idealistic proposal since the one was generally known as Canada's biggest businessman of the past five years and the other as the shrewd operator of one of the most efficient airlines of the world.

When the committees started on 7 November to take our draft convention as the basis of discussion they made rapid progress. On 8 November I wrote to Ruth: 'Yesterday at two committees we went through the Canadian convention clause by clause and got about half way through. Today we got through the rest. Symington is magnificent and, to quote Mr. Berle, I dearly love him.' What we went through in the committees were the non-controversial parts of our convention, and by 11 November it became clear that the committees could not make progress on the controversial parts, those on freedoms of the air, rates, and frequencies of service, as long as the positions of the United States and Britain remained so far apart. Berle, as president of the conference, therefore arranged that the three delegations which had submitted complete plans to the conference – the United States, Britain, and Canada – should meet in private in an effort to work out agreed proposals. In his diary for 11 November Berle wrote: 'There is at least reasonable probability that anything these countries agree on will go through the conference.'[9]

---

8 *Navigating the Rapids 1918–1971*, edited by B.B. Berle and T.B. Jacobs (New York: Harcourt Brace Jovanovich 1973), 499

9 Adolf Berle's diary of the Chicago Conference, September – December 1944, Roosevelt Library, Hyde Park, N.Y.

The American, British, Canadian (ABC) group had nine members, three from each country. The Canadians were Howe, Symington, and I. It met for ten days from 12 to 20 November. The meetings were, as Berle has put it, 'brutal in their length,' and 'strenuous in the extreme.' I certainly found them so. The day before they ended I wrote to Ruth: 'For a good deal of the past two weeks I have been working about a sixteen-hour day. Wake up about 6:30; do some work in bed; breakfast about 7:30 and then on till 1:30 in the morning ... The last week has been nightmarish. When I wasn't in the three-power committee – passing notes to Symington – I was drafting and redrafting our convention to meet the arguments of the U.S.'

The central issue was how many of the six freedoms of the air each contracting state would grant to the other contracting states in respect of scheduled international air services and under what conditions. (Canada has been given the credit, notably by Berle, for the formulation of these six freedoms but the credit belongs to the British who set them forth in a message to us in July 1943.[10]) The six freedoms are:

1 Freedom to fly across another state's territory without landing (the right of innocent passage).
2 Freedom to land in another state's territory for non-traffic purposes (refuelling, repair, and in emergency).
3 Freedom to put down in another state traffic (passengers, mails, and freight) taken on in the aircraft's country of origin (the country whose nationality the aircraft possesses).
4 Freedom to take on in another state traffic destined for the aircraft's country of origin.
5 Freedom to convey traffic between two states, neither being the aircraft's country of origin.
6 Freedom to convey traffic between two points in the territory of another state.

A gross over-simplification of the differences between the American and British positions at the opening of the conference was that the Americans stood for freedom in the air and the British for order in the air. The Americans did not stand for freedom in the air: under their original proposals the contracting states would grant each other only the first two freedoms; other freedoms could be obtained only by countries negotiating bilateral agreements with each other. Unlike Britain and Canada, the United States proposed no regulatory powers for the international aviation organization; its functions would be limited to the collection of information, study, and review and its powers would be wholly advisory.

The British proposed the reciprocal granting of the first four freedoms on condition that the international civil aviation organization would eliminate uneconomic competition by allocating routes, determining the frequencies of service each country would maintain on a route, and fixing rates. The British proposal did not set forth the criteria the aviation organization would follow in making these decisions.

The Canadian draft convention also proposed the reciprocal granting of the first four freedoms and control of routes, frequencies of service, and rates by an international air authority but it differed from the British by setting forth the criteria the authority would follow in making its decisions. Thus rates should 'permit the most economical operator to cover the full cost of operation and reasonable profit.' Rates would be fixed in the first instance by the airline companies which were operating on a route. If they failed to agree or an interested government took exception to their decision, the authority could fix the rates. As for frequencies of service, we proposed an escalator clause: if an airline company had been operating on a route 'with an average payload over a year of more than 65 per cent of carrying capacity,' it would automatically receive the right to run additional services on that route. The official conference summary of the Canadian proposals said that this escalator clause 'would reward efficiency and stimulate healthy competition, encourage improvements in the arts and services of flying, and offer free choice for the traveller between competing airlines and competition in services but not in subsidies.'

The first meeting of the ABC group on Sunday afternoon, 12 November, was nearly the last. After an hour the discussion degenerated into acrimonious debate between Berle and Lord Swinton, the head of the British delegation, on what each contended was the basic principle behind his proposal, Berle saying that the United States stood for freedom in the air and Swinton saying that Britain stood for order in the air. Tempers got so high that we proposed an adjournment on the ground that the leader of our delegation, Howe, had just arrived in Chicago and we had not had an opportunity to discuss with him the recent developments at the conference. At our meeting I suggested that I might go to Berle and Swinton to propose that instead of arguing about general principles, the ABC meeting should discuss the section on traffic capacity in the Canadian draft convention. Howe agreed. I pleaded for fifteen minutes with Berle, who was in a raging temper. He agreed to our proposal, which I then sold to Swinton, who was in a state of anger equal to Berle's, and the talks were resumed. Within half an hour the precise points of difference between the United States and Britain were beginning to emerge and the large measure of agreement between them was apparent.

After another few days of meetings it looked as if the Canadian escalator clause had provided a bridge between the United States and Britain and that the ABC group would propose to the conference a convention based on the granting of four freedoms of the air and control by the international authority over rates and frequencies of service subject to an escalator clause. Then Berle came to an ABC meeting one morning tense and drawn. We found out later that he had been arguing into the early hours of the morning at a meeting of his delegation with the advisers on the delegation from the American airlines (Pan American, American, and Chicago and Southern) and with the four members of the delegation from Congress. He proceeded in a masterly fashion to put forward a new proposal: that a grant of four freedoms was insufficient; the fifth freedom must be added – the right of an airline to take on and put down traffic at intermediate stops along a through route traversing a number of countries, subject to the right of a country to reserve traffic between two points in its territory. Berle's presentation was dispassionate and lucid, but I noticed that while he was making it his knuckles were white.

I said to Symington after Berle had finished that it was a masterly performance. Symington said that Berle's insistence on five freedoms rather than four made agreement almost impossible. Symington was right. The problem which could not be resolved was how to apply the escalator clause to fifth-freedom traffic.

While the ABC talks were taking place, meetings of the full conference on the questions being considered by the ABC group were suspended and the conference was kept 'in idleness, ignorance and an uncomfortable hotel,' as Godfrey Boyd-Shannon of the British delegation put it in his report on the conference.[11] The Stevens Hotel (now the Hilton), described in its stationery as 'World's largest hotel,' was certainly uncomfortable. I said in my report on the conference that it was 'a mammoth second-rate hotel whose lobby was like the lobby of the Grand Central Station in New York, a hotel in which it was necessary to waste an hour a day waiting for elevators and probably half an hour a day waiting to complete telephone calls.'

Informal consultations between Berle, Swinton, and Symington went

11 Public Record Office, DO 35/1236, XN 074.27

on after the ABC talks were terminated and I kept on drafting one new compromise after another on how to apply the escalator clause to fifth-freedom traffic. By this time the formulas were becoming more and more complicated, esoteric, and lengthy. Our final proposal on traffic capacity, entitled 'Full Planes,' was two thousand words long. I could not possibly have drafted these complicated formulas if Ed Warner, acting in a personal capacity, had not been my technical adviser. Warner was the vice-chairman of the Civil Aeronautics Board of the United States. We worked for long hours together, one time till 1:40 in the morning. I had other confidential advisers from the American delegation acting also in their personal capacities: Colonel S.E. Gates of Air Transport Command helped with revision of the traffic capacity article, and Congressman A.L. Bulwinkle revised the ABC draft article on rates.

Towards the end of the conference Berle, Swinton, and Symington met in a last desperate effort to bridge the narrow gap which by then separated the United States and Britain on the traffic capacity article. If they reached agreement on this article they would submit it to the full conference for approval. It would be embarrassing if before they did so the conference had approved of an earlier incomplete draft of the section of the convention of which this article would form a part. Symington therefore instructed me to make sure that this did not happen. I was to conduct a filibuster. So I jumped up to talk at length on every issue that came up at the meeting. My filibuster was successful but the meeting of the heads of the ABC countries was not.

The result of this failure was that the convention agreed to by the conference contained no reciprocal grant of any freedoms of the air, and no provisions on rates or on frequencies of service. An accompanying agreement which was open to members of the International Civil Aviation Organization provided for a reciprocal grant of the first two freedoms of the air. This agreement, called the International Air Services Transit Agreement, is now accepted by a hundred states. The other supplementary agreement, the International Air Transport Agreement, under which contracting states would grant each other four or five freedoms of the air, never had more than twelve member states and is now for practical purposes dead.

One of the undercurrents at the conference of which I knew little at the time was Berle's opposition to the ambitions of Pan American Airways (PAA). He believed that it wanted to be the sole or at least the dominant American international airline. He despised PAA. In April 1940 he wrote that it had been helping to run a German airline in Colombia and 'had been using it to train German pilots – presumably to bomb the Panama Canal, when the time comes'; and five months later he wrote, 'I do not trust Pan Am any farther than I can see it.' He considered that Senator R.O. Brewster, one of the two senators on the American delegation at Chicago, was a 'stooge' for PAA and was communicating the delegation's decisions to it.[12]

Though I did not know this at the time, I did know that Berle was insistent that the international convention should contain a provision aimed at PAA. This provision, included in the draft of the convention submitted by the ABC powers to the conference on 20 November, stated: 'No state shall be bound to grant any of the privileges of this Convention to an airline of any state unless it shall be satisfied that substantial ownership and effective control are vested in the nationals of that state.' This would make it impossible for PAA to set up airlines in foreign countries and secure rights for these airlines which it could not secure as a United States company. In spite of the importance Berle attached to this provision, it would sometimes be omitted from drafts of the convention prepared by the American delegation and I began to suspect the hidden hand of PAA within the delegation. Whenever I noticed the omission I would draw it to the attention of a member of the American delegation. Once when I did this the official angrily exclaimed, 'I take my instructions from the head of my delegation, not from you.' The provision does not appear in the convention adopted at Chicago since that convention does not grant any rights to scheduled air services to operate over or into the territory of a member state, but it does appear in the International Air Transport Agreement.

At the conference I made my first attempt to simplify the language of international agreements. I found this a pleasant diversion from intractable substantive problems. In order to have expert advice I got in touch with Dr I.A. Richards, one of the principal authors of Basic English, and he sent me Basic English versions of some of the principal sections of the Canadian draft convention. When I was charged with preparing revised versions of these sections I would do my best to insert as much Basic English as possible and it had considerable influence on the preamble, on some of the early chapters of Part II of the final convention, and on some of the provisions of the Air Transport Agreement. Thus the principal objective of the International Civil Aviation Organization is 'to meet the needs of the peoples of the world for safe, regular, efficient, and economical air transport.' Richards had suggested 'cheap' instead

12 *Navigating the Rapids*, 301, 337, 488, 501

of 'economical' but this was rejected as sounding, as a British official put it, like an advertisement for a Chinese laundry. Instead of aircraft embarking and disembarking passengers, mail, and cargo, the words 'to take on' and 'to put down' were used. And, as I said in a letter to Richards after the conference was over, 'One of the most useful contributions which your Basic English version made to the Convention was the substitution of "undertakings" for "obligations". The latter word carries with it much more connotation of supra-national authority than the other and is, consequently, a bad word to use in an international agreement.'

There were many reasons for the failure of the United States and Britain to reach agreement at the conference on a comprehensive international civil aviation convention. One of the principal reasons was that Swinton, who had succeeded Beaverbrook as the cabinet minister in charge of civil aviation only two weeks before the conference, had gone to the conference with little knowledge of the complexities of the problems of international civil aviation and bound by precise instructions from the War Committee of the Cabinet – instructions which could be amended only by the War Committee which received advice from a committee chaired by Beaverbrook. If Swinton had had more knowledge he might have been prepared to argue with the War Committee. This he did not.

Berle was suspicious of Swinton from the outset. As soon as he learned that Swinton had replaced Beaverbrook, he said 'rather gingerly' to an officer of the British embassy that he 'was a little worried' about Swinton's appointment since he had the reputation 'in some quarters here of being anti-American.' He did not indicate that that was substantiated by a good many reports from Africa where Swinton had for the two preceding years been the British cabinet minister in West Africa.[13] Berle and Swinton certainly rubbed each other the wrong way. This is evident from Berle's account of his first meeting with Swinton at the opening of the conference. Berle states that Swinton said to him that the British desired that 'they should have roughly one-half of the Atlantic traffic, and that in general they felt that United States lines should not play any great part beyond the Atlantic gateways.' The general conception of the British, according to Berle, 'appeared to be that American aviation had no particular reason to exist on the continents of Europe, Africa and Asia, beyond the seacoast.'[14] (It is scarcely likely that Swinton said anything as extreme as this. Berle must have given to something Swinton said the most damaging interpretation possible.) Berle reports himself

13 FRUS, 555
14 Ibid., 601

as having replied that it did not seem to him 'that United States airmen would take kindly to the proposition that they were only of use when they were fighting to liberate other countries, after which they were to be asked to get out of the air.' This was hardly an auspicious opening for Anglo-American talks at Chicago.

The main negotiations between the British and the Americans on the larger issues which separated them did not take place in Chicago but through exchanges of telegrams between Roosevelt and Churchill.[15] One of Roosevelt's telegrams, that of 24 November, was so brutal that it evoked an emotional response which increased the difficulties of reaching agreement. Roosevelt made the mistake of not following the advice of the other Roosevelt president to speak softly while carrying a big stick. He began his telegram by stating that he was afraid that Churchill did not yet 'fully appreciate the importance of reaching a satisfactory agreement':

Our people have gone as far to meet yours as I can let them go. If the conference should end either in no agreement or in an agreement which the American people would regard as preventing the development and use of the great air routes the repercussions would seriously affect many other things. We are doing our best to meet your lend-lease needs. We will face Congress on that subject in a few weeks and it will not be in a generous mood if it and the people feel that the United Kingdom has not agreed to a generally beneficial air agreement ... [This statement Churchill correctly characterized as pure blackmail.[16]]

At a meeting of Commonwealth delegations in Chicago three days later all the Dominion delegations pressed Swinton to agree to a Canadian compromise which the United States had accepted. According to the British minutes of the meeting, Symington said that the 'political aspect was now uppermost ... Was it to go forth to the world that the United Kingdom was willing to face all the political consequences of a break, simply for the sake of a formula about a few hundred or even a few thousand passengers a year between Cairo and India?' Swinton replied 'that he had had most explicit instructions from the War Cabinet not to budge an inch on the question of conceding to the United States more fifth freedom traffic than they would have got under the earlier United Kingdom formula.' Five days later the Dominion delegations

15 Ibid., 584–99
16 Jordan A. Schwarz, *Liberal: Adolf A. Berle and the Vision of an American Era* (New York: The Free Press 1987), 248

again pressed on the British the political implications of rejecting the new compromise offer by the United States, but Swinton 'dismissed the political arguments as having been considered and decided by Mr. Churchill, with fuller knowledge and greater wisdom than anybody at Chicago, and he would not presume to question the decision.'

Five weeks after the conference Lord Cranborne, the British cabinet minister for Dominion affairs, wrote on a departmental minute after reading Boyd-Shannon's report on the conference from which these quotations have been taken: 'One gets the impression that it was unfortunate that Lord Swinton was not given a freer hand. He felt he was tied by instructions from London, and we, in London, were unaware of many of the detailed facts of the constantly changing position.'[17]

Normally when two countries such as Britain and the United States differ on an important and urgent issue, each keeps its embassy in the other's capital fully informed so that it can assist in efforts to reach a satisfactory compromise. Not in this case. J.G. Winant, the distinguished American ambassador in London, complained on 1 December to the president and the secretary of state: 'Once the President and twice the Department have asked me to intervene in support of our position at the Conference. I did everything I could to persuade the Prime Minister to accept the President's wishes ... I could have been far more effective ... if I had been properly informed ... I had nothing beyond the President's messages.'[18]

The British embassy in Washington and the State Department were equally uninformed. When an officer of the British embassy called on an officer of the State Department to discuss the British and American positions at the conference, the American officer reported that the hour and a half's discussion had been 'rather pointless' since both 'knew very little' about the position of his government.

The Dominion high commissioners in London were as ill-informed as the American and British embassies, but this unfortunately did not inhibit them from giving advice to the British government – advice the opposite to that which the representatives of their governments in Chicago were giving to the British delegation there. At a meeting with Cranborne at the end of November the high commissioners, according to the British account of the meeting,[19] 'commented in the strongest terms' on Roosevelt's brutal telegram to Churchill of 24 November and 'heartily endorsed'

---

17 Public Record Office, DO 35/1236 XN 074.27
18 FRUS, 597
19 Public Record Office, CO 35/1235 XN 07H.27

the terms of Churchill's reply of 28 November. In London as in Chicago the Canadian representative took the lead. While Symington in Chicago was leading the attack against British inflexibility, Vincent Massey, the Canadian representative in London, was leading the appeal to the British to be inflexible. The British account reports him as stating that 'if he knew the Americans at all, the only course was to stand absolutely firm and not concede an inch ... [He] remarked that the United States had come to regard the air as something created by Divine providence for them to dominate. We should rudely disabuse them of this illusion.'

If Mackenzie King had known of this he would have been furious. He had forbidden Massey to agree to a British position on an issue of foreign policy unless so instructed from Ottawa. What was even worse, Massey had supported a British attempt to create a common Commonwealth policy on an issue in foreign affairs. He had, moreover, expressed an opinion contrary to the policy of the Canadian government enunciated by its spokesman at the Chicago conference.

The Americans appreciated our efforts at Chicago. Roosevelt in his telegram to Churchill of 30 November said that the Canadians 'have labored tirelessly to bring us together.' Berle, who probably drafted the telegram, said in his closing address to the conference: 'Let me pay tribute with particular affection to the Delegation of Canada which tirelessly worked to reconcile the different points of view.' The British were not so appreciative. Boyd-Shannon, the representative of the Dominions Office on the British delegation, reported that one view in the British delegation of the Canadian efforts to help the British 'to see the light' was that 'they were impudent and unintelligent obstruction of the highest policy of the United Kingdom War Cabinet ... [and] that the Canadians were concerned too much with modifying United Kingdom views to meet the United States than *vice versa.*' Another British view of the Canadian efforts to reconcile Anglo-American differences, which Boyd-Shannon indicated was more widely accepted, was that 'it seemed at times as if they cared more about securing a convention and some basis of agreement ... than about the substance of such convention and agreement.'[20]

At the meetings of the interdepartmental committee in Ottawa Symington had led the opposition to proposals for the international operation of the main international air routes and, since I strongly favoured this, his opposition prejudiced me against him. But within a few days of the opening of the Chicago conference I had become his devoted admirer. After his brilliant press conference on 9 November I wrote to Ruth, 'I

20 Ibid., DO 35/1236

wish to God he was ambassador at Washington. He has brains, charm and kindness.' At the conference he worked himself to the point of exhaustion in his efforts to bridge the gap between the United States and Britain. When Berle and Swinton on 27 November declared that they could not reach agreement, Symington pleaded that they should make another effort. He came through, I wrote, 'with everything in him and the battle was won.' The battle for another effort was won, but the effort was a failure. Berle said to me afterwards that Symington was one of the great world leaders. After the conference I wrote to Frank Underhill that Symington had 'taken the place in my affections formerly held by J.W. Dafoe. He is a grand and lovable man and was willing to risk his life at Chicago in order to get a first-class aviation convention.'

A few months after the conference I was present at a demonstration of the trust which Symington could inspire in such a tough politician-businessman as Howe. Howe, Symington, John Baldwin, and I were meeting in New York with an American delegation to work out an agreement on the division of trans-border air routes between American and Canadian airlines. Within a few minutes of the opening of the meeting Howe made statements which indicated that he was prepared to give away one of our best bargaining counters without getting anything in return. Symington, on the ground that we had not had time before the meeting to discuss matters with Howe who had just arrived in New York, asked for an adjournment. When the four of us were alone together he explained to Howe why the line he had taken at the meeting was mistaken. Howe said, 'I don't understand what you are saying.' Symington repeated his argument twice again. Howe then said, 'I still don't see what you are getting at, Herbie, but if that's the way you feel I accept what you say.'

I was so deeply involved at the conference in its first committee on the aviation convention that I paid no attention to the two other important committees, one on the provisional civil aviation organization and the other on technical standards and procedures. The technicians on the ten subcommittees of the technical committee produced unanimous reports which were adopted by the conference. They covered such matters as rules of the air, the licensing of pilots, the airworthiness of aircraft, and the collection, preparation, and use of weather reports and aeronautical charts. In his closing address to the conference Berle said that by reaching agreement on such matters the conference had 'begun to put an end to the era of anarchy in the air ... We have established a base for common air practice throughout the world. This will mean that a plane from whatever part of the world can fly safely throughout the earth, and land safely in any port on any continent, following signals and practices established and understood everywhere. This may be called the technical freedom of the air.'

When Fiorello La Guardia was making an eloquent but fruitless appeal during the conference for a renewed effort to reach agreement on the freedoms of the air, he said that he did not underestimate the value of these achievements in the technical realm but 'there was no difficulty in agreeing on technical problems: everybody is against bad weather and everybody wants safe planes.'

In my report to Ottawa on the conference I said: 'The Chicago conference worked a minor miracle. It failed, however, by a hair's breadth to work a major miracle.' The accomplishments of the conference were indeed miraculous though small in comparison with what it might have accomplished. The international convention agreed to at Chicago created a new international organization, the International Civil Aviation Organization (ICAO), and established codes of operation for aircraft and personnel and health and safety rules for aviation. The convention plus the accompanying International Air Services Transit Agreement created the foundation of a new law of the air.

An important accomplishment of the ABC talks, for which Berle was responsible, was a formula for creating an effective international regulatory authority with the least possible risk of offending national susceptibilities. In our draft of the convention we proposed that the international civil aviation authority would have power to issue and withhold certificates to airline companies desiring to operate international air services and to cancel the certificate of an airline company which failed to abide by the international rules of the game. In my report I said that Berle substituted for this an undertaking by each contracting state to 'agree to the international rules of the game, agree on how the rules should be changed, and on who should be the referee, and agree to see to it that its airlines played according to the rules, that its airlines accepted the decisions of the international referee, and that, if any one of its airlines didn't play according to the rules it and every other [contracting state would] be obliged to refuse that airline the use of its air space.' Thus, instead of an international authority enforcing rules of the game, national governments would enforce the rules. This would not only be 'more palatable to the United States Senate but more sound under present conditions of international society.' The Berle formula could 'be made use of in many fields of international politics and economics. It is a statesmanlike contribution to the building of an effective world order.'

The major miracle which the conference just failed to work was to agree on a convention under which the member states of ICAO would grant each other four or five freedoms of the air and would give ICAO the ultimate authority to set rates and establish frequencies of services. The way to this agreement had been impeded by

the backstairs intrigues of a few powerful, ambitious, wealthy, experienced and unscrupulous airline companies [Pan American and B.O.A.C.] who with the confidence and energy usually shown by new capitalist enterprises, probably agreed with the Canadian Government that a failure of the conference would result in the emergence of a powerful international cartel which they could dominate. We are here dealing with the frustrated ambitions of an influential United Kingdom politician [Beaverbrook] who, having been unable himself to reach an accord with the United States, was jealous lest a colleague's [Swinton's] efforts be crowned with success. We are here dealing with the subconscious motives of the leaders of two great nations [Churchill and Roosevelt] who, because they have done so much for mankind, are in danger of believing that to them alone is reserved the right to cut Gordian knots, even if the knot is a small one and could easily be unravelled.

Part of the difficulty at the conference was that Berle and Swinton rubbed each other the wrong way. The United States should have arranged at least one long weekend in a gracious country house near Chicago for the dozen top men at the conference. During the weekend Swinton might have shown himself to Berle 'not as a stupid, reactionary representative of a stupid and reactionary regime, tied hand and foot by his instructions, but as an honest, well-intentioned, intelligent but far from brilliant barrister ... who, because of his own limited knowledge of the problems of international air transport, floundered badly and occasionally blustered when confronted suddenly by a new idea emerging from Mr. Berle's teeming brain.' And Berle might have shown himself to Swinton

in those hours of release of tension which can follow a small pleasant dinner between people who have wrangled with each other for a week and have accomplished much not as a bitter anglophobe and a devious combination of Machiavelli, Talleyrand and Fouché, but as a man with the virtues and faults of a great renaissance statesman, a man with encyclopedic knowledge, with a lucid, fertile and inquisitive mind, a man who can see visions and dream dreams of a better world and try to make those visions and dreams come true ... [a man who] finds most Englishmen unsympathetic [but] whose policy toward the United

Kingdom is rooted in a firm conviction – driven deep into his soul in the dark months of the summer of 1940 – that the national interests of the United States demand that there be a powerful Great Britain.

The International Civil Aviation Convention came into force in 1947 following ratification by the required twenty-six states. ICAO now has 157 members. It has made a number of attempts to complete the work of the Chicago conference by an agreement for the reciprocal granting of four or five freedoms of the air accompanied by international control over rates and frequencies of service but has failed, and governments secure third, fourth, and fifth freedoms for their airlines as the result of bilateral agreements.

14

Creating the United Nations
1944–1946

One of my principal duties at the Canadian embassy in Washington in 1944 and 1945 was to help L.B. Pearson, who had succeeded Leighton McCarthy as ambassador, in his discussions with the State Department on the proposed United Nations organization.[1] Our task was to find out all we could about the proposals the United States was likely to put forward on the U.N., and to try to influence United States' thinking when we had enough guidance from Ottawa on the tentative Canadian views. We also, of course, tried to influence the thinking in Ottawa. The high point in this period was our reporting on the Dumbarton Oaks conference from 21 August to 28 September 1944 at which the United States, Britain, and the Soviet Union produced the Dumbarton Oaks charter of the United Nations, a charter which was adopted by the San Francisco conference nine months later with relatively few substantial changes. The British gave us the proposals of the three great powers to the Dumbarton Oaks conference on the strict condition we were not to let the Americans know we had them, and during the conference they gave periodic briefings to all the Commonwealth missions.

The principal expert in the State Department on the proposed United Nations was Leo Pasvolsky. After the Dumbarton Oaks conference I used to call on him occasionally. One time I displayed too much knowledge and he, I think, concluded that the British had given us full information about the conference. This is a constant problem in intergovernmental discussions when one has read documents or received information of which the other government is supposed to believe one is ignorant. In another talk with Pasvolsky I said, 'I have an indiscreet

1 This chapter incorporates material from my book *On Duty: A Canadian at the Making of the United Nations, 1945–1946* (Toronto: McClelland and Stewart 1983).

question to ask.' He replied: 'No question is indiscreet. It is only answers which can be indiscreet.'

At the beginning of March 1945 the Department of External Affairs asked Pearson to comment on a lengthy departmental memorandum on what the prime minister might say in a statement to the House of Commons on the Dumbarton Oaks charter and the San Francisco conference which was to open at the end of April. I prepared 'comments' which Pearson sent to Ottawa. He commended a paragraph in my paper in which I contended that the statement in Ottawa's memorandum that a great power could under the Dumbarton Oaks charter block punitive action against it was a half-truth. The great power could, I said, by using its veto block punitive action by the Security Council but it could not block punitive action by the other great powers on the Security Council.

Surely ... the lesson to be drawn from the history of the thirties is that if a great power should, in future, act in such a way as to convince the other great powers that it is determined to dominate the world by force, the only way to prevent a world war from breaking out will be for the other great powers to form immediately an alliance against it and to declare that the moment it commits aggression they will in combination wage total war against it until it surrenders unconditionally. Such a threat might conceivably bring the state which is planning aggression to its senses and so prevent the war from breaking out.

This contention I was to bring forward again a year and a half later when I was attacking Bernard Baruch's insistence at the meetings of the U.N. Atomic Energy Commission that an international agreement on atomic energy should provide that there be no great power veto over the imposition of what he called 'condign' punishment on a state which violated the agreement, provisions Dean Acheson, the secretary of state, opposed because they 'added nothing to the treaty and were almost certain to wreck any possibility of Russian acceptance of one.'[2] I brought forward the contention again a year later when I was suggesting a security pact to supplement the U.N. charter, a suggestion which had in it the germ of the idea of the North Atlantic treaty.

The passage I have quoted above from my memorandum of March 1945 was taken from a complete rewriting of the Dumbarton Oaks proposals which I had sent to Ottawa in January. A quarter of a century later James Reston in his column in the *New York Times* called my rewriting of Dumbarton Oaks my 'personal charter for world sanity.' I

2 Dean Acheson, *Present at the Creation* (New York: Norton 1969), 155

wrote it in the hope that the Department of External Affairs might use it as the basis for a document which would be published by the Canadian government before the San Francisco conference and circulated to the governments which would be attending the conference. I said that the Chicago conference on international civil aviation, from which I had just returned, had 'demonstrated that the influence of a delegation at an international conference called to draw up an international instrument is greatly increased if, before the conference opens, the state which the delegation represents publishes a well worked-out complete draft of the international instrument. Unless there are competing drafts, equally well worked-out and complete, the chances are good that the state's draft will be taken as the basis of discussion at the conference.'

The Department of External Affairs turned my suggestion down, Hume Wrong, the second-in-command, arguing that it would be a 'wasted effort for Canada as a secondary country to attempt to plan from the foundation upward.' The department, however, gave me permission to have my draft charter published anonymously. It was published as a forty-page pamphlet by the Free World Research Bureau and was circulated to the delegates at San Francisco. It sank without a trace. My preamble and five chapters were published at the same time in the periodical *Free World*.

I did not know at the time of Hume Wrong's rejection of my proposal as a 'wasted effort.' If I had I would have countered by asking whether our planning 'from the foundation upward' in the discussions leading to the creation of the International Monetary Fund (IMF) and the International Civil Aviation Organization had been wasted efforts. Before the Bretton Woods conference on the IMF and the World Bank, the Canadian government published a twelve-thousand-word pamphlet entitled 'Tentative Draft Proposals of Canadian Experts for an International Exchange Union.' Eight months before the Chicago aviation conference the Canadian government published a tentative and preliminary draft of an international air transport convention. A month before the conference the government published a 'revised preliminary draft.' If the government had, before the San Francisco conference, published and circulated to other governments a well-worked out revision of the Dumbarton Oaks proposals this would, I believe, have raised the level of discussions at the conference and improved the final result.

Though my pamphlet sank without a trace at San Francisco the chapter in it on human rights which was published in *Free World* may have had some influence. Pearson, then under-secretary of state for external affairs, called me in to see him on 23 February 1947. He said that the minister, Louis St Laurent, was to give a speech on human rights the next day to the Montreal branch of the United Nations Association at which Eleanor Roosevelt was to be present. She was the chairman of the U.N. Commission on Human Rights which was preparing a tentative draft of an international bill of human rights. Unfortunately, by some inexplicable error, no speech had been prepared for St Laurent. I therefore would have to write the speech and have it ready the next morning. He apologized for giving me this difficult assignment. There was, he said, not time for me to consider the kind of speech St Laurent would like to give. I should write the speech which I would give if I were the principal speaker at the meeting. I took advantage of this opportunity to include in St Laurent's speech my formulation of the basic principles of human rights:

The individual man, woman and child is the cornerstone of culture and civilization. He is the subject, the foundation, the end of the social order. Upon his dignity, his liberty, his inviolability depend the welfare of the people, the safety of the State and the peace of the world. In society complete freedom cannot be attained. An individual possesses many rights but he may not exercise any of them in a way which will destroy the rights of others. No right exists in isolation from the other rights. The liberties of one individual are limited by the liberties of others and by the just requirements of the democratic state. The preservation of the freedom of the individual requires not only that his rights be respected, preserved and defended but also that he respect, preserve and defend the rights of others by fulfilling his duties as a member of society. The state exists to serve the individual. He does not exist to serve the state. The state exists to promote conditions under which he can be most free.[3]

Two weeks before the opening of the San Francisco conference I was appointed a technical adviser to the Canadian delegation. This was a signal honour, for only five members of the Canadian external affairs service below the rank of ambassador were appointed to the delegation. I was at the conference from the day it opened, 25 April, to 20 June, five days before it ended.

I have never been able to understand how anyone who was at San Francisco could have had high hopes for the United Nations if he had known what was going on there and what was happening at the same time to the relations between the Soviet world and the western world in Europe. Yet some eminent and intelligent participants in that confer-

3 Department of External Affairs (DEA), *Statements and Speeches*, 47/6

ence, including L.B. Pearson, have repeatedly said that they had high hopes. I remember that towards the end of the conference a number of us in the Canadian delegation were talking about the results of the conference. We bemoaned the errors the conference had committed and the weaknesses in the Charter and we expressed our deep pessimism about the future of the United Nations. Norman Robertson, after listening to this litany of woe, commented that we must be careful not to talk that way outside our own group; people in general had high hopes for the U.N. and we must not do anything to undermine their hopes.

The roots of our pessimism went deep. The secret telegrams which were transmitted to us from Ottawa about what was happening in Europe depicted a brutal Soviet occupation of half of Europe, the imposition of a puppet Soviet regime on Poland, and the breakdown of Allied cooperation in Europe. In every committee of the conference, except the Coordination Committee, the Soviet delegates seemed intent to do all they could to ensure that the United Nations would be as weak as possible. Our custom in the Canadian delegation was that the principal Canadian official on a committee would report after each committee meeting to the *de facto* head of the delegation, Norman Robertson. Once when I had just begun my report, Robertson interrupted me by exclaiming, 'I wish to God somebody would come into this room and not start his report by saying, "those goddamned Russians".' In the middle of the conference the intransigence of the Soviet Union on the veto nearly resulted in the conference breaking up in confusion without agreement on the Charter.

I was exasperated at San Francisco by the restraints under which the Canadian delegation operated. After two weeks there I wrote to Ruth: 'In general New Zealand and Australia are doing the things which we would do if we had any guts. We would also, I think, do them better.' Two weeks later I wrote that the committees I attended were boring but 'We would not be bored if we weren't gagged and unable to say anything but that is pretty much our position.' Mackenzie King, the leader of the delegation, would never have said that he had gagged the delegation. His line, as I reported to Ruth, was 'that the Canadian delegation is to be helpful and not commit itself to rigid positions or, as Grant Dexter [of the Winnipeg Free Press] puts it, it is to have no principles.' Australia, under its ebullient foreign minister, H.V. Evatt, assisted by New Zealand, assumed the leadership of the middle and small powers in efforts to curb the special position which the great powers had given themselves under the Dumbarton Oaks proposals. If we had had a John Diefenbaker and not a Mackenzie King as prime minister, foreign minister, and head of the delegation he might have behaved like Evatt. But King was no Evatt. Evatt gloried in being the flamboyant leader of the middle and small powers; he enjoyed oratorical contests. King did not. Norman Robertson, who headed the delegation during most of the conference after the politicians had left to fight a general election, would have carried out the instructions of a John Diefenbaker though he would have counselled caution. But King's instructions suited Robertson's cautious temperament. An example of his caution was his reluctance to have Canada oppose the proposal of the great powers that each of them have a veto over the appointment of four deputy secretaries general as well as the secretary general. Louis Rasminsky and I had to argue with him for an hour one evening to persuade him not to instruct us to withdraw our opposition.

The restraints under which the Canadian delegation at San Francisco operated made me impatient. What was happening in Europe made me fearful. In May I wrote in letters to my family:

We all have a feeling here that what we are doing is merely writing marginal notes on the pages of history. The substance of history is being written not in San Francisco but in Poland, Germany, Czechoslovakia, Yugoslavia and so on. That is where the world is taking shape with terrifying speed ... It looks very much as if the world is beginning to jell into two rival groups – the Soviet and the Anglo-American ... Something big has to be done to stop the steadily increasing speed with which we are setting about to construct two rival, heavily armed camps in the world ... The new League being established here can work only if there is an extremely high degree of cooperation between the three great powers. The chances of our getting that cooperation seem pretty slim from what is going on today throughout the world.

I reiterated that conclusion in October after five more months working on the making of the U.N.: 'The new organization of the United Nations can work only if the big three can cooperate and they demonstrate little capacity to cooperate.'

Early in the conference I wrote to Ruth: 'The conference is full of dullness and discussion that only slowly gets anywhere. Making peace is like making war. It is ten parts boredom and one part excitement.' Occasionally something would happen to relieve the boredom. The committee on the secretariat on which I was representing Canada appointed a subcommittee to make a four-power proposal less objectionable and the subcommittee brought in a very slight revision. Unfortunately the United States' member of the subcommittee had forgotten to clear the report with the Soviet delegation. None of us knew this and the committee was taken aback when the Soviet delegate proposed that the committee take as its basis of discussion not the relevant paragraphs in the sub-committee's report but the original four-power proposal. This led to confusion and annoyance which reached its apex when the chairman exploded and asked four rhetorical questions of the committee which could be paraphrased: 'Why in bloody hell should we go to drafting subcommittees and work until midnight preparing a revised text when we might be having fun going to dances or whatnot (loud cheers at this point) if the results of our labours are to be disregarded because of the bloody Russians.'

The New Zealand delegate on the committee on the preamble told me that the Ukranian chairman of the committee attacked the use of the term 'fratricidal strife' to describe the Second World War; he said he could not bring back to Ukraine a document which said that the Germans were brothers. The Belgian representative defended the use of the term on the Christian ground of the brotherhood of all men and said that the fact that Cain and Abel were brothers made Cain's crime the more odious. The translator wearily in his translation referred to Abel killing Cain. At this point the Soviet representative who was sitting beside the New Zealander turned to him in exasperation and said, 'This younger generation knows nothing about the scriptures.'

My main accomplishment at San Francisco was launching a successful attack on the proposal of the great powers that each of them have a veto not only on the appointment of the secretary general but also on the appointment of four deputy secretaries general. The intent of the Soviet delegation was that each of the five permanent members of the Security Council would designate a national as one of those five senior officials and that each of them would in turn be secretary general for two years. The secretariat would have been run by a five-man executive committee of the five great powers. When this proposal came up at the committee on the secretariat at which I was representing Canada, the chairman of the committee insisted that he would put the proposal to a vote without debate. Perhaps he was being stupid, like so many of the committee chairmen at San Francisco, but more probably he had been instructed by one or more of the great powers to ram the proposal through. I had been instructed to oppose the proposal and I protested the chairman's ruling. After many rebuffs I managed to secure permission to give a speech. This started off a heated debate which went on for many weeks and the proposal was eventually defeated.

One committee at San Francisco gave cause for some hope for the

future of the United Nations, the fourteen-nation Coordination Committee on which Norman Robertson was the Canadian representative
and I his adviser. As soon as one of the twelve main committees of the
conference approved of a paragraph of the charter it was sent to the
Coordination Committee. The task of the committee was to revise the
paragraph if it did not clearly express the intent of the main committee
and to review all the paragraphs to ensure that they were consistent
with each other in terminology, form, and substance and to arrange
them in logical sequence by articles and chapters. The Coordination
Committee had direct links with the Dumbarton Oaks conference. Its
U.S. chairman, Leo Pasvolsky, the Soviet representatives, A.A. Sobolev
and S.A. Golunsky, the United Kingdom representatives, Gladwyn Jebb
and C.K. Webster, had all helped to draft the Dumbarton Oaks proposals
which were the basis of discussion at San Francisco and, as Paul Hasluck,
the Australian member of the committee, has written: 'It was only necessary for someone to question the use of a comma in such and such a
line of such and such a paragraph for them to produce immediately the
high reasons of state that had led to the insertion of the comma in the
first place.'[5]

The committee was guarded as if it were a supreme directorate of a
war. Its meetings were held on the top floor of the Opera House, reached
only by one elevator. To get on the elevator one had to be checked by
armed soldiers and by a civilian official. On the balcony off the committee
room a soldier marched up and down on patrol while the committee
was meeting.

The committee owed much of its success to its chairman, Leo Pasvolsky. He realized that in this kind of committee it was essential not
to take votes but to weigh opinions. If discussion showed that a proposal
was opposed by a great power he would say, 'Since there is not general
agreement I suggest we let this matter stand over till our next meeting,'
hoping that by then the great power would have withdrawn its opposition
or that a compromise would have been worked out. If a smaller power
was in a minority he would say, 'I assume that in the light of the general
agreement on this point the delegate of —— will not wish to press his
objection.' This ploy did not always work. We were discussing the preamble. There was general agreement that 'we the peoples of the United
Nations' would not only be 'determined' to do certain things but would
also 'agree' to the Charter of the U.N. The Netherlands' delegate, Adrian

5 Paul Hasluck, *'Twelve Months on the Security Council,'* address at the University of
Western Australia, 9 September 1947, 2

Pelt, objected: under Netherlands law it was only the monarch who could agree to a treaty; the Netherlands government could not sign a Charter which said that the people of the Netherlands agreed to a treaty. At first most of the members of the committee were not inclined to take this nice constitutional point seriously; but Pelt persisted and the committee was forced to find a formula which would satisfy him: the peoples of the United Nations would be determined to do certain things but it was their governments which would agree to the Charter.

At the Dumbarton Oaks conference, when the great powers could not reach agreement on a provision to be included in the Charter, they would mask their disagreement in deliberately obscure language. One example is article 107: 'Nothing in the present Charter shall invalidate or preclude action, in relation to any state which during the Second World War has been an enemy of any signatory to the present Charter, taken or authorized as a result of that war by the Governments having responsibility for such action.' Norman Robertson suggested at a meeting of the Coordination Committee that something should be done to elucidate the meaning of this article. Pasvolsky said, 'Norman, if I were you I would let sleeping dogs lie, particularly when they are such very large dogs.'

A panel of language experts met next door to the committee. Their task was to translate the English text agreed to by the committee into equally authentic French, Russian, Spanish, and Chinese texts. The only one of these translations on which the Coordination Committee kept a careful eye was the French, but on one occasion it got involved in the Russian text. We were discussing chapter II of the Charter on membership. The question was whether we should refer to the member states of the U.N. as member states or simply as members. There was general agreement that we would call them 'Members.' The Soviet representative said that he could go along with this decision provided it was understood that in the Russian text the term 'Member States' would be used and not 'Members,' since the word member meant in Russian the male sex organ.

We tried to improve the preamble to the Charter which had been approved by a main committee. It was based on a draft submitted by Field Marshal Smuts which had been added to by C.K. Webster of the British delegation. It was so bad that when a newspaper published the committee's version and attributed it to Smuts and Virginia Gildersleeve of the United States delegation, Dean Gildersleeve declared at a meeting of the delegation that as a professor of English she protested against this draft being attributed to her. One night Norman Robertson organized a small dinner in a private room at our hotel to try to reach agreement on a new version of the preamble. He invited Archibald MacLeish, the librarian of Congress, Kenneth Bailey of Australia, Etienne Gilson of the Collège de France, Gladwyn Jebb, and Georges Demolin, the chief adviser on the French version of the Charter. We dined, drank, and talked from 7:30 to 12:30 and produced a new version. In order to avoid a public row, Robertson called on Smuts the next morning but Smuts refused to bless the new draft and it was stillborn.

The official Canadian report on the San Francisco conference contains in a slightly disguised form the preamble which most members of the Coordination Committee wanted. It is, I think, a good deal better than the longer preamble in the Charter:

We, the peoples of the United Nations, believe in the worth and dignity of the individual, in the rule of law and justice among nations and in respect for the pledged word. We are persuaded that men and nations can by their joint and sustained efforts live together as good neighbours free from fear and want and with liberty of thought and worship. We are resolved to save ourselves and our children from the scourge of war which twice in our time has brought us untold loss and sorrow. Therefore we unite our strength to keep the peace.

At the San Francisco conference Canada put forward substantial amendments to the proposals of the great powers on the Economic and Social Council and on the secretariat of the U.N. Many of these were accepted and improved the Charter. But three other amendments which we succeeded in making to the proposals of the great powers and to which we attached great importance turned out to be of no importance. We insisted that a state which was not a member of the Security Council should have the right to sit and vote as a member when the council was discussing the employment of the armed forces which it had agreed to provide for peace enforcement by the council. No such agreements to provide armed forces have ever been made. We insisted that the General Assembly when it was electing the non-permanent members of the Security Council should pay special regard to the contribution which member states were making 'to the maintenance of international peace and security and to the other purposes of the organization' and that equitable geographical distribution should be a secondary consideration. The Assembly has never paid the slightest attention to this directive. We urged that if a general conference of the U.N. for the purpose of reviewing the Charter had not been held before the tenth annual assembly, such a conference could be convoked by a majority vote of the Assembly and by a vote of any seven of the members of the Security Council. This provision was redundant, since a majority of the members of the U.N. can at any time under article 20 of the Charter have the Assembly convoked in special session and the purpose of such a session could be to consider a general revision of the Charter.

My first task after the conclusion of the conference was to write a draft of the Canadian report on the conference. In nine days ensconced in a room at the Chateau Laurier hotel in Ottawa I wrote a thirty-thousand-word report. The greater part of it was not included in the final printed report. I had tried to make the report interesting and intelligible, and not like the dry-as-dust reports which the Department of External Affairs had published on the meetings of the League of Nations. It was not until Pearson took over the direction of the department that I succeeded in writing and having published what I considered to be the right kind of report.

One of the sections in my report which was omitted from the final version was the peroration, entitled 'The task before us.' It was, no doubt, considered too rhetorical.

The San Francisco Conference ... laid the foundation of a just and stable world order in which men may be able to achieve freedom from fear and from want, freedom of thought and of worship ... That was a great accomplishment but it is only a beginning. It is the task of the living generation of men to strengthen that foundation and to build on it a great structure. The task will be heavy. It will be long and dreary. It will be full of set-backs and heart-breaks. There will be periods of joy but there will also be periods of despair. Some parts of the foundation, some bits of the structure, will turn out to be badly planned or badly constructed and will collapse. Other bits will need to be shored up. If we, the peoples of the United Nations, are to succeed in our task we must be willing to experiment, and to run great risks to attain great objectives. We must be resolute and display in our just cause a holy obstinacy. We must have faith in ourselves and in each other.

This passage was not wasted. I kept in those days a folder containing passages which I had written for speeches and reports which had not been used. At the U.N. General Assembly in New York on 4 December 1946 I was asked to write a speech on disarmament for Paul Martin, the head of the delegation, to give four hours later at a plenary meeting of the Assembly. I had in the preceding three days written two speeches for him for plenary meetings. I was out of ideas. I had recourse to a stiff whisky and to my folder of rejections, and dictated a speech consisting at least in half of rejections. One was 'The task before us.' The speech was warmly received by the Assembly. A member of the American delegation who admired it said to me that he was, however, puzzled that at several places in the speech he thought it was about to come to an end. I did not tell him that this was because it contained three perorations.

In July 1945 I was appointed to the Canadian delegation to the fourteennation Executive Committee of the Preparatory Commission of the United Nations which was to meet in London in August. I remained in London until the beginning of February, attending the Executive Committee, the Preparatory Commission, and the first part of the first session of the General Assembly. The Executive Committee and the Preparatory Commission were instructed by the San Francisco conference to 'prepare the provisional agenda for the first sessions of the principal organs of the Organization, [to] prepare documents and recommendations relating to all matters on those agenda and to make recommendations on the location of the permanent headquarters of the U.N.' The Executive Committee met from the middle of August to the end of October, the Preparatory Commission from the end of November to 23 December, and the General Assembly from 10 January to 14 February. In a memorandum I wrote at the conclusion of the Executive Committee's work I said that the U.N. Charter was similar to a written national constitution which had to be supplemented by constitutional statutes. The job of the Preparatory Commission was to prepare the constitutional statutes to supplement the constitution.

I was on board ship in the middle of the Atlantic on the way to London when I learned on 7 August that an atomic bomb had been dropped on Hiroshima. I wrote that day to Ruth:

I am in despair today about the kind of world our children are going to live in. I have hoped against hope until today that the atomic bomb would not be discovered. Now all the vistas of Titanic glooms of chasmèd fears open up ... I just haven't enough faith in man or god to believe that we have enough time or intelligence or goodwill to reach the goal of a world government before we obliterate civilization in another war. But there's nothing to do except to live as if it were possible, and to try one's best to make it possible.

Two weeks later I wrote:

One thing which relieves an otherwise sombre outlook is that the atomic bomb is so revolutionary that even the thickest-headed realizes that a revolution has taken place to which we have to readjust all our thinking on international political organization. As soon as the bomb fell all the security articles in the Charter became archaic.

At the end of October I wrote that the year had been 'cut in two by an event which has made all history ancient except that of the last three months – the use of the atomic bomb.'

In London at the Executive Committee I found myself working with colleagues I had worked with in San Francisco on the Coordination Committee: Gladwyn Jebb of Britain, who had become executive secretary of the Executive Committee and the Preparatory Commission (Alger Hiss had held the corresponding position at the San Francisco conference), C.K. Webster of Britain, Paul Hasluck of Australia, Cyro de Freitas-Valle of Brazil, and Adrian Pelt of the Netherlands. These had been among the most constructive members of the Coordination Committee. I was particularly happy that Hasluck was my Australian colleague. I, like him, look back on our association in the Executive Committee and the Preparatory Commission as a 'pleasant feature of my work.' We became, as he puts it in his memoirs, 'what in those days was called "a ginger group", throwing up many suggestions which some other delegates thought were good ideas.'[6]

In San Francisco I had the feeling that all we were doing was writing marginal notes on the pages of history and that the substance of history was being written in Poland, Germany, Czechoslovakia, and Yugoslavia. There the new world of two rival heavily armed camps was beginning to take shape with terrifying speed. I had the same sort of feeling in London. I could feel the wartime alliance with the Soviet Union rapidly eroding under my feet. It seemed to me that the widespread wartime enthusiasm of the people of Britain for the Soviet Union was turning into contempt and fear. British soldiers brought home stories of the wholesale atrocities of the Soviet armies in occupied territories in Europe and of the way the Soviet authorities treated their own people returning home from prisoner-of-war camps and displaced persons' camps. The newspapers were full of these stories and of how the Soviet government was imprisoning, torturing, and killing the leaders of the agrarian and social democratic parties in Eastern Europe.

While public support in Britain (and presumably in other western countries) for close relations with the Soviet government was dwindling, the relations between western governments and the Soviet government

6 Paul Hasluck, *Diplomatic Witness, Australian Foreign Affairs 1941–1947* (Melbourne: Melbourne University Press 1980), 229

were becoming increasingly strained. My recollection is that in 1944 the western powers did not have high hopes of co-operation with the Soviet Union in dealing with the problems of the post-war world but that they did not contemplate that the borderline in Europe between the Soviet troops advancing from the east and the western troops advancing through France and Italy would become the boundary between a Soviet empire and the western world. They believed that a buffer zone would be created between the two spheres consisting of Poland, Czechoslovakia, Hungary, Romania, and Bulgaria. These states would be friendly to the Soviet Union but they would not be dominated by it. As the year 1945 drew to a close it was becoming increasingly clear that the Soviet Union intended to establish puppet regimes in these states.

I had been in London two months when Norman Robertson came to London with the prime minister. One night after dinner he told me in the strictest confidence that the Canadian government had just learned of the existence of an extensive Soviet spy ring in Canada through the defection of Igor Gouzenko, a cipher clerk at the Soviet embassy. This spy ring had been operating since 1942. Seventeen members of the Soviet embassy in Ottawa were members of it. There was proof that it included a cipher clerk in the Department of External Affairs and it was possible that other members of the department were in the spy ring. Now, when we take the existence of spy rings as a matter of course, it is hard to comprehend the shattering effect in October 1945 of learning that, at the very time we had been allies in war, the Soviet government had been operating in our country a spy ring whose Canadian members were mainly idealistic supporters of communism.

The worsening relations between the Soviet Union and its former allies in the autumn of 1945 were reflected in the work of the Executive Committee. As the meetings of the committee went on I found it difficult not to conclude that the Soviet government was deliberately trying to sabotage efforts to make the U.N. into an efficient and effective organization for fear that it would be used against the Soviet Union by the United States and Britain and that, if its efforts at sabotage were unsuccessful, it would refuse to ratify the U.N. Charter. More and more often at the meetings of the committee and its subcommittees Andrei Gromyko would assert that some proposal which was clearly going to be adopted was a violation of the Charter. I had an uneasy feeling that he was under orders from Moscow to accumulate a list of so-called violations of the Charter which could be used by the Soviet government as justification for a decision by the Soviet Union not to ratify it. What was also strange and perturbing was that Gromyko, though he could count on only three votes out of fourteen (his own and those of Czechoslovakia and Yugo-slavia), often gave the impression that he believed he spoke for the majority of mankind. Whether the Soviet government was in fact in September and October 1945 contemplating not joining the U.N. I do not know. I do know that when Gromyko returned to London from Moscow for the opening of the Preparatory Commission on 24 November he agreed to many proposals he had previously opposed.

Paul Hasluck had the same sort of apprehension. In his memoirs he writes:

From July to October 1945 there were indications of uncertainty in the Soviet Union's attitude towards the United Nations. I can only guess at the possible reasons – a reaction to the change in calculations of power following the launching of the atom bomb, an internal crisis in the Soviet Union itself, preoccupation with the immediate post-war diplomatic task of building security on their western frontier and adjusting boundaries and creating buffers between the Soviet Union and Germany. As it seemed to me in the work of the Executive Committee, the Soviet Union was stalling until about mid-October. At that time their stiffness eased a little and the prospect of their continued membership of the United Nations and active participation in its affairs became clearer.[7]

At the San Francisco conference Andrei Gromyko was so rigidly con-trolled by instructions from Moscow that Adlai Stevenson in a letter to his wife said: 'Poor Gromyko can't spit without permission from Mos-cow.' Much the same was true in the meetings in London. He was told how he was to vote. He was seldom told the reasons he could give to explain his vote. That resulted in his delivering the following sort of speech time after time: 'The Soviet delegation has studied carefully the amendment proposed by the delegation of A to the proposed rule X of the rules of procedure of the General Assembly. In the opinion of the Soviet delegation the proposed amendment would not improve the rule of procedure. The Soviet delegation believes that rule X is a very good rule. Therefore the Soviet delegation will vote against the amendment.' Gromyko also sorely tried the patience of the Executive Committee by his stubborn refusal to admit defeat and by his insistence on raising again and again questions which had already been determined by the committee against Soviet wishes. What we did not realize was that he needed to be able to send to his masters in Moscow official records of the meetings which clearly demonstrated that he had fought as hard as

7 Ibid., 230

he possibly could to defeat a proposal which Moscow disliked. Fortunately by the end of the Preparatory Commission Gromyko and his able assistant, Alexei A. Roschin, became more self-confident and, as I reported to Ottawa, they were 'much more able to hold their own in discussion without having to fall back on the simple negative repeated monotonously for three hours.'

The most bitter battle in the Executive Committee and the Preparatory Commission was over where the headquarters of the United Nations should be located. The first engagement in the battle was on whether the headquarters should be in the United States or in Europe. The United States and the Soviet Union won this engagement in the Executive Committee against Britain, France, and the Netherlands with the help of such countries as Australia, Brazil, Chile, and China which wanted San Francisco as the headquarters and would probably not have voted to locate the headquarters in the United States if they had realized that a decision in favour of the United States would mean not San Francisco but somewhere in the eastern part of the United States. Rather than that they would probably have preferred a site in Europe. Having secured a decision in favour of the United States with the help of such countries, the United States and the Soviet Union put through a resolution in the second engagement of the battle that the headquarters should be in the eastern part of the United States.

Canada favoured Europe because we believed that the most urgent problems with which the Security Council and Assembly would have to deal related largely to Europe. I believe we were right in our decision to support Europe but wrong in our reason for doing so. In the first three years of the U.N. only five of the urgent problems were European (Spain, Greece, Berlin, Czechoslovakia, and Trieste) and six were non-European (Iran, treatment of Indians in South Africa, Palestine, Kashmir, Korea, and Indochina).

When I was in San Francisco in June 1985 at celebrations of the fortieth anniversary of the signing of the U.N. Charter I was astounded to hear the French ambassador to the United Nations state in his speech that the British had proposed Washington as the U.N. headquarters and that the Russians wanted Vienna. Nothing could be further from the truth. Perhaps ghost-writers maliciously put statements such as these in the speeches they write for their superiors in order to make their superiors look foolish.

Because the United States and the Soviet Union put great pressure on the members of the Preparatory Commission to vote in favour of the headquarters being established in the United States, countries such as

Canada which favoured Europe proposed that voting on the headquarters be by secret ballot. This proposal was defeated, twenty-six to twenty-four. The committee then voted on a resolution in favour of Europe; twenty-three voted for Europe, twenty-five against, and two abstained. In the subsequent vote in favour of the headquarters being in the United States, thirty voted for the United States, fourteen against, and six abstained. The resolution had secured the necessary two-thirds majority of the votes cast. I believe that if the voting had been by secret ballot the resolution would have failed to secure a two-thirds majority. According to Philip Noel-Baker, the chief British delegate, Czechoslovakia and Yugoslavia wanted Europe but voted for the United States under an ultimatum from the Russians.[8] Presumably on a secret ballot they would have voted against establishing the headquarters in the United States. In the open ballot Ethiopia, New Zealand, and Syria abstained though in the immediately preceding ballot they had voted for Europe. An abstention by a country friendly to the United States on a resolution which the United States is strongly supporting usually means that the abstainer is opposed to the resolution but does not wish to carry its opposition to the point of openly voting against the United States. These three countries might therefore in a secret ballot have voted against locating the headquarters in the United States. Thus, even if the United States had in a secret ballot voted for itself rather than abstaining, the vote on the resolution, if by secret ballot, might have been twenty-nine to nineteen with three abstentions, and the resolution would have been defeated. Out of the negotiations which would have followed the deadlock the result might have been the highly desirable one of the establishment of the permanent headquarters near the borderline in Europe between East and West, possibly Vienna or Copenhagen, and the use of Geneva as temporary headquarters pending the construction of the necessary facilities at the permanent site.

The best presentation of the arguments against stationing the headquarters in the United States was made by J.D. Hickerson in a memorandum of 22 August 1945 to the secretary of state. Hickerson at the time was deputy director of the office of European affairs in the State Department, and one of the wisest foreign service officers of his generation. The reasons Hickerson advanced for preferring Europe to the United States were:

8 Thomas M. Campbell and George C. Herring, eds, *The Diaries of Edward R. Stettinius, Jr. 1943–1946* (New York: New Viewpoints 1975), 433

(1) The headquarters should be in the territory of a state other than one of the 'Big Five', otherwise the state in which it was located would be suspected of exercising too much control over the organization; (2) location in the United States would tend to give the impression that the United Nations Organization was 'an American affair'; (3) Europe has been traditionally the trouble center and headquarters should be near the trouble zone; (4) if located in the United States there will be a tendency in this country to say: 'Oh yes, Stalin agreed to give the United States its world organization but took care to see it to that it was moved to an ivory tower in the United States far from the scene of the strife where it would not interfere in any way with his writing his own ticket in Eastern Europe'; (5) the location in the United States would tend to promote a European regional organization; and (6) the interest of the American people is sufficiently strong for our Government to give its full support to the organization irrespective of where the headquarters may be located.[9]

The choice of the United States was a serious error. The choice of Trygve Lie as the first secretary general was another serious error. On 30 January 1946, immediately after his election, I wrote to Ruth: 'Nobody is very happy about the choice of Lie as Secretary-General. He seems to be no better than second-rate. He may not have enough courage or independence or integrity and he may also be subject to Soviet pressures exerted against Norway which is in a vulnerable position. Scotty Reston tells me that his qualifications were never discussed by the Security Council. The whole discussion was on equitable distribution of honours between North America and Europe and so on.'

The United States and British governments when they concurred in his appointment knew he was not first-class. Dean Acheson said before his appointment that he did not consider him a very impressive candidate. Noel-Baker was much disturbed over the prospect of his being selected; in his opinion he was all right in Norway, where he was quite a good foreign minister, but he was not nearly quick enough or astute enough to tackle the work of secretary general. Noel-Baker wanted Ernest Bevin to support a last-minute move to draft Eisenhower for a couple of years, with the hope that Pearson would succeed him. Stettinius, the head of the United States delegation, had pressed for Lie's appointment but four months later he told the president that 'we had made a mistake

9 *Foreign Relations of the United States Government* (FRUS), Department of State Publications, 1945; vol. 1: General: U.N. (Washington: U.S. Government Printing Office), 1440n

in picking a dud as secretary-general.'[10] Brian Urquhart, who was on the U.N. secretariat at the London meetings and served on it in New York for forty years, states in his memoirs that Lie was an undistinguished choice and that in his new and demanding job he was confused, temperamental, insecure, and out of his depth.[11]

I had fun at the London meetings leading a crusade for the use of simple, direct, forceful language in the resolutions passed by U.N. bodies. I launched the crusade with a memorandum to the drafting committee of the Preparatory Commission criticizing the language of a resolution to be put before the first session of the General Assembly:

The resolution is couched in the standard League form: Considering ...; and Having been informed ...; Reserves ...; Records ...; and Declares ...; Considering ...; Considering ...; The General Assembly is willing ...; Considering ...; Considering, however; the General Assembly of the United Nations decides. The new organization of the United Nations is making a fresh start. It would be most valuable if that fresh start were reflected in the form and language of the resolutions which it adopts, if the United Nations were to make a clean break with Geneva jargon and League lingo and write its resolutions as simply and directly as possible. The issue raised is more important than one of stylistic preferences or prejudices. Our confident hope is that the United Nations is going to be a forceful, decisive body, not a body in which the emphasis is on 'considerings', 'notings', 'reservings', 'recordings', but which uses, when necessary, the strong language of the Charter, 'decide', 'determine', 'call upon', 'take action'.

I would not have won the battle for good English in U.N. resolutions if I had not had the support of the most distinguished Australian lawyer who was chairman of the drafting committee of the Preparatory Commission, Kenneth Bailey. Our success won us a public accolade from that defender of the English language, A.P. Herbert.[12] But our triumph was short-lived. The first part of the first session of the General Assembly passed some resolutions in the new form, because these resolutions had been put in that form by the drafting committee of the Preparatory Commission but from then on the organs of the U.N. relapsed into error.

One of our tasks in the Executive Committee and the Preparatory

10 Campbell and Herring, *Diaries*, 474
11 Brian Urquhart, *A Life in Peace and War* (New York: Harper and Row 1987), 99–101
12 A.P. Herbert, 'The Battle of Bunkum,' *Sunday Times* (London), 23 December 1945

Commission was to make recommendations on what languages were to be used in discussions in U.N. bodies and in U.N. documents. I was a member of the subcommittee on this matter. The other members were the five great powers and the Netherlands and Brazil, which had no hope that their languages would be included among the working languages of the United Nations. It was not unnatural therefore that they should jointly move a resolution that there should be only one working language – English. They knew that such a proposal had no chance of success but their hope was that if they rallied sufficient support for it, they might force a compromise under which there would be only two working languages – English and French. This was indeed the outcome. I well remember the speech which the Dutch delegate, P.S. Gerbrandy, gave in support of the Brazilian-Dutch resolution. He said: 'People who oppose this resolution say that it is impossible that the U.N. should have only one working language because foreign languages are too hard to learn. There is a great deal of exaggerated talk about the difficulty of learning foreign languages. I know this from my own experience. I was born in Friesia. My mother tongue is Friesian. When I went to school I had to learn Dutch. When I got involved in international affairs I had to learn English. It wasn't difficult. The only difficulty is that I speak in English, I think in Dutch and I dream in Friesian.'

At a reception at the Soviet embassy in London I had an experience which was not uncommon in those days. I was chatting with the pleasant alternate Yugoslav representative, Vladimir Rybar, when Alexei Roschin of the Soviet delegation, whom we both liked, joined us. He suggested we have a competition drinking vodka. We agreed on condition that the Soviet embassy provided a car to drive us to our hotels. A waiter kept coming up with a tray on which were three glasses. When the tray came up for the fourth time Rybar picked up the glass nearest Roschin, sipped it, and said, 'Roschin, you're drinking water.'

At the U.N. meetings in London in the autumn of 1945 I worked long hours under great pressure week after week with the result that I frequently became exhausted. I knew that when I was exhausted I was apt to be bad-tempered and arrogant – weaknesses to which a diplomat should never succumb. I usually wore an ordinary dark business suit to the meetings but if, when I woke up in the morning, I felt that my temper was likely to be short, I would put on the diplomatic armour of short black chancery coat and striped trousers. Then when at the conference I felt irritation mounting in me I would look down at my striped trousers and remember that I was a diplomat and expected to behave like one.

On a Sunday in the middle of October during a committee meeting at Church House I started scribbling a letter to Ruth. I wrote: 'Our committee meeting is taking place in a horrible din. The workmen are knocking away the brickwork built up outside the windows as protection against bombs. A fine theme for a speech. The protection against the last war being removed while we build up protection against the next. A fine theme and I wish it turns out to be true but our ...' I was interrupted and never finished the letter.

When I now look back at the making of the U.N. in 1945 and early 1946 I ask myself, Could we have done better? What avoidable errors of omission and commission did we make? The principal obstacle in the way of a better Charter was the necessity of doing nothing which would result in the Soviet Union deciding not to join the United Nations. Perhaps the mistake the western powers made at San Francisco in their disputes with the Soviet Union was to conclude sometimes that the Soviet Union was not bluffing when it was and its bluff could have been called. We did not then realize that negotiating with the Russians was like bargaining in an Indian bazaar. The seller puts his price at about twice what he hopes to get; the buyer puts his offer at about one half of what he is prepared to pay; and bargaining begins. I think that at San Francisco the Soviet Union demanded more than it expected to get and that it would have accepted some compromises if the opposition had been stubborn.

The Soviet Union did accept defeat at San Francisco on two issues which it considered important. The Americans by appealing to Stalin got the Soviet Union to withdraw its demand that each great power have the right to veto mere consideration by the Security Council of a threat to the peace under the chapter in the Charter on peaceful settlement. The middle-sized and small powers forced them to accept defeat on their proposal that the great power veto should extend to the appointment of four deputy secretaries general as well as to the secretary general. Perhaps if the western powers had pushed hard enough they might have secured other limitations on the veto. They might, for example, have succeeded in taking it away from the admission of new members other than ex-enemy states. There is a slim chance that they might have succeeded in taking it away from the operation of the whole of the chapter on the peaceful settlement of disputes.

The veto on the admission of new members has in practice not had a serious effect. All it has done is to delay the entry of a number of states. The veto on the operation of the chapter on the peaceful settlement of disputes has had serious effects. The Security Council has not been as effective in helping to settle international disputes by peaceful means as we had hoped at San Francisco it would be. The Charter provides that a party to a dispute shall abstain from voting when the Security Council is making decisions under the provisions on peaceful settlement. This means that a great power cannot veto decisions on disputes to which it is a party; but it can, and frequently does, veto decisions on disputes in which a state is involved which for some reason or other it wishes to protect against condemnation by the Security Council. The United States, for example, has used its veto to protect Israel twenty-one times in the last seventeen years.

There was never any expectation at San Francisco that the U.N. could keep peace among the great powers. The expectation was that the great powers, with support from the other nations on the Security Council, would impose on middle and small powers the settlement of disputes or situations the continuance of which was 'likely to endanger the main-tenance of international peace and security.' We knew that, since the willingness of the great powers to co-operate was slight, this would happen only rarely. But we assumed that occasionally there would be a coincidence of interest among the five permanent members of the Security Council which would enable the council to recommend the terms of settlement of a dispute under article 37 of the Charter and, if this recommendation was not accepted, to impose the settlement by the threat or use of force. We assumed that occasionally the parties to a dispute which had been unable to settle it by negotiation would welcome an imposed solution. We did not foresee that never would the Security Council impose a settlement of a dispute – not, for example, in the disputes between Israel and Palestine, or in the disputes between India and Pakistan over Kashmir.

On many important issues at San Francisco it was not just the Soviet Union which demanded restrictions on the authority of the U.N. All five great powers, for example, wanted the veto to cover the imposition of sanctions. On some issues the unity of the five powers was based on a bargain between them; one or two of them would receive support of the others on an issue they considered important in return for their support on some other issue. Thus Britain and France, the principal colonial powers, demanded weak provisions in the Charter on non-self-governing territories and got the other great powers to support them. The interests of the people of the non-self-governing territories, and indeed of the colonial powers themselves, would have been better served if the Charter had put all non-self-governing territories under the trusteeship system. Then the progress of these territories towards independence might have proceeded at more deliberate speed – faster in some cases, slower in others – and the colonial powers would have been under pressure to make better preparations than many did for the time when their colonies would become independent.

Another principal error at San Francisco was that we did not contemplate the possibility that the membership of the United Nations would more than triple in the next forty years – from the fifty-one states which signed the Charter at San Francisco to one hundred and fifty-nine today (1988). Because so many of these states are small – sixty-two have a population of less than a million and of these thirty-six have a population of less than two hundred thousand – a resolution can be passed by a two-thirds majority in the General Assembly even if it is opposed by countries containing 90 per cent of the population of the U.N. This debases the currency of resolutions of the Assembly and is responsible in large measure for the decline in its authority and respect. If at San Francisco we had contemplated the possibility of such an increase, we might have done something to limit the ill effects. Perhaps the Charter could have provided that only countries with a population of at least a million could become voting members; the other countries would become associate members without a vote. Or the provisions on voting in the General Assembly might have provided that the two-thirds majority required for the adoption of a resolution on an important question should include states representing a majority of the population of the United Nations and contributing at least half of its regular budget. This would have provided a rough and ready way of weighting voting in the Assembly. If such a provision had been included in the Charter it might have been possible to get it included in the constitutions of those U.N. agencies where each state has one vote. This would have gone far to prevent the deterioration which has taken place in UNESCO and other agencies.

Even now when it is impossible to amend the provisions in the U.N. Charter on voting in the Assembly it might be possible to secure agreement on amending the rules of procedure to provide that when the chairman of a plenary meeting of the Assembly announces that a resolution has been passed by a two-thirds majority he should then or at the earliest opportunity announce at a plenary meeting the proportion which the population of the states which had voted for the resolution bore to the total population of the U.N. and the proportion of the regular budget contributed by these states. States which knew that they had a two-thirds majority for a resolution might decide not to press for a vote on it if after the vote the chairman would announce that the states voting for the resolution contained, say, only 20 per cent of the population and contributed, say, only 15 per cent of the regular budget.

My senior colleagues at the meetings on the U.N. in 1945 and the beginning of 1946 were the four brightest stars in the External Affairs galaxy: Norman Robertson, L.B. Pearson, Hume Wrong, and Dana Wilgress. I was then forty and they were all older than I: Robertson by only a year, Pearson by eight, Wrong by ten, and Wilgress by twelve. Of the four, the one I was fondest of and the one with whom I was most in agreement was Wilgress. Indeed, I cannot recall any issue concerning the United Nations on which we differed in 1945 and 1946 or subsequently. One incident in New York in December 1946 illustrates how closely our instinctive reactions to these issues coincided. We both wanted Canada to oppose Bernard Baruch's efforts to bulldoze his proposals through the U.N. Atomic Energy Commission before they had been adequately examined because this would eliminate the possibility, however slim, of working out an agreement with the Soviet Union on the control of atomic energy. We did not know that one reason Baruch insisted that the U.N. commission approve the proposals before the end of 1946 was that he had decided to resign at the beginning of 1947 from his post of United States representative on the commission. Baruch was an arrogant old man in a hurry and in difficult international negotiations, where patience is essential, an arrogant old man in a hurry is even more dangerous than an arrogant young man in a hurry. Wilgress and I were sitting behind General Andrew McNaughton, the Canadian delegate, when he gave a speech before the commission on 20 December accepting a compromise. As he spoke we unconsciously kept pushing our chairs farther and farther back from him, separating ourselves from what he was saying.

Wilgress did not play a leading role at San Francisco but he was one of the most influential members of the Preparatory Commission. He was also, as chairman of the Canadian delegation, the best chairman of delegation I have ever served under. He brought out and used the special abilities of each of the members. He got the delegation working together as a team.

At the beginning of June 1945 it looked as if Soviet intransigence on the veto might result in the San Francisco conference breaking up without agreement on a Charter. In a letter of 6 June on this crisis I said that Robertson was better than Wrong 'in the kind of serious crisis the Conference – or rather the world – has been going through in the past week. His dislike of making a final decision one way or the other, of slamming doors shut, his phlegmatic qualities, which are often annoying weaknesses when he is dealing with small matters, are sources of strength in a real crisis.'

Thirteen years later when Robertson was appointed under-secretary for external affairs for the second time, after ten years in other posts, I wrote him to say how delighted I was: 'It is the place where you are most needed. We need your creative imagination and well-stocked mind and most of all your habit of applying a disciplined scepticism to the old orthodoxies of international politics. And we also need your extraordinary ability to expound and persuade. In this post you should be able to use all your talents and I know you are not happy unless you can do that.'

Wrong had been Canadian delegate to the League of Nations at Geneva in the second half of the thirties. The League was not at its best then but I think he found the atmosphere of the League Council and Assembly less distasteful than the atmosphere of the U.N. Security Council and Assembly at the beginning of 1946. On his return from the London Assembly he wrote a lengthy, closely argued, penetrating memorandum on 'the atmosphere which prevailed [at those meetings] and the political factors which gave the proceedings the form that they took.'[13] It was, he thought, 'debatable whether the advantages of open discussion of issues dividing the Great Powers outweigh the disadvantages caused by the public fixing of positions on delicate questions, with the consequence that the area of negotiation is reduced.' In the final sentence of his memorandum Wrong set forth his sombre conclusion:

Without a great alteration, therefore, in the attitude towards each other of the great powers – and it should be emphasized that this alteration is required not only on the part of the Soviet Government – the first meetings of the Security Council and the Assembly leave open the question whether the establishment of the United Nations has in fact furthered its primary purpose – the maintenance of international peace and security.

Wrong sent me a draft of his memorandum and asked for my comments. I urged him to modify this statement. In order to justify it he would have to be able to argue

that the present situation would be no worse if the United Nations had not been

13 Hume Wrong's memorandum in its final form is in DCER, vol. 12, 1946: 673–80. I have not been able to find the draft of the memorandum on which I commented.

established. Is it possible to maintain this? Presumably 'the attitude towards each other of the great powers' would have been about the same if the United Nations had not existed. They would either have continued to meet at five or three-power meetings and quarrelled (with the quarrels getting out into the press) or they would not have met and would have quarrelled through diplomatic channels and by open Soviet abuse in their press and radio countered by public statements by the leaders of the Western powers. So far as I can judge the quarrels would have gone on anyway, and the existence of the United Nations has not made them worse. On the other hand the existence of the United Nations has already done some good and may do much more good in matters not directly related to their quarrels.

At the United Nations General Assembly in New York in the autumn of 1947 I was given the job of taking a press conference at 9:45 every morning. At 9:00 we had our daily meeting of the delegation when we would go over what had happened at the plenary meetings and in the committees of the Assembly during the previous day, and discuss what line the Canadian delegation would take on issues expected to arise in the near future. On 26 September Andrei Vishinsky, the leader of the Soviet delegation, gave the Soviet statement in the general opening debate in the Assembly. It was a vituperative attack on the West, and especially on the United States. No such speech had ever been given in the Assembly. The cold war had not by then broken out. I knew that the first question I would be asked at my press conference would be, 'What does the Canadian delegation think about Vishinsky's speech?' I had talked to enough members of the delegation, Liberal, Conservative, and CCF, to know how they felt. I had, therefore, jotted down the general lines of the reply I proposed to make. I brought the subject up at the meeting. The delegation approved unanimously of my reply – adding to it comments even more pungent. The formula which I was to use was: 'The general impression of the Canadian delegation is ...'

I opened the press conference. The question was asked. I gave my reply. I said, 'Anything I say you can use provided you preface your story with some such formula as that "in your conversations with members of the Canadian delegation you have gathered that the general impression of the delegation of Vishinsky's speech is as follows." ' I said: 'To be prepared for a speech by a Soviet representative, what you should do is to write the kind of speech which the critics of Soviet policy could with justice make against the Soviet government and then change a few words in that speech in order to turn it into an attack by the Soviet Union on other governments.' The Soviet government had ordered

Czechoslovakia to withdraw its acceptance of the invitation to attend the first Marshall Plan conference. Now Vishinsky attacked the Marshall Plan as making the European nations in need of relief give up their inalienable right to dispose of their own economic resources. I drew the attention of the correspondents to a statement in the morning's *New York Times* that 'veteran correspondents' had said that if you had closed your eyes in the United Nations Assembly hall when Vishinsky had been speaking 'you could hear the voice of Hitler in the Sportspalast.' I also reminded them of the famous paragraph in *Mein Kampf* about 'the big lie.'

That day was a particularly heavy one for me. I was chairman of a fifteen-nation committee of the Assembly which had been charged with revising the Assembly's rules of procedure in order that the Assembly should not waste time in debates on procedure. We were trying to finish our work before the Assembly went into committee and that night we sat well after midnight. By the time I got back to the Biltmore Hotel from Lake Success it was one in the morning. I was sound asleep in a few minutes. I was wakened by the telephone. It was the Toronto *Globe and Mail* calling. They had a story from New York quoting me as saying – and then followed the remarks I had made that morning about Vishinsky's speech. They were sure that it must have been in error that these remarks had been attributed to me by name. I said that they were entirely right. I had made the statements, but the rule governing the press conference was that statements such as these were not to be attributed to me but to the Canadian delegation. The *Globe* said they would make the necessary change in the story. I thanked them for calling me, looked at my watch, saw it was two o'clock, and went to sleep again.

About seven hours later my telephone rang while I was having breakfast in my room. Again it was long distance. This time from Ottawa. It was Gerry Riddell from the Department of External Affairs. The department had just sent off a telegram to St Laurent, as head of the delegation, asking for an explanation of the grave infraction which I had committed of the rules governing civil servants by making to the press in my own name such forthright statements on a matter of foreign policy. Riddell explained that my remarks were bound to arouse controversy in Canada. The department had to send this telegram in order to keep the record straight. He was phoning me to warn me that this telegram was coming and to say that Pearson knew there must be a satisfactory explanation. I asked where the story had appeared. It was in the early edition of the Toronto *Globe*, though not in the later editions, and it was front-paged in all the editions of the Montreal *Gazette*. The stories in both papers were by the same correspondent.

When the telegram came I went with it to St Laurent. I explained to him what had happened. The department feared there might be newspaper controversy over this. There might be questions in the House of Commons when it met in two months' time. St Laurent did not pause for one second. He said, 'Send the following telegram to Ottawa: "Everything Reid said he said under my instructions. St Laurent." ' He added, 'I think the thing will blow over. If it doesn't I will make a public statement to that effect.'

With those words St Laurent made me his devoted admirer. I knew that here was a man who deserved loyalty because he was loyal. I had done what I had been authorized to do. One newspaperman had failed to respect my anonymity. Because my remarks were probably in advance of public opinion in Canada, this might damage the government. In such circumstances many politicians would have been careful not to commit themselves to support a civil servant until they had had time to find out which way the cat would jump at home. If it turned out that the party's interests would be served by repudiation, they would repudiate. Not St Laurent. If it had been King I had been dealing with and not St Laurent, I would have feared that he might sacrifice me if he considered that the national interests demanded this – and King was not accustomed to make a clear distinction between his own interest, the party interest, and the national interest.

While in the first years of the United Nations the complaints of Canadian delegations were directed mainly at the Soviet states, it was not long before it was the Asian and other underdeveloped countries which most irritated Canadian delegates. This was reflected in the delegation's assessment of the Assembly held in Paris at the end of 1951. When I read this assessment I was concerned, as I said in a memorandum in January 1952, that this irritation might be clouding the judgment of the delegation on tactics and strategy and making it difficult for it to understand the Asian approach to problems before the Assembly.[14] The Asians seemed to be judged by one standard and we by another. We supported otherwise futile resolutions because they are good propaganda in the western world

14 Canadian Delegation to U.N. Assembly, Paris, to SSEA, telegrams 252 of 21 December 1951 and 272 of 29 December 1951. E.R. memorandum of January 1952, E.A. file 5475-DW-14-40

but when the poor countries insisted on passing a resolution about an international development fund we say that it is futile and will debase the currency of United Nations resolutions and machinery, but we do not accept the fact that from their point of view it is good propaganda in the underdeveloped world. When we refused to accept compromise proposals, we were opposing wishful thinking which assumes that a clever form of words could eliminate vital differences of principle but when the poor countries refused to water down their resolutions they were being intransigent and unrealistic and irresponsible. Presumably they could retort that what we were asking them to do was to assume that a clever form of words could eliminate vital differences of principle between rich and poor countries on how much assistance rich countries should give to poor countries. We called the poor countries irresponsible, but was it irresponsible for them to put pressure on the rich countries in the debates over Morocco, Southwest Africa, economic development, and human rights? 'While this pressure is annoying to the West, if it is kept up it is probably going to make it increasingly difficult for the West to refuse to increase the pace of the granting of self-government and to increase the pace and extent of the economic aid which it grants.' The delegation seemed to assume that the rise of Islamic nationalism in areas of strategic importance to the western world could be satisfied only at the expense of the defence requirements of the Western world but there

may be cases where the defence requirements of the Western world require us to satisfy Islamic nationalism at the expense of a metropolitan power. We have, for example, to weigh the possibility that a continuation of present French policy in Morocco might provoke so much disorder there as to constitute a greater strategic danger to us than a grant of self-government to Morocco ... I suggest that the policy of the Western countries on Morocco at this Assembly was contrary to our own interests and was unrealistic and sentimental.

Throughout the fifties Canadian policy on racial and colonial issues in the U.N. continued, in my opinion, to be mistaken. At the end of the fifties John Holmes, then an assistant under-secretary, asked me to comment on a memorandum on the U.N. which he had written. In my reply I said that I was depressed by

the line which Canadian delegations to the Assembly had been taking in the last years of the Liberal regime on racialism, colonialism and trusteeship questions ... I think it would be easy to demonstrate that on all the complex of racial and colonial issues in the U.N. Canadian policy has not been in our national interest but has been based on sentimentalism, racial arrogance or a Europocentric view of the world. The West is likely to be so weak and vulnerable in the next decade or two that it cannot possibly afford the luxury of supporting the claims of South Africa or of the Portuguese in Africa. As for supporting the French in Algeria that is a typical Gadarene swine policy [a policy of rushing down a steep place into the sea and being drowned].[15]

Whether my arguments had any effect I do not know, but gradually in the next two decades the Canadian government came to comprehend better the demands of the poorer half of the world. The arguments insistently put forward by delegates of the third world in the Assembly helped Canada to this better comprehension. The government also had to acknowledge that the strident third world demand for more economic aid from the rich countries had not been a futile exercise but had resulted in concessions from the rich countries. It was, for example, one of the reasons the International Development Association was established, the branch of the World Bank which gives interest-free loans to the very poor countries. The pressure from the third world in the Assembly for speeding up the pace of the advance of non-self-governing territories to self-government did, I think, speed up the pace. The constant attacks on the apartheid policy of the government of South Africa helped to rally most of the nations of the world against South Africa on this issue. The Security Council and the General Assembly have hitherto done less than we hoped at San Francisco to reconcile differences between the western world and the Soviet world. They have done more than we contemplated to reconcile differences between the rich white world of the northern hemisphere and the poor coloured world of the southern hemisphere.

In the report I wrote in the summer of 1945 on the San Francisco conference I said that the conference by reaching agreement on the Charter of the United Nations had laid the foundation of a just and stable world order. Here I committed an error which many writers on the U.N. have fallen into. I should have said that the San Francisco conference had laid part of the foundation of a new world order, for other parts of the foundation had been laid by the conferences which had created the World Bank, the International Monetary Fund, the World Health Organization, the Food and Agriculture Organization, the International Civil Aviation Organization, and UNESCO.

If we now try to assess the extent to which the international agencies and organs created in the last years of the war and the first years of the

15 John Holmes to E.R., 25 February 1959; E.R. to Holmes, 13 March 1959

peace have served the people of the world we must balance the decline in the authority and respect of the U.N. Security Council, Assembly, and Secretariat with the rise in the power and influence for good of the specialized agencies, especially the World Bank, the International Development Association, and the International Monetary Fund. There is still no world order but the governments and people of the world, building on the foundations which have been laid, can by their joint and sustained efforts create a world order in which men and nations can live together as good neighbours free from fear and from want and with liberty of thought and of worship.

15

Creating the North Atlantic Alliance

1947–1949

When I came back to Ottawa in February 1946 after nine months in San Francisco and London I was appointed head of the European division of the Department of External Affairs[1] and the next year I was made an assistant under-secretary and became the principal adviser to L.B. Pearson, who had by then become the under-secretary. I was principal adviser to the Canadian delegation to the U.N. General Assembly in the autumn of 1946 and attended meetings of the Assembly, the Security Council, and the U.N. Atomic Energy Commission. Their proceedings demonstrated to me that the gap between the Soviet world and the western world was deepening and widening. I divided the blame for this between the Soviet Union and the United States. I was appalled by Bernard Baruch's behaviour in the Atomic Energy Commission at the end of 1946, where it seemed to me he was doing his best to sabotage whatever slight possibility there might be of agreement with the Soviet Union on the control of atomic energy. I was contemptuous of the way United States' delegations to the Assembly were constantly forcing votes so that they could put through resolutions opposed by the Soviet Union by the two-thirds majority which, in those days, they could almost always whip together – what we then called their mechanical majority. Because of this conflict between the Soviet Union and the western world, the United Nations was becoming an increasingly less effective organization for maintaining international peace and security. At the same time as this was happening to the United Nations, Soviet power was spreading in

---

1 This chapter incorporates material from my book *Time of Fear and Hope: the Making of the North Atlantic Treaty, 1947–1949* (Toronto: McClelland and Stewart 1977; Totawa, N.J.: Allenheld & Osmun 1981).

Europe. The cables and despatches that crossed my desk told the story of how the states of Eastern Europe were being incorporated into a Soviet empire.

Fear of the Soviet Union and anger at what we then called the Soviet abuse of their veto in the Security Council led at the beginning of 1947 to a mounting demand by many leading supporters of the U.N. in the United States, Britain, and Canada that the organization be 'strengthened' by amendments to the Charter which would drastically reduce or even eliminate the veto rights of the five permanent members of the Security Council. Those who sought this change knew that the Soviet Union would veto the proposed amendments and that this might precipitate the breakup of the United Nations, and the creation of two rival international security organizations, one dominated by the western countries and the other by the Soviet Union. By the summer of 1947 I had become convinced that the western world, instead of pressing for amendments to the veto provisions of the Charter, should establish its own security organization. I asked Pearson for permission to say this in a speech I was to give in the middle of August at the annual Couchiching conference of the Canadian Institute of Public Affairs. Most heads of foreign offices would have refused permission on the ground that it was inappropriate for a foreign service officer to make in public a proposal so far in advance of government policy. Pearson, after consulting St Laurent, gave me permission but suggested that the passage in which I made the proposal should be omitted from the copies of the speech given to the press at the conference. (A few months later the speech was published in full by the Department of External Affairs and the unexpurgated version was included in the printed proceedings of the conference.)

In my speech I first attacked proposals for amending the U.N. Charter which, I said, 'would mean destruction of the only constitutional structure which includes both the two worlds into which our one world has now so tragically been divided. As long as that structure remains in existence there is some hope that the two worlds can learn to live together. If that structure goes, the possibility will become much more remote.'

Since I was a civil servant putting forward in public ideas not yet adopted by the government I used guarded language when I went on to say:

The world is now so small that the whole of the western world is in itself a mere region. If the peoples of the western world want an international security organization with teeth, even though the Soviet Union is at present unwilling to be a member of such an organization, they do not need to amend the United

Nations charter in order to create such an organization; they can create it consistently with the United Nations charter. They can create a regional security organization to which any state willing to accept the obligations of membership could belong. In such an organization there need be no veto right possessed by any great power. In such an organization each member state could accept a binding obligation to pool the whole of its economic and military resources with those of the other members if *any* power should be found to have committed aggression against any one of the members.

This, James Eayrs has written, 'is almost certainly the first public statement by a government official advocating a collective defence organization of the western world.'[2]

At the same time as I was preparing my speech to the Couchiching conference I was drafting a lengthy top secret departmental memorandum on 'The United States and the Soviet Union: a study of the possibility of war and some of the implications for Canadian policy.' I circulated it on 30 August 1947 to St Laurent and to the senior officers of the department at home and abroad. I said of the Soviet Union that it was attempting with considerable success to establish 'a zone of exclusive Soviet influence' in Poland, the Soviet zone of Germany, Austria, Hungary, Romania, Bulgaria, Yugoslavia, and Albania. 'In Czechoslovakia, Soviet influence is strong but not as yet exclusive.'

It seems probable that the practical result of Soviet policy in Germany will be the creation of a closely integrated Eastern German state with a communist or near-communist system of government, well-organized and possibly even powerful. Such a state would have a very considerable attraction for western Germans, and the Soviet Government must be expected to do everything in its power to increase the communist influence in the zones occupied by the western powers. Nor will the struggle for the allegiance of western Europe be confined to Germany; the political future of France and Italy is also in doubt.

Both the Soviet Union and the United States wanted to expand their defence areas because each side 'fears the threat to its security which results from the other's expansionist moves [and] believes that the other constitutes a menace to its way of life.' This 'brings them into conflict in all the borderlands between their present defence areas from Korea to Finland.' But the conflict need not result in war. 'The Soviet leaders

2 James Eayrs, *In Defence of Canada: Growing up Allied* (Toronto: University of Toronto Press 1980), 17

believe that, by a process of gradual expansion of power, they can, in the long run, secure their ends without the necessity of risking a first-class war.' The United States was most unlikely to embark deliberately on a course which would lead to war with the Soviet Union unless

it was generally believed in the United States that the balance of power between the United States and the Soviet Union was constantly tilting more and more against the United States and that, unless the United States precipitated a preventive war while it was still stronger than the Soviet Union, it would soon be at the mercy of the Soviet Union ... The danger of war diminishes if the forces on the United States side of the balance are much greater than the forces on the Soviet side, provided that the Soviet leaders are not driven by too relentless an increase of United States power to risk a desperate gamble.

The proposals I put forward for strengthening the United States' side of the balance and so lessening the chances of war were an elaboration of what I had advocated in my Couchiching speech and in the memorandum I had written in February of the previous year after attending the U.N. meetings in London. Much of what I proposed is conventional wisdom now but it was not in August 1947.

Economic assistance, I said, should be given to 'that part of Europe which is outside Soviet control in order to restore stability, prosperity and hope and thus to lessen the possibility of pro-Soviet elements capitalizing on discontent in order to get power.' The western powers must do everything they can to prevent a serious economic depression which 'would raise doubts in the minds of many people, especially in the borderlands [between the Soviet and the western worlds], whether western civilization is in fact preferable to Soviet civilization.' The specialized agencies should be changed 'into international federal institutions to deal with international economic and social questions ... in order to strengthen the western world in its struggle with the Soviet Union ... The veto on these changes is not a Soviet veto; it is usually a United States veto.' (I found that I was too far ahead of government policy. In commenting on the memorandum, St Laurent said, 'I would not care to state, as a matter of policy, ... that the specialized agencies should be transformed into international federal institutions.')[3] The states of Western Europe should be given a guarantee 'against the establishment by force of pro-Soviet governments.'

3 St Laurent, memorandum, 'Re Draft "The United States and the Soviet Union",' 13 October 1947, DEA file 52 FS

In order to gain the allegiance of Western Europe, western civilization, and particularly that of the United States, must 'demonstrate by actions that it really believes in and practises the democratic faith. About two-thirds of the peoples of the world are coloured. The Russian section of the white race can make a successful appeal to the coloured peoples of the world because the Russians do not practise racial discrimination. In order to save itself from Soviet domination, the western section of the white race must meet this challenge by removing racial discriminations. The longer the giving of independence to colonial peoples is delayed, 'the greater are the chances that the colonial independence movements may come under Soviet influence or control.'

The adoption of these proposals, plus the maintenance of the 'armed forces of the western world ... at a level which is reasonable in relation to the armed forces of the Soviet world' and the establishment of a western collective defence organization, would enable the western powers to create and maintain the necessary overwhelming preponderance of power relative to that of the Soviet Union. 'The policy of firmness and of "containing" the Soviet Union should not be pushed too hard and too fast and ... we should keep our heads,' and I quoted with approval from the article by 'X' (George Kennan) which had just appeared in *Foreign Affairs* for July 1947: 'Demands on Russian policy should be put forward in such a manner as to leave the way open for a compliance not too detrimental to Russian prestige.'

An important advantage to Canada of membership in a western collective defence organization of which the United States was a member was that it would increase Canada's ability to moderate American policy on relations with the Soviet Union. The fact that we would be in the same boat with the United States would make it

wholly proper for us to tell the United States to stop rocking the boat or driving holes in its bottom. When we are compelled to differ with the United States publicly on an issue which the United States Government considers important, we should always remember that ..., in view of the similarities between the people of the United States and Canada, it will be a conflict between certain groups of Canadians and Americans who will support United States policy, and other groups of Canadians and Americans who will support Canadian policy ... If we play our cards well we can exert an influence at Washington out of all proportion to the relative importance of our strength in war compared with that of the United States. The game is difficult; the issues will be delicate; but with skill we can play it effectively.

J.L. Granatstein rightly concludes that my campaign for the North

Atlantic treaty indicates that in my own way I 'had scarcely changed since the 1930's': 'The world still needed effective international organization; security could be guaranteed only by an efficient joint defence system; and Canada could remain independent only if its relations with the United States were subsumed in some broader multilateral arrangement. The North Atlantic Treaty Organization of 1949 was a logical outgrowth of his concerns over two decades.'[4]

I was greatly encouraged when I read in the *New York Times* a month after I had delivered my Couchiching speech an article by the influential editor of *Foreign Affairs*, Hamilton Fish Armstrong, making much the same proposal as I had made for a collective defence organization but in greater detail. He proposed a protocol supplementing the U.N. Charter. The protocol would establish a new international organization. The obligation of each member of the new organization to come to the defence of other members would come into effect if two-thirds of the members were to decide that collective action had become necessary under the U.N. Charter and if the Security Council had failed to act. Before signing the protocol the member nations would agree on the armed forces which each would put at the disposal of the new organization. This 'international force actually in being' might have the atomic bomb at its disposal.

At the General Assembly in the beginning of October 1947 I wanted St Laurent to say in the opening debate very much what I had said at the Couchiching conference and I included a statement to this effect in the speech I prepared for him. Pearson disagreed. He wanted to maintain in St Laurent's speech an ambiguity between whether Canada was proposing a radical revision of the U.N. Charter, even at the cost of driving the Soviet Union out of the United Nations, or a collective security pact to supplement the Charter. The speech which Pearson wrote and St Laurent delivered was heavily weighted on the side of a supplementary agreement; and when the Canadian government agreed six months later to support a supplementary agreement, it was this part of the speech which the government emphasized:

Nations in their search for peace and co-operation will not, and cannot accept indefinitely an unaltered [Security] Council ... which, so many feel has become frozen in futility and divided by dissension. If forced they may seek greater safety in an association of democratic and peace-loving states willing to accept more specific international obligations in return for a greater measure of national security. Such associations ... if consistent with the principles and purposes of

4 J.L. Granatstein, *The Ottawa Men* (Toronto: Oxford University Press 1982), 250–1

the Charter, can be formed within the United Nations. It is to be hoped that such a development will not be necessary ... If, however, it is made necessary, it will have to take place. Let us not forget that the provisions of the Charter are a floor under, rather than a ceiling over, the responsibilities of member states.[5]

This statement was the first public suggestion by a member of a western government that it might be necessary for 'democratic and peace-loving states' to establish a security association within the United Nations which would not be subject to a Soviet veto over the imposition of sanctions. The significance of this statement was not appreciated at the time by the newspapermen who were covering the Assembly and it received little publicity. It seems likely that it also did not, immediately at least, make much impression on foreign offices. Armstrong's article of 14 September did, however, make an impression on at least two of the men who were to become principal architects of the North Atlantic treaty – J.D. Hickerson of the United States State Department and Gladwyn Jebb (later Lord Gladwyn) of the British Foreign Office. When I learned of this I arranged for St Laurent's speech and my own statement to be brought to their attention. At the end of October Hickerson told Hume Wrong, then the ambassador in Washington, that he thought it quite likely that the United States government would in time come out in support of the Armstrong proposal, perhaps if the four-power Council of Foreign Ministers failed to reach agreement on Germany at its meeting in December, and he expected failure.

In mid-January 1948 the British took the initiative in top secret messages from their prime minister, Clement Attlee, to Mackenzie King and to Washington: 'If we are to stem further encroachments of the Soviet tide, we should organize the ethical and spiritual forces of western Europe backed by the power and resources of the Commonwealth and the Americas, thus creating a solid foundation for the advance of western civilization in the widest sense.' The British government had concluded that they should seek to form a western democratic system, a Western Union of the states of Western Europe. This was substantially what Ernest Bevin, the foreign minister, said in a speech eight days later in the House of Commons. In this speech, as Gladwyn Jebb has put it in his memoirs, Bevin did not positively suggest any wider grouping than that of Western Europe, since this 'might at that stage have disturbed

5 St Laurent speech, 18 September 1947, *Canada at the United Nations 1947*, DEA, 178–80

the Senate of the United States ... [H]e knew perfectly well what he was after, but he had to achieve his end by stages.'[6]

Attlee and Bevin were careful in these messages to use language which would not disturb the United States Senate. They were not equally careful to refrain from language which would disturb Mackenzie King. They should have known that the words 'the power and resources of the Commonwealth' would arouse all his deep suspicions of British desires to centralize the Commonwealth and dominate it. King told the British high commissioner, according to his diary, that he 'took decided exception' to these words. They 'might mean military power, finance, resources, etc. ... and [he] did not like the use of the word Commonwealth as though it was one entity instead of several nations.' King said that he was, however, 'in general sympathy with the point of view expressed' in Attlee's message.

Pearson was delighted that the British had by their messages to Washington and Ottawa launched a campaign for a western security pact. It was, he believed, essential that Canada should welcome this initiative. He feared that the offending words in the British message might stand in the way. Pearson prepared for King's consideration a favourable reply to Attlee's message, secured St Laurent's approval, and girded himself for a struggle. King Gordon was visiting Ottawa at the time. Pearson and I had arranged that he would have dinner with our wives and us in the grill room at the Chateau Laurier. Pearson was late arriving. He looked drawn and tired. He whispered to me: 'I got the reply through. But it was the worst struggle I've ever had. I had no support from anyone in my arguments with King.' Three years later I wrote in a departmental memorandum that Pearson's success was 'his most important accomplishment as under-secretary.' (He was under-secretary from 1946 to 1948.)

During the next six weeks or so it seemed to me that no progress was being made towards the conclusion of a western security pact. One reason was that the British tried at the beginning of February to press the State Department too hard and too fast. They proposed that the United States 'enter with Great Britain into a general commitment to go to war with an aggressor.' The State Department immediately rejected 'consideration of a military alliance' with Britain: it could not consider the part it might appropriately play in support of the British proposal for a Western European union until it knew more about the proposal and, in particular, about the extent of the determination of the Western European countries to act in concert to defend themselves. 'You are in

6 *The Memoirs of Lord Gladwyn* (London: Weidenfeld and Nicolson 1972), 210–11

effect asking us to pour concrete before we see the blueprints.' The British countered with the complaint that 'without assurance of security, which can only be given with some degree of American participation, the British government is unlikely to be successful in making the Western Union a going concern.' This argument might have gone on interminably and there might have been no treaty of Brussels and no North Atlantic treaty had it not been for the Soviet seizure of Czechoslovakia on 25 February which resulted in the opening of negotiations on the Brussels treaty on 7 March. Then on 8 March came the catalytic message from the Norwegian government to the British and American governments that Norway might soon face Soviet demands for a pact which would reduce it to the level of a Soviet satellite. Two days later came news of the murder or suicide of Jan Masaryk, the pro-western foreign minister of Czechoslovakia. The next day Attlee proposed to the United States and Canada that officials of the three countries meet in Washington without delay to explore the possibility of establishing a regional Atlantic approaches pact of mutual assistance under article 51 of the u.n. Charter. All the countries directly threatened by a Soviet move on the Atlantic could participate in this pact: Norway, Denmark, Iceland, Ireland, France, Portugal, Britain, the United States, Canada, and Spain once it had a democratic regime.

This time there was no hesitation in Ottawa. The very day we received the British proposal for a three-power meeting in Washington, we accepted it. The United States accepted it the following day. Mackenzie King, Louis St Laurent, Brooke Claxton, and Lester Pearson, who were responsible for this decision, had lived through two world wars. They were convinced that Canada could not escape being an active belligerent in a third world war. They believed that the first and second world wars would not have broken out if Germany had known that it would eventually face a coalition of the United States, Britain, and France, and that the way to prevent a third world war was to convince Stalin that in such a war he would face from the outset an even stronger coalition than those of 1917 and 1941. The grand coalition should, therefore, be created now.

On 17 March King declared in the House of Commons, 'The peoples of all free countries may be assured that Canada will play her full part in every movement to give substance to the conception of an effective system of collective security by the development of regional pacts under the Charter of the United Nations.'

In spite of this public statement I feared that King would, when the time came for a decision, refuse to agree that Canada become a member of a North Atlantic alliance. I did not know until the middle of June that

St Laurent shared this apprehension. On 19 June the estimates of the Department of External Affairs were being debated in the House of Commons. Pearson was absent from Ottawa and I was acting under-secretary. As such I sat in the House across from the desk of St Laurent. In his statement on the negotiations for a North Atlantic pact St Laurent said that if the United States were willing to join in an alliance with the United Kingdom, France, and the Benelux countries, 'we think the people of Canada would wish that we also be associated with it ... We do not think that anything that the United Kingdom and these western European democracies and the United States would be in is something that we could avoid being in.' He sat down. He leaned across to me and said, 'I wonder how that will go down.' I said, 'I think it will go down very well in the country.' St Laurent said, 'I wasn't thinking of the country. I was thinking of Laurier House.' (Laurier House was King's residence.)

Looking back now on this incident, it is clear to me that St Laurent had decided that he would in the debate commit Canada to membership in a North Atlantic alliance if one were formed. By doing this he would make it impossible for King to refuse to agree that Canada become a member, since the price of refusal would be St Laurent's resignation from the cabinet.

The fear in 1948 which precipitated the negotiations on the North Atlantic treaty was not of an overt armed attack by the Soviet Union on Western Europe. In communications between the foreign ministers of the United States, Britain, and France in April, May, and June 1948, Marshall said that the Soviet government did 'not want war at this time'; Bevin that the Soviet government did not intend to push 'things to the extreme of war'; and Georges Bidault that there was 'no clear indication that the U.S.S.R. is now prepared to make war.'[7]

Hickerson in a memorandum to the secretary of state on 8 March said: 'The problem at present is less one of defense against overt foreign aggression than against internal fifth-column aggression supported by the threat of external force, on the Czech model. An essential element in combatting it is to convince non-Communist elements that friendly external force comparable to the threatening external force is available.'[8]

7 *Foreign Relations of the United States Government* (FRUS), 1948 (Washington: U.S. Government Printing Office), vol. IV: 858, 844; ibid., vol. III: 142
8 Ibid., vol. III: 40–1

Seven weeks before the Italian elections in April 1948 the State Department believed that a victory for the People's Bloc, 'exploiting legitimate economic grievances, social unrest, and the pervading fear of vengeance in the event of communist domination,' would result in the communists getting control of Italy and the end result would be a totalitarian police state subservient to Moscow. George Kennan believed that this would have resulted in a sweep by the communists through the territories lying along the western Mediterranean, a sweep accomplished without the use of armed force by the Soviet Union.

George Marshall believed 'that the fears and dissensions of the Western European countries are unlikely to be overcome without a greater appeal to the imagination and hopes of the people.' Bohlen said in July that 'the first benefit which should derive [from the treaty] would probably be a psychological one, a certain confidence [in Western Europe] in the future.' Kennan said in August that 'he felt it would be a mistake, politically and psychologically, to put forward before the world at this time a pact or a regional arrangement which proved to be a strictly military alliance.' And in November he said that what value the treaty possessed was 'insofar as it operates to stiffen the self-confidence of the western Europeans in the face of Soviet pressures.'

St Laurent had made his decision in favour of a North Atlantic treaty by the end of March 1948. Once he made up his mind he became the leader of what he himself called a 'crusade' for the treaty – a crusade conducted by seven speeches in April, May, and June. I wrote most of the references in those speeches to the proposed North Atlantic treaty. In those speeches St Laurent said that the purpose of a new collective security league would not be merely negative; it would create a dynamic counter-attraction to communism – a free, prosperous, and progressive society as opposed to the totalitarian and reactionary society of the communist world. The formation of such a defensive group of free states would not be a counsel of despair but a message of hope. It would not mean that we regarded a third world war as inevitable; but that the free democracies had decided that to prevent such a war they would organize so as to confront the forces of communist expansionism with an overwhelming preponderance of moral, economic, and military force and with a sufficient degree of unity to ensure that this preponderance of force was so used that the free nations could not be defeated one by one. No measure less than this would do. We must at all costs avoid the fatal repetition of the history of the pre-war years when the Nazi aggressor picked off its victims one by one. Such a process did not end at the Atlantic.

In his speech of 29 April St Laurent insisted, contrary to views held at that time in Washington, that

the western European democracies are not beggars asking for our charity. They are allies whose assistance we need in order to be able successfully to defend ourselves and our beliefs ... The spread of aggressive communist despotism over western Europe would ultimately almost certainly mean for us war, and war on most unfavourable terms. It is in our national interest to see to it that the flood of communist expansion is held back ... We must constantly remember that the Union of the Free World which is now rather painfully struggling to be born will possess the necessary overwhelming strength only if it is based on moral as well as material force; if its citizens are bound together not merely by their opposition to totalitarian communist aggression but by a positive love of democracy and of their fellow men, by a determination to make democracy work for the promotion of mutual welfare and the preservation of peace, for others as well as themselves.

Now when I read the speeches given in 1948 by St Laurent and Pearson on the necessity of a North Atlantic treaty I am struck by the constant use of such terms as 'communist expansionism' and 'aggressive communist despotism' when what we feared was not communism but the Soviet Union, albeit a Soviet Union supported by the then strong communist parties of Western Europe. Part of the reason for our using these terms was that Mackenzie King deplored cabinet ministers stating in public that the Soviet Union was our potential enemy. In his diary for 30 October 1948 King stated that he had spoken to Pearson about 'Claxton's speech which I said was ill-advised, his continuous references to Russia and our preparations for war against Russia. Said I thought he should use general terms of our wishing to do our part with other nations in being prepared against aggression from whatever source it might come etc.'

Though we did not know it at the time, St Laurent's speech of 29 April helped to win George Kennan over from his opposition to a North Atlantic treaty. Kennan was then one of the most influential officers in the State Department. He and Charles (Chip) Bohlen, who was also opposed, were senior to the treaty's two chief advocates in the State Department, Jack Hickerson and T.C. (Ted) Achilles. On 24 May, four weeks after the speech had been given, Kennan informed the secretary of state, George Marshall, and the under-secretary, Robert Lovett, that St Laurent's speech and a message from Ernest Bevin of 14 May had added a 'new and important element' to the problem of a North Atlantic security pact and that in the light of these statements, 'we must be very careful not to place ourselves in the position of being the obstacle to further progress toward the political union of the western democracies.'[9]

Kennan's goal was the political union of the western democracies. St Laurent said in the spring of 1948 that the creation and maintenance of an effective North Atlantic alliance may 'require the establishment of new international political institutions which will appear to trench much more upon old-fashioned concepts of national sovereignty than any of the international institutions which have been established in the past.' Pearson's memorandum to cabinet on 6 October 1948, his first as foreign minister, stated that the proposed North Atlantic alliance would create a new international institution which would 'have within itself possibilities of growth and of adaptation to changing conditions. The North Atlantic community is today a real commonwealth of nations which share the same democratic and cultural traditions. If a movement towards its political and economic unification can be started this year, no one can forecast the extent of the unity which may exist five, ten or fifteen years from now.'

Because St Laurent and Pearson hoped that the North Atlantic treaty would establish a basis for the gradual political and economic unification of the North Atlantic community, they wanted the alliance to be more than a military alliance. They therefore pressed in the negotiations for what became article 2 of the treaty and for strengthening in other ways the non-military obligations in the treaty. Our efforts to get article 2 into the treaty would have failed if Hickerson and Achilles had not, as they themselves have said, strongly favoured its inclusion 'as the basis upon which a true Atlantic Community, going far beyond the military field, could be built'; they were for article 2 'almost to the point of crusading for it.'

In the negotiations it was not only article 2 on which we in Ottawa dug in our toes; it was also the wording of article 5, in which each ally promises to come to the assistance of an ally which is attacked. At the very end of the negotiations leading members of the United States Senate demanded that this article should give rise to no obligation, moral or otherwise, to go to war. When Dean Acheson pressed for a weak pledge in order to avoid difficulties in the Senate, he argued that what mattered was the substance of the treaty and the words were of secondary importance. Oliver Franks, the British ambassador, replied that strong

9 Ibid., 128

words – an undertaking by the parties to take military action if one of them were attacked – were necessary to give confidence to people in western Europe.

This was certainly our feeling in Ottawa and we authorized Wrong to tell the State Department that a weak pledge would reduce the treaty 'almost to the level of a Kellogg-Briand peace pact,' and that if there were no satisfactory pledge in the treaty, 'we might have to re-examine our whole position [and it] might be that in the light of such re-examination we will be compelled to decide that the Canadian national interest involved in this kind of treaty ... is not sufficiently direct and immediate to warrant the government recommending to Parliament our adherence to it.' Wrong did not have to use this threat because President Truman intervened and the recalcitrant senators agreed that the article should include a reference to the use of armed force.

Some of the principal architects of the treaty hoped that it would restrain not only the Soviet Union but also the United States from pursuing impatient or provocative policies towards each other. In April 1948 Bevin made a guarded reference to British apprehensions about American attitudes to the Soviet Union in a message to Marshall. The United States and Britain, he said, must be careful, while remaining firm, not to provoke the Russians into ill-considered actions from which it would be difficult for them to retreat. The motto of the United States and Britain must be moderation, patience, and prudence combined with firmness and toughness.[10] Four months later the French used more forthright language. Armand Bérard, the second-in-command at the French embassy in Washington, speaking under instructions from Paris, said to Bohlen that the French government felt that 'the developments in regard to Germany and in particular [the United States'] attitude thereto might well bring matters to a head in Europe' before the western European countries had been strengthened by the United States' support and especially military supplies. What his government had in mind were the 'very strong statements from Berlin about armed convoys and not getting out of Berlin short of war,' which General Lucius Clay, the commander-in-chief of the United States forces in Europe, had been making.[11]

At that time the French were hesitant and negative about the very idea of a treaty and Pearson, in an effort to encourage them to be more forthcoming, said in a message to the French government on 13 August 1948 that one of the reasons France should support the treaty was that

10 Ibid., vol. IV: 843–4
11 Ibid., vol III: 206–7

'the United States may press the Russians too hard and too fast and not leave them a way out which would save their faces. To lessen this danger, the western European powers will have to exert a steady and constructive influence on Washington. The establishment of a North Atlantic Union will give them additional channels through which to exert this moderating influence.'

When Pearson a month later gave his first public speech as foreign minister, he contended that one of the purposes of the proposed treaty was to restrain the United States. This time, since he was putting the argument in public and not in private, he used veiled language but the meaning was clear. In the alliance 'the sharing of risks, resources and obligations must be accompanied by, and flow from, a share in the control of policy ... Otherwise, without their consent, the policies of one or two or three may increase the risks and therefore the obligations of all.'

Article 2 gave rise to three of the six non-military obligations in the treaty. The other three were created by the provisions of articles 1 and 4. The two military obligations were set forth in articles 3 and 5. The eight obligations are:

1 To 'settle any international disputes in which they may be involved by peaceful means in such a manner that international peace and security, and justice, are not endangered' (article 1).

2 To 'refrain in their international relations from the threat or use of force in any manner inconsistent with the purposes of the United Nations' (article 1).

3 To 'contribute toward the further development of peaceful and friendly international relations by strengthening their free institutions [and] by bringing about a better understanding of the principles upon which these institutions are founded' (article 2), principles defined in the preamble as 'democracy, individual liberty and the rule of law.'

4 To 'contribute toward the further development of peaceful and friendly international relations ... by promoting conditions of stability and well-being' (article 2).

5 To 'seek to eliminate conflict in their international economic policies and [to] encourage economic collaboration between any or all of them' (article 2).

6 To 'consult together whenever, in the opinion of any of them, the territorial integrity, political independence or security of any of the Parties is threatened' (article 4). This provision 'is applicable in the event of a threat in any part of the world, to the security of any of the Parties' (interpretation of the treaty agreed to on 15 March 1949).

7 To 'maintain and develop their collective capacity to resist armed attack ... by means of continuous and effective self-help and mutual aid ... in order more effectively to achieve the objectives of this Treaty' (article 3).

8 To consider an 'armed attack against one or more of them in Europe or North America ... [as] an attack against them all; and ..., if such an attack occurs ... [to] assist the Party or Parties so attacked by taking forthwith, individually and in concert with the other Parties, such action as it deems necessary, including the use of armed force, to restore and maintain the security of the North Atlantic area' (article 5). This and the other provisions of the treaty are to be 'carried out by the Parties in accordance with their respective constitutional procedures' (article 11).

We who took part in the struggle for the treaty know that there was nothing inevitable about the treaty. There might have been no treaty, or a better treaty or a worse treaty. We know that what we felt and thought and did at the time, that our insights and our errors, are reflected in its text. It was not the result of American cold war policies; it was not an example of the United States persuading other countries to support its cold war policies. Britain, not the United States, took the initiative in proposing the treaty. When in the next three months the American State Department was divided about the proposed treaty Britain, supported by Canada, put the arguments for it to the United States in confidential messages and in public statements.

The treaty created the first multilateral military alliance to span the North Atlantic Ocean in time of peace. The last time a comparable grand alliance had been created in peace-time was in 1815 after Waterloo when Britain, Austria, Prussia, and Russia formed the quadruple alliance to keep Napoleon and his family off the throne of France and to defend the territorial settlement of the Congress of Vienna. That alliance lasted only seven years. The entry of the United States into the North Atlantic alliance constituted a revolutionary change in American foreign policy. During the century and a half since the termination in 1800 of the Franco-American alliance, the United States had never in time of peace made a military alliance with a European power. After the First World War, it had refused to ratify the treaty of alliance with France which Woodrow Wilson had signed in June 1919. What the United States refused to do after the First World War, it did after the Second. Great Britain had, for thirty years or more, been hoping to entangle the United States in a military alliance; it succeeded in 1949. It was not only the United States which made a revolutionary change in its foreign policy when it joined the North Atlantic alliance; Norway, Denmark, and Iceland had never since the Napoleonic wars been involved in military alliances in peace-time, and Canada had consistently refused to pledge itself in peace-time to defend any other country.

The hope of St Laurent, Pearson, Kennan, Hickerson, and Achilles that the North Atlantic treaty would in time be transformed into a North Atlantic federation was frustrated and it is easy now to dismiss the holders of this hope as unrealistic visionaries. Visionaries they were, but they were not the kind of people to be unrealistic. They had for years been leading practitioners of diplomacy; they knew from first-hand ex-perience the realities of world politics. For historians now to say that their hopes were bound to be frustrated is to my mind to fall into the error of thinking that what has happened was bound to happen, an error which the historian Sir Percival Spear has warned against: 'What has occurred in time cannot be undone, but it does not necessarily follow that nothing else could have happened, or that the actual course of events was the only possible or even probable outcome of the interplay of historical forces and personalities.'[12]

At the beginning of 1947 virtually all experts on foreign affairs would have dismissed as unrealistic a proposal to create a military alliance of the North Atlantic countries; the inertia, scepticism, doubts, hesitations, fears, and opposition were too great to be overcome. If there had been no Atlantic alliance many of those historians who now assert that those who hoped in 1948 for a North Atlantic federation were unrealistic vi-sionaries would today be asserting that those who hoped in 1948 for a North Atlantic alliance were unrealistic visionaries.

Those who hoped in 1948 for a North Atlantic alliance were not unrealistic visionaries but they were highly fortunate visionaries. Fortune smiled on the negotiations. I doubt, for example, that the negotiations could have succeeded if the State Department had not been headed for the first ten months of negotiation by George Marshall and Robert Lov-ett. Dean Rusk has said of this partnership that Lovett was Marshall's alter ego and that the 'combination of Marshall and Lovett at the lead-ership of the Department of State has never been equalled in our history and is not likely to be again.' Marshall had the full confidence of President Truman and Lovett was a friend of Senator Vandenberg and persuaded Vandenberg to support the idea of a treaty. So once the administration

12 Percival Spear, *The Oxford History of Modern India 1740–1975*, 2nd ed. (Delhi: Oxford University Press 1973), 2

decided it wanted a treaty there was unity of purpose between the White House, the State Department, and the chairman of the Senate Foreign Relations Committee.

Britain had a similarly fruitful combination of two strong, creative politicians, Attlee and Bevin, a forceful, wise adviser in the Foreign office, Gladwyn Jebb, and two first-rate negotiators in Washington, Oliver Franks and Hoyer Millar. Canada, like the United States, had a partnership in foreign affairs between St Laurent and Pearson never equalled in Canadian history and it had in Washington the formidable Hume Wrong.

Fortune also favoured the treaty because shortly before the negotiations began Britain granted independence to India. During the negotiations Dean Rusk warned the British that if they were not more forthcoming on Palestine the feeling in the United States against Britain might make the conclusion of a treaty impossible. What would feeling in the United States against Britain have been if during the negotiations Britain had been suppressing the Indian independence movement and the American press had been full of stories of Britain imprisoning Gandhi, Nehru, and other Congress Party leaders and of British troops and police brutally putting down demonstrations and riots? This would have caused such an upsurge of anti-British feeling in the United States as to make impossible the mere discussion of a possible alliance with Britain.

The birth of the North Atlantic alliance demonstrated that miracles can take place in international affairs. That is why I called my article in the *NATO Review* in 1980 'The Miraculous Birth of the North Atlantic Alliance.'

When at the beginning of September 1948 negotiations were going through a bad period Robert Lovett, who was presiding at a meeting of the negotiators, said: 'If domestic politics were the art of the possible, international politics might be called the art of the almost impossible.' The negotiations on the North Atlantic treaty succeeded because the North Atlantic governments practised the art of the almost impossible. If they had continued to practise that art we might by now have created a federation of the countries bordering on the North Atlantic in spite of the many obstacles in the way. The principal obstacle was the change in the nature of the alliance which was precipitated fourteen months after the coming into force of the treaty by the outbreak of the Korean War or, more accurately, by the response of the United States to the invasion of South Korea by North Korea in June 1950.

The coming into force of the North Atlantic treaty was followed by only a small increase in the defence expenditures of the alliance. Indeed, there was general agreement within the alliance at the time that an increase was unnecessary and undesirable. In 1949 the Canadian white paper on defence stated that the North Atlantic treaty would not result in an increase in the defence expenditures of the alliance. 'By pooling resources the effect of the pact should be to reduce the total expenditures which each of the twelve countries would have found necessary for their security had there been no pact.'[13] Hickerson believed that the mere commitment of the United States to the alliance would be enough to deter the Soviet Union from committing aggression. The United States administration hoped that there would be 'some increase' in the defence expenditures of the Western European allies but it also believed that 'economic recovery must not be sacrificed to rearmament.' In 1950, the first year of the alliance, the defence expenditures of the alliance increased in real terms by only 7 per cent over the preceding year. Within two years of the outbreak of the Korean War the defence expenditures of the alliance almost tripled.[14]

It is normal for the nature of alliances to change as the years pass. What is unusual in the North Atlantic alliance is how quickly the change occurred and how profound it was. Not only did the defence expenditures almost triple from 1950 to 1952 but in those years the United States insisted on the admission of Greece and Turkey to the alliance, on the armament of West Germany, and on the appointment of a supreme commander. The North Atlantic alliance gave birth to the North Atlantic Treaty Organization. Charles Bohlen has called these developments an unwise militarization of the alliance.[15] Pearson in July 1951 deplored this growing concentration on the military aspects of the alliance which, he wrote in his diary, 'would endanger the "Article 2" idea of the Pact, the development of a North Atlantic community,' and he cast about for a substitute for the alliance as a starting-point for the development of the community. In his diary he describes how on a visit to Western Europe in July 1951 he very tentatively put forward the idea that two treaties be substituted for the North Atlantic treaty; one would be purely military and would be open to any member of the United Nations; the other would promote political, economic, social, and cultural co-operation among countries which were in fact part of the North Atlantic community. The new organ of the North Atlantic community would not include Italy, Greece, and Turkey but it would include the other countries which had

13 Department of National Defence, *Canada's Defence Programme 1949–1950*, 8
14 The defence expenditures in constant 1950 U.S. dollars are given in Reid, *Time of Fear and Hope*, 278.
15 Charles Bohlen, *Witness to History* (New York: W.W. Norton 1973), 304.

been members of the North Atlantic alliance, plus Switzerland and Sweden. According to Pearson, the response of the foreign ministers of the Netherlands and Norway was encouraging but nothing came of this.[16]

St Laurent and Pearson in 1949 would have rejected as highly improbable the idea that thirty-nine years later Canada would be spending on defence in real terms five times[17] what it was then spending, that Canada would be maintaining armed forces in Europe, and, indeed, that the alliance would still be in existence. Pearson in 1949 believed, or at least hoped, that the North Atlantic alliance as a security organization was a temporary expedient. He looked forward to the time when the relations between the western world and the Soviet world had so improved that the U.N. Security Council, assisted by its Military Staff Committee and with forces at its disposal provided under special military agreements between the Council and member states, would become the effective security organization contemplated in the Charter and the security aspects of the alliance would wither away. St Laurent at the beginning of 1949 wanted a conference of the alliance in eight or ten years to discuss whether a continuation of the treaty was necessary to assure international security. These and similar views held by other participants in the negotiations led to the inclusion in the treaty of article 12, which provides that after the treaty has been in force for ten years, or at any time thereafter, it might be reviewed, having regard among other things to 'the development of universal as well as regional arrangements under the Charter of the U.N. for the maintenance of international peace and security.'

Though I was often frustrated and disappointed in the course of the negotiations on the North Atlantic treaty I found my participation rewarding since it gave me an opportunity to use to the full whatever abilities I possessed on an important creative task. I look back with pride on the part I played in the making of the treaty since I believe the world would be worse off today if there had been no treaty in 1949.

---

16 Diary entry for 2 July 1951, in L.B. Pearson, *Mike: The Memoirs of the Rt. Hon. Lester B. Pearson* (Toronto: University of Toronto Press 1973), II:70
17 In the year 1949–50 Canadian expenditures on defence were $372 million, the equivalent in 1988 dollars of about $2,100 million. The expenditures on defence in 1987–88 were $10,340 million.

16

*D*epartment of External Affairs
1946–1952

I had the great good fortune to be a senior officer in the Department of External Affairs in the six years from 1946 to 1952 when a revolution took place in Canadian foreign policy. In periods totalling a year I was acting head of the department and for almost all the rest of the time I was second in command. And for all but the first six months of these six years I worked directly under L.B. Pearson, under-secretary from September 1946 to September 1948 and then foreign minister. This was a great privilege.

The rapid promotions I received in this period were for me a heartening indication of Pearson's confidence in me. When I came back to Ottawa in February 1946 from the United Nations meetings in London I had the rank of counsellor. The next year I was made an assistant under-secretary and in March 1949 deputy under-secretary. In 1951 my salary was increased to $12,000, which made me one of the four highest-paid officers in the External Affairs service. Two other officers, the high commissioner in London and the ambassador in Washington, were likewise paid $12,000. The under-secretary was paid $15,000. These officers are now treated more generously. The under-secretary, for example, now receives in real terms about 70 per cent more than his predecessor.

I later learnt that Pearson's confidence in me was not unqualified. In April 1947, the very time he was having me promoted to be an assistant under-secretary, he wrote to Norman Robertson:

Escott is as busy and active and useful as ever but is emotionally unstable, and I sometimes get worried about him. He came back from the Assembly as you know in very bad shape – almost a nervous wreck – and he is showing signs the last two or three weeks of mental fatigue. This always means for him a certain irrationality of conduct and an intolerance of viewpoint. He has become quite obsessed lately over the export of arms, having exalted it into a crusade against evil and, when the Cabinet decided the other day to permit such export in certain circumstances, he was acutely distressed.

It was a joy to be from 1946 to 1952 a member of a brilliant team of officers in the Canadian foreign service at home and abroad. The level of knowledge, intelligence, judgment, charm, and devotion to the public welfare was high. They possessed outstanding ability in preparing at short notice lucid analyses of international problems and recommendations on policy in memoranda, telegrams, despatches, and speeches to be given by the minister. This is not surprising since one out of eight have written books: memoirs, poetry, diaries, novels, histories.[1] This must constitute a record in national foreign services. If the present corps of Canadian heads of mission and foreign service officers were to follow their example about 190 would write books – a daunting prospect for Canadian publishers.

On 9 September 1948 Pearson summoned me to his office to tell me that he had decided to enter politics, that his appointment as secretary of state for external affairs would be announced the next day, and that I would be acting under-secretary until a new under-secretary was appointed. Some people would have left it at that and I would have lived in hope that if I did well as acting under-secretary I would be appointed under-secretary. Not Pearson. He said that I would not be appointed under-secretary. In this talk Pearson said that one reason he had agreed to be foreign minister was that he could fight better for the North Atlantic treaty as foreign minister than as deputy foreign minister. Then, as soon as he had won his election to the House of Commons, he went to Paris for the annual meeting of the U.N. General Assembly and stayed there for seven weeks. This was a crucial period in the negotiation of the North Atlantic treaty. If he had spent those weeks in Ottawa and Washington we might have had a better treaty. This is the only occasion I can remember when he sacrificed a more important interest in order to play

---

1 In 1952 there were 276 heads of mission and foreign service officers. Of these, 37 have written books; Arthur Andrew, Paul Beaulieu, Marcel Cadieux, Jean Désy, Pierre Dupuy, Robert Ford, James George, James Gibson, George Glazebrook, John Hadwen, Arnold Heeney, John Holmes, George Ignatieff, H.L. Keenleyside, James Langley, Jules Léger, Douglas LePan, T.W.L. MacDermot, Graham McInnis, R.A. MacKay, Léon Mayrand, Herbert Norman, R.A.J. Phillips, J.W. Pickersgill, Wynne Plumptre, Maurice Pope, Escott Reid, Charles Ritchie, Gordon Robertson, Basil Robinson, E.B. Rogers, Chester Ronning, John Starnes, Frank Stone, Pierre Trottier, Georges Vanier, Dana Wilgress.

the game of international politics at the United Nations, a game he loved playing and at which, as in the Suez crisis in 1956, he was brilliant.

The day after Pearson had told me of his entry into politics I went to Mackenzie King's press conference to hear his announcement that Pearson had joined the cabinet as secretary of state for external affairs. On King's right at the conference was St Laurent, on his left Pearson. Was King basking in the glory of having succeeded in choosing not only his successor but his successor's successor? I think so. He was about to give up power but here for history to note was a final revelation of his power.

I thought at the time that I would be acting under-secretary for only a month or so until Hume Wrong took over, but Wrong was not appointed as he should have been – he would have been the best of all the under-secretaries in the fifties and sixties – and my tenure lasted six months until Arnold Heeney became under-secretary on 15 March 1949. It was a demanding period: the last six months of the negotiation of the North Atlantic treaty; the negotiations on the entry of Newfoundland into Confederation; financial relations with Britain; the Berlin blockade; the establishment of the state of Israel; the advance of communist power in China; the government's apprehensions about the declaration of human rights which was being discussed at the U.N. General Assembly because much of the subject-matter came under provincial jurisdiction; problems relating to the new nine-nation Commonwealth, especially how to reconcile India's decision to become a republic with its desire to remain in the Commonwealth; the attitude to be adopted to Ireland when it left the Commonwealth.

Not all the problems which piled up in my in-basket were as solemn as these. One day I received an invitation from the Czechoslovakian legation to a reception 'in honour of the fifth anniversary of the liberation of Czechoslovakia *by the Soviet army*' (my italics). My recommendation that cabinet ministers and civil servants should not accept the invitation was adopted. I wrote my mother:

To put propaganda in invitation cards especially when it involves re-writing history is too galling ... It opens vistas of paying off official social obligations at no cost by inviting people to parties in such a way that they could not accept, e.g., inviting Americans to a celebration of the defeat of the American aggressors at Queenston Heights; French to a party in honour of the liberation of Canada from French tyranny by the defeat of France on the plains of Abraham; Russians to celebrate the expulsion of Russia from the soil of North America by the U.S. purchase of Alaska.

To deal with the many problems which demanded consideration in the late 1940s, the Department of External Affairs had only seventy-one officers in Ottawa and of these only twenty-seven had been in the external affairs service for at least three years. (Thirty years later nine times as many foreign service officers in Ottawa had served for three years or more.) My difficulties as acting under-secretary were compounded because I did not inherit the office and staff of the under-secretary; Pearson kept them. It took me time to create a staff but fortunately I chose well: Herbert Moran, Bruce Williams, Sybil Rump, Ruth Hyde.

General Charles Foulkes, the chairman of the chiefs of staff, and I were neighbours. I told him once that my wife often complained to me that she did not see why I did not get home from the office till 6:30 or later whereas Charles got home a little after four. Charles said: 'Brooke Claxton [the minister of national defence] has also talked to me about my going home so early. He said to me one morning: "Charles, I tried to get you by phone yesterday a little after four and they said you'd gone home." I said: "I always leave my office at four. If I can't organize my office well enough that I can leave at four you'd better get yourself another chairman of the chiefs of staff." ' By thus conserving his resources Foulkes was able to serve for the fifteen tumultuous years from 1945 to 1960, first as chief of the general staff and then as chairman of the chiefs of staff. I have never profited by Foulkes's example. If I had, Arnold Heeney might have been able to make a more favourable assessment of my six months' tenure as acting under-secretary when he wrote to Norman Robertson in February 1949 just before he took over the department from me:

In the Department, Escott has really done a remarkably good job under very difficult circumstances. On the whole, too, he has managed under great pressure to restrain his natural impulses and his natural dispositions to carry the torch high in every direction simultaneously ... Mike, because of his necessary preoccupation with the Cabinet and the House and politics generally, cannot give the time required to Departmental personnel and other problems. At the same time, Escott is constantly pressing him for decisions with that sense of urgency which he manages to attach to so many matters of varying importance.

It is no exaggeration to characterize as revolutionary the changes which took place in Canadian foreign policy from 1947 to 1951. At the beginning of 1947, Canada was virtually a disarmed nation. Its armed forces had totaled 800,000 during the war; by the beginning of 1947 they had been reduced to 43,000. At that time there were no countries with which Canada was joined in a formal mutual undertaking to go to war if the other were attacked; Canada had no allies. The few troops it had were all at home. It had no thought of making regular contributions to the economic development of poor countries. Within five years Canada's defence expenditures had tripled; for the first time in its history, it became in peace-time a member of a military alliance; as a member of that alliance, it had armed forces stationed in Germany as part of the North Atlantic forces; as a member of the United Nations it had an army brigade and naval units fighting in Korea under the United Nations command; and it had become a member of the Colombo Plan for co-operative economic development in South and Southeast Asia.

In 1967 I advanced a related thesis, that the years from 1941 to 1951 constituted a golden decade in Canadian foreign policy.[2] I said that in those years, from shortly after the fall of France to the early years of the North Atlantic alliance, Canada, because of a peculiar and temporary set of circumstances, became one of an inner group of three countries which moulded the shape of the future:

The issues on which we became one of the top three Western powers along with the United States and Britain had to do, not with the waging of war, but with the creation of post-war international institutions. It was Canadians who helped the British and Americans to create the International Monetary Fund and the World Bank. The same was, I know, true of the international conference at Chicago in 1944 which founded the International Civil Aviation Organization. It was, I think, true of the formation of UNRRA and the Food and Agriculture Organization. It was most certainly true of the long negotiations on the formation of the North Atlantic Alliance.

One of my happiest memories of my time in External Affairs was going with Pearson to the conference of foreign ministers of the Commonwealth held in Colombo, Ceylon (now Sri Lanka) in January 1950 – the one and only conference of Commonwealth foreign ministers – and visiting with him Pakistan, India, Burma, Singapore, Hong Kong, and Japan. When Pearson announced at a press conference the names of the advisers who were to accompany him on his round-the-world trip he said that P.M. Beaupré of the Department of Trade and Commerce was an expert on trade, Arthur Menzies an expert on the Far East, Douglas LePan an

2 'Canadian foreign policy 1967–1977: A Second Golden Decade,' *International Journal* (Spring 1967); this article was a slightly revised version of speech given at the annual dinner of the Canadian Centenary Council, Ottawa, 1 February 1967.

expert on economics, and Escott Reid an expert on – and he paused for what seemed to me an excruciatingly long period – everything.

We left Ottawa in a pelting rain storm on 2 January 1950. The plane was an unpressurized North Star. As soon as it left the ground we knew that it was noisy and it was not long before we discovered that the constant vibrations had a worse effect on us than the noise. It took us five days to get to Colombo; we made refuelling stops at Gander and the Azores, and we stopped overnight at Gibraltar, Malta, Suez, and Karachi. By the time we reached Colombo my brain had turned into a soggy mass of damp cottonwool. Pearson asked me to draft a speech for him to give at the opening of the conference. Normally I could have done it in half an hour; it took me two hours.

I was charmed by my first glimpse of semitropical South Asia and its people, and the land and people have never lost their charm for me. The day after we arrived in Colombo I wrote: 'Ceylon, we all liked from the moment we saw its green coconut palm plantations from the plane and we all fell in love with it after we had driven only about two of the fifteen miles from the airport to the city of Colombo ... The road is one long village and the houses are close to the road. The road was lined with people who grinned at us as we drove by ... Every one from small child to gaunt old man or woman carries himself superbly. It comes from carrying pots on their heads. And they are cheerful and clean.'

A few weeks later at a dinner in Karachi I met members of the Pakistan governing class: cabinet ministers, members of parliament, senior civil servants and their wives. 'Many of the men,' I wrote, were 'outrageously handsome and many of the women very beautiful and in lovely saris.' They were 'homesick for Delhi which contains "their" historic Muslim buildings.' They lived in 'beautiful houses in beautiful walled gardens with refugees living in things which we wouldn't use for chicken coops between the walls of their gardens and the street.' A garden party at Government House in Karachi 'had all the pomp of the British vice-regal regime – six-foot Punjabis in scarlet Lancer uniforms, ... military band in kilts, waiters in red tunics and white baggy trousers.'

In New Delhi we attended the dinner given by Prime Minister Nehru in honour of the retiring governor general, C. Rajagopalachari, two days before India was to become a republic. In those days, in India as in Canada, women curtsied when presented to the governor general. Before the dinner we were all lined up around the vast drawing-room so that the governor general could walk along the line and be introduced to the guests. I was standing beside Lady Nye, the wife of the British high commissioner. When her turn came she made a deep, deep curtsy. Rajagopalachari said, in his piping high voice, 'That will be your last opportunity to do that, my dear.'

This was the biggest state dinner I had ever been at, about 110 people with about fifty servants dressed in crimson with gay headgear. No alcohol, before, during, or after dinner. I sat beside Raghavan Pillai, who was about to become secretary of cabinet. He began smoking immediately after the dessert. I said to him that clearly in New Delhi they didn't have the same trouble about smoking at state dinners as we had in Ottawa where you couldn't smoke until after the toast to the king. A minute later Nehru rose and said, 'Your Excellency, ladies and gentlemen, the King.' The band played the first bars of 'God Save the King' and we drank the last toast to the sovereign of India to be drunk in the vice-regal palace in India. I wrote the next day: 'I had a feeling that if they had been able to put off their decision [to become a republic] for a year, they would have been so happy at working themselves the symbols of royalty that they might not have become a republic.'

The event in our visit to Tokyo which stands out most clearly in my mind is the briefing we received from a general on MacArthur's staff on the United States' occupation of Japan. Beside the general was a stand on which placards were put. On the other side of the stand was a major. When the general tapped the lectern with his pointer the major would change the placard. A placard would list the principal objectives the United States had when it occupied Japan. The general would say, 'The principal objectives we had when we occupied Japan were' and he would recite what was on the placard. Subsequent placards would deal with how the United States had achieved each objective. According to the briefing the United States knew from the start exactly what it wanted to achieve and it had achieved all its objectives. No objective was modified in the light of experience. Everything went according to plan. I had never heard anything more unconvincing.

After the Colombo conference was over Pearson sent a long telegram to Ottawa which I had drafted giving his preliminary impressions.[3] The conference had accomplished its main objective, providing the non-Asian members of the Commonwealth with an opportunity to gain a better understanding of the points of view of the Asian members on some of the main questions of foreign policy, especially those relating to Southeast Asia, Burma, Indo-China, and Malaya. 'I was, myself, greatly impressed by the arguments put forward by both the United Kingdom and

3 Pearson to Heeney, telegram 133 of February 1950, DEA file 299, Ds

India for recognition of the Communist government of China. Mr. Nehru advocated with support from Mr. Bevin that recognition should be followed by adoption of a cautious but not unfriendly policy which would have the best chance of encouraging the new government to pursue a policy independent of the Soviet Union.' When at one meeting Nehru was asked what advice he would give the French about Vietnam, 'he said he would be inclined to urge them to try to bring about a rapprochement between Bao Dai [the emperor of Vietnam] and Ho-Chi-Minh on the basis of arranging for free elections with a view to the appointment of a constituent assembly which might devise means of establishing a new single government.' What tragedies would have been averted if Nehru's advice had been taken.

Pearson in his telegram went on to say that one useful purpose which the meeting served was to provide an intensive course in the realities of present Commonwealth relations for the new Australian and New Zealand ministers of external affairs:

Their parties have been out of office during a period in which there have been very great changes in the nature of the Commonwealth and the new ministers might, therefore, have been expected to have a rather out-of-date view of Commonwealth relations. The New Zealand representative, Doidge, at the beginning of the conference, was talking about New Zealand being 'a daughter in her mother's house but mistress of her own.' I think he now realizes that this view of the Commonwealth is not held by any of the other Commonwealth external affairs ministers.

Three incidents at the conference stand out in my memory. Norman Brooke, the secretary of the British cabinet, was secretary of the conference. He had been the secretary of many of the meetings of Commonwealth prime ministers and had been responsible for having full summaries of discussions prepared and circulated. He told me one morning, when we were breakfasting together, that one of the younger British assistant secretaries of the conference had come to him and said: 'I am so disappointed by the level of the discussion at this conference. I have read the minutes of recent conferences of Commonwealth prime ministers. Those men spoke like statesmen.' Norman Brooke replied: 'Don't you realize that it is the task of those who write the minutes of Commonwealth meetings to make all the ministers sound like statesmen. Some can sound even more statesmanlike than others.'

The chairman of the Colombo conference was the prime minister of

Ceylon, who was also foreign minister, Dudley Senanayake. Whenever the discussion was in danger of becoming too heated he would say: 'I think it is time we all had a cup of tea.' A bevy of dignified liveried servants would come in with tea. The formal discussion would be automatically adjourned. There would be opportunities for quiet informal talks and fifteen minutes later the meeting would resume with temperatures back to normal.

At the final meeting of the conference each of the foreign ministers summed up his views. Ernest Bevin had been a mountain of wisdom at the conference and his British civil servants were proud of him, but when it came to his turn to speak he said that until recently Asia had been 'queeshunt.' His British advisers, who were usually impassive at the meetings, could not disguise their bewilderment. They did not know what he was saying; they had never before heard this pronunciation of quiescent.

During the six years prior to the Colombo conference I had attended many international meetings at which about fifty nations were represented. It was a relief to find myself in Colombo at a conference of only eight nations: Britain, Canada, Australia, New Zealand, South Africa, India, Pakistan, and Ceylon. This made informal discussion much easier, much more illuminating. But it was not just the small number of participants which made the difference; it was that the participants all spoke the same language (and the best English was spoken by Nehru whose mother tongue was Urdu) and there was not that barrier to comprehension which exists when speeches have to be interpreted. Moreover, all the participants in Commonwealth meetings at that time had, as Nehru put it in a talk during his visit to Ottawa in 1949, been trained within the framework of constitutional structures very closely allied to the British parliamentary system and on the basis of British rules of parliamentary discussion. There were no procedural debates at Colombo, unlike the United Nations at that time where there were interminable debates on procedure.

I was also impressed by the fact that these nine nations constituted a fairly representative group of the non-communist world: the most important nation in Western Europe; a North American nation; two Australasian nations; a South African nation; the second most populous country of Asia; one of the two most populous Muslim states of the world; a Buddhist nation; rich white countries; poor coloured countries. I knew that every view of the world suffers from distortions; the Colombo conference made me realize better how we in Ottawa could be helped to a less distorted view of the world by seeing it through the eyes of nations with different traditions from ours, different concepts of national interest, different emotional reactions to world events, different views of the world.

One of the strengths of the Commonwealth as we saw it at Colombo lay in the calibre of its leaders. The two who stood out were Nehru and Ernest Bevin. Nehru dominated the conference by his charm, his knowledge and intelligence, his capacity for lucid exposition of his views. My friend and colleague at the conference, Douglas LePan, scholar and poet, wrote immediately after the conference:

Nehru sat at the conference table at Colombo impassive, reflective, smoking cigarettes in a long black holder and blowing the smoke through his nostrils. An air of elegance informed the way he wore his close-fitting, mulberry-coloured ashkan and the way he spoke. His contributions to the discussion were always even-tempered and philosophical. He combined, in his own person, at least as wide a knowledge of the whole range of western civilization as any of his Western colleagues along with a passionate concern for the nationalist aspirations of Asian peoples and for their economic advancement ... Even when he was not speaking he was often the centre of interest, partly because of the importance of the country he represented and partly because such great issues depend on his strength and wisdom and magnanimity.[4]

A year and a half after the Colombo conference I sent F.H. Soward, then an officer in the department, comments on a memorandum he had prepared on Canada and the Commonwealth. I said that I thought he had not sufficiently emphasized the changes which had taken place in the attitude of the Canadian government to the Commonwealth. Would it have been possible to imagine five years before that Canada would agree to a permanent Commonwealth secretariat (the secretariat in Colombo of the Colombo Plan), that there would be a Commonwealth army division which included Canadian troops (the Commonwealth division in Korea), that Canada would have participated in more meetings of Commonwealth cabinet ministers in the past three years than in the preceding ten, and that the ministers who attended those meetings were convinced of their value, especially as a bridge between the democratic nations of the west and the democratic nations of the east?

4 D.V. LePan, 'Around the World in 1,500 Words,' unpublished, undated memorandum, written at the request of the Department of External Affairs for one of its official publications but not used. NAC, Escott Reid Papers

To my mind the watershed in Canadian policy was India's decision to remain in the Commonwealth. This has resulted in the creation of a new Commonwealth. It is no wonder, therefore, that Canadian policy has changed towards the Commonwealth since it is a different Commonwealth which we are dealing with in 1951 than the one we were dealing with in 1946 ... My guess is that [these] tendencies ... will probably become more marked during the next few years and this will partly be the result of an almost unconcious reaction to the increasing power of the United States in the world.

At the Colombo conference the Colombo Plan for Co-operative Economic Development in South and Southeast Asia was conceived. It had pre-natal care at a conference in Australia and was brought to birth at a conference in London. If anyone had asked me before I left Ottawa whether it was practical politics to suggest that Canada should make a gift of $25 million a year to the Commonwealth countries in South and Southeast Asia to help them speed up the pace of their economic development, I would have replied that it certainly was not. What made it possible was that the Colombo Plan was a Commonwealth concept, that the countries to which the gifts were to be given were Commonwealth countries in Asia, and that the membership in the Commonwealth of these new Asian nations had struck the imagination of the Canadian people. In many ways the acceptance by Canada of the Colombo Plan is the most revolutionary of the changes in Canadian foreign policy which took place from 1946 to 1952. Alliances and rearmament are familiar patterns in history. Organized regular giving from the governments of wealthy countries to the governments of poor countries for the purpose of helping them speed up their economic development is an unfamiliar pattern in history.[5]

It was not easy for Pearson to persuade his colleagues in cabinet to agree that they should take the unprecedented step of asking Parliament to vote money to be given to poor countries. Almost all the senior civil servants concerned with the government's economic policy were initially opposed to Canada's giving $25 million a year to the Colombo Plan. Almost all the cabinet was opposed or uninterested. It was three men who finally succeeded in persuading a reluctant cabinet to approve the grant – St Laurent, Pearson, and Robert Mayhew. Mayhew, the cabinet

---

5 D.V. LePan has written about the beginnings of the Colombo Plan in his essay entitled 'A Problem Broached' in his book of memoirs, *Bright Glass of Memory* (Toronto: McGraw-Hill Ryerson 1979).

minister from British Columbia, had accompanied Pearson to India and Pakistan after the Colombo conference. He and Pearson had seen with their own eyes something of the terrifying, indescribable poverty of the Indian subcontinent. They had seen something of what India and Pakistan were trying to do to lift themselves out of their poverty. They were convinced that Canada should help them.

In the 1950s membership in the Commonwealth helped Canada to break out of the confines of Canadian isolationism, North American isolationism, North Atlantic isolationism. It helped to inoculate Canada from some of the misleading simplicities of much of the cold war propaganda of the time. It helped us realize, sooner than we otherwise would have, that most of the crucial problems before the world are not in their pith and substance aspects of a struggle against communism. It helped us to face these crucial problems: colonialism and its aftermath, racial discrimination, cultural imperialism, the misery of half of the people of the world.

During the discussions in the United Nations from 1947 to 1949 of the future of the British mandate of Palestine I was so deeply involved in the Canadian crusade for the North Atlantic treaty that I tried to keep on the sidelines in discussions on the Palestine problem within the Department of External Affairs. My efforts met with so little success that I was attacked by Prime Minister Mackenzie King because he thought I was critical of the British government for not supporting the pro-Zionist policy of the United States and attacked by an envoy of the Israeli government for being hostile to Israel. I am proud of this evidence of my impartiality.

My most vivid memory of this period is not of these two attacks on me but of King's attack on Pearson on 23 March 1948 in a talk with St Laurent and me. St Laurent was then foreign minister and Pearson was under-secretary for external affairs. Pearson was in Washington for the top secret talks between the United States, Britain, and Canada on the possibility of creating a North Atlantic alliance and I was acting under-secretary. I had to have a few minutes' talk with St Laurent on an item on the cabinet agenda for that day. He agreed to meet me outside the cabinet office just before the meeting of cabinet. We had our talk. King came up and joined us. Almost immediately he launched on a scathing attack on Pearson's activities on the problem of Palestine. Look where his ignorant activities have got us! Why does he think he knows anything about the Palestine problem? Why hasn't he enough sense to follow the lead of the British with their long and profound knowledge of the Near and Middle East? He went on and on. I took my cue from St Laurent and said nothing.

St Laurent as foreign minister was responsible for the activities of his senior civil servant, Pearson. When King attacked Pearson he was reprimanding St Laurent for failing to curb Pearson's activities. King could have done this in a private talk with St Laurent. Why did he reprimand him in front of me? I do not know. I did not understand King then. I do not understand him now.

In his diary for that day King wrote of the discussion in cabinet on Palestine which took place immediately after our talk outside the cabinet office and referred to that talk: 'Next came the question as to what was to be done at the U.N. in regard to Palestine. The officials of the Dept. [of External Affairs] had prepared something along the lines of our continuing to give support to what the Americans are now proposing. Notwithstanding that Britain is holding rigidly aloof ... I had talked privately with St Laurent about our not again committing ourselves on matters that we know nothing about.'

After the meeting of cabinet Arnold Heeney, the secretary of cabinet, sent me the record of this discussion in the cabinet minutes and on the basis of this I dictated a telegram to Norman Robertson, our high commissioner in London, instructing him to discuss the Palestine question with Ernest Bevin, the British foreign minister.[6] Before sending the telegram I showed it to St Laurent and he approved it. When he approved it he obviously believed that it faithfully reflected the discussions in cabinet that morning – but not King. In his diary three days later he wrote: 'I reread the statement sent by Reid to Norman Robertson. I felt quite incensed on reading it over.'

In my message to Robertson I had said that we found it difficult to believe that the policy of the British government on Palestine was as negative as their public declarations and the private conversations of their representatives would lead us to believe and I asked Robertson to press Bevin to let us know what he felt was the best policy for countries like Canada to support in the Security Council now that partition with economic union could not be carried into effect. What incensed King about this statement was, as he put it in his diary, our 'talking about Britain's attitude as negative ... [when it was] positive, based on the

6 Telegram 418 of 23 March 1948 to high commissioner in London, DEA files, File 74B(s)

sound maxim that while speech was silver, silence was golden.' Nor did he think it was fair of us to press Bevin to answer our question about the policy Canada might follow in the Security Council.

In his diary King did not allude to what St Laurent and I believed was the most important passage in the telegram to Robertson: 'We feel that in the present grave international emergency it is just not possible that the United Kingdom and the United States are going to continue to be divided' on the Palestine question, especially with the discussions on the proposed North Atlantic treaty going on in Washington. It was then touch-and-go whether the State Department, let alone the president and the Senate, would support the idea of a treaty, and we feared that the possibility of support would be greatly lessened if the British and American governments continued to differ over Palestine. We received confirmation of our fears six weeks later when Dean Rusk told Pearson that an understanding between the United States and Britain over Palestine was necessary if the North Atlantic treaty was to be concluded.[7]

The attack on me by the Israeli ambassador in Washington, Eliahu Epstein, took place on 7 February 1949, eleven months later. I was once again acting under-secretary, Pearson having become foreign minister. Before Epstein called on Pearson, he had an hour's talk with me on whether Canada, now that it had on the previous 24 December granted *de facto* recognition to Israel, would support Israel's application to be admitted to the United Nations instead of abstaining as it had when the issue had been voted on in the Security Council on 17 December. I said I could not answer his question but I could say that it would be easier for us to support Israel if Israel were to co-operate with the United Nations on three issues. In the armistice negotiations at Rhodes, Israel was apparently insisting on retaining all the territory it had won since 14 October of the previous year by its violations of the truce. Israel had installed a civil administrator in the Israeli-occupied new city of Jerusalem in place of the military governor, apparently with the intention of forestalling action by the United Nations Conciliation Commission leading to the establishment of an international administration of the whole of Jerusalem, new and old. We were concerned by repeated indications that the Israeli authorities intended to settle Jewish immigrants on properties belonging to Arab refugees in disregard of the Assembly's resolution of 11 December 1948 on their repatriation. (Our information at the time was that 910,000 Arabs in Palestine had been displaced.[8])

7 Escott Reid, *Time of Fear and Hope* (Toronto: McClelland and Stewart 1977), 52, 111
8 *Canada and the United Nations 1949*, DEA, 56

In my report to Pearson on my talk with Epstein I said that Epstein had given the usual Israeli replies to these criticisms: nothing which Israel was doing prejudiced the final peace settlement; Israel did not want an international administration of Jerusalem; Israel did not want the Arab refugees to be repatriated with the exception of Christian Arabs and the Druse.[9]

Epstein in his report to the Israeli foreign minister on his talk with me,[10] said that he found me extremely unfriendly on the question of Canadian support for Israel's admission to the United Nations. 'He accused us of rejecting and counteracting decisions of the Security Council, especially the resolution on Jerusalem ... He was very critical of our attitude to the Arab refugee question.' Epstein did not give me credit for independent thinking. He wrote that when he saw Elizabeth MacCallum after his talk with me he easily discovered that 'she inspired Mr. Reid's views on Israel and the Arabs ... She is the main source of anti-Israeli influence in the Ministry of External Affairs.'

After seeing me Epstein saw Pearson. In his report on this interview Epstein said: 'In the course of the conversation, I mentioned cautiously the unfavourable impression I got from my talk with Reid. Pearson smiled and said that I should not consider Mr. Reid's views as those of the Ministry, and should completely disregard his opinion on the subject of our admission to the United Nations.' My respect for Pearson is such that I do not believe he would have made to a representative of a foreign government so unqualified a repudiation of what his senior adviser in his department had said to that representative.

Epstein's report of Pearson's views on Israel's admission to the United Nations was that 'as things stand today' Canada would support admission 'provided that nothing happened in the meanwhile which could be interpreted as a violation of the cease-fire order by Israel.' Pearson's account of what he said to Epstein differs only slightly. He wrote at the end of my memorandum on what I had said to Epstein that he had told Epstein that 'Unless Israel took some action which would make it impossible for us to recognize her as a "peace-loving state" I would recommend to the government that we support her application for membership in the U.N. when it next was made.' He made no comment on the three issues on which I had told Epstein we felt particular concern.

The debate in the U.N. Assembly on Israel's admission took place three months later. The Canadian representative, Gerry Riddell, in sup-

9 Two memoranda for s.s.e.a. from e.r., 7 February 1949, dea files, File 47B(s)
10 Israeli Foreign Office, box 2414, file 19, Elath (Epstein) to minister of foreign affairs, 24 February 1949

porting Israel's admission, said on 6 May 1949 that he thought the Assembly should avoid debate on the three issues with which the Conciliation Commission, which was meeting in Switzerland, was dealing (the issues I had raised with Epstein): 'final boundary adjustments, Arab refugees, and the future of Jerusalem.' He referred to the 'undertakings' which the Israeli representative had given the Assembly 'concerning the protection of the holy places' and to the Israeli government having 'pledged itself to full cooperation' on the issue of Arab refugees, and he concluded by stating that the Canadian delegation expected that the parties which were then engaged in the negotiations in Switzerland would so act that solutions to the problems of boundary adjustments, Arab refugees, and the future of Jerusalem would 'be reached within the meaning and spirit of the resolutions of the Assembly and the Security Council and of the aims and purposes of the United Nations.'[11]

No such solutions were reached then or later. The only boundary adjustments which have been made have resulted from successful Israeli military activities. Arab refugees have not been permitted to return to Israel. There is no international regime for Jerusalem. I wonder whether the world, and especially Israel, might not be better off if the Assembly had in 1949 decided to postpone consideration of Israel's application for membership in the U.N. until it had given satisfaction on boundaries, refugees, and Jerusalem.

The vote on 11 May on Israel's admission to the U.N. was thirty-seven in favour, twelve against, and nine abstentions, including Britain, Belgium, Denmark, Greece, and Sweden. Twelve of the eighteen Asian and African states voted against the resolution; the only ones which voted in favour were China (Taiwan), Philippines, Liberia, and South Africa and at that time the first three were client states of the United States; Siam and Turkey abstained. Of the thirty-seven supporters of the resolution, eighteen were Latin American republics and six were members of the Soviet bloc. This line-up in the vote presaged difficulties for Israel in the Assembly once the number of Asian and African member states increased and Israel no longer had the support of the Soviet bloc.

Sunday, 25 June 1950, was a particularly lovely day. It was our older son's nineteenth birthday and we were having a family celebration at our farm in the Gatineau hills northwest of Ottawa. Our younger son had just finished converting a rowboat into a sailboat and he and I went

---

11 Telegram of 6 May 1948 from Riddell to External Affairs, RG 25 84-85/019, box 143, F.5475-CR-2-40

sailing on it that afternoon on Lac Gauvreau. There was little breeze and we were becalmed. A rowboat approached us. In it to my surprise was Mary Macdonald, Pearson's secretary, who had a cottage on the other side of the lake from our farm. She told me that she had just heard over the radio that North Korea had invaded South Korea.

I was not greatly perturbed by the news. It never crossed my mind that the United States might intervene with military force in support of South Korea. I do not recall what I thought at the time the invasion would lead to. Perhaps my forecast was similar to that of my friend Gladwyn Jebb of the British Foreign Office. He, like me, heard the news while he was at his place in the country. In his memoirs he writes that he thought 'the probability surely was that somehow or other the invasion of South Korea – if it were an invasion – would result in the collapse of the rather unpopular and seemingly not very democratic Syngman Rhee and the formation of a new government that would make a new deal with the North, thus unifying the country.'[12]

For the next four years as deputy under-secretary in Ottawa and as high commissioner to India I was deeply involved in the crises piled upon crises precipitated by the North Korean invasion, crises which carried with them the threat that the Korean War might lead to the third world war. I believe that the two occasions we have come closest to a third world war were the Cuban missile crisis in 1962 and the ten months from the outbreak of the Korean War in June 1950 to the dismissal of General MacArthur in April 1951.

The rapid unpredictable swings between near defeat in Korea and near victory intensified the strains imposed by the war. In the first few weeks of the war North Korea overran almost the whole of South Korea, only a small perimeter around Pusan in the southeast corner of the peninsula remaining unoccupied. Four months later the U.N. forces drove the North Koreans back almost to the Chinese border. Within another month the Chinese and North Korean forces pushed the U.N. forces so far back that the United States joint chiefs of staff contemplated the possible evacuation of the U.N. forces to Japan.

On 26 June, the day after the invasion, we still believed in the Department of External Affairs that the United States would not intervene with military force in Korea. This was the belief of Pearson, of Hume Wrong, our ambassador in Washington, and of John Holmes, our acting representative to the U.N. in New York. This belief was shattered the next morning when the United States informed us that it had decided to

12 *The Memoirs of Lord Gladwyn* (London: Weidenfeld and Nicolson 1972), 228

give air and naval support to the South Korean forces and was asking the U.N. Security Council to pass a resolution that afternoon recommending 'that the Members of the United Nations furnish such assistance to the Republic of Korea as may be necessary to repel the armed attack and to restore international peace and security in the area.' The last three words, inserted by Jack Hickerson of the State Department, were the joker in the resolution and we unsuccessfully objected to them; they enabled the United States government to contend later that the 'area' was the whole of Korea and that the U.N. had authorized military action in North Korea, not merely the expulsion of the invaders from South Korea.

News of the passage of the resolution reached us on the evening of 27 June, not long after we had learned that the North Korean forces had occupied Seoul, the capital of South Korea. Douglas LePan and I immediately went to work and by midnight he had produced a speech for Pearson and I a draft of a memorandum to him entitled 'The extent of the obligations of Canada, as a member of the United Nations, to participate in United Nations police action to restore peace in the Republic of Korea.' The conclusion of my memorandum was:

Canada has conferred on the Security Council primary responsibility for the maintenance of international peace and security and has agreed that in carrying out its duties under this responsibility the Security Council acts on behalf of Canada. Canada conferred this power on the Security Council in order to ensure prompt and effective action by the United Nations ... The Security Council, under a specific power given to it by Article 39, has determined that the armed attack upon the Republic of Korea by forces from North Korea constitutes a breach of the peace ... [and] has made a recommendation to Canada that Canada furnish such assistance to the Republic of Korea as may be necessary to repel the armed attack and to restore international peace and security in the area. Canada has undertaken to give to the United Nations every assistance in any action it takes in accordance with the Charter. It has also undertaken to fulfill in good faith the obligations assumed by it under the Charter.[13]

By 30 June I had become convinced that it was essential that the members of the North Atlantic alliance, including Canada, should greatly increase their expenditures on defence. The reasoning which led me to this conclusion was that the North Koreans would not have invaded

13 Memorandum of 30 June 1950, sent to the minister by Arnold Heeney on 6 July 1950, DEA file 11073-40

South Korea without the blessing of the Soviet Union; that the Soviet Union must have known that there was a possibility a war in Korea might spread and might ultimately lead to a third world war; that to deter the Soviet Union from taking more such dangerous risks the North Atlantic alliance must rearm.

I now think I was probably mistaken in believing in 1950 that when the Soviet Union gave its blessing to the North Korean invasion of South Korea it knew it was running a risk of precipitating a third world war. If, as Denis Stairs has put it in his book on the war, we in Ottawa 'so closely familiar with the American policy-making community ... [believed] after the war had broken out that the United States would not intervene militarily, the Soviet Union probably made the same mistake.'[14] Charles Bohlen, at that time one of the principal American experts on the Soviet Union in the State Department, believes that 'Stalin never dreamed the United States would intervene.'[15] If Stalin did not dream the United States would intervene then he did not consider that the war between North and South Korea could lead to a third world war. If I was mistaken in this, was I likewise mistaken in believing that a vast program of rearmament by the North Atlantic alliance was required to deter Stalin from running risks of precipitating a third world war? I now think that a more modest program would probably have sufficed. Charles Bohlen believes that all that was required was 'a slight increase in the American military budget.'[16]

The vast program of rearmament was accompanied, under pressure from the United States, by the admission of Greece and Turkey to the North Atlantic alliance, the armament of West Germany, the appointment of a supreme commander, and the creation of the North Atlantic Treaty Organization. The North Atlantic alliance was militarized and it became less and less likely that it would lead to the political and economic unification of the North Atlantic community. I sometimes wonder whether one reason Dean Acheson advocated American armed intervention in Korea was that he hoped it would have these results.

On 14 July, the secretary general of the United Nations thanked Canada for providing three destroyers for the U.N. forces in Korea and appealed for a contribution of ground forces. It took us three weeks to agree to this and during these three weeks the United States government

14 Denis Stairs, *The Diplomacy of Constraint: Canada, the Korean War and the United States* (Toronto: University of Toronto Press 1974), 41n
15 Charles Bohlen, *Witness to History* (New York: W.W. Norton 1973), 295
16 Ibid., 304

put ever-increasing pressure on us to agree. General Charles Foulkes, the chairman of the chiefs of staff, told me at the time that the government had doubted whether it would be possible to get sufficient recruits to man a brigade and that he had said: 'There will be no difficulty at all. The war has been over for four years. There are plenty of men who served in the war who are now so sick and tired of their wives and children that they would welcome an opportunity to enlist for service overseas.' The three weeks' delay in agreeing to send ground forces to Korea was unfortunate. I think we would have got more credit in Washington for offering one battalion in mid-July than a brigade three weeks later. An American general in the civil war said that the secret of success in battle was to get there firstest with the mostest men. Our motto in mid-July should have been to get there firstest with the fewest men.

The next crisis occurred in September and the first week of October when the United States pressed the U.N. Assembly to approve a resolution which could be interpreted as authorizing U.N. forces to cross the 38th parallel, the border between North and South Korea. I was acting under-secretary at the time and Pearson was in New York at the Assembly. I bombarded him with telegrams, mostly written by Arthur Menzies, setting forth the arguments against crossing the border. Since I seemed to be getting nowhere I appealed for support to Norman Robertson who was then secretary of cabinet. He entirely agreed with me on the folly of the United States' proposal and said he would telephone Pearson to urge him not to support it. A few hours later he told me that Pearson said to him, 'Norman, you have no idea what the pressure is like here. I can't possibly oppose the resolution.' A demonstration of the nature of the situation which confronted Pearson in New York was the overwhelming support for the resolution when it came to the vote on 7 October: forty-seven in favour, five against, and seven abstentions.

We had no inkling at the time that both the policy planning staff of the State Department and the Central Intelligence Agency opposed the crossing of the 38th parallel. The policy planning staff in a draft memorandum of 22 July said: 'The risks of bringing on a major conflict with the U.S.S.R. or Communist China, if U.N. military action north of the 38th parallel is employed in an effort to reach a "final" settlement in Korea, appear to outweigh the political advantages that might be gained from such further military action.' The conclusion of the CIA study of 18 August was that 'the military success of the operation is by no means assured because the U.S. ... might ... become involved in hostilities with Chinese

Communist and Soviet troops. Under such circumstances there would, moreover, be grave risks of general war.'[17]

If only one of the people who had access to these memoranda had considered that the public interest required him to leak them to the press, or if an intelligence agent of a country opposed to the crossing of the parallel had got hold of them and had them published, the disastrous error of the crossing of the 38th parallel might have been avoided. For the U.N. forces to stop at the 38th parallel made political sense; to stop at the narrow waist of Korea half-way between the parallel and the Chinese border made military sense; to advance to the Yalu River, the boundary between North Korea and China, made no sense. General MacArthur's advance to the Yalu resulted in China intervening in the war on 26 November with massive armed forces which drove the U.N. forces back in disorder far beyond the 38th parallel and, as the CIA had warned, created 'grave risks of a general war.'

I had no success in this crisis, but I did have some success in the next crisis. On 14 November Arnold Heeney told me that the American ambassador had just left with him an aide-memoire stating that the United States government considered that it might soon become necessary for United Nations aircraft to pursue attacking enemy aircraft over the Yalu River into Chinese airspace and that he had told the ambassador that the Canadian government would recognize the justification of such action. I was appalled by the United States' proposal and by Heeney's concurrence in it, and I put to him the arguments against concurring. He asked me to telephone Pearson who was in Windsor. Pearson's immediate reaction that there should be no pursuit of hostile planes into Chinese airspace until the Communist Chinese government had been warned that if hostile planes continued to use Chinese airspace the U.N. command would have to permit hot pursuit; the warning should preferably be given through the United Nations. I wrote an answer to the American aide-memoire embodying Pearson's views and we gave it to the American embassy in Ottawa and to the State Department.[18]

A few days later an officer of the American embassy complained to me that we had shown no independence of judgment in our comments but had merely echoed what the British had said. I retorted that we had drafted our comments within two hours of receiving the American aide-memoire, well before we had learned of the views of the British.

17 *Foreign Relations of the United States Government* (FRUS) 1950 (Washington: U.S. Government Printing Office), vol. VII: Korea, 453, 600
18 The American ambassador's account of his talk with Heeney on 14 November is in ibid., 1155–6, and the Canadian aide-memoire of 15 November is on pp. 1159–60.

The Americans gave in to the unanimous opposition of their allies and did not authorize hot pursuit.

On 26 November, twelve days after this incident, China, which had been sending a comparatively few members of its armed forces across the border into Korea, sent in masses of troops and began the offensive which drove the U.N. forces back beyond the 38th parallel. We entered a nightmarish period in which we were haunted by the possibility that the Soviet Union might enter the war in support of China and the third world war would break out. I sweated blood doing what I could to reduce the risk of this happening. Pearson told me at the time that I was a diplomatic dynamo. But I was no piece of machinery. One evening in December, coming home exhausted from the office, I threw myself down on my bed sobbing with fear and frustration – the only time in my life I have broken down in this way.

Our fear in Ottawa that we might be on the edge of the abyss of a third world war was shared by the United States and by many other countries. Dean Acheson on 28 November, two days after Chinese troops had crossed the border in large numbers, said at a meeting with President Truman that 'we were much closer to the danger of general war.' On 2 December the CIA concluded that 'the U.S.S.R. is prepared to accept, and may be seeking to precipitate, a general war between the United States and China, despite the inherent risk of global war. The possibility cannot be disregarded that the U.S.S.R. may already have decided to precipitate global war in circumstances most advantageous to itself through the development of general war in Asia. We are unable, on the basis of present intelligence, to determine the probability of such a decision having in fact been made.'[19]

We shared the American government's fears. We did not share its belief in the wisdom of asking the U.N. Assembly to declare China an aggressor and we put the argument against this in a memorandum we gave the State Department on 27 December. I did a draft of this memorandum and Charles Ritchie and Douglas LePan came to my house on Sunday afternoon 17 December to go over it with me. I am proud of this memorandum which reads in part as follows:

With China on the march and all of Asia striking out on new paths, the strengthening of the free world which is now taking place [by the rearmament program] may provoke the leaders of the Soviet Union to strike within the next few months before our defences reach the point where the Soviet leaders can no longer believe

19 Ibid., 1310

in the possibility of an easy victory in Europe and Asia ... The necessity of doing nothing which might increase the danger of the Soviet Union precipitating a general war during this period ... means that our diplomacy must be wise and unprovocative and that, in playing for time in which to get stronger, we must continue to be as conciliatory as possible ... In order to leave the door open for negotiations the United Nations has so far deliberately and wisely refrained from naming Communist China an aggressor. The United Nations should continue this careful course as long as possible ... [After the next year or so] the strength of the free world, although still less than that of the Soviet Union, should be sufficient to deter the leaders of the Soviet Union from precipitating war. The uneasy equilibrium thus established may then make possible the working out of a *modus vivendi* with the Soviet Union.[20]

In spite of repeated efforts, Pearson failed to persuade the United States not to press the Assembly to declare China an aggressor, and when a resolution to this effect came to a vote on 1 February he declared that though it was 'premature and unwise' he would vote for it. The resolution was passed by a vote of forty-four in favour, seven against, and eight abstentions. I thought at the time that Pearson should not have voted for the resolution and I still think so. I believe before the vote was taken he should have informed countries which we knew shared our views that we intended to abstain in the vote and that we hoped they would abstain.

This decision by the Assembly strained the meaning of the term aggression. Gladwyn Jebb has written: 'The Chinese had after all not backed up the North Koreans at the beginning of the latter's undoubted aggression: all they had done, after due warning, was to intervene in order to save the North Koreans from total defeat involving the occupation of the entire country by the forces of the U.S.A.'[21] The branding of China as an aggressor was used by the United States for years afterwards to defend their absurd and costly policy of opposing the seating in the United Nations of representatives of Communist China.

Our constant fear in the course of the Korean War was that the United States government would pursue impatient and provocative policies in its relations with China and the Soviet Union. Our fears that General MacArthur would pursue such policies were much greater. We came eventually to believe that he was out of control of Washington and that he wanted to provoke a full-scale war with China. On 1 April 1951 I

20 Our memorandum of 27 December is in ibid., 1618–19.
21 Gladwyn, *Memoirs*, 243

wrote: 'MacArthur's insolent insubordination is getting worse and worse but he is too powerful politically to be fired. A German submarine saved the British from the much more minor embarrassment of Kitchener in 1915.' I underestimated President Truman; he dismissed MacArthur eight days later.

For the rest of that year there were no serious crises in the Korean War and at the beginning of 1952 I wrote my father:

I am beginning not to be afraid to be hopeful. If we can get through this year safely – and I think we can – the road ahead is going to be much less terrifying than the journey we have been making for the past four years. It was almost exactly four years ago that the first of the real postwar scares burst on us – the scare that precipitated the negotiation of the North Atlantic Treaty. For three years after that it was one scare after another, culminating in the terror of a year ago when it looked as if we might stumble into a general war by way of Korea and China. Something has saved us. I think that many righteous men must have been praying.

When I wrote this letter I thought there would be no more Korean crises. I was mistaken. In May 1952 a crisis broke out over the sending of a company of the Canadian brigade in Korea to help guard a prisoner-of-war camp on Koje island where about 44,000 prisoners were held by the United States army. The press had been full of stories about the chaotic conditions in the camp, which culminated in February 1952 in riots in which seventy-five prisoners were killed and over one hundred wounded, the capture by the prisoners of the American brigadier-general in command of the camp, and his release after his replacement had stated in writing that there had been 'instances of bloodshed where many prisoners of war have been killed and wounded by U.N. forces ... [and that] in the future the prisoners of war can expect humane treatment in this camp according to the principles of international law.'

On the afternoon of 22 May, Brooke Claxton, the minister of defence, telephoned me (I was acting under-secretary) to say that he had just learned from General Foulkes that the Commonwealth division in Korea had been ordered to provide two companies for Koje and that one Canadian company and one British company had been chosen. Claxton asked me to request Wrong to tell the United States that we did not like the proposal to send a Canadian company to Koje. Pearson was out of town and unreachable by telephone. I therefore telephoned St Laurent and he instructed me to ask Wrong to get in touch immediately with the secretary of state in an effort to get the order countermanded before the

Canadian company had left for Koje. We hoped that if this happened the incident would not become public. (We learned later that the Canadian company had started to move to Koje only one or two hours after Foulkes had been informed of the order to move.)

I gave St Laurent's message to Wrong by telephone at 6 p.m. and confirmed it by teletype:

You should inform Mr. Acheson that in the Prime Minister's opinion it would be more difficult to have our people agree to any additional contribution that may be required of them in Korea if a Canadian company were to be sent to help guard the Koje Island prison camp. It was, therefore, in his opinion, in the general interest of the United Nations that the Canadians should not be asked to do this.

After speaking to Wrong I telephoned St Laurent to tell him that Pearson had been in touch with Wrong and had suggested that we put off speaking to the State Department until we had learned what the British were doing about the sending of a British company to Koje. St Laurent said that the presence of a British company at Koje would make some difference but would not dispel his fear that the sending of a Canadian company to Koje 'might result in quite a reversal of feeling in Canada about our participation in the Korean war. There was a lot of anxiety in Canada about what has taken place at Koje Island and, regardless of what the government did, the sending of a Canadian company to Koje might have a considerable effect on opinion.'

We knew that there was no military reason for sending a few Canadian soldiers to Koje; the reason was political. The United States officers in Korea responsible for the order to the Commonwealth division wanted Canadian and British participation in guarding the camp as a demonstration that the guarding of the camp was a U.N. commitment, not a purely American one; we objected to being involved in the mess at Koje for which we bore no responsibility.

On 23 May, the day following our representations to the State Department, we learned that Reuters had issued a story from Tokyo that 'troops of the Commonwealth division may go to the U.N. prison camp on Koje island to keep order.' I immediately sought advice from Jack Pickersgill, the prime minister's principal secretary. I said we now had to assume that if the order to send the Canadian company to Koje were countermanded the story would become public. Pickersgill said that he thought the best argument to use in public, and Wrong could use it in Washington, was that traditionally the Canadian government had taken the line that its troops should serve as an entity and that our units should not be split up without political consultation. Pickersgill's advice was taken. We presented a note to the State Department on 26 May setting forth this argument and Pearson read the note that day to the House of Commons.

The position of the Canadian government on the Koje incident aroused anger in some Americans, notably Dean Acheson. It is ironic that Pearson, who had nothing to do with St Laurent's decision to protest to the United States and who, as soon as he heard of it, counselled caution, should have been the main recipient of Acheson's wrath.

In 1952 many Canadians were infuriated by the charges which James Endicott had been making both abroad and in Canada that the United States forces in Korea had been conducting bacteriological or germ warfare. Endicott had been a missionary in China and was an ardent supporter of the communist revolution there. His critics in Canada demanded that he be deprived of his passport. I am happy that I marshalled the arguments against this in a memorandum to Pearson in May 1952. When after thirty years this memorandum became public, a reporter in the Toronto *Globe and Mail* described it as eloquent. I was flattered, but I would have been even more flattered if he had said that it was closely argued as well as eloquent. I contended that to deprive a citizen of his passport was to impose a penalty on him and 'no government, no minister or no official should, without express statutory authority, have the right to impose a penalty on a citizen for expressing his opinions, if the expression of these opinions does not constitute a criminal offence, no matter how offensive the opinions may be.'

We are all agreed that in the free world, in spite of the cold war and even because of it, we want to maintain as much freedom of speech and freedom of movement as possible. The leader of the free world, the United States, is peculiarly subject to temptations to limit freedom of speech and freedom of movement. It would be unfortunate if Canada were to encourage these tendencies in the United States ... In countries such as France and Italy there must be Endicotts by the thousands making declarations against the United States and their own governments in much more violent terms than those used by Dr. Endicott. So far as I know, no attempt is made to prosecute them or to refuse them passport facilities. I suggest that we bear our Endicott with patience as part of the price we have to pay to maintain our democratic traditions.

It was in the period from 1946 to 1952 that I worked most closely with L.B. Pearson. I am proud to have worked under him.

For his accomplishments in foreign affairs alone he richly deserved
the double honour no one else has received, the Nobel Peace Prize and
the Order of Merit. Among his accomplishments were: his contribution
to securing a cease-fire in the Korean War; his brilliant intervention in
the Suez crisis; Canadian membership in the Colombo Plan; strengthening Canada's relationship with India; and the negotiation of the North
Atlantic treaty. He demonstrated his skill in foreign affairs by the way
he confronted the most difficult task which faces any Canadian government, that of weighing in the balance the cost to Canada of offending
the government and people of the United States by opposing it on an
issue in foreign affairs it considers important against the costs to Canada
and the world of our not doing our utmost to dissuade the United States
from pursuing an unwise policy in its foreign relations. He knew that
Canada must do its best to avoid being left alone with the United States
in dealing with an important controversial multilateral problem in foreign
policy because of the great disparity in power between the two countries
and he tried to call in the United Nations, the Commonwealth, and the
North Atlantic alliance to redress the balance in North America.

Mackenzie King in the twenties and thirties sought for a foreign policy
that divided us the least. St Laurent and Pearson in the late forties and
fifties sought for a foreign policy that united us the most. The widely
held belief in Canada in their time that under their leadership Canadians
were doing great things together in foreign affairs, that Canada was a
nation with a mission, was a sustaining myth that helped to define
Canadians as a people and strengthened our will to endure.[22]

Among the reasons for Pearson's success as a professional diplomat
and as foreign minister was his brilliant sense of timing. A few days after
he became a cabinet minister in September 1948 there was a meeting of
cabinet defence committee of which he, as foreign minister, was a member. This was his first appearance as a cabinet minister at a cabinet
committee. I, as acting under-secretary, sat behind him as his adviser.
We had the day before discussed the main issues on the committee's
agenda. We came to the principal item, which had serious implications
for our foreign policy. After the discussions had gone on for about five
minutes I leaned forward and whispered in Pearson's ear, 'What about
making the point we discussed yesterday?' He said, 'Not yet,' and let
the discussion go for another ten minutes before intervening. The timing
was perfect. The intervention was successful.

Pearson did not, when under-secretary for external affairs, possess

22 Sandra Gwyn put this point well in her article in *Saturday Night*, August 1978.

that passion for anonymity which is the mark of most distinguished senior civil servants; he gave many press conferences and speeches both in Canada and at the U.N. General Assembly. In an interview in 1970 he said that as deputy minister he had made almost as many speeches as when he was a cabinet minister and that this was 'really quite preposterous in the tradition of a silent, non-partisan civil servant.'[23] Preposterous it may have been, but by his press conferences as deputy minister, minister, and prime minister, by his speeches and articles, and by his interviews with makers of opinion in Canada, he educated the Canadian people on foreign affairs.

In the nine years from 1937 to 1946 Ruth and I and our three children moved six times, from Toronto to Halifax, back to Toronto, Toronto to Washington, Washington to Ottawa, back to Washington, back to Ottawa. This was hard on Ruth and on the children, who were buffeted about from school to school. Patrick, after going to nine schools from 1937 to 1945, decided that he wanted stability in his school life and tried the scholarship examinations for Upper Canada College in Toronto. He succeeded and lived in residence there for four years and then in residence at Trinity College in the University of Toronto. Morna went to eight schools and Timothy to seven before enrolling in Lisgar Collegiate in Ottawa in 1946. Lisgar was for Morna and Timothy a happy ending to their pilgrimage. Morna was chosen in her final year as the most attractive girl in the Ottawa secondary schools and became Miss Rough Rider, the mascot for the Ottawa football team. Timothy became expert at football, basketball, track and field.

When we went to India in 1952 Timothy went to Ridley College in St Catharines. There, in the tough 'Little Big Four' league, he perfected his skills in football, with the result that at the University of Toronto he was an all-star player for three years on the varsity football team. He graduated *cum laude* and the next year went to Yale on a Ford management fellowship and received an MA there. We were very proud when in 1960 he was awarded a Rhodes scholarship to Oxford, thus following in my footsteps.

For me the years from 1946 to 1952 were the most exhausting six-year period of my life. I would have broken under the strain if Ruth had not insisted as soon as we returned to Ottawa at the beginning of 1946 that we buy a farm near Ottawa. This is one of the many debts I owe

23 York University oral history project; interview on 7 May 1970 by Tom Hockin and Gerald Wright, revised by Pearson on 9 November 1971

her. She rightly felt that we and the children needed a place in Canada of great natural beauty where we could strike roots, needed the assurance that wherever we were in the world we had a home in Canada to return to.

We bought the farm in the summer of 1946, eighty acres in the lovely Gatineau hills twenty miles northwest of Ottawa, with a river as the southern boundary and a lake as the northern boundary. To begin with we lived at the farm only on weekends, at Christmas, and in the summer. Since the early seventies the farm has been for Ruth and me our year-long home. At first we lived in the log farmhouse, now we live in the barn. When we have returned to the farm from travelling abroad we have often exclaimed, 'This is lovelier than anything we have seen on our travels.' Wooded hills, meadows, long views, woodland paths. The farm was beautiful when we bought it. It becomes lovelier every year as the thousands of trees we and the children planted mature and the woods recover from decades of being grazed by sheep and cows. For more than forty years our farm has been for Ruth and me a place of refuge and of refreshment for body and for mind and spirit, a very present help in trouble.

17

Envoy to India
1952–1957

In 1951 I was offered a choice between being ambassador to Japan and ambassador to the Netherlands. I knew that the post in India would be vacant in about six months. I said that India was the post I wanted. My wish was granted.[1]

When my appointment was announced, someone (I do not now remember who) said: 'Reid's appointment is not surprising. Mr. Nehru will find him a most congenial spirit in the field of anti-imperialism.' The comment, though malevolent, was shrewd. My views of what should be done to make the world safer and saner were much the same as Nehru's. During my stay in India a number of my colleagues in the Department of External Affairs in Ottawa used to complain that I almost never found fault with Nehru's views on foreign affairs (though I often found fault with his diplomatic methods). They might more justly have complained that I never found fault with the views I had expressed in a departmental memorandum of 30 August 1947 in which I had urged that the western world should make rapid progress in granting self-government to colonies and in removing racial discrimination. Otherwise,

the western powers may have the great majority of the colonial and coloured peoples hostile or unfriendly to them in the event of war with the Soviet Union or at least doing their best to fish in troubled waters. In this context the term 'colonial peoples' may well include a considerable section of Latin America, as well as the whole of Asia and Africa and the South West Pacific ... There are

---

1 This chapter incorporates material from two of my books: *Envoy to Nehru* (Delhi: Oxford University Press 1981), and *Hungary and Suez 1956: A View from New Delhi* (Oakville, Ont.: Mosaic Press 1987; New Delhi: Allied Publishers 1987).

dangers in giving colonial peoples self-government before they are ready for it. But the dangers in not giving them self-government quickly are probably greater, since the longer independence is delayed the greater are the chances that the colonial independence movements may come under Soviet influence or control.

My wife Ruth, our eighteen-year old daughter Morna, and I proceeded by slow stages to India. We stopped in Washington, New York, and London where I had talks with Indian, American, and British officials. In London I met Sir Raghavan Pillai who was about to take up his appointment as secretary general of the Ministry of External Affairs in New Delhi. This was the beginning of a deep lifelong friendship. In Bombay we stayed for two days with the governor of the state of Bombay, Sir Girja Bajpai, whom I had known in Washington during the Dumbarton Oaks conference (which he called at the time the Dumbarton hoax conference), and at the Chicago conference on international civil aviation. Bajpai had just retired as secretary general of the Ministry of External Affairs. His opinion of the cabinet and of the senior officials in External Affairs was uncomplimentary. There were only three men of ability in the cabinet in addition to Nehru: Gopalaswami Ayyangar, C.D. Deshmukh, and T.T. Krishnamachari. By singling out these three Bajpai displayed his prejudice against Congress Party politicians, since none of the three had been members of the Congress Party during the struggle for independence. Ayyangar had been a provincial civil servant, Deshmukh a member of the Indian Civil Service, and Krishnamachari a successful businessman in Madras. Of the three senior officials in External Affairs, Bajpai said that one was deaf and dumb, one he had little respect for, and one was sound, had views, and was willing to express them but was not capable of filling the highest posts.

We arrived in Delhi on 17 November. Five days later I plunged into discussions with the Indian government on the issue of the Chinese prisoners of war in Korea who refused to be repatriated to North Korea or China. This was helpful to me because it meant that in my first two and a half months in New Delhi I had occasion to discuss important official business with Nehru himself, with the two top officials in the External Affairs ministry (Raghavan Pillai and R.K. Nehru), and with Mrs Vijayalakshmi Pandit and V.K. Krishna Menon when they returned in January to New Delhi after having attended the U.N. General Assembly in New York. The business I had to discuss arose from Pearson's efforts as president of the Assembly to get through a resolution on the Chinese prisoners of war which would be acceptable to India and its uncommitted Asian friends and satisfactory to the United States. In these efforts Pearson was working hand-in-glove with Krishna Menon so that my task was to facilitate co-operation between my country and the country to which I was accredited – always a pleasant task for an ambassador, particularly when he has just arrived at his post.

In the middle of January I wrote Pearson about my introduction to diplomacy in New Delhi:

Sor far as I can make out, the situation is simple. Krishna Menon has no use for Pillai and R.K. Nehru. Pillai has little use for Menon and considers that his anti-American speeches in the United States were stupid. Mrs. Pandit has no use for Krishna Menon. The relations between Pillai and R.K. Nehru are strained. I am not certain what Pillai and R.K. Nehru think of Mrs. Pandit and she of them, except that Pillai and R.K. Nehru undoubtedly consider that she is a lesser evil than Krishna Menon. Mrs. Pandit and Krishna Menon compete for the Prime Minister's favour.

My introduction to Indian diplomacy was followed immediately by an introduction to Indian villages. Before we left for India Ruth and I had decided that, instead of starting our discovery of India by visiting the big cities, as most if not all ambassadors did, we would start by visiting villages. Since it was in the villages that 80 to 85 per cent of the people of India lived, it seemed obvious to us that, unless we saw something of what life was like in the villages, we would have no inkling of what life was like for the average Indian and would have little chance of understanding India. The Indian authorities suggested that we start by visiting the village of Bichpuri, about half-way between Agra and Fatehpur Sikri, and then go to villages in the Etawah project.

In all Ruth, Morna, and I visited sixteen villages ranging in size from 130 people to 1,500. We walked through the fields near the villages; we visited schools, hospitals, rural workshops; I talked to about sixty officials; we heard stories of successes and failures in efforts to help the villagers improve their conditions of life. Some years later I told Kenneth Galbraith that I had learned on this tour how to make a good impression on the agricultural development officers when they escorted us through fields of grain. I would pick a few grains, bite them, and say 'oomf' and then take a little earth into the palm of one hand, rub it, and again say 'oomf.' Galbraith said I would have made an even better impression if I had spat on the earth in my hand before rubbing it.

In an essay I wrote at the end of our village tour and sent to Ottawa I said:

We fell in love with the Indian countryside we visited. It is flat country but it combines much of the loveliness of our prairies with the loveliness of the sleepy canals in rural England. My memories of it are full of colour, of fragrance and of music. The rose of sunrise turning to gold. The golden glow of late afternoon turning to the rose of sunset. The gold of the mustard fields. The fragrance of the flowering fields of peas and mustard. The sweet smell of boiling sugar cane that met us in a country lane. The long shadows of late afternoon and early morning. The bells of the bullock carts. And the gay singing of villagers heard across the fields or from the villages at night.

Shortly after we had returned to Delhi a leading Indian newspaper-man, Durga Das, used me as a stick with which to beat the group which surrounded Nehru, which, he said, was so westernized that it was aloof from the problems facing India. 'Even foreign diplomats are tired of the so-called social technique of New Delhi. The new High Commissioner of Canada recently undertook a strenuous, village-to-village tour to understand real India.' I certainly did not understand real India as the result of one village tour in one part of India. But I had had an introduction to life in some Indian villages.

This tour was one of my accomplishments in my first year in India. Another which pleased me greatly and which likewise had nothing to do with international problems was my contribution to finding a name for the recently established diplomatic enclave in New Delhi. Early in September 1953 Chopra, the chief of protocol in the External Affairs ministry, told me that the Indian authorities were trying to find a suitable name for the enclave. I suggested it be called after the Indian Machiavelli, Chanakya, who had been the principal adviser to Emperor Chandragupta, a contemporary of Alexander the Great. A few days later, after looking up what Nehru had written about Chanakya in his *Discovery of India*, I wrote to Chopra:

Chanakyapur, it seems to me, would not be an inappropriate name for the enclave. Chanakya certainly seems to have been the kind of man diplomats might aspire to be. He was no mere 'humble adviser' of his emperor and he 'looked upon the emperor more as a loved pupil than a master'. Some heads of mission, however, might not like to live in an area called after a man who, according to Mr. Nehru, was 'simple and austere in his life, uninterested in the pomp and pageantry of high position.'

The next day Chopra showed Nehru my letter. An hour or so later

Nehru telephoned him to say that the ending should be 'puri' not 'pur' and that he was going to take the matter up with cabinet that morning. Cabinet agreed with his recommendation. I said to Chopra that surely I was not the first to suggest the name. He replied, to my chagrin, that K.P.S. Menon had also suggested it.

At the end of August 1953, a month after the armistice agreement in the Korean War had been signed, the U.N. General Assembly voted on a resolution that India should be a member of the peace conference on Korea which was to be held in Geneva. In the debate which preceded the vote Canada urged the United States not to block the membership of India. Pearson considered the American opposition to India as 'almost pathological ... due in part to their feeling that India and Krishna Menon are the same thing at international conferences.' The resolution failed by one vote to secure the required two-thirds majority. The United States rallied to its side, as it was usually able to do in those days in a United Nations of only sixty members, a blocking group of one-third plus one (seventeen Latin American republics, Pakistan, Greece, and Taiwan). Pillai told me that the opposition of the United States was 'a terrible mistake' – the effect on Indo-American relations would be 'deplorable.'

On 18 February 1954 the foreign ministers of the United States, Britain, France, and the Soviet Union agreed that the international conference to be held in Geneva in April should discuss not only Korea but also Indo-China. Four days later, Nehru in a speech in Parliament appealed for an immediate cease-fire in Indo-China. St Laurent was in New Delhi when Nehru made this appeal. At his press conference two days later he was asked about Nehru's appeal. He replied that he was in favour of it: it was practicable; it was apt to have considerable influence since it would be 'listened to very attentively and with very respectful consideration by the heads of all the governments with whom' he had had any contacts. The Canadian government endorsed the appeal 'without any reservation or hesitation whatsoever.' Anthony Eden in his memoirs states that he 'was not very happy' about Nehru's proposal for a cease-fire before the Geneva conference.[2] Presumably he was not very happy about St Laurent's support of it. If Eden was not very happy, John Foster Dulles was probably angry. As for the French, they were 'furious,' the term the French ambassador in New Delhi used to describe to me the tone of the telegram on St Laurent's statement which the French Foreign Office had sent to the French ambassador in Ottawa.

During the Geneva conference Eden, then British foreign minister,

2 Sir Anthony Eden, *The Memoirs of Sir Anthony Eden: Full Circle* (London: Cassell 1960), 90

proposed a kind of Locarno Pact for Southeast Asia and Dulles, then the United States secretary of state, proposed the formation of a Southeast Asia treaty organization, SEATO. What Dulles was proposing was an alliance against aggression by the Vietminh, China, and the Soviet Union in Vietnam, Laos, and Cambodia. What Eden was proposing was an agreement by all the countries immediately concerned, plus the five great powers and India, to guarantee the Geneva settlement on Indo-China. I reported to Ottawa that I was certain that Nehru was prepared to join an Eden pact provided it was accompanied by independence for the Indo-Chinese states and regimes in those states based on popular support. Such regimes would not exist until, in accordance with the Geneva settlement, elections had been held in Laos and Cambodia in 1955 and in Vietnam in 1956. The elections in Vietnam would result in a united Vietnam. I reported to Ottawa:

The advantages to the western world of having India become a co-guarantor of the Indo-China settlement are substantial. It would lessen the chances that the other side would commit aggression in Indo-China; it would mean that if they did commit a flagrant act of aggression which resulted in war, India would be on our side from the outset. Our own experience and that of the United States in the past six years indicates that it is the first step in the acceptance of guarantees outside of one's borders which is the most difficult. The taking by India of this first step might, if the western world is patient and imaginative, result in the next few years in an increasingly closer association between India and the West.

Dulles succeeded in getting his SEATO. Eden failed to get his Locarno-type pact. I told Ottawa that this was 'one of the tragic lost opportunities of the middle fifties.'

At the Geneva conference Krishna Menon and Pearson worked closely together on all aspects of the discussions on Indo-China. At the conclusion of the conference in July both countries accepted membership in the three-member international supervisory commissions for Vietnam, Laos, and Cambodia which the conference set up. Poland was the other member. During this period from February to July 1954 Indo-China was an example of co-operation between India and Canada on foreign policy. Within six months the Geneva settlement on Indo-China was collapsing and Indian and Canadian policy on Indo-China began to diverge. Within a few years Indo-China became a major irritant in Indo-Canadian relations and one of the principal causes of the erosion of the special relationship between India and Canada.

I attended the preliminary meeting of the international supervisory commissions for Vietnam, Laos, and Cambodia held in New Delhi at the beginning of August. The morning after the conclusion of the meeting I got up at four to say goodbye at the airport to the Canadian advance mission to Indo-China. I saw them off and was about to return home when I was told that a group of half a dozen Canadian army officers had just arrived at the airport and would be leaving in a few minutes. They had been flown in from Korea where they had been serving in the United Nations forces and were being transferred to Indo-China to serve on the inspection teams of the international supervisory commissions. I had a pleasant time talking to them and waved them goodbye when their plane left. I then discovered that the British high commissioner would be arriving in twenty minutes. He had been away from Delhi for a month on holiday. To his surprise he found me waiting at the bottom of the runway of his plane to welcome him back to Delhi. Entering into the spirit of the game, my British colleague said to me, 'There's a Canadian colonel on the plane you might like to greet.' I introduced myself to the colonel. He was on his way to Kashmir to serve as a United Nations observer. At the New Delhi airport on that early morning in August 1954 was demonstrated the extent of the participation of the Canadian armed forces at that time in U.N. peace-keeping activities. Here were army officers who had just served or were just about to serve in U.N. activities in Korea, Kashmir, and Indo-China.

At the end of January 1955 when it was clear that the Geneva settlement on Indo-China was collapsing I cabled Ottawa:

The Indians, as you know, suspect that the United States intends to torpedo the settlement in Vietnam and that in particular the United States will use its best efforts to see that a free election does not take place. The Indians also believe, on the basis of reports from their own people in Vietman, that in a free election the Democratic Republic [Vietminh] would receive up to three-quarters of the vote in the south. The Indians consider the Geneva settlement as a package deal under which the North gave up the possibility, or indeed the probability, of a complete military victory in the South in return for a promise of free elections. They consider Ho Chi Minh an intelligent statesman and they would find it hard to believe that he will not be willing to agree to any reasonable requirements for free elections, since in their opinion he is certain to win them. Because of these Indian beliefs they have for some time assumed that Vietnam would be unified under Ho Chi Minh and that the problem which they and their friends face is to prevent an extension of his influence into Laos and Cambodia which they would consider disastrous.

I did not realize how far the Indian and Canadian views on Indo-China had diverged until I was in Ottawa on leave in the summer of 1955 and was asked to give a report on India at a meeting of the senior officers of the Department of External Affairs. In my talk I spoke of the intent which I understood lay behind the acceptance by France and Britain of the Geneva settlement: that it was not possible to hold a line against communist expansion in Vietnam, but that it was possible to hold a line at the border between Laos and Cambodia on one side and Vietnam on the other, and that France and Britain had implicitly acquiesced at Geneva in Ho Chi Minh taking over the whole of Vietnam as the result of elections. This, I said, was the Indian view and I agreed with it. The roof fell in on me. Officer after officer at the meeting attacked me for my callous, immoral proposal which would betray millions of anti-communist people in South Vietnam into the clutches of the communists of North Vietnam. (Twenty years and millions of deaths later not only they but also the Laotians and Cambodians would be 'betrayed' into the hands of the communists.)

In 1953 and 1954 the special relationship between India and Canada and, indeed, in India's relations with the West reached its high point. A process of erosion then set in. It was caused by the resentment aroused in India by the U.S. military aid agreement with Pakistan concluded early in 1954; the differences of opinion between the West and India over Indo-China and Kashmir; the resentment aroused in the West by the treatment accorded by India to Krushchev and Bulganin on their visit to India in the autumn of 1955; and the attitude of the Indian government to the Hungarian revolution of 1956 and the Soviet-imposed counter-revolution.

In October 1953 I learned from the British high commissioner that the United States was proposing to announce, probably before the end of December, that it was giving Pakistan military aid worth $25 million. When I reported this to Ottawa I said that both the United States embassy in Delhi and the United Kingdom mission had put in strongest terms to their governments the deplorable effect this would have on Indo-Pakistan relations and that the United Kingdom mission was particularly concerned that this announcement should not be made while India and Pakistan were discussing the appointment of a plebiscite administrator for Kashmir the following April. I said that I concurred in these views. 'There is now some hope of a settlement of the Kashmir problem but this hope would, I am afraid, vanish if the United States persists in its proposed policy.'

Since I knew that Ottawa would find it difficult to understand why the Indians were getting so excited about military aid to Pakistan of only $25 million a year, I said that the Indians believed that the United States would find itself involved in a large and continuing program. The Indians were right. In the ten years following the conclusion of the military aid agreement, the United States gave Pakistan about $1.5 billion (U.S.) in arms, equivalent to $6 billion in 1988 dollars.

I told Ottawa that the envoys of the United States, Britain, France, and Australia were making much the same arguments as I in their efforts to persuade their governments of the folly of the United States' making a military aid agreement with Pakistan. I said I had an uneasy feeling that the attitude of the United States administration to India was not 'based on a cool calculation of the long-run national interests of the United States,' or on 'a careful weighing of military, political, economic and "moral" considerations, and of long-run against short-run factors' but on wholly understandable but nevertheless irrational factors – in particular a resentment against Nehru for his moral lectures to mankind, his general attitude of moral superiority, his criticisms of United States policy, his organization of an opposition to the United States in the United Nations, and his failure to show gratitude to the United States for the economic aid it had given India.

William Bundy, who had been a senior officer in the CIA at this time and who later became editor of *Foreign Affairs*, wrote me in 1982 about my book *Envoy to Nehru*. He said he was especially interested in the chapter on American arms to Pakistan. 'For many years I have regarded that decision [of the United States to make the military aid agreement] as perhaps the single most clearcut mistake of American policy in the 1950s and 1960s. I exclude Vietnam which was not a single decision but a cumulative series.' These are strong words – 'the single most clearcut mistake of American policy in the 1950s and 1960s.'

I sweated blood thirty-five years ago in the crisis over American arms aid to Pakistan. I got very excited. I am sure that many of my colleagues in Ottawa thought I was too excited. Pearson himself wrote me that he believed that 'in itself and within its limits' United States arms aid to Pakistan 'is not altogether a bad thing, especially when viewed in relation to forces at work elsewhere.' I am happy now to be assured on excellent authority that I was right in urging that Canada should in its own national interests do whatever it could to dissuade the United States from making the agreement.

In the summer of 1953 Nehru visited Karachi to talk to the new prime minister of Pakistan, Mohammad Ali. On 17 August Mohammad Ali returned his visit. Two days before I had attended the Indian independence day celebrations in Old Delhi. In his speech to the hundred thousand people gathered in front of the Red Fort, Nehru appealed to the people to give the prime minister of Pakistan a warm welcome when he arrived at the airport. They responded with an excess of enthusiasm. When Mohammad Ali descended from his plane they surged onto the tarmac to greet him and Nehru had to try to clear a way for the visitor by waving his baton at the crowd and shouting angrily at them. A day or so later I mentioned this incident to him. He said, 'You can do anything to an Indian crowd, even curse at them, and they won't mind, provided you do it in a friendly way.'

On the day the talks between the prime ministers ended Pillai and his wife dined alone with us. He was so optimistic about the results of the talks as to be euphoric. The impression I gathered from him was that Nehru had told Mohammad Ali that it should be possible to hold the plebiscite in Kashmir in April 1955 or at least between April and October 1955. The only qualification which Pillai put on his optimism was 'provided the atmosphere in Karachi remains good': that is, provided the governor general of Pakistan (Ghulam Mohammad) and Mohammad Ali could hold the line against extremists in the Pakistan cabinet.

I reported to Ottawa that the references in the joint communiqué issued at the end of the talks to the plebiscite in Kashmir meant that though the plebiscite would extend throughout the whole of the state of Jammu and Kashmir, its practical effect would be limited to the Vale of Kashmir since the mountainous area occupied by Pakistani troops would go to Pakistan, and Jammu and Ladakh would go to India. The Vale of Kashmir constitutes only about one-eighth of the area of the whole state. Its population in 1956 was about a million and a quarter of whom 90 per cent were Muslims. I was convinced that Nehru was prepared as a price for better relations with Pakistan to run the risk that the plebiscite would result in India losing the Vale. In believing this Walter Crocker, the Australian high commissioner, and I were in a small minority in the diplomatic corps. Most of the ambassadors and high commissioners, including the American ambassador (and the State Department), believed that Nehru never intended to make a settlement and that he used the American arms agreement with Pakistan as an excuse for getting out of his commitment to a plebiscite on Kashmir.

When in 1979 I read the authoritative biography of Nehru by Sarvepalli Gopal, which is based on access to Nehru's private papers, I found to my delight that Gopal believes from his study of these papers that Nehru was prepared in August 1953 to agree to a plebiscite in Kashmir even though this might result in India losing the Vale of Kashmir. 'The evidence,' he writes, 'suggests that [Nehru's] offer [of a plebiscite] had been genuine and would have held if the prospect of a military alliance between Pakistan and the United States had not impinged on it.'[3]

My belief that Nehru in August and September 1953 was prepared to make a settlement with Pakistan over Kashmir even though this involved the possible loss of the Vale to Pakistan and that the settlement was frustrated by American military aid to Pakistan did not mean that I believed that it was right or prudent of Nehru to allow the issue of American military aid to Pakistan to frustrate the possibility of a settlement. I said to Ottawa, 'I cannot see any logical connection between United States military aid to Pakistan and a denial by India of the right of self-determination for the people of Kashmir.'

The next development which widened the gap between India and the West was the two-week visit to India of Krushchev and Bulganin at the end of 1955. New Delhi gave them a highly organized tumultuous welcome. About a million people lined the twelve-mile route from the airport to the president's residence and about six hundred thousand were present at the civic reception the next day.

Many people in the West were irritated by this enthusiastic welcome, by the crude anti-western statements the Soviet leaders made in India, and by Nehru's failure to take public exception to them. Thus the Soviet leaders charged that the western powers had precipitated the Second World War in 1939 and Hitler's attack on the Soviet Union in 1941. Pearson was so irritated that he made a statement in New York about the visit which resulted in Nehru instructing Subimal Dutt of the External Affairs ministry to speak to me about it. In his statement Pearson had wondered what would happen if two government leaders from the West were to go around India and make the kind of speeches which the two Soviet leaders had made. I said to Dutt that I had raised this point in a telegram to Pearson three days before and I read to him from the telegram.

The Soviet leaders have done about six things in India which western diplomats here would have warned similar western leaders against doing. They have used the Indian parliament as a forum for attacking countries friendly to India. They have in public speeches called India an 'ally'. They have boasted of the aid they are going to give India whereas we would not think it wise to boast of the aid

3 Sarvepalli Gopal, *Jawaharlal Nehru: A Biography* vol. II: 1947–1956 (Delhi: Oxford University Press 1979), 185

we have given India. They have criticized Indian projects they were visiting, whereas our advice would be that a westerner who is new to India should be chary of giving advice because there may be a good reason for the Indian practice being different from the western and even if his advice is correct it would be resented if given publicly. They have in a public speech given full support to India on a controversy with a foreign government (Portugal over Goa). They have twice – at Bakhra and at Calcutta – warned India about what a nuclear bomb might do to the dam or to the city ... The commission by western statesmen in India of any one of the six gaffes would have precipitated considerable public criticism in India and the commission of all six would have raised a tempest. The Russians have not raised a tempest.

A year later Nehru's attitude to the Hungarian revolution widened the gap between India and the West. For me the three weeks between the high point of success of the Hungarian revolution on 30 October 1956 and 19 November when Nehru belatedly came down on the side of the revolution and denounced the Soviet-imposed counter-revolution were the most crowded and demanding period of my posting in India. The strain came at a bad time for me. I was recovering from a severe attack of jaundice which had left me tired and depressed. During the critical week beginning 4 November, instead of having six officers on duty at the High Commission, I had only one and he had been in India for only two months. Two officers were travelling in South India on official business, two were ill, and one was attached to the Canadian delegation to the UNESCO conference which was being held in New Delhi.

Once Britain and France had embarked on the use of armed force against Egypt at the end of October and Australia had a few days later supported them at the United Nations, Nehru was not prepared to listen to urgings from their governments or their representatives in New Delhi that he denounce the use of force by the Soviet Union to suppress the Hungarian revolution; he suspected them of wanting to divert his attention from what he considered to be the dangerous, arrogant, imperialistic aggression of Britain and France against Egypt. If the United States had had at that time an ambassador in New Delhi of the stature of ambassadors it had had, or was about to have, in New Delhi – Chester Bowles, Sherman Cooper, Ellsworth Bunker, Kenneth Galbraith – he would have been the spokesman of the western world in talking to Nehru about Hungary and he would have had the weight of a great power behind him. But the United States had had no ambassador in New Delhi for seven months. Canada, by not supporting Britain in the voting at the U.N. General Assembly on the first resolution on Suez, did not forfeit its special relationship with India, and Nehru continued to have confidence in and respect for St Laurent and Pearson. A special responsibility therefore descended on me during the crises over the revolution in Hungary.

My spirits soared in October when the success of Poland under Gomulka in securing greater freedom was followed by the early successes of the revolution in Hungary. I saw new vistas of hope opening up for greater freedom in Eastern Europe and within the Soviet Union and for better relations between the Soviet world and the western world. But when the Soviet Union suppressed the revolution on 4 November and Britain and France invaded Egypt the following day, these hopes were dashed and vistas of fear took the place of the vistas of hope. I was shaken by feelings of terror, pity, and anger: terror at the thought of the dangers of a third world war breaking out, pity for the people of Hungary, anger at the actions of the Soviet Union, Israel, Britain, and France. To these emotions were added my apprehensions that a failure by Nehru to denounce Soviet aggression in Hungary would make a Soviet withdrawal from Hungary less likely, would damage his reputation and India's, and would weaken the links between India and the West – links which I believed served the interests of the West and India. I was a devoted admirer of Nehru; indeed, I had been captivated by him and I did not want him to damage his reputation.

On 23 October the Hungarian revolution had broken out against the Stalinist-type government which the Soviet Union had imposed on Hungary in 1949. The government called on Soviet troops for help. The rebels fought against the superior Soviet forces with incredible gallantry and by 30 October the Stalinist government had been replaced by a coalition government under Imre Nagy which included representatives of the non-communist parties. On that day the Soviet government declared that troops of one member of the Warsaw Pact should be stationed in the territory of another member only with the consent of the host state and that the Soviet government would withdraw its troops from Budapest as soon as the Hungarian government considered withdrawal necessary. This was the high point in the Hungarian revolution. Two days later, on 1 November, Nagy, on learning that more Soviet military units were entering Hungary, demanded their withdrawal and announced that the Hungarian government was repudiating the Warsaw treaty, was declaring Hungary's neutrality, was turning to the United Nations, and was requesting the help of the four great powers in defending Hungary's neutrality. On 4 November Soviet troops seized Budapest and installed a puppet regime under Janos Kadar.

At the very time this tragedy was unfolding the crisis resulting from

Egypt's nationalization of the Suez Canal came to a head. In accordance with a secret agreement reached on 24 October between Israel, France, and Britain, Israel invaded the Sinai on 29 October and the next day Britain and France issued an ultimatum to Egypt to serve as a pretext for their invasion a few days later, an invasion which had as its objective the overthrow of Colonel Nasser.

On 31 October Nehru issued a statement attacking the actions of Israel, Britain, and France against Egypt as a flagrant violation of the U.N. Charter. Pearson immediately cabled me: 'A press despatch just received carries the story of Indian condemnation of the Israeli attack on Egypt. I have no quarrel with the Indian government's decision on this matter but the contrast between its quick and strong denunciation of Israeli action with its complete silence over events in Hungary, and Russian intervention in these events, will have a very bad effect in this country.' Pearson's reference to the Indian condemnation only of Israel is puzzling because Nehru in his statement had also condemned Britain and France.

During the next two weeks I did what I could to persuade Nehru to support the Hungarian revolution and to denounce the Soviet aggression against Hungary. As soon as I received Pearson's message I called on Pillai, read it to him, and urged that Nehru break his silence over Hungary. Pillai rebuffed me. He said I was the only diplomat in Delhi who had expressed to him criticism of Indian inaction on Hungary. He would not pass my message on to Nehru because it would have an unfortunate effect. The next day, 2 November, he learned that his belief the day before that the Russians were withdrawing from Hungary had proved to be false and he passed my message to Nehru and warned Nehru against an application of double standards to Hungary and Suez. From then on Pillai and I worked together on the Hungarian issue.

On the evening of Sunday 4 November I heard from a BBC broadcast that Soviet armed forces had launched an attack on Budapest, had overwhelmed the Hungarians, and had installed a puppet regime. I knew that Pillai was dining at the German embassy. I phoned him there and asked him to drop in to see me on his way home. I told him of the news from Budapest. The UNESCO conference was opening in New Delhi the next day. Could not Nehru in his speech at the opening of the conference pay tribute to the Hungarian people, express sorrow at their suffering, and demand that every Russian soldier get out of Hungary immediately? He could also demand that every Israeli, French, and British soldier get out of Egypt immediately. The next day Nehru did bracket the aggression in Hungary with that in Egypt.

The following morning I was able to draw Nehru aside for a couple of minutes at the airport where he was welcoming the emperor of Ethiopia. I expressed my pleasure at his reference to Hungary the previous day. To my dismay he replied:

One difficulty about the Hungarian situation is that there are disputes about the facts. Apparently there were not only Russian troops in Hungary but also technicians and it is said that a thousand of the Russian technicians were murdered. There seem to have been massacres on both sides. The Russians had agreed to withdraw but came back when new developments took place in the rebellion. It is said, for example, that people were streaming across the border to help the rebels and that planes were landing in Hungary from outside the country to help the rebels.

(Years later I learned that Nehru's remarks were based on what the Soviet foreign ministry had told the Indian ambassador in Moscow the day before.[4])

In order to counteract the false stories Nehru had been fed by the Soviet government I telegraphed to Ottawa:

I wish it were possible to fly to India immediately for the express purpose of seeing Nehru about four of the active leaders of the abortive Hungarian rebellion. It would be best if the group included a communist, a socialist, a small holder and a non-party man and if one of the members were a poet, one an artist and one a university student. Nehru might sense in them the kind of people who fought beside him for Indian independence. With his feeling for history he might also sense the continuity of the Hungarian rebellion of 1956 with the Hungarian revolution of 1848, both of which were put down by the armed forces of reactionary Russia. He must be helped to realize that the ancient forces of nationalism in Europe are as worthy in themselves as the new forces of nationalism in Asia and that the nations of Europe have as great a right to national freedom and independence as the nations of Asia.

I passed this suggestion on to the American chargé d'affaires when he called on me the following day. Nine days later the State Department was still 'actively discussing it' with other agencies of the American government. Nothing emerged from this active consideration. I also suggested to the chargé that the State Department should furnish Nehru with a blow-by-blow account of what had been happening in Hungary

4 K.P.S. Menon, *The Flying Troika* (Bombay: Oxford University Press 1963), 172–3

since the outbreak of the revolt. The chargé said he had already recommended this to Washington. The account did not, however, reach
Nehru until after he had given his appalling Calcutta speech on 9 November.

A few hours after my talk with Nehru at the airport I called on Pillai
at the External Affairs ministry. He had just come from a discussion
with Nehru about the messages which Bulganin had, the day before,
sent to Eisenhower, Eden, Mollet (the premier of France), and Nehru.
Bulganin had proposed to Eisenhower that the United States should join
the Soviet Union in naval and air action backed by the United Nations
to stop the Anglo-French aggression in Egypt. In his messages to Eden
and Mollet, Bulganin referred to his message to Eisenhower and warned
them that if they did not end hostilities immediately they risked attack
by a stronger power capable of committing rocket weapons. 'We are
filled with determination to use force to crush the aggression and to
restore peace in the [Middle] East. We hope you will show the necessary
prudence and will draw from this the appropriate conclusions.' Pillai
said to me, presumably reflecting Nehru's views, that the situation created by the Soviet government's messages was one which the great
powers would, no doubt, settle among themselves; India had no influence. I disagreed and I urged that India should use its influence with the
Soviet government immediately since there was danger of a world war
breaking out. Could not the Soviet ambassador be called immediately
to the External Affairs ministry and told that in India's view there was
no justification for Soviet intervention? My parting shot as I was leaving
Pillai's office was: 'If I were in India's position I would do this even if it
were just so that the last document in the Indian government white paper
on the outbreak of the third world war might begin with "I summoned
the Soviet Ambassador and told him ... " '

That evening Pillai had a long talk with Nehru and Nehru wrote a
reply to the message from Bulganin. His reply was a strong criticism of
the Soviet message to the British and French governments.

While we entirely agree with you that aggression of all kinds must be put an
end to we feel strongly that any step that might lead to a world war would be
a crime against humanity and must be avoided ... I agree with you fully that the
situation [in Egypt] is serious and delay may lead to disaster. Urgent and effective
measures have to be taken. But I earnestly hope that they will be measures to
bring back and ensure peace rather than to enlarge the circle of war and disaster.

The low point in Nehru's attitude to the Hungarian revolution was
his speech on 9 November to the All-India Congress Committee in Cal-

cutta in which he accepted as valid the Soviet defence of their actions in Hungary which he had received from Bulganin the previous day. On the same day Krishna Menon voted against a resolution of the U.N. Assembly calling for the withdrawal of Soviet troops and free elections in Hungary. India and Yugoslavia were the only countries outside the Soviet bloc to vote against the resolution.

As soon as I read Nehru's speech I asked for an appointment with Pillai to express my dismay. I had told Ottawa in advance what I was going to say to him and that I was prepared to say much the same thing to Nehru, with whom I had an appointment for 13 November. On 12 November Malcolm MacDonald, the British high commissioner, said to me that he wished he could speak to Nehru to try to convince him of the deplorable effects on the West of the Calcutta speech and the Menon vote, but his position in Delhi was now so weak because of the British aggression against Egypt that there was no use in his speaking to Nehru. He hoped I would speak to Nehru since I was the only western ambassador in Delhi who was in a position to speak frankly to him. Ottawa, however, cabled me that it would be unwise for me to continue my campaign on the Hungarian question any longer. I was not to 'take any further initiatives except on express instructions.' I was also rebuked in another telegram sent on the same day for placing too high a priority on two telegrams I had sent to Ottawa on the crisis. The tone of the telegrams from Ottawa was curt. They evoked a protest from Norman Robertson, then the high commissioner in London, in which he shrewdly analysed one of my 'difficulties' as a diplomat. In a 'strictly personal' letter to Pearson on 13 November he said he had been 'rather shaken' by the telegrams and that he was afraid that 'Escott will be badly hurt and feel himself rather humiliated by them.'

One of Escott's qualities which much of the time is a source of strength is his faculty for identifying himself unreservedly with the fortunes of the issue or the idea which is uppermost in his mind. This means that he sometimes overdoes things and needs pulling up, but I don't think he should ever be pulled down quite so severely as in these two telegrams. I think he has been doing a remarkably good job in India, and he probably wouldn't be doing such a good job if he did not believe it the most important place in the world. That is one of Escott's difficulties.[5]

In his statement to Parliament on 19 November Nehru repudiated his

5 Robertson to Pearson, 13 November 1956, NAC, Pearson Papers, MG26 NI, vol. 13

Calcutta speech. The Socialist opposition referred to this about-face as the 'debulganisation of the Prime Minister.' Nehru said that the revolution in Hungary against 'an imposed government' and against the Soviet armies which were there 'against the wishes of the Hungarian people' had 'the great masses of the people behind it, with the workers, with the young people in it.' Nehru had at long last accepted the view of the liberals and social democrats throughout the world with whom he was normally in agreement. But his conversion came too late to restore his reputation. It had been permanently impaired by his wavering on an issue which had stirred the hearts and minds of masses of people in the non-communist world as had no issue since the Spanish Civil War.

Many more memories of India crowd in on me when, thirty years later, I think back on my years there, years which were among the happiest of my life. General de Gaulle once described India to Scotty Reston as 'a dust of peoples, living in misery and meditation.' He would have been nearer the truth if he had said, 'misery, beauty, and meditation.' I remember heart-breaking misery which I saw in the slums of Calcutta and some villages and heart-breaking beauty which I saw in the plains and in the mountains, at ancient monuments and holy shrines. I have seen two of the seven wonders of the world, the Taj Mahal and Fatehpur Sikri, at their loveliest, the Taj Mahal under a full moon and the gate of victory at Fatehpur Sikri at sunrise – that gate whose inscription is a monument to the religious eclecticism of the founder of Fatehpur Sikri, the great sixteenth-century Mughal emperor Akbar: 'Thus said Jesus, on whom be peace, The world is a bridge. Pass over it but build no dwelling place on it. The world exists only for an hour. Spend it in prayer.' I have seen the deep rose of sunrise over Kangchenjunga from the hill behind the residence of the Indian representative in Gangtok, the capital of Sikkim, and from the place at Vulture's Peak in Rajgir where the Buddha used to meditate I have gazed over the valley below bathed in the light of a full moon. And I remember the riot of colour in the gardens of the president's residence in New Delhi and the colours in the sky which come with the dust storms in Delhi in June. After being driven through one of the worst of these storms on my way to the External Affairs ministry I said to the secretary general, 'It looks like the last day of judgment.' Pillai replied, 'How strange to describe the known by the unknown.'

I used to go for a walk in the early morning along the streets near our residence in New Delhi. I was constantly delighted to pass on this walk groups of Rajasthan women on their way from their hovels to their hard manual labour, walking with magnificent carriage in their gaily coloured clothes, chattering, laughing, singing. To me these women became a symbol of India. In my farewell speech in New Delhi I spoke of these women and went on to say 'It is the dignity and gaiety of the mass of the people of India which make India rich – not just the wisdom of its teachers and saints and scholars, and the beauty of its landscapes, its monuments and its shrines.'

One afternoon at the end of 1956 I went to the final session of the international Buddhist conference held to celebrate the twenty-five hundredth anniversary of the death of Buddha. There were speeches by the Dalai Lama, the Panchen Lama, and Nehru. I went on from there to Parliament to hear a speech by Chou En-lai. I reported to Ottawa that that afternoon I had heard speeches by two incarnations of God and by two prime ministers who between them represented a billion people. This, I said, must be a record in the Canadian diplomatic service. Sardar K.M. Panikkar tried to deprive me of my record by telling me that the two Tibetan lamas were not incarnations of God, but I call to my side *Everyman's Encyclopedia* which states that the Dalai Lama is 'reverenced as the living incarnation of deity.'

My favourite summit story is of the three-hour talk in Delhi in 1956 between Nehru and John Foster Dulles, then U.S. secretary of state. Before the talk the press in India and abroad had been full of speculation about which important international problems they would concentrate on when they met under four eyes, as the Germans say. The meeting took place in the afternoon. That evening at dinner at the prime minister's house I sat on the left of Indira Gandhi; Dulles was on her right. Halfway through dinner she turned to me and whispered, 'I saw my father immediately after the meeting and can you imagine what he told me? He said that for the first two hours and three-quarters they chatted about nothing important. Just before the meeting was to end Mr Dulles asked a question about Indian policy and there was fifteen minutes of useful discussion.'

Above all else, the memories of India which crowd upon me are memories of Nehru. In May 1957 just before I left India I sent Ottawa a lengthy assessment of Nehru. The following consists of extracts from this assessment.

Nehru has great personal charm. All the arts of the charmer come naturally to him and appear, and perhaps are, spontaneous. There is an elegance about him. Not just his well-fitting Indian clothes and his red rose, but the way he smokes a cigarette, the way he greets a visitor or sees him off at the door of his home. He is an actor like all those who have to live a good deal of their lives in public with the spotlight turned on them, and who have to exercise charm in order to get their way. When the spotlight is on him, he puts on his actor's mask – handsome, smiling, alert, young for his sixty-seven years.

He is thoroughly westernized; he probably dreams and thinks in English. The things in India which make him impatient are the things which make westerners impatient: the microphone which doesn't work; the concert that goes on and on; the speeches that go on and on; shoddy workmanship; unnecessary filth and smells. His socialism is in large part the socialism of the generous-hearted and imaginative aristocrat in a poverty-stricken country who is revolted equally by the vulgar conspicuous consumption of the rich and the filth and misery of the poor. He has the suspicion, the superior attitude, the lack of understanding of the United States which most upper-class leaders of the British Labour party had in the late twenties and which some still have – not much more, not much less.

Though Nehru lives in constant danger of assassination, he appears not to live in fear of it or in any event he shows no fear. As Churchill has said of him, he has mastered fear and conquered hate. He seems to have no bitterness against the British though he struggled against them for twenty-five years, though they kept him in jail for a total of ten years, and though almost all his loved ones were imprisoned by the British and some were beaten by their police. He seems to have no hatred or bitterness against any group of people – except perhaps the extremist Hindus, the kind who murdered Gandhi. His motto is, confidence begets confidence. In order that someone may have confidence in you, you must show him that you have confidence in him. He says that this works with the masses of India. He carries this thesis over to international affairs. If Eisenhower wants his confidence, Eisenhower must show that he has confidence in him.

In his speeches Nehru tries to communicate to the people of India his feeling of excitement at what he considers to be the high adventure of economic development in which they are engaged. Nehru understands the profound truth about economic advance in an underdeveloped country: that it is not only good in itself, it is good because it gives the people of India more confidence in themselves and in their country. And the more confidence they have, the easier it is for them to withstand the divisive forces of regionalism, language, religion and caste, and the corrosive forces of underemployment, unemployment, sickness, hunger and hopelessness.

The person who has had the greatest influence on him is Gandhi. He keeps remembering that Gandhi emphasized the necessity of distinguish-

ing between the evil thing and the evil-doer: in the struggle for independence, the Indians should hate the evil of imperialism, but they should
have no bitterness or hatred in their hearts for the individuals who served
that evil thing. He often recalls that it was the obedience of so many
Indians to this teaching of Gandhi – plus, he is always generous and
honest enough to add, the very moderate way in which the British used
force to suppress the independence movement, and their decision to leave
when they did – which made it possible for the final parting between
India and Britain to take place 'gracefully, graciously and with a minimum of bitterness.' It has been the persistence of Gandhi's influence
which has, ever since India became independent, prevented him from
accepting the regimes in Russia or communist China as really 'good'
regimes. He says there is 'too much coercion and suffering' in the 'methods employed in certain communist societies' and these are 'not the right
methods.'

Nehru finds it exciting to be the creative, practical politician who
prods, pushes, pulls, cajoles, and leads India out of the bullock-cart and
cow-dung age into the age of jet airplanes and nuclear energy. Because
he is the leader of India in a high adventure of national development,
he lives in a pleasurable state of whirling, restless activity, a state he
himself has called 'continuous excitement.'

Sometimes I have had the feeling watching Nehru that he is a magician
who conjures up a vision of a united, progressive India and that when
he passes from the scene, the vision will disappear. It is a vision which
he conjures up and he conjures it up deliberately. He doesn't do it to
mislead the foreigner. He does it because he knows that India can advance only if it can see visions and dream dreams, if it draws on the
best in its past, if it breaks with the worst.

He loves India in a poetic, almost mystical way. He loves the land
of India, and it is a land which is easy to love. He grows rhapsodical
about India, the mountains, the plains, the backwaters of Travancore,
the ancient monuments, and the lovely shrines. He is enchanted by the
great vistas of Indian history. Whenever he mentions Benares, he talks
of how moving it is to any Indian to walk in a city which for three thousand
years has been a holy city of India. As an Indian living in 1957, he is
patriotically proud of the Buddha who died 2,500 years ago, whom he
calls India's greatest son.

Anyone who tries to describe Nehru must feel very much the way he
felt when he tried to describe Gandhi. He said recently of this, 'It's always
difficult to describe a man who is rather unusual and a tremendous
personality, and who gave an impression of enormous strength and inner

reserves of power ... And then his career was one of success ... in moulding the Indian people ... in making them better than they were, stronger,
braver, more disciplined.'

This assessment of Nehru did not, I think, enhance my reputation in
Ottawa. Rather, it confirmed the suspicion that I had been so captivated
by Nehru as to be incapable of weighing judicially his demerits against
his merits, his weaknesses against his strengths, his failures against
his accomplishments. I was indeed captivated by Nehru. How far this
affected my judgment of his policies is another matter. But in being
captivated I was in good company. Arnold Toynbee in an obituary
essay on Nehru used the word captivation to describe the effect Nehru
had on him.[6] Walter Crocker, who was for many years Australia's high
commissioner to India, wrote, 'Most people found Nehru captivating. I
certainly did.'[7]Asoka Mehta, economist and politician, in his book of reflections published thirteen years after Nehru's death, wrote, 'His lone-
liness was no bar to his ability to charm, captivate those who came in
contact with him.'[8]

My impression when I was in India in the winter of 1978–79 was that
there had been a considerable increase in the number of people in India
who denigrated Nehru. This is not surprising. Many of the hopes and
dreams and visions of a quarter-century before had not been fulfilled
and it was tempting to make Nehru the scapegoat. The question which
tantalizes me is not so much what people now think of Nehru's record
but what Nehru himself would have thought of it if he had lived until
1979 and had realized at the age of ninety that in over thirty years of
independence the conditions of life of the poorest people of India had
improved little if at all. This would assuredly have broken his heart.
How far would he have blamed himself?

Nehru's accomplishments and failures have to be seen against the
daunting problems he had to deal with when he became prime minister.
There were the problems of partition, communal violence, refugees, and
the princely states; but far transcending all these in importance was the
fact that 'on the eve of Independence, India was still stamped with the
sharp disparities of the most deeply stratified society in human history,'[9]

6 *Encounter* magazine, June 1964
7 Walter Crocker, *Nehru* (London: Allen and Unwin 1966), 11
8 Asoka Mehta, *Reflections on Socialist Era* (New Delhi: S. Chand 1977), 403
9 Francine Frankel, *India's Political Economy, 1947–1977: The Gradual Revolution*
  (Princeton: Princeton University Press 1978), 18

stratified by caste, economic class, language, religion, and region, and
that it was a society where grinding poverty was the lot of most of its
people and had been their lot for centuries. India may be in a parlous
state today, but if Nehru had been assassinated in 1946 how much more
parlous would India's state be? For Nehru fought for the things which
are most likely to hold India together and to bring its people in time out
of the morass of their poverty – secularism, protection of the rights of
minorities, respect for democratic parliamentary institutions, insistence
on the necessity of social reform, faith in the essential goodness and
intelligence of the people of India, contempt for lavish expenditure by
the rich, sorrow and anger because of the misery of the poor, pride in
India's past, visions of India's future greatness.

India was a life-enhancing experience for Ruth and me and our children.
For me India was the university of my middle years. Ruth complemented
her activities as a brilliant diplomatic hostess by working in a free medical
clinic for the poor. We both fell in love with India. Morna was with us
for our first two and a half years. She was then at her loveliest, in the
golden years from eighteen to twenty-one. She came with us on most of
our tours of India. She went to the University of Delhi for a year. She
learned to ride and was presented with a prize for her riding by the
president of India. She brought many young Indians to our house. Her
years in India were among the happiest of her life.

Patrick spent eight months with us between graduating from the University of Toronto and going to Cambridge, and Timothy was with us
for almost a year between graduating from Ridley College and going to
the University of Toronto. They joined Ruth and me on some of our
official travels but they enjoyed more their travels on their own. Patrick
and Morna trekked in Kashmir. Morna and Timothy did an eight-week
tour of southern India and Ceylon. Patrick and Timothy each stayed for
some weeks with David Hopper, later a senior vice-president of the
World Bank, in a poor village in Uttar Pradesh where he was doing
research for his PhD. They saw there the misery and injustices suffered
by poor villagers and became conscious of the daunting problems of
development in a poor country.

The longer Timothy lived with us in New Delhi the more impatient
he became with the way in which distinguished Canadian visitors to
India were shielded from seeing the miserable conditions in which so
many Indians lived, and when Paul Martin, then minister of health and
welfare, stayed with us at Christmas 1956, Tim took him sightseeing in

Delhi. He showed him the worst slums of Delhi and Paul came back to the residence visibly shaken.

The high point of our stay in India was in the summer of 1954 when all five of us and our dog, a Tibetan hound, trekked in the Himalayas above Almora on the way to the Pindari glacier. The children reached the glacier. Ruth and I stopped about three-quarters of the way there in a rest-house where we and the children celebrated our twenty-fourth wedding anniversary with a bottle of champagne.

18

Ambassador to Germany
1958–1962

In mid-April 1958 I wrote our children a long letter about my impressions of our first two and a half months in Germany and the differences between life in Cologne and Bonn and life in Delhi. In those days the ambassador's residence was in Cologne and the office in Bonn.

I said that in Delhi I spent about a third of my time in negotiations with the Indian government on projects we were financing or might finance under the Colombo Plan. 'Every one of the negotiations used to involve protracted and often heated discussions with our people in Ottawa and protracted but less heated discussions with the Indians ... Here in Bonn we have few negotiations with the Germans on anything ... There are also virtually no diplomatic negotiations in the sense of discussions in which the Canadian ambassador, under instructions from Ottawa, tries to persuade the German government to modify its policy on some matter of common concern. I've been looking over our files for the past couple of years before I arrived here and can find no occasion with the exception of a protest over German commercial policy.'

I contrasted this with India where I carried out instructions to try to persuade the Indians to modify their policies on a very considerable number of questions. 'Some were connected with the Korean armistice; many were connected with the work of the supervisory commissions in Indo-China; there were a number of interventions relating to the U.N.; and one or two on Goa.'

In Bonn our job was not negotiating but reporting on German views and policies. 'Our reports help Ottawa to frame instructions to our representatives on NATO, OEEC and GATT ...[and occasionally] to frame instructions to our embassy in Washington to try to persuade the Americans to try to persuade the Germans to modify their policies. This may be a useful clue to the difference between Bonn and Delhi. If we in Canada wanted the Indian government to modify its policy on some important matter, the last thing we would think of doing would be to ask Washington – or London – to talk to the Indians ... For India is not a country where United States influence is paramount. Germany is. Germany is clearly out to establish itself in the eyes of the Americans as the strongest and most dependable ally the United States has.' In Delhi Canada had a position of greater magnitude than its importance in international affairs warranted; in Bonn it has less. 'In Delhi Canada ranks in influence among the first half dozen powers. In Bonn Canada ranks among the second dozen.'

Then, I said, there is the business of living with ghosts and among murderers and torturers: 'In both countries you do that. The streets of Delhi must contain thousands of people who took part in cold-blooded, organized mass murder at the time of partition ... But there was nothing in India comparable with the twelve-year-long purgatory of Hitler's concentration camps, the methodical extermination of six million Jews, the bestialities of the occupation of Poland and the Ukraine, the horror of mass murder and torture organized by government and acquiesced in by all but a minute proportion of the population.'

I concluded by asking our children not to take my depression too seriously. 'The experts say it takes six months to adjust to the climate here. Until then one is apt to suffer from prolonged fits of depression ... I hope that before then I will get caught up in what should be a fascinating intellectual problem of trying to understand the complexities of what is happening here.' I did get caught up in that fascinating intellectual problem but I continued to feel frustrated in my posting to Germany. A year after arriving in Germany I wrote to Norman Robertson, then undersecretary at External Affairs, 'I'm not the kind of person who is interested in jobs which are mostly reporting and representation. If I stay in External Affairs I want to be in a place where I have a good chance to influence the thinking of the government on the bigger issues of foreign policy.'

My hope that my stay in Germany would be brief provided me with an excuse for not learning to speak German. My stay was not brief. It lasted four years.

A few weeks after my arrival in Germany, I visited Berlin to present my credentials as head of the so-called military mission in Berlin, which was really a sort of consulate general. My credentials were addressed to the Allied Control Commission composed of representatives of the United States, Britain, France, and the Soviet Union. The commission had not functioned for years and the presentation of the credentials was pure farce. The chairmanship of the commission alternated every month among the four powers and in February the chairman was France so that the French protocol officer headed the group to receive my credentials. He met me and the officers of the Canadian mission accompanying me at the entrance to the Allied Control Commission building, conducted us through a vast entrance hall reminiscent of a deserted Grand Central Station and along long corridors to a small room. There we lounged in shabby chairs and chatted informally for fifteen minutes. At exactly 12:15 the Frenchman said with a deadpan expression that the Soviet authorities had been warned two weeks before of the meeting, that we had now waited fifteen minutes for their representative to appear, that our place of meeting was only five minutes from his office, and that it therefore appeared that our Soviet colleague was unable to attend. (A Soviet delegate had not attended any such meeting for at least five or six years.)

The Frenchman then rose to his feet and stood solemnly at attention. I, of course, did the same, and we exchanged the ponderous platitudes appropriate to the occasion. I then handed to him my letter of accreditation. I handed copies to the British and United States representatives. One copy was left over, that addressed to the Soviet representative, and, playing my part in the farce, I handed this to the Frenchman with the request that he pass it on to his Soviet colleague.

The Frenchman then suggested that he take me to the room in the building where the Allied Control Authority used to meet and where the Four-Power Conference on Germany met in 1954. We retraced our way along the long corridor, ascended a grand staircase, and entered a vast, unfurnished and cold room. After I had gazed at this historic site for a minute my guide threw open the doors to the next room which was as large, if less imposing, likewise unfurnished and even colder. This, he told me was where refreshments used to be served after Allied Control Authority meetings. One connecting door after another was thrown open and we passed from one cold, unfurnished room to another. He explained that there were several hundred rooms in the building, all but a dozen of which were unoccupied and unfurnished. Even though office accommodation in Berlin was scarce it was necessary that the rooms should remain unused since otherwise the western powers would be giving the impression that they thought that the four-power government of Germany had irretrievably broken down. I hazarded the suggestion that perhaps keeping four of the rooms empty would be a sufficient gesture for this purpose.

We were all so frozen after our tour through this ghost-ridden structure that we welcomed with great warmth a lunch which the French protocol officer gave for us at the Maison de France. My host had carried his passion for farce to his arrangements for lunch for he had reserved a seat for the Soviet protocol officer. This seat having been removed, the eight of us sat down for a two and a half hour luncheon party.

The next day I called on the Soviet commandant in Berlin and the general and I toasted each other in brandy. He proposed a toast to the abolition of all armed forces. I replied with a toast to the abolition of all passports. He proposed peace. For the next toast I said I would use the words of Mr Krushchev when I was introduced to him in India at the end of 1955, 'Ah, the ambassador of our great neighbour to the north.' I proposed the toast 'Our great neighbour to the north.'

The high point of my visit to Berlin was my call on Willy Brandt, who had the year before become mayor of Berlin. I was so impressed by the intelligence and charm of this handsome forty-five-year-old that when I returned to Bonn I said to my colleagues at the embassy that I was sure he would be the next Social-Democratic Party candidate for the chancellorship of Germany. My forecast was greeted with profound scepticism. I have been better at forecasting developments in the politics of other countries than in my own. When Ruth and I heard over the radio in November 1948 that the voters of Illinois had elected Adlai Stevenson governor by a majority of 480,000 and had given President Truman a majority of only 20,000, I said to Ruth that I would be willing to place a bet that Stevenson would be the Democratic candidate for the presidency in four years' time. I told Stevenson this a few weeks later and when he became the presidential candidate in 1952 I reminded him of it. He replied, 'I have not forgotten your curious prophecy of 1948. I hope you didn't omit something – "and that he will be the worst President in history." '

Shortly after my return from my first visit to Berlin we gave a dinner in honour of Franz Joseph Strauss, the minister of defence. I mentioned to Frau Strauss who was sitting beside me at the dinner table my feeling that Brandt would be the next Social-Democratic Party candidate for the chancellorship. She exploded: 'That bastard. He was a communist when he was young. He fought against us in Spain. He wore a Norwegian uniform during the war.' When some years later Brandt was campaigning for the chancellorship Strauss said in a public speech: 'We know what we were doing during the war. What was Willy Brandt doing?'

Christian Democrat attacks on Brandt for having been an anti-Nazi exile were so vicious and so well reported by American correspondents in Germany that they helped, along with anti-semitic outbursts in Germany and the trial of Adolf Eichmann in Jerusalem, to rekindle dislike of West Germany in the United States. The attacks on Brandt were composed of lies and half-truths. He was illegitimate; he did not know who his father was. He had never been a communist but he had in 1931 at the age of eighteen left the Social-Democratic Party to join a left-wing splinter group, the Socialist Workers Party. He was in Spain for five months during the civil war, not as a soldier, but as a correspondent for Scandinavian newspapers. When Hitler came to power he fled to Norway; when Germany occupied Norway he fled to Sweden. He worked in the underground resistance in Norway and in Germany. He did wear a Norwegian uniform during the war; he put it on so that when he was taken prisoner by the German occupation forces he would be treated as a prisoner of war and his real identity would not be discovered. He became a Norwegian citizen. After the war he came to Berlin as press attaché at the Norwegian mission in Berlin. In 1947 he gave up his Norwegian citizenship to become head of the Berlin office of the Social-Democratic Party. Ten years later he was elected mayor of Berlin.

We enjoyed our visits to Berlin which we made two or three times a year. I always had a talk with Willy Brandt and he and his very charming wife would usually come to dinner with us. Sometimes there would only be the four of us at the dinner. Sometimes we would give a dinner party. Florence Bird in her memoirs describes one such party. She arrived too late to study the seating plan for the dinner and was surprised to find that Brandt was on Ruth's left at the dinner table and that the guest of honour on her right was 'a tall, loud-voiced, arrogant-looking man.' When she was talking to Brandt after dinner this man came over to them and began talking excitedly about the Soviet Union. She quotes him as saying: 'It's no use trying to reason with them or work with them. The only way we can settle the mess here in Berlin is to have a preventive war right away before the Russians get any stronger.' Florence Bird was furious. She attacked him vigorously: no Canadian in his right mind favoured a preventive war; he should be ashamed to talk that way in front of the mayor of Berlin. Brandt listened to the heated argument with a deadpan expression on his face. When the other guests had left Florence asked me who this unpleasant man was. I said he was General Hamlet, the United States member of the four-power Allied Control Commission in Berlin who as such outranked the mayor of Berlin. The next day at the end of her interview with Brandt 'I told him I owed him an apology as I had not known who the American was and certainly had no intention of embarrassing him in front of the general. Brandt's face lit up and for a moment a broad grin wiped away the lines of worry and fatigue. "You didn't know who he was?" he said. "You didn't know. Well, you were wonderful. You said all the things I wanted to say and couldn't say. Thank you." [1]

When Davie Fulton, then minister of justice, came to Germany with a parlimentary delegation I took him to call on Brandt. He asked my advice on how best to start the conversation. I said – it was during one of the Berlin crises – that everyone who called on Brandt would ask him about the crisis. Why not ask him, as one politician to another, about the changes which the recent congress of his party in November 1959 had made in the party's program? Fulton took my advice. Brandt said that when the socialist party was founded, the regime in Germany under Bismarck was based on the support of the church and the army. It was therefore natural that the socialist party would be anticlerical and anti-militarist. If it was to gain power it had to break with both these traditions. It was now trying to make clear to the voters that socialism was no surrogate for religion. I was delighted with the use of the precisely correct word, surrogate. (In his autobiography Brandt states that to his grandfather 'socialism was more than a political programme; it was rather a kind of religion.' His grandfather subscribed to the militant anticlericalism of the founders of the Social-Democratic Party.)[2]

We took pleasure in the humour of the Berliners. I wrote our children:

The Berliners pride themselves on their own special type of humour which is, I am told, similar to London Cockney humour. There was an international building exhibition in Berlin a year or so ago. Two churches were put up, one Roman Catholic and one Protestant, both in very modern styles. The Roman Catholic one is called by the Berliners, the Jesus Christ power house. Another new church in West Berlin looks like a Nissen hut. It was easy for the Berliners to christen this St. Nissen. The Americans built a congress hall for the Germans. There is a dispute among the Berliners as to whether it is a pregnant butterfly or a pregnant oyster. The Hochschule for music is called by them either the music aquarium or the symphony garage. There is a big office building which is occupied entirely by offices of the clothing industry. The third floor is not closed in. It is an open space. This building is therefore called the Bikini building.

The attack by Frau Strauss on Willy Brandt because 'he fought against us in Spain' was an indication of the failure of many Germans to realize that most of us in the West believed that it was Germany which had

1 Florence Bird, *Anne Francis: an autobiography by Florence Bird* (Toronto: Clark Irwin 1974), 249–50
2 Willy Brandt, *My Road to Berlin* (London: Peter Davies 1960), 23, 50

fought against us in Spain. Frau Strauss's blindness to this was shared by her husband and by other cabinet ministers. In February 1960 Strauss, as minister of defence, sent a mission to Spain to negotiate for military facilities there for the German armed forces, what was commonly called at the time an effort to establish German bases in Spain. This set off protests in western countries, including Canada. A German cabinet minister said to me about these protests, 'The Americans have bases in Spain, why shouldn't we?'

Most Germans were unable to comprehend the depth and intensity of the hatred aroused against Nazi Germany because of its alliance with Franco and the persistence of this feeling twenty years later. They were likewise unable to comprehend the much greater hatred and loathing of Nazi Germany because of its murder of the Jews and the atrocities committed in Poland and Ukraine and why the West felt that post-Hitler Germany had failed miserably to show that it was ashamed of these crimes.

I wrote half a dozen despatches and telegrams to Ottawa on what I called 'Penitence, punishment, purging and pedagogy.' I said that in the immediate post-war years the responsibility for punishing crimes committed under the Nazi regime was assumed by the Allied powers and consequently Germans were not forced to face the problem themselves. Moreover they were compelled in those years to concentrate their energies almost exclusively on securing food and shelter and rebuilding their shattered economy. For those Germans who knew the enormity of the crimes committed by Germans under the Nazi regime there was every desire to forget. For those who knew only a little of the era's evils, there was no desire to know more. The German people repudiated the doctrine of collective guilt as morally untenable but gave little evidence of having a sense of collective shame or even collective grief or collective responsibility. The authorities in West Germany were slow in punishing Nazi criminals and little protest was made at the return of former Nazis to positions of importance in public life. The Hitler era was largely ignored in the schools of Germany and most parents remained silent about their life under the Third Reich, with the result that most German youths knew little or nothing of the Nazi past.

The German conscience began to awaken in the late 1950s but it was not until the wave of anti-semitic outbreaks perpetrated by youths at the beginning of 1960 and the violent reaction abroad to these outbreaks that the government and people of West Germany were shocked into realizing how far they had allowed themselves to suppress memories of the past and what a frightening gap existed in the knowledge of young

Germans of the recent past of their country. It became evident that West Germany had not done enough to show penitence for Nazi crimes, to punish those who could be convicted of direct participation in them, to purge the organs of the state of those who had been involved in the crimes, and to educate the German people, and especially German youth, about them. During the year and a half after the anti-semitic outbreaks much was done to correct these errors. The Eichmann trial in 1961 gave further impetus to these efforts.

Films and television programs were especially effective. One influential film was a two-hour-long Swedish documentary, 'Mein Kampf,' made up of news films taken at the time. It was played to crowded cinemas throughout the country. I wrote to my mother: 'It was very moving and horrible. The worst scenes were the slow starvation of the Jews in the ghetto in Warsaw and the fortunately brief shots of the extermination camps for Jews and others. For the last hour there was not a sound in the crowded theatre. When it ended people filed out in complete silence not even daring to look at each other.' Even more influential was a series of fourteen television programs called 'The Third Reich.' Between eight to twelve million West Germans followed the series, which starkly portrayed the excesses of Nazi barbarism and stated that the crimes had been committed 'by Germans in the name of Germany.'

Prime Minister Diefenbaker visited Germany in the autumn of 1958. His talk with Adenauer, instead of lasting the hour and a half allotted to it on the program lasted two and a quarter hours. The first thing they talked about was how much each of them loved politics and loved political campaigning. (When talking to me afterwards Diefenbaker made fun of statesmen who talked about the heavy burdens of office.) Most of the rest of the talk was about the crisis in negotiations for a free-trade area. Then Adenauer gave a survey of how the world seemed to him. He had grave worries about the American presidential elections in 1964 and 1968. Afterwards I said to Diefenbaker that it was paradoxical that the oldest of the western leaders was the one who was most worried about the situation ten years from now. Diefenbaker said that he had made a practice of not worrying about anything that might happen the day after tomorrow.

In a letter I wrote immediately after the visit I said that Diefenbaker had been very impressed by Adenauer,

not so much his views and his intellect but his youthfulness, his energy, his pleasure in good food and good wine, his gaiety when he relaxes as he did at our dinner [for Diefenbaker]. ... My guess is that the most important result of Mr. Diefenbaker's visit to Germany is that he is now turning over in his mind the thought that if Dr. Adenauer can be as vigorous as this at the age of 82 there is no reason why he cannot be equally vigorous at the same age and, therefore, no reason why he cannot be prime minister for another twenty years.

At the dinner we gave for Diefenbaker I had on my right Frau Gerstenmaier, the wife of the president of the Bundestag. She said to me that what had struck her in Diefenbaker's speeches and in talking to him when she had sat beside him at dinner the previous night was that he had faith in people. 'It is difficult for us in Europe to have faith in people after seeing the horrible things that people can do to each other.'

After two and a half days in Bonn we went to Soest to visit the Canadian brigade. There were fifty-five hundred Canadian soldiers there and about thirty-five hundred wives, making nine thousand voters. During that one day in Soest, beginning with a parade in the morning and lasting until about eleven o'clock at night, Diefenbaker must have talked individually to over a thousand Canadians. He would break away from the official program to mingle with women and children who were bystanders. He insisted on adding two items to the already heavy schedule, both of them visits to sergeants' messes. Indeed, we broke away from an officers' ball after we had been there about an hour in order to go to a sergeants' mess where there were about 160 sergeants with their wives. There were more votes in the sergeants' mess than at the officers' ball. After I saw him performing I could understand the success of his political campaigning in Canada.

Diefenbaker impressed me by his inexhaustible energy, his fund of anecdotes, and his ability as a mimic. He mimicked R.B. Bennett, George Drew, and Gordon Churchill, the minister of commerce. When we were sitting alone in the car driving to the parade at Soest he told me about George Drew's weaknesses as a politician. Drew could never turn an embarrassing incident into a source of strength. In British Columbia the most popular person among all parties was Howard Green who had been a captain in the First World War. George Drew, who was then the Conservative leader, was being introduced at a big public meeting by Leon Ladner, an old British Columbia politician. After a great buildup about the merits of the leader of the Conservative party in which George Drew's name was never mentioned, Ladner ended by saying, 'And I now introduce Captain George Green.' Diefenbaker said that Drew got up (and here he started imitating him), biting his lower lip and looking very embarrassed and even angry. The result was that the audience burst into laughter at him. I said to Diefenbaker, 'What would you have done?' He said, 'I would have told a story which would have got the audience laughing with me instead of against me.' He then produced two stories, either of which he would have used, but I have no doubt if I had pressed him and we had had enough time he would have produced six stories which would have been suitable for the occasion.

The one which, according to Mrs Diefenbaker, was a favourite of his was of a Canadian Club meeting in Vancouver at which he was speaking. The chairman was a man of no experience in chairing public meetings. He was head of the Ford organization in British Columbia and was a good automobile dealer, but not a good public speaker. He was introducing Diefenbaker just after Diefenbaker had been made leader of the Conservative party. His introductory speech went on and on. He shovelled the compliments on the new leader. After the introduction had gone on for some time Diefenbaker became certain that the reason it was going on so long was that the chairman couldn't remember his name. Finally, a look of intense relief passed over the chairman's face. He had remembered the name he was searching for. He brought his speech hastily to a close with the words, 'And I now have the pleasure of calling on Mr. John G. Studebaker.'

He told me that the article about him in the *Saturday Evening Post* had about twenty errors. One was that he had defended twenty people charged with murder and that only two of them had been hanged. He said it was twenty-six and that one of the two hanged was innocent. It was because of this that since he had been prime minister almost all sentences of hanging had been commuted by cabinet.

When the second volume of Diefenbaker's memoirs was published in 1976 I discovered that I had had more influence on his thinking about international affairs than I had thought. In his memoirs he wrote that when he had looked ahead into the sixties the major problems had seemed to him to be:

one, how to work out effective international agreements to reduce the dangers resulting from the development of methods of mass destruction; two, how to minimize the dangers to the free world created by the rise of China to the rank of a first-class power; three, how to maintain an effective balance of military power with the Russo-Chinese bloc; four, how to reduce the dangers created by the division of Europe into a Soviet zone and a Western zone, particularly the division of Germany and Berlin; five, how to organize effective help to India to speed up its economic development; six, how to prevent independent Africa south of the Sahara from relapsing into chaos and how to facilitate the orderly progress of the remaining dependent territories in Africa (including Angola and Mozambique) to independence; seven, how to deal with the population explosion; and eight, how to work out equitable international arrangements under which the Western industrialized countries would each accept its fair share of a rapidly increasing flow of low-priced manufactured goods from the underdeveloped countries.[3]

The language sounded strangely familiar and I soon discovered why. It reproduced word for word a passage in a memorandum I had sent the Department of External Affairs from Germany in September 1960.

I wish that in his memoirs Diefenbaker had gone on to state his agreement with the immediately following paragraph in my memorandum:

These problems are, of course, related. They exacerbate each other. But even if communism did not exist, if Russia and China did not exist, or if Russia and China were liberal democracies, would not many of these problems be intractable and endanger the peace and welfare not only of the advanced countries but of the whole world? Is not this, for example, true of the problems of India and of Africa? Would not the present explosive growth in the population of the world, the difficulty of obtaining acceptance by Western nations of cheap manufactured goods from underdeveloped countries, and the control of methods of mass destruction constitute serious problems? While problems like these have significant implications for the struggle between the Russo-Chinese bloc and NATO, surely they have their core and origin in circumstances not directly related to that struggle.

Hasso von Etzdorf was German ambassador to Canada and was about to be posted back to the Foreign Office in Bonn when my appointment as ambassador to Germany was announced. He immediately invited Ruth and me to have dinner with his wife Katharina and himself. We saw a good deal of them before we left Ottawa for Germany and we became friends. On our last talk before we left Ottawa Etzdorf said to me, 'Let us agree now to stop calling each other Mr Ambassador and Herr von Etzdorf. If we don't stop this now while we are in Canada we never will once we are both in Germany. Let us call each other by our Christian names.' So from then on it was Hasso and Escott, Katharina and Ruth.

We soon discovered in Germany how right Etzdorf was. We found

3 John G. Diefenbaker, *One Canada: The Years of Achievement, 1957–1962* (Toronto: Macmillian of Canada 1976), 146–7

that Germans called very few of their German friends by their Christian names and virtually no foreigners. Evangeline Bruce, the charming wife of the American ambassador, disliked this intensely. She organized an outing in the country for a party of about ten, equally divided between wives of ambassadors, including Ruth, and wives of senior German officials. Before they set forth Evangeline Bruce said, 'Let us stop calling each other Frau so-and-so and Mrs so-and-so. Let us call each other by our Christian names. I am Vangy.' Everyone agreed and during the outing they did so. But never again.

During much of the war Etzdorf was the liaison officer between the Foreign Office and the high command of the German army. He was privy to the plots which German generals made to kill Hitler. After the failure of the Stauffenberg conspiracy the general with whom he had been most closely associated spent two days going through his papers to eliminate anything which might implicate others and then shot himself. This saved Etzdorf from execution.

One of Etzdorf's colleagues in the upper ranks of the Foreign Office was George F. Duckwitz. He was known as Dookey and his wife was Annemarie. We met them through the Etzdorfs and became friends. Sometimes they would join the Etzdorfs and us in the walks we took every Sunday morning in the Eiffel hills above Cologne. Duckwitz had been attached during the war to the German mission in occupied Denmark. He learned that the Jews in Denmark were about to be rounded up and sent off to Germany to be killed. He warned some Danish friends and they organized the escape of the Jews to Sweden. Hitler was enraged. If he had learned of what Duckwitz had done, Duckwitz would have been executed, probably after prolonged torture. His act demonstrated courage of a high order. During the Eichmann trial the Israeli government paid tribute to him.

I was fortunate to have two such good friends as Etzdorf and Duckwitz in the senior ranks of the Foreign Office. They were my guides and informants on developments in German foreign policy. Etzdorf was on the whole a supporter of the foreign policy of Adenauer and Brentano; Duckwitz was a severe critic of the rigidity of that policy. He believed that Germany should seek an accommodation with East Germany and Poland. His views were considered dangerous and heretical until Willy Brandt became chancellor. Duckwitz was then recalled from retirement and made head of the Foreign Office, the state secretary, so that he could assist Willy Brandt in his Ostpolitik. If Duckwitz had been especially indiscreet in talking to me I would not, in my report to Ottawa, name him as the source of my information but would say it had come from a top official in the Foreign Office. I cherish a letter he wrote me at the end of January 1970: 'Having been by now State Secretary for about two and a half years, the moment is approaching when I will leave this office and return to Bremen for the second time. Before doing so I shall have to lead rather difficult talks with Poland, an assignment for which nobody envies me. But, why should a career always end with a success and not sometimes with a failure?' Duckwitz's courageous career ended with a success.

Another of my good fortunes in Germany was to be there when David Bruce was American ambassador. He was charming, well informed, and intelligent and he helped me to understand what was happening in Germany. He, like two of the American ambassadors I served with in India, Chester Bowles and Sherman Cooper, was not a professional foreign service officer. Another non-career American ambassador I have known, Kenneth Galbraith, came to India as an economic adviser to the Indian government during my time as high commissioner, and I later used to draw on his wisdom whenever I came to India on behalf of the World Bank during his ambassadorship there. My association with these four non-career ambassadors has made it impossible for me to maintain that outsiders should never be appointed ambassadors, provided – and the proviso is essential – that they are up to the standard of Bowles, Cooper, Bruce and Galbraith – and that is a very high standard.

When I arrived in Germany at the beginning of 1958 German foreign policy on the main issues of relations with the Soviet bloc was inflexible. On the question of a possible recognition by West Germany of East Germany (the DDR), Brentano, the foreign minister, said to me in December 1958 that it was impossible. The seventeen million Germans in East Germany would say, if West Germany recognized the DDR, 'This is our death sentence.' They would be left without hope. There was no use in speaking to the DDR; their government was not composed of German politicians but of Russian policemen. As for recognizing the Oder-Neisse line, only an all-German government formed following free elections in all Germany would have the moral authority to make an agreement on Germany's eastern border. The German government had, however, time and time again declared that it would never use force to obtain a change in the existing *de facto* German border. It was also, he said, clear that Germany could not hope to get back the lands east of that border from which twelve to fourteen million Germans had fled, since Poland had to have compensation in the west for its loss of territories in the east to the Soviet Union. At this time Germany adhered to the Hallstein doctrine: it would not maintain diplomatic relations with any government other than that of the Soviet Union which had diplomatic relations with the DDR, as Poland, Czechoslovakia, and Yugoslavia had.

One possible explanation of the inflexibility at that time of German foreign policy on relations with the Soviet Union is that Adenauer believed that the West must hold the line firmly in Europe against the Russians until the Russians became so frightened of the growing might of China that they would make peace with the West on terms favourable to the West in order to be able to strengthen their flank against the Chinese. Then Germany would be unified in peace and freedom; then the eastern satellites of Russia would become free. Adenauer did not, so far as I was aware, talk about the 'yellow peril,' but the partner of his closest intimate did and sometimes this man echoed Adenauer. He told me that Kaiser Wilhelm II was right when he called fifty years ago for Europe to unite against the yellow peril. I said I could see no necessity for us to ally ourselves with Russia when Russia and China fell out. Why not let them kill each other off? He was visibly annoyed. When I reported this to one of my German friends he said the reason he was so annoyed was that he thought I was alluding to the belief of many people in Britain in the thirties that we should welcome a German war against the Soviet Union since they would kill each other off.

In December 1958 I participated in a meeting in Paris of the Canadian ambassadors in Western Europe with the minister, Sidney Smith, and senior officers of the department in Ottawa. We discussed whether it would be wise to try to persuade Germany to retreat from this no-no policy on the recognition of the DDR and of the Oder-Neisse line. Some of those present shared the views which Charles Ritchie, my predecessor as ambassador in Bonn, had expressed a few months after his departure from Germany. In March 1958 he had said that there survived in Germany an element of nostalgia for the days of the Ribbentrop-Molotov pact, and we must beware of policies which would leave an embittered Germany with a new legend of a stab in the back and ripe for entanglement with Russia. Others at the meeting in Paris considered that the risks of pushing Germany into agreeing to concessions would be worth taking if they resulted in a more tolerable *modus vivendi* with the Soviet Union.

In March 1959, three months later, I sent Ottawa a memorandum setting out a possible *modus vivendi*. Norman Robertson commented: 'I think something like Mr. Reid's "hypothetical" nine points makes a good deal of sense – though the Germans have not been prepared for anything like it. They have been encouraged in their complacency by Allied policy over the years – naturally have not begun to think in other terms.'

My nine points were: (1) Renunciation by West Germany of the territories beyond the Oder-Neisse line, which belonged to the Reich in 1939 and which were now under Soviet and provisional Polish administration. (2) *De facto* recognition of the DDR by West Germany and its allies. (3) Admission of both German states to the United Nations. (4) Establishment of diplomatic relations between West Germany and Poland and Czechoslovakia. (5) The 'thinning out' of an area in Central Europe comprising the two Germanies, Poland, Czechoslovakia, and Hungary. In this area there would be no nuclear arms, that is to say, neither nuclear warheads nor the means of their delivery. There would be a limitation of other armaments and there would be international inspection and control. (6) Maintenance of western troops in West Berlin with better assured rights of access. (7) Maintenance of United States and other western troops in West Germany. (8) Continued membership of West Germany in NATO and of the DDR in the Warsaw Pact. (9) Reiteration by all the powers concerned, and perhaps also by the United Nations General Assembly, of the paramount importance of the reunification of the two Germanies as soon as possible in peace and freedom.

My second-in-command, Llyn Stephens, took the opposite view and I appended his comments to my memorandum. He argued lucidly and persuasively, (though he did not persuade me) that the policy I advocated violated the deep, abiding, and highly emotional German will for the re-establishment of German political and cultural unity; that it did not enhance and might indeed diminish the strength of the defence of Germany and of Western Europe; that it wounded German national pride; that the longer-run danger of the policy was that a resentful and bitter Germany, labouring under a sense of betrayal by the United States and other western countries, might embark on a course which would seriously damage western interests. He went on to warn against the error of gauging probable German reactions on the assumption that Germans were just like other people and would therefore not cut off their nose to spite their face. He reminded us of the German potentiality for national folly and international mischief, and of the influence which emotion and chauvinistic patriotic fervour could play in German national life. The kind of policy I recommended could result ultimately in an accommodation between West Germany and the Soviet Union with disastrous implications for the West.

I had no success in carrying with me my seconds-in-command at the embassy in my unorthodox views on western policy on Germany. When I put forward another full statement to Ottawa two years later, I said, after summarizing Llyn Stephen's views, 'My present counsellor, Frank Hooton, sharing these concerns, regards the policy I advocate as a dangerous one.'

Discussions on the German problem, especially during my last two years in Germany from 1960 to 1962, were haunted by the fear that the western powers and the Soviet Union might stumble into war as the result of a crisis over Berlin. On instructions from Ottawa we at the embassy worked out plans under which if fighting broke out the wives and children of the members of the embassy would be evacuated, probably along with the wives and children of the members of our army brigade at Soest. It was against this background of fear that formal and informal discussions about the Berlin problem within governments and between governments took place.

One of the proposals which emerged was that the whole of Berlin, East and West, should become an internationalized city under the United Nations and that the U.N. headquarters should be transferred to Berlin from New York. I first heard of this proposal from David Bruce, the American ambassador, at the beginning of March 1959. The American embassy obviously attached importance to selling this idea to me. First Bruce's second-in-command mentioned it; then a week later Bruce urged it on me at a lunch party; and when I called on him to draw him out on his proposal he spoke earnestly and forcefully to me for about forty minutes. He was relatively optimistic that it might be possible to sell the proposal to the Soviet Union. The Soviets, he said, had dropped hints in many capitals of the world of their willingness to modify their proposals for a free city of West Berlin by having them apply to the whole of Berlin.

When I sent Ottawa an account of my talk with Bruce and asked Ottawa to give his proposal sympathetic consideration I said: 'This is the only time in the year since I have known Bruce that he has talked to me in apocalyptic terms and with the fervour of a prophet ... As far as I know he has not a reputation of vigorously advocating unrealistic solutions to intractable problems.'

The more I thought of Bruce's proposal the more I was attracted by it, but I believed it needed some revisions. I believed that if ever Germany were reunified, Berlin should become its capital. Bruce did not. I believed that Berlin should by administered by a freely elected government; Bruce believed that the United Nations should administer the city.

Two and a half years later, in October 1961, I learned from Etzdorf, who was then German ambassador in London, that Lord Home, the British foreign minister, had told him that Berlin might become the Vatican City of the entire world: the U.N. headquarters would be moved to Berlin from New York, as would its Geneva office, UNESCO from Paris, and FAO from Rome.

Just before the abortive four-power summit meeting in 1960 the Soviet Union formally proposed that if the four powers were unable to agree on the terms of a peace treaty with a united Germany, West Berlin should be set up as a free city and the United Nations should in some way be connected with the guarantees which the four powers would give for the defence of the interests of the population of West Berlin. The western powers rejected this proposal out of hand. Duckwitz told me that he believed it would have been wiser if they had replied that they could consider a proposal for a free city only if it applied to the whole of Berlin.

Etzdorf accompanied Brentano on his visit to Washington in February 1961, a month after Kennedy had become president, and Brentano had a talk with Kennedy. Etzdorf and Duckwitz told me that they thought the United States was now prepared to support the establishment of a free city of the whole of Berlin, which would be self-governing, have its rights of access to West Germany guaranteed by the four powers, and not be part of West Germany though it would be able to make cultural and economic agreements with other countries, including West Germany. Six months later, however, Dean Rusk and other leading advisers to the president gave no indication that they favoured these proposals.

In 1945 the four principal Allied powers had secured *de jure* sovereignty over the whole of Berlin as the result of conquest. By mid-1959 I had become convinced that the rights of the four powers in Berlin should no longer be derived from conquest but should be derived from a new contract between them, a contract which would take the form of an international statute, and I put this proposal to Ottawa. The two Germanies would be associated with the statute; the statute would be approved by the Security Council and the General Assembly of the U.N.; it would set forth in clear and precise terms western rights in Berlin and the rights of access to Berlin for western military and civilian traffic; it would not be subject to denunciation by any of the parties to it; any dispute between the parties on its interpretation would go before the International Court and its decision would be final and binding. The association of the DDR with the statute would constitute a long step toward *de facto* recognition of the DDR by the West. The West Germans would resist *de facto* recognition but surely it was possible to find a formula for the association of the DDR with the statute which the East Germans would claim constituted *de facto* recognition and the West Germans that it did not and both sides would have the support of a respectable number of respectable international lawyers. Moreover, many Germans would consider that a new agreement which unified Berlin under a free democratic government, and thus brought freedom to a million East Berliners, was worth the price of a move toward *de facto* recognition of the DDR.

In June 1959 Ottawa instructed me to go to Geneva to report on the foreign ministers' conference of the United States, Britain, France, and the Soviet Union with the two German states in attendance. My four days there were filled with talks: lunch with Selwyn Lloyd, lunch with Brentano, dinner with Duckwitz, calls on Herter, the secretary of state, and his principal adviser, Livingstone Merchant, and meetings with the representatives of the *New York Times* and of the London *Times*.

I reported to Ottawa that I had been struck by the repeated references by Gromyko during the last week of the conference to the juridical question of the basis of future western rights in West Berlin; he had insisted that the occupation of West Berlin was outmoded, that it was impossible for the Soviet government to underwrite the occupation status, that it was inadmissible to perpetuate the regime. Was this, I asked, a hint that the Soviet Union might be prepared to agree that the western powers should, until Germany was reunified, have reasonable rights in Berlin, provided that these rights derived from a new contract with the Soviet Union and that the West renounced its present rights based on conquest? I said that I had discussed with Lloyd, Herter, Brentano, and their advisers the idea of substituting contract for conquest and that my impression from what Lloyd said to me was that he would be happy if this were done. A few weeks later the British ambassador in Bonn told me that this was indeed the British position; the British would prefer to have new title deeds instead of the dog-eared ones they now possessed. Selwyn Lloyd, however, seemed to me to accept as a fact of life that he could not at present overcome the opposition of the United States and France. The fact that he did not mention opposition from West Germany confirmed the feeling I had after talking in Geneva with Brentano and Duckwitz that the West Germans did not have strong views one way or the other. Was there not, I asked Ottawa, a possibility of a bargain with the Soviet Union which would save the faces of both sides: the Soviet Union would get the end of the occupation regime, the West would get more precise and assured rights? 'The USSR would get the shadow, we would get the substance.'

I was in Canada on home leave in the summer of 1961. While I was there the Berlin wall was put up. This did not change my views on the kind of Berlin settlement the West should seek. I had within about a month of my arrival in Germany concluded that the West should accept the probability that the East Germans would take steps to stop the flow of refugees and emigrants from East Germany to West Germany. By the time the wall was put up more than two million had fled and this had greatly weakened East Germany. I knew that Willy Brandt believed this. The erection of the wall, however, greatly increased tensions between East and West and increased the risk of armed clashes. It emphasized the importance of reaching what I called 'some tolerable and honourable accommodation with the Soviet Union on Berlin.'

I discussed with Diefenbaker and with the Department of External Affairs the ideas on such an accommodation which I had been putting up to Ottawa during the preceding two years and Diefenbaker authorized me to go to Washington to discuss them with the State Department on condition that I made clear that they were my personal views and that I was not putting forward the views of the Canadian government. This visit to Washington was the high point in my ambassadorship to Germany.

Arnold Heeney, our ambassador in Washington, gave a dinner party on 23 August to enable me to discuss the Berlin problem informally with the State Department. Dean Rusk, the secretary of state, was there and two senior officers of the State Department, Charles Bohlen, Rusk's senior adviser on Soviet affairs, and Foy Kohler, assistant secretary of state for Eastern European affairs. The fourth American guest was McGeorge Bundy, national security adviser to Kennedy. I had known Rusk and Bohlen for fifteen years or so and was on first-name terms with them. I had not previously met Kohler or Bundy.

I remember vividly that hot Washington August evening. Almost as soon as we sat down at the dinner table Rusk, addressing Heeney, said that he did not usually bring up serious business at the beginning of a diplomatic dinner but this time he would. The United States had just received another note from Krushchev which he characterized as 'gross impertinence.' It accused the United States of abusing its access rights to Berlin by facilitating the entry into West Berlin of spies and saboteurs. Kohler thought this might presage Soviet interference with western access to Berlin by air. Rusk said that the United States thought it important that the West be in a position to impose a complete economic embargo against the Soviet Union and its eastern European satellites should access be denied. The United States had already taken the necessary legal action to permit an embargo to be proclaimed. He urged that the Canadian government do likewise. Heeney, speaking in accordance with instructions he had received from Ottawa, said that we thought consideration of whether or not to apply an embargo should take place only after the Soviet Union had interfered with western access to Berlin. Rusk was impatient with this; he considered that the NATO powers should agree now that if a collapse of talks with the Soviet Union were followed by a Soviet blockade of West Berlin they would impose a complete economic embargo on the Soviet Union and its satellites; this would reduce the risk that armed force would have to be used to break a blockade of West Berlin.

After dinner we settled down to discuss the Berlin question and Heeney asked me to outline my personal ideas. I started by putting the case for substituting contract for conquest as the basis for western rights in Berlin. The Americans vehemently opposed this. As a lawyer Heeney was aghast at their contempt of rights based on contract compared with rights based on conquest and the discussion on this issue between Heeney and the Americans was prolonged. I then brought up the other parts of my proposals: an independent, self-governing, democratic free city of the whole of Berlin; the transfer of the U.N. headquarters to Berlin; and a willingness to use as negotiating counters *de facto* recognition of the DDR and *de jure* recognition of the Oder-Neisse line. This precipitated a discussion which went on for about two hours. Heeney in his report to Ottawa described it as very informal, very private, personal, and uninhibited. I found the discussion to be all of this and also profoundly disturbing.

I dictated a note on the discussion the next morning. I said that Rusk and Bohlen had expressed complete disbelief in the usefulness of informal exploratory talks with the Soviet Union. Their definition of negotiation appeared to be formal confrontations at formal conferences, when surely the essence of negotiation was that it was a long, slow, patient process of bargaining at which tentative ideas were exchanged in quiet confidential talks. Having ruled out all methods of negotiation other than formal confrontations, Rusk came close to ruling out the possibility of anything useful resulting from formal consultation. He said that the Soviet Union had presented proposals on Berlin which were unacceptable to us; we would present counter-proposals which would be unacceptable to them. He must have seen our dismay at this statement, for the fourth time he made it he qualified it by saying that this was the worst that might happen. The West was not going to pay the Soviet Union every year for the right to remain in Berlin which the West had already paid for by its victory in the war. Bohlen expressed complete disbelief in the usefulness of any negotiation with the Soviet Union over anything. He repeated three times the statement, 'The Soviet approach to negotiation is that what is ours is ours and what is yours is negotiable.'

On the central question of what kind of concessions each side might be prepared to trade for counter-concessions by the other side, the discussion was most confused. Some of the Americans argued some of the time that there was nothing the West wanted from the Soviet Union other than respect for our existing rights and why should we pay for that. Some argued some of the time that there was nothing Krushchev would be prepared to give, some that there was nothing the West was prepared to give which the Soviet Union would consider to be worth much, some that all possible ideas had been tried out on the Soviet Union and rejected. The Soviet Union would not be prepared to give much in return for *de jure* recognition of the Oder-Neisse line. A move by the West towards *de facto* recognition of the DDR would be worth more to the Soviet Union. The United States was not prepared to use the bargaining counter of agreeing to end the occupation status of Berlin.

When Rusk dismissed the possibility that the Soviet Union might agree to the creation of a free city of the whole of Berlin I said that there had been hints dropped in many capitals of the world by Soviet spokesmen that they would be willing. He said he had never heard of this. It is hard to believe that this important fact had not been brought to his attention by his advisers. David Bruce had told me that the British had mentioned it in their report to the North Atlantic Council on 5 March 1959. An officer of the policy planning staff of the State Department whom I saw the next day confirmed that there had been hints early in 1959 that the Soviet Union might accept an all-Berlin solution.

I suggested that the key to successful negotiations with the Soviet Union was to uncover the concessions which side A might make to side B which were relatively unimportant to side A but of considerable importance to side B. Rusk could not understand how a concession might be more important to one side than the other. Such a statement from a foreign minister of a major power is incredible since the essence of intelligent bargaining is to uncover just this kind of concession. Bohlen said that it did not matter if public opinion in the NATO countries was not prepared to risk war over minor or symbolic interferences by the Soviet Union with western access to Berlin. The only thing that was important was what the NATO governments were prepared to do and they should be willing to risk war to prevent the Soviet Union from using the salami tactics of successively taking away thin slices of western rights. The Americans showed no concern over the failure of the United States,

Britain, France, and West Germany to discuss among themselves the substance of the Berlin and German problems. Their ambassadors in Washington were supposed to discuss these problems with the State Department but so far these discussions had been concerned only with questions of tactics and of sanctions. The British ambassador in Washington told me that the presence at these meetings of a dozen or more people meant that they could not be used to discuss the delicate problem of establishing an initial western negotiating position and western fall-back positions.

The discussion with Rusk and his colleagues could, I felt, have scarcely been more discouraging. Heeney in his memoirs writes that I

was left with the impression ... that the administration had virtually given up the idea of any modus vivendi with the USSR, that they were totally fed up with their allies and with the uncommitted countries, and that they were going to drive right ahead with their own policies whatever the results on the alliance ... While I did not share my guest's black pessimism as to the attitude of the U.S. administration, I did understand how he had obtained his impression from the conversation that evening.[4]

My black pessimism was somewhat abated by the talks I had the day of the dinner and the following day with Senators Sherman Cooper, Fulbright, and Mansfield and an officer in the policy planning staff of the State Department.

Senator Cooper and I had become friends when we were representing our countries in India. He was a personal friend of President Kennedy. Fulbright was Democratic chairman of the Senate Foreign Relations Committee. Mansfield was Democratic leader in the Senate. I had an hour's talk with Cooper at his home one evening and the next day I had lunch with him and Fulbright in the Senate and afterwards Cooper took me to meet Mansfield. Cooper had spent the day before I saw him with the president, first on his yacht and then at the White House. Kennedy had said to him something like, 'I realize that the time will come when I will have to stand up to public opinion on the Berlin question and move from the present fixed positions.' (My friend Marquis Childs, the well-informed columnist, told me the same thing; he said that Kennedy was prepared to negotiate but that he had not yet prepared the American people for negotiation.) Cooper said that Senator Mansfield had given

4 Arnold Heeney, *The Things That Are Caesar's: Memoirs of a Canadian Public Servant* (Toronto: University of Toronto Press 1972), 177–8

a speech in the Senate advocating a free city of Berlin. The reaction in the United States to the speech had been very bad and this had discouraged others from supporting his proposal. In the last month, however, public opinion had moved a long way and 'negotiation' was no longer a dirty word.

Fulbright, on the other hand, was afraid that public opinion in the United States was so inflamed on the Berlin issue that it might not be prepared to support proposals for a free city of Berlin. He himself remained a convinced believer that we should try to get the Soviet Union to agree to the setting up of a free city of greater Berlin; he was in favour of moving the United Nations headquarters to Berlin, especially since he considered that New York was not an appropriate place for the headquarters; he was also willing to contemplate the vesting in the United Nations of sovereignty over Berlin until Germany was reunified. He realized that the setting up of a free city would mean the abolition of the occupation status of Berlin. He was also prepared to pay the price of *de jure* recognition of the Oder-Neisse line and *de facto* recognition of the DDR. When I asked him what countries like Canada could do, he said that just because the issue of peace and war did not rest in the hands of Canada, whereas a mistake by the United States might precipitate nuclear war, Canada had more freedom of action. If it turned out that the advice we gave was wrong, then only our *amour propre* would suffer. He therefore urged that Canada should put its ideas to the president and the secretary of state. He also thought that public speeches by the Canadian government might do more good than harm. (I suspect that this was the kind of advice Fulbright later gave to Pearson to encourage him to criticize openly United States policy in the Vietnam War.)

The officer I spoke to in the policy planning staff of the State Department told me that five or six officers had been engaged, for the past three months, in working out ideas on the substance of a possible accommodation on the Berlin problem. They were considering all possible negotiating positions and fall-back positions. They had been consulting a number of persons with special expert knowledge on Germany and the Soviet Union such as George Kennan, David Bruce (now ambassador to London), and John J. McCloy. The general view of those who had been consulted was that Krushchev's aim in precipitating a crisis over Berlin was to try to stabilize the Soviet empire in Eastern Europe by securing *de jure* recognition of frontiers and by enhancing as much as possible the status of the DDR. As a result of this assessment of Krushchev's motives, a 'lot of people' were thinking about what the United States might contribute to the stabilization of Eastern Europe since, while it could not be stated publicly, it was common sense that the stability of Eastern Europe was in the long-range interests of the West. The policy planning staff had been thinking about ideas similar to those which I had put forward to him as my personal views. He agreed that one could not rule out the possibility of the Soviet Union agreeing to a united Berlin. The policy planning staff had also been thinking of the possibility of moving the headquarters of the U.N., or at least its European office, to Berlin. Recognition of the Oder-Neisse line should occasion little difficulty and could help stabilize Eastern Europe. Granting the substance of recognition to the DDR would be another stabilizing factor.

The puzzling question is why Rusk, Bohlen, Kohler, and Bundy took such a harshly negative line so remote from the views of leading senators, of the State Department's own policy planning staff, and of the very intelligent American ambassador in Moscow, Llewellyn (Tommy) Thompson, who had told the Canadian ambassador in July that he did not rule out the possibility of finding a political solution of the Berlin and related problems which would safeguard western interests and prove acceptable to the Soviet Union. Why did Rusk and Bundy, both of whom reported direct to the president and were his principal advisers on foreign affairs and must have known how his mind was moving, take a line contrary to the president's realization that the time would come when he would have to stand up to public opinion on the Berlin question and move from the present fixed positions? One clue may lie in a phrase in a letter Bundy sent to Heeney the day after the dinner, 'you really don't think of us as Germans or Russians – and you must never suppose that we think of you as appeasers.' Perhaps Bundy did not think of the Canadian government as appeasers in the Berlin crisis but my guess is that Rusk, Bohlen, and Kohler did and they were determined to slap appeasers down. Another possible clue lies in Marquis Child's flat statement to me, 'Rusk and Bundy don't trust each other.' Mutual mistrust might mean that neither would be frank in expressing before the other views which departed from the publicly stated position of the American government.

Bundy in his letter to Heeney said: 'And on one point you are entitled to the clearest reassurances: if there *is* mileage in one or another of the notions we discussed, we plan to get it in whatever way we can ... Nor did we in any way cover the waterfront of possibilities ... or even discuss all the combinations of those we did mention. I believe, for example, that there is ground between "occupation rights" and "a mere contract." '

Though I did not know it at the time, President Kennedy did, a fortnight after Heeney's dinner, indicate that he was seriously considering new

ideas on Berlin. On 5 September at a meeting with Rusk and Adlai
Stevenson, then the American representative to the U.N., Kennedy suggested that he might propose a four-point program for Berlin in his speech
to the General Assembly in three weeks' time: 'the submission of the
legal dispute over Berlin to the World Court, transfer of the U.N. to
Berlin, internationalization of the autobahn to Berlin under U.N. control,
and a U.N. plebiscite in Berlin.'[5] He did not, however, mention these
ideas in this U.N. speech.

When I returned to Ottawa I reported to the department on my talks
in Washington by memorandum and orally. I also had a number of talks
with Diefenbaker. My recommendation, as I put it in a memorandum
of 29 August, was:

It seems to me clear that no final decision has been made in Washington and
that the President is being subjected to conflicting advice. In such circumstances
it is possible for a country such as Canada to exercise considerable influence by
strengthening the hands of those in Washington with whose views it is in general
agreement. The possibility of our exercising influence is greater the sooner we
present our views. I therefore recommend that we should, as soon as possible,
give to the authorities in Washington a carefully reasoned exposition of our
views on the questions of substance which will arise in negotiations with the
Soviet Union. Perhaps these views could be put as the tentative and provisional
views of the Canadian Government. I suggest that this statement of our views
should also be given to Mr. Macmillan and Lord Home, to Mr. Lange of Norway,
Mr. Spaak of Belgium and possibly Mr. Fanfani of Italy. I was told by a senior
official in the German Foreign Office a month ago that Mr. Lange is about the
only European statesman in whom Dr. Adenauer has confidence. Because of
this and because of the reputation he has in Washington we might discreetly
encourage Mr. Lange to make a visit to Washington as soon as possible for
quiet informal exploratory talks with the President and the Secretary of State.
It may be – though I am not certain about this – that a visit by Mr. Spaak to
Washington would also be useful.

How far I influenced Diefenbaker by my reports I do not know, but
the speeches he gave on 1 and 11 September reflected some of the considerations I had put to him. Thus he said that the freedom of West
Berlin and the right of the West to uphold that freedom were not negotiable but other things were, and that consideration might be given to

5 John Bartlow Martin, *Adlai Stevenson and the World* (New York: Doubleday 1977),
660

internationalizing the city of Berlin under the United Nations. Then in mid-September Howard Green sent a telegram to the embassy in Washington which began as follows: 'If preliminary soundings indicate there is any likelihood of the USSR's readiness to negotiate on basis of a reunited Berlin, elements of such a statute might include ...' and there followed a ten-point summary of the proposals I had been putting forward.

So ended my efforts to help shape Canadian policy on Berlin.

Ten years later, in 1970 and 1971, the West did what it had refused to do in 1961: it gave to the DDR not the *de facto* recognition which it boggled at giving in 1961 but *de jure* recognition, and it gave *de jure* recognition to the DDR and the Oder-Neisse boundary. It did not in return secure the freedom of all Berlin. Berlin remains divided. Wiser statesmanship by the West in the early sixties might have secured the freedom of all Berlin in return for these concessions, and Berlin would today be a united, independent, democratic city-state.

19

Officer of the World Bank

1962–1965

John F. Kennedy in a speech in the United States Senate on 19 February 1959 proposed that I be a member of a three-man international mission representing potential donor nations to examine India's needs and plans for economic development and to make recommendations to governments on how they could more effectively support India's development. 'Such a mission – particularly if it drew upon men of both national and international stature such as John McCloy of the United States, Sir Oliver Franks of the United Kingdom and Escott Reid of Canada – would be uniquely effective in providing a fresh approach – avoiding misunderstandings on both sides – encouraging the Indians in their association with the West – stimulating effective, efficient plans and appropriate lending criteria.'

I was immensely pleased to be called by a possible president of the United States a man of national and international stature and to be nominated by him to a position where I would be able to help a country I loved – India. But it was not to be. The three men who were appointed to the World Bank mission were Oliver Franks, Joseph M. Dodge of the United States, and Herman Abs of Germany.[1]

According to Chester Bowles, then a member of the House of Representatives, he and Kennedy and Senator John Sherman Cooper 'had hoped that the commission would be expanded to five and that you and Jean Monnet would be included. However, my friends in the State Department tell me that Secretary of the Treasury Anderson insisted that

---

1 This chapter incorporates material from my book, *Strengthening the World Bank* (Chicago: Chicago University Press, 1973).

the commission be limited to three on the ground that you and M. Monnet might support "too bold" a program.'[2]

Louis Rasminsky, the deputy governor of the Bank of Canada and Canada's representative to the World Bank, had a different explanation for my exclusion. He wrote me that Eugene Black, the president of the World Bank, and Burke Knapp, his second-in-command, had told him that 'they had come to the conclusion that if they went beyond the three they would have to have at least a Frenchman and a Japanese as well as a Canadian, and they thought it would become too cumbersome.' He added the cryptic sentence: 'As you know the Canadian Government at no time expressed any interest in having a Canadian included.'[3] Perhaps the Diefenbaker government believed that my membership on a mission which was bound to recommend more help to India would embarrass them by increasing the pressure on them to give more.

Kennedy did not know me but his two associates in his campaign for more help for India – Senator Cooper and Congressman Bowles – did, and it was they who persuaded him to nominate me. They had been ambassadors to India when I was high commissioner there and we had become friends united in our determination to do what we could to help India lift itself out of its poverty.

The mission to India proposed by Kennedy became a mission to Pakistan as well. Its members were known as the three wise men. Rasminsky in a letter to me called them 'the Three Wise Bankers,' perhaps to soften the blow to me of being left off the mission since I certainly did not qualify as a banker. Each of the three wise men had an expert adviser. According to the German adviser they called themselves the three half-wits.

When I learned that I was not to be a member of the mission I decided to do what I could to influence its deliberations and I sent Rasminsky an abbreviated version of my despatch to Ottawa in the spring of 1957, just before leaving India, in which I had assessed India's prospects for sustained economic growth and suggested to Rasminsky that he might propose to Eugene Black that he transmit it to the members of the mission. This he did.

Then when Rasminsky sent me in April 1960 the confidential report which the mission had submitted to Black I wrote a five-thousand-word commentary on the report which the World Bank passed on to the mission and to the senior staff of the Bank. I sent copies to senior officers

2 Chester Bowles to E.R., 30 March 1960
3 L. Rasminsky to E.R., 1 March 1960

in the Department of External Affairs and to Sherman Cooper, Chester Bowles, and Douglas Ensminger, the representative in India of the Ford Foundation. A few months later, with the World Bank's approval, I sent a slightly revised version to Prime Minister Nehru. Burke Knapp, the vice-president of the Bank, told me that my commentary was 'helpful and perceptive as well as interesting' and that the Bank had received appreciative letters from some of the wise men.

I confined my commentary to those parts of the report which dealt with India, since that was the country of which I had first-hand knowledge. I commended the report's emphasis on the limitations on the freedom of action of the Indian government imposed by the scarcity of managerial ability and technical skills, by its determination to maintain and extend democracy and individual freedom, and by the extreme poverty of most of the Indian people. I said: 'The task which the government and people of India face is enormous. What is required of them is creative political leadership, hard work and a willingness to break with the past. All these are scarce commodities in any country. And what is required from donor nations is also scarce – creative imagination, respectful sympathy, capital, technical skills, and a willingness to allow domestic industries to suffer from competition from cheap Indian exports.'

The central thesis of my commentary was that the main task before the government of India was to increase agricultural production. This should become 'a first charge not only on capital resources but also on that commodity which is scarcest in all countries – skilled, enthusiastic, imaginative, sympathetic, masterful administrators ... For it is only on the foundation of a healthy agriculture that an industrialized India can safely be built.'

The other main thesis of my commentary was that substantial aid from donor countries to India could be maintained only if the governments of the donor countries could assure their legislatures that the aid which came out of the taxes and savings of their people was well used,

that the total of resources available to the government of India from domestic and foreign sources is spent to the maximum advantage ... If this were to mean a series of unfriendly, ignorant, arrogant inquisitions into the domestic affairs of India, the price which India and its western friends would pay for the necessary aid would be incalculably high ... What is required, I suggest, is to seek Mr. Nehru's views on how the inquiries by the donor countries into India's economic situation and development programmes can best be pursued and how the assurances from the Indian government to the donor countries can best be given. I take it for granted that Mr. Nehru would consider that if inquiries are to be made it would be best if they were made by an international agency and that the most appropriate international agency would be the International Bank for Reconstruction and Development [the World Bank].

During the year 1961 when I was in my fourth year as ambassador to Germany I pondered my future in the Canadian foreign service. I was fifty-six years old. It would be nine years before I reached retirement age. If I were to stay in the service I wanted to spend those years in posts where I could exercise my talents to the full and which would be close to our children and our farm. Those posts were the under-secretaryship in Ottawa and the ambassadorship in Washington. We had been away from Canada for nine years and that was too long. It became clear to me that my chances of being appointed to Ottawa or Washington were slight. I therefore wrote to Rasminsky telling him this and asking whether there was a possibility of a post opening up in the World Bank in 1962 for which I might be suitable. Rasminsky spoke to Eugene Black; this, he generously assured me twelve years later, was 'one of the best pieces of business that I ever did as a director of the World Bank.' I had a talk with Black when he visited Bonn in January 1962 and a few weeks later he offered me an appointment as consultant to the Bank 'at a very senior level to undertake special assignments as they arise.'

I am not in a position now to tell you precisely what assignments we would wish you to undertake, but our experience indicates that we are almost continuously involved in delicate and important negotiations of one type or another, as for example, the Indus Basin negotiations, the Suez Canal compensation matter and the like, which can only be handled by a member of the management [the president and the two vice-presidents] or by a senior-level consultant of your stature. I feel confident that this will continue to be the case and, indeed, indications are that this type of activity is likely to increase.

Black invited Ruth and me to drop in to see him at his summer place in Cape Cod when we were driving from Ottawa to Washington in July to take up my appointment with the Bank. He told me he would be leaving the Bank in October and that Sir William Iliffe, one of the two vice-presidents, would also be leaving in the autumn. Iliffe's post would be filled by Geoffrey Wilson, the director of the South Asian Middle Eastern department of the Bank. He had discussed with Knapp and Iliffe how best to use my services. Their opinion, with which he concurred, was that it would be in the Bank's interests and mine that I take over Wilson's department which was by far the most important of the five geographical departments rather than, as he had originally suggested, be available for special diplomatic assignments. My guess is that he had come to realize that his successor might not follow his practice of involving the Bank in 'delicate and important' international negotiations and that I might find myself as consultant without useful asssignments. He was right in this forecast. I was happy to agree to Black's proposal, especially since it would mean that I would be able to influence the Bank's policies towards India and would be visiting India on Bank business.

The organization I joined in July 1962 was very different from today's Bank. It consisted, as it does today, of three institutions: the Bank proper which provides loans at conventional rates of interest guaranteed by the government concerned; the International Development Association which provides interest-free loans to the poorer countries also guaranteed by the government concerned; and the International Finance Corporation which makes loans and investments in private industry without government guarantee. But these institutions were much smaller then than they are now. The professional staff which served the three institutions numbered less than four hundred; now almost four thousand. The staff was accommodated in one building; now in seventeen. The Bank then lent in real terms less than one-quarter what it now lends and IDA less than one-eighth.[4] I am glad I worked in the Bank when it was a comparatively small institution. I am fortunate that I have never had to work in a vast bureaucracy.

When I started attending meetings of the senior officers and executive directors of the Bank I was overwhelmed by the terms that were used: seasoning portfolios, rolling paper over, debt-equity ratios, cost-benefit ratios, debt-service ratios, net farm benefit investment ratios, shadow rates of interest. Then there were such statements as 'The cost-benefit ratio of this proposed project is favourable but it is not economically viable.' I gradually began to comprehend what these terms meant. It took me longer to realize that when officials spoke of Bank loans to relatively well-to-do member countries which were certain to repay their debts to the Bank as 'seasoning the Bank's portfolio', they were using a term appropriate to private investment banks, but not to the World Bank.

One reason they fell into this error was the misnaming of the twin institutions, the Bank and the International Monetary Fund. The Bank,

---

4 In 1961–62 the Bank lent $880 million (U.S.) and IDA $134 million (equivalent in 1988 dollars to $3.4 billion and $516 million). In 1987–88 the Bank lent $14.8 billion and IDA $4.5 billion.

as Maynard Keynes insisted at the inaugural meeting of the two institutions, should have been called a fund and the Fund should have been called a bank. This would have made it less likely that those in charge of the Bank's lending program in its early years would apply criteria for its lending appropriate to private investment banks. This retarded the metamorphosis of the Bank from a conservative semi-commercial investment bank into a development assistance agency, a metamorphosis which did not take place until the presidencies of Eugene Black's successors, George Woods and Robert McNamara.

In my first six weeks in the Bank, before taking over the South Asian Middle Eastern department, I had long talks with ten of the senior officers of the Bank. I was impressed by their courtesy in speaking frankly to a newcomer and by their competence. When I took over my department I was equally impressed by its seventeen officers. Their ability seemed to me very high, higher on the average than officers of corresponding rank in the Canadian external affairs service. They were of nine nationalities: American, British, French, German, Italian, Belgian, Dutch, Swiss, Chinese. In those days few officers of the Bank came from its poorer member nations.

I was not impressed by the pace at which the Bank moved to make decisions. In the Department of External Affairs we were constantly working to deadlines: the deadline of the last cabinet meeting before an international conference at which approval could be secured for instructions to the Canadian delegation; a question on the order paper of Parliament had to be answered within a few days; the minister needed a draft of a speech in so many days; he had to be briefed to explain and defend the department's estimates which were shortly to come before the House of Commons; an important controversial resolution was about to come to the vote in a U.N. committee; an ambassador had asked for instructions for a talk with the foreign minister; an ally had asked for comments on a course of action it proposed to take in a few days. In the Bank it seemed to me that there were few such built-in incentives to speed.

I assumed that an International Bank for Reconstruction and Development would have the flavour of an international institution. It did not. It was aggressively Anglo-American. Of the three top officers – the president and the two vice-presidents – two were Americans and one was British. Half the senior staff were American and one-fifth were British. (Now the nationality of the five top officers is two Americans, one Canadian, one German, and one Pakistani; only one-quarter of the senior staff are American and one-tenth British, half the previous proportions.)

The Bank's strong ideological prejudice against public ownership of manufacturing industry and of national development banks indicated a subservience to predelictions and prejudices peculiar to the United States. New member countries signed the Bank's articles of agreement at a ceremony in the United States State Department presided over by an assistant secretary of state. (One of Eugene Black's last acts as president was to do away with this absurdity.) Lunches given by the president of the Bank to non-Americans were American: iced water not wine, coffee served in the middle of lunch.

Within a few weeks of my arrival in the Bank Burke Knapp told me that the Bank wanted me to visit Egypt. The coming departure of Black and Iliffe would result in the Bank losing 95 per cent of its knowledge of Egypt; it was important that some senior person have direct knowledge of the country. Therefore I was to leave for Egypt in a fortnight. In the two weeks I would spend there I was to get someting of the feel of the country and of the people who ran its economic policies – were they serious about economic development? How far could you trust what they said?

The Bank, Knapp said, had been willing to lend $250 million to Egypt for the Aswan Dam provided the United States and Britain lent similar amounts. It had stood aside from the U.S.-U.K. break with Egypt over the dam; it had mediated the dispute over compensation for the nationalization of the Suez Canal; it had assisted in repairing the canal after the invasion of Egypt in 1956 by Britain, France, and Israel and had given a loan for improving it. The Bank was now considering more loans to Egypt, but Egypt would first have to compensate the French and the Belgians for property it had nationalized. Black and President Nasser had at one time been buddies; Black would be paying a farewell visit to Egypt while I was there and would be calling on Nasser.

My visit to Egypt from 23 October to 3 November 1962 coincided with two first-class international crises: the Cuban missile crisis and the Chinese invasion of India. The missile crisis reached its peak during my first few days in Cairo and was resolved on the fifth day. The Chinese invasion was launched three days before I reached Cairo and during my stay in Egypt the newspapers were full of stories of Chinese victories over the Indians. The day after I arrived in Cairo I wrote Ruth: 'The international news from India is saddening, from Cuba frightening.' I did not, however, realize when I was in Egypt how close the Cuban crisis had brought the world, in Robert Kennedy's words, 'to the abyss of nuclear destruction and the end of mankind.'[5] During a serious confrontation between the

5 Robert F. Kennedy, *Thirteen Days* (New York: W.W. Norton 1969), 23

superpowers there is an advantage in working hard on an unrelated matter in a third world country remote from the area of confrontation.

I did have to work hard on my visit to Egypt, but the most difficult part of my work had nothing to do with the economic problems and prospects of Egypt: it had to do with securing an appointment for Eugene Black with Nasser. Black as president of the Bank had done much for Egypt but gratitude is sometimes a lively sense of favours to come; Black could grant no more favours to Egypt and Nasser showed no interest in seeing him. I had to plead, cajole, storm, at meetings with cabinet ministers and senior officials, before I could get Black an appointment with Nasser.

This was the first time in my life I had been charged with the task of finding out what was happening in a totalitarian state. I soon found out how much more difficult it was to do this in a totalitarian state than in a democracy. In India it was possible for an intelligent visitor to get clues within a week of his arrival to differences of opinion and struggles for power within the government, and to the main areas where the program of economic development was running into difficulties or where errors of judgment were being made. There were many sources of information and opinion: newspapers, periodicals, public statements by leaders of opposition parties, talks with civil servants who considered the policies of their political chiefs to be mistaken, talks with newspapermen and businessmen. In Egypt not only was there no free press and no opposition parties, but civil servants and the surviving businessmen were very guarded in what they said to a new acquaintance.

The six cabinet ministers I called on impressed me as able, experienced, keenly interested in economic development, and with an excellent grasp of the work of their departments. But it was obvious that they were not cabinet ministers in any real sense of the term but more like senior civil servants corresponding to state secretaries in Bonn, permanent under-secretaries in Britain, and deputy ministers in Ottawa. The Egyptian equivalent to a cabinet was the presidential council, which consisted for the most part of the colonels who had made the revolution with Nasser ten years before. What was disheartening was the probability that there was inadequate communication between the so-called cabinet ministers and the presidential council and that the council made decisions without weighing the advice of senior civil servants. Politicians should certainly not always do what civil servants recommend, but before making decisions they should always seek their advice. I was impressed by the intelligence and charm of the minister of finance, Kaissouni, but I doubted whether the presidential council consulted him enough or that when they did consult him he was sufficiently blunt and forceful. Kaissouni appeared to me to be the most influential and courageous of the cabinet ministers I met.

I asked myself whether under such conditions the real facts of the economic and social situation and the arguments for and against alternative policies got to the top level of Nasser and his presidential council. Absolute power corrupts; it also isolates. The World Bank, it seemed to me, could help to breach this isolation. The president of the Bank could, as Eugene Black had done on his last visit, tell Nasser some of the facts of life which his cabinet ministers might be reluctant to tell him or which he might be reluctant to believe when cabinet ministers told him. If Nasser and his council were to read the forthcoming report of the Bank's economic mission they would learn much from which they had been shielded or from which they had shielded themselves.

I had discovered the importance of the role the Bank could play in non-democratic countries which wished to borrow from it.

Not all my time was spent in Cairo. I was taken to see a drainage project in the Nile delta which the government wanted to expand with the assistance of a loan from the International Development Association. Open drainage ditches were being replaced by buried tile drains. This increased the cultivable area of the peasant's plot of land and improved the fertility of the soil. There was no problem of teaching the farmer new methods of cultivation, the obstacle which has to be surmounted in most schemes to increase agricultural production in poor countries. The farmer could farm the way he had always farmed and his crops would increase. They would increase even more if he adopted new methods of cultivation. This was obviously a high priority project for financing by IDA, but because of unsettled claims of foreigners for compensation for their property that had been nationalized it was eight years before IDA gave a loan for it. This was to be the first loan from the Bank Group to Egypt since its loan in 1959 for improving the Suez Canal.

The Nile delta project impressed me but I was not so impressed with another agricultural project I was taken to in the New Valley in the middle of the desert, where water for irrigation was being drawn from the vast aquifer deep below the desert. It was a superb engineering accomplishment but I wondered if the army engineers in charge had asked themselves whether the agricultural production resulting from the project would justify the high costs. They had certainly not asked the peasants who had migrated to the New Valley the kind of village in which they would like to live and the kind of house they would like to live in, and the peasants disliked the villages and the houses the government had built for them. If the administration had consulted the peasants they could have built on the site of each new village a few improved houses as models and let the peasant build his own house with a government grant. This would have slashed the costs of the project and increased its chances of success. The villages might also have been attractive, not ugly like the long rows of concrete boxes the army engineers had built.

I had the feeling that in Egypt engineers and especially army engineers had too much influence on development policies, programs, and projects and economists and sociologists too little.

I ended my report to the management of the Bank on my visit to Egypt with my answer to the central question I had been instructed to consider:

My brief visit to Egypt gave me no reason to doubt the conclusion of almost all careful students of the Egyptian scene that Nasser and his associates are seriously concerned with economic development, that the development program is in the hands of men who, in general, are able and devoted, and that Egypt is the key country in the Middle East. Nasser and his associates are also, of course, seriously concerned with promoting revolution in the neighbouring Arab countries and they may devote too much of their energy and Egypt's scarce resources to this task. I should think that during the time I was in Egypt the attention of Nasser and his associates was concentrated on the revolution in Yemen and the earth tremors which it has caused throughout the whole of the Middle East.

When I returned to Washington I found that all six senior officers in my department were away on missions to the countries of the Middle East and South Asia. They drifted back over the next six weeks. By then I had learned something the hard way about the work of my department.

After five months in the Bank I wrote to a friend in Ottawa:

I miss the Cadillac and breakfast in bed and having my shoes shined every day at home but little else of diplomatic life. In five months we have been to only six or seven diplomatic cocktail parties and evening receptions compared to forty or fifty in Bonn in a similar period ... What I miss is not diplomatic life but membership in the Canadian External Affairs service. Here was something I had grown up with and helped to create and fashion. It still had the feeling of an intimate club. It would have been worse if so many of the people I liked and respected the most had not left before I did – Hume Wrong, Gerry Riddell, Don Matthews, Doug LePan, John Holmes, Dana Wilgress, Gordon Robertson ... I am glad I made the change to the Bank. Here there is a chance to do something useful. And my colleagues are able and pleasant and have given me a warm welcome unclouded so far as I can sense by any feeling of resentment at the appointment of an outsider to a senior position.

My next foreign assignment for the Bank was to Pakistan and India. The first few days of my visit to West Pakistan in February 1963 were spent in Karachi. There I learned an important difference between visiting a country like Egypt on behalf of the Bank and visiting Pakistan (and subsequently India). Pakistan, unlike Egypt, had been lent much money from the Bank and IDA and hoped for much more. The authorities wanted me to visit projects which the Bank and IDA had helped to finance so that they could show me they had made good use of the money. They also wanted me to visit projects they hoped the Bank and IDA would help to finance so that I would be impressed by what they intended to do. For Pakistan, as for India, a consortium had been set up consisting of governments which were contributing to its develoment and I had discussions in Karachi with the ambassadors of six of the members of the consortium.

My most interesting meeting in Karachi was with a group of nine leading industrialists associated with the privately owned development bank to which the Bank had lent money. In my report on my visit to Pakistan I said of this group of industrialists:

I had not realized how new the wealth and power of most of them is, or that most of them came to West Pakistan after Partition from what is now India, or that almost all had no experience in industry but were traders. That such a group have become leading industrialists in a few years is a tribute to their abilities to adjust to changed circumstances and to seize opportunities. They possess entrepreneurial qualities of a high order ... A potential source of weakness ... is that they have become accustomed to an extremely high rate of profit ... from the highly protected and expanding internal market ...[and this makes] them disinclined to struggle for markets abroad. And, of course, a high rate of profit on a protected expanding domestic market can make industrialists flabby.

In my first morning in Lahore, the next city I visited in West Pakistan, I was rushed through six calls on cabinet ministers and senior civil servants, accompanied by a top civil servant. The Pakistan authorities in their lengthy press release on these calls attributed to ministers what had in fact been said by civil servants, an inexpensive tribute by the civil servants to the ministers whom they controlled.

I was amused by this. I was angered by a deliberate distortion of what I had said at another meeting a few days later. At that time Pakistan was pressing the Bank to help finance the construction of a dam at Tarbela on the Indus River and senior Bank officials were privately sceptical of Pakistan's claims that it would be wise to embark on this project, which it was then thought would cost about $900 million but which actually cost $1,500 million. Tarbela came up at a meeting I had with Ghulam Ishaq, the head of the government's Water and Power Development Authority. I was scrupulously non-committal, but the next day the newspapers carried an obviously inspired story headed 'Indus Pact without Tarbela meaningless. World Bank help for project assured. Reid meets Governor and Wapda chief,' and going on to say that I had stated at the meeting that the World Bank was as much interested in the building of the Tarbela dam as Pakistan and would make every effort to convince friendly countries to help finance it. I had to tell the Bank that this story was nonsense and at my request the West Pakistan authorities said they would rebuke Ghulam Ishaq.

My most pleasant memory of my tour of East Pakistan (now Bangladesh) was a visit to Comilla, where Akhter Hameed Khan was conducting a pilot agricultural development which he hoped would demonstrate how to get greatly increased agricultural production throughout East Pakistan. Ruth and I were charmed and impressed by this handsome, dedicated man with a keen sense of humour. He seemed to us a younger version of the saintly Indian agricultural expert Boshi Sen with whom we had become friends in India: the same burning zeal, the same belief in the peasant. He was contemptuous of the system followed in the community development projects in rural India under which a young man trained and paid by the government was sent to a village as a village-level worker to show the peasants how to increase the yields on their plots of land. Under his system the farmers in a village chose and paid one of themselves to do the job. Once a week he would come to the agricultural institute at Comilla for training.

His plan for the salvation of the villagers was more than helping them increase their agricultural production. He believed that in the past seventy years or so the villager in the subcontinent of India had lost his sense of security and of belonging to a community; and when he borrowed from a money-lender he lost his self-respect. These he must get back. He could get them back if he organized his village into a co-operative for economic development and if he saved regularly, even though it might be a very small amount, and got rid of his debt to money-lenders. He told us with glee what had happened in one village where the villagers had for long been browbeaten by tough money-lenders from a neighbouring village. He had persuaded the members of the village co-operative to swear on the Koran that they would band together to resist paying more on their loans than 12-1/2 per cent a year instead of the 80 per cent the money-lenders demanded. When the money-lenders came to the village at four one morning to beat up a defaulting debtor all the members of the co-operative gathered together and threatened to kill them.

When a month later I was having a talk with Indira Gandhi before lunching with her father I contended, as I had in Pakistan, that it was absurd that India and Pakistan refused to learn from the other's successes and failures in economic development – in community projects, small industries, road research, and in cheap methods of building houses for the poor. Each seemed determined to learn only from its own successes and failures. I told her about the Comilla project. When I said that at Comilla the village-level worker was one of the villagers chosen and paid for by the villagers she said, 'That's the only sensible system.' I said that no one from India had gone to Comilla to study their system. I learned many years later that at Indira Gandhi's insistence Indian officials had shortly afterwards been sent to Comilla.

I had stumbled on another way the World Bank could help the poorer countries – by warning them not to make the mistakes other comparable countries had made and urging them to study the failures and successes in economic development of those countries.

Following our visit to Pakistan, Ruth and I spent three weeks in India. We first visited Calcutta and steel plants in West Bengal and then Delhi and Bombay. I talked in Delhi to leaders in public life I had been friendly with during my time as high commissioner: prime minister, president, vice-president, half a dozen cabinet ministers, and many senior public servants, including L.K. Jha, I.G. Patel, S.K. Dey, and Tarlok Singh. I talked with ministers in the governments of the states of West Bengal and Maharashtra, with the governor of the Reserve Bank, and with Homi Bhabha, India's expert on atomic energy.

Whatever diplomatic talents I possessed I had to use to the full on this visit in the kind of task I had never before been concerned with: to persuade the national government and the two leading privately owned steel plants to reach agreement on outstanding issues which divided them so that the Bank could give loans to the companies to help finance their expansion. The companies were Indian Iron and Steel (IISCO) and Tata Iron and Steel (TISCO). This introduced me to another of the useful roles the Bank could perform in the poorer countries. The head of IISCO, Sir Biren Mukerjee, with whom I had many long talks, had bad relations with the government and this increased the difficulties of my task. Morarji Desai, the minister of finance, told me that it annoyed him that Mukerjee, whom he called a black Englishman, made such intemperate attacks on the government.

I had three meetings with Nehru – one as soon as I arrived in Delhi, one just before I left India, and one in between, a family lunch at his house with Nehru and his daughter. I knew that Nehru had been shocked and grieved by the recent successful Chinese invasion of India and though he was as ever courteous, charming, and intelligent, he lacked the vigour of six years before. When we had lunched with him then he had always conducted us downstairs afterwards and accompanied us to the door of his residence. Now he apologized for saying goodbye at the top of the stairs.

I said to Nehru that I knew that Barbara Ward and other friendly visitors to India had made the point to him that the scarcest of all commodities in any country was able, imaginative, sympathetic, administrators and managers who had the capacity to create and head a team. I had met on my recent visit to the IISCO plant in Burnpur, McCracken, the manager of the plant, an engineer from Glasgow, who had impressed me as a great administrative manager. I had expected to see an efficient industrial undertaking but I had not expected to see as well model workers' quarters, free medical services, and an institute for training Indian university graduates of twenty-two who had never seen the inside of a factory to become in two years self-confident, efficient factory supervisors. I hoped that saying this might help reduce Nehru's prejudices against IISCO and foreign experts.

I explained the difficulty the Bank and IDA were having in continuing loans to India at the level of the past two years – the Bank because India's creditworthiness for more loans was reduced by its soon having to use 18 per cent of its exports to service its foreign debt, IDA because its resources were not going to be as great as we had hoped. The more India could export, the more creditworthy it would become. One important invisible export was tourism. A great increase in tourism would have distasteful effects within India, but an India willing to give up so much for development might make this sacrifice. India would need to secure advice from foreign experts on tourism and, for a time, foreign assistance in managing its tourist industry. It would also need to substitute for prohibition some sensible system of liquor control.

Nehru was generous in the time he spent with me. He knew that I would do my best to get the World Bank to give all possible help to India and that it was important that I make an accurate report to the

Bank on what I had found in India to be encouraging and what discouraging. In our last talk I asked him to read a memorandum I had just prepared on this and to comment on it. This he did.

Eight months later, in November and December 1963, I spent a month visiting Iran, Iraq, Syria, Jordan, and Lebanon, the first time I had been to those countries. After a few days in Teheran I wrote Ruth: 'The Persians are very charming but in our business they are elusive. Nobody wants to take responsibility for agreeing to the Bank's unpleasant conditions on the proposed road loan to them. We have to force the discussions on them.' They asked that we not insist that the contracts for constructing the roads be subject to international competitive bidding. I said it was impossible for us to give Iran what we had refused to Spain and Syria.

The Iranian authorities gave a lavish dinner in my honour, starting with vodka and royal caviar. I had to tell my host that because of an attack of dysentery, which I was careful to say I had contracted in Pakistan not in Iran, I was able to eat only yoghurt, rice, and bread, and drink only clear tea. A few minutes later a dish of fried rice arrived swimming in butter. I apologized for not making clear that it was plain boiled rice I needed. A year later when I was again in Teheran I said to my host at a similar lavish dinner which I greatly enjoyed that at the dinner a year before I had been able to eat only plain boiled rice. 'Yes,' he said, 'and the only way we could get plain boiled rice for you was to send a car to the hospital.'

I went on from Teheran to Baghdad. A few days before I left Washington on this Middle-Eastern tour Iraq had had another military coup and it was possible there might soon be more fighting for power between rival military factions. I had no desire to be an innocent bystander killed in such fighting so I sent a telegram addressed to the minister of finance in which I said that I assumed the Iraqui authorities would wish me to postpone my visit. They wired back not at all. I comforted myself that I had friends in Baghdad and I let them know when I was arriving. They rallied. I was met at the airport not only by four Iraqi officials but also by the Indian ambassador, Sadath Ali Khan, by the second-in-command of the American embassy, Wesley Adams, and by the former Iraqi ambassador to India, Mohamed Al Radi and his wife. The resulting lightening of my spirits was short-lived. On the drive in from the airport to the hotel we drove around four traffic circles. On each were two tanks. My memory is that the tanks in each circle were facing each other, a sign they belonged to rival military groups, but I can scarcely believe this was the case.

The next day the government gave a dinner in my honour. About two-thirds of the cabinet turned up, including two generals in uniform, one accompanied by two military guards with machine-guns. When I showed my displeasure the guards were withdrawn. Fortunately it was only after the dinner was over that I realized that the presence of two-thirds of the cabinet had provided their opponents with a superb opportunity to overthrow the government by tossing a few bombs into the dining-room.

It soon became apparent to me that the newly established government wanted a loan from the Bank not for economic but for political reasons; a loan would demonstrate that the Bank believed in the stability of the new regime. Indeed, the president said to me that he hoped our visit was an indication of stability in Iraq. He assured me that he was not in favour of revolution. (What revolutionary leader who has seized power is?) He expressed his belief in principles which he must have been told the Bank held dear: he wanted the Bank's help to conquer poverty, illiteracy, and disease; he was in favour of encouraging the private sector and we could assure foreign investors that they could invest safely in Iraq.

On my return to Washington after visiting Iran, Iraq, Syria, Jordan, and Lebanon I reported to the Bank that all five countries had difficulty in attracting and keeping capable civil servants because of low salaries, antiquated administrative procedures, and insufficient delegation of authority. In Iraq and Syria the principal obstacle to rapid economic growth was chronic political instability resulting in a lack of continuity in government policy and administration. Iran, Iraq, Jordan, and Syria suffered from devoting 35 to 60 per cent of their ordinary budget to defence and it was difficult for their governments to reduce these excessive expenditures because their existence depended on the active support of the armed forces. In all five countries receipts from taxation were lower than they should be because of corruption and inefficiencies in tax administration. In all five, and particularly in Iran and Iraq, insufficient use was being made of many of the development works constructed in the previous ten or fifteen years. Expensive irrigation dams had inadequate networks for distributing the water; the peasants wasted the water; there were too few agricultural extension officers. Iran had a development plan but not enough development projects. Syria and Iraq had more than enough projects but lacked a good plan. Jordan and Lebanon had problems on both scores. 'What this area needs from the Bank and IDA is not, to any great extent, capital ... The chief purpose of Bank loans and technical assistance and IDA credits is to give the Bank opportunities to influence government policies and to improve government administration over the whole field of economic development.'

I greatly enjoyed two visits to Israel with the usual combination of extensive tours and intensive talks. Israel demonstrated how brains, determination, vision, and massive financial help from the United States could result in impressive economic development. Poor countries could learn from Israel non-capital-intensive techniques it had worked out to increase production. But they could learn little else from Israel's economic success because they had no hope of getting anywhere near the extremely high foreign aid per capita which Israel received.

When I visited Israel it was being run by the generation which created the kibbutz, European Jews who were agnostics and therefore did not believe in the tribal myth that God had given Israel the whole of the West Bank of the Jordan River. It is tragic that this group when it held power did not make peace with Israel's Arab neighbours.

I had dinner in Beersheba with the general in charge of the potash works on the Dead Sea which the Bank had helped to finance. At the next table in the hotel dining-room was a noisy group of about a dozen Jewish tourists from the United States. Our main course at dinner was beef. When dessert came it was water ice. The general said, 'You know why you can't have ice cream. It's because the Bible says you mustn't have meat and milk at the same meal. We don't believe in this nonsense but we have to obey these rules in hotels like this or otherwise those people over there [and he gestured with contempt at the people at the next table] would object.' I could not resist saying that the Bible did not say do not have meat and milk at the same meal, but do not boil a kid in its mother's milk.

Shortly before I left the Bank in 1965 I told the president, George Woods, that the Arab countries in the Bank believed that the Bank discriminated against them and that, by contrast, it was generous to Israel. One reason they gave for this was the strength of Zionist influence in the governments of our three largest shareholders, the United States, Britain, and France; another reason was that so many of the senior officers of the Bank were personally prejudiced against the Arab countries, the Arab way of referring to the large number of Jews in top posts in the Bank and IDA. I never found them prejudiced in their dealings with our Arab member countries, but it was not unnatural for the Arabs to believe they were.

In the summer of 1965 when I was preparing to take leave of the Bank after serving in it for three years, I decided to do what I could before leaving to influence the Bank's trinity of institutions. I gave the president a confidential memorandum on the administration of the Bank which was discussed in the President's Council and may have had some influence. I wrote a long essay on the relations between the Bank and India.

I wrote a twenty-thousand-word booklet on the future of the Bank which the Bank published.[6] The Bank had ten thousand copies printed and distributed it widely. In my talk at the farewell lunch the Bank gave for me I summed up much of my advice.

I praised George Woods for his many accomplishments since becoming president two and a half years before, especially his starting the process of converting the Bank from a conservative investment bank to a development assistance fund. Under his presidency the staff had become more international, less predominantly Anglo-American; the Bank had become more experienced in co-ordinating the activities of the countries which were giving aid to a poor member country; it had made partnership agreements with the FAO and UNESCO under which these institutions helped poor countries identify and prepare agricultural and educational projects for Bank financing; the Bank had improved its relations with the IMF, the Economic and Social Council, the U.N. Special Fund, the Inter-American Development Bank, and the European Development Fund. By doing this Woods had done what no other head of a United Nations specialized agency had done – broken with the bad tradition of specialized agencies going in for empire-building, separatism, and jealousy of each other.

I paid a tribute to Woods as a great diplomat. He did not, I said, use the traditional diplomatic formula for avoiding saying no, which was to say perhaps, but he had invented a wonderful set of formulas:

When you say, 'I hear what you say' it means 'I disagree with what you say. I've heard quite enough from you and I don't want to hear another word on the subject.' You have another formula when that doesn't work which is, 'It's a question of taste.' That means, 'I'm right. You're wrong and I'm not going to argue with you.' And the third, 'Your ideas and mine are 180 degress removed.' That means, 'There's no point in your arguing.' You are also a believer in another of the great precepts of diplomacy which is that you never say 'never'; you always leave doors open. And I have begun to believe that often when you use one of your formulas for no, what you are really saying is, 'If I were you I would go back to your office and think this problem through again and the next time you talk to me about it, you'd better be able to marshal your argument a little better than you have this afternoon.'

George Woods was, I think, surprised by my tributes to him, for he and

6 *The Future of the World Bank* (Washington: International Bank for Reconstruction and Development 1965)

I had had a number of disagreements. I had repeatedly questioned the wisdom of the Bank financing the Tarbela dam in West Pakistan which he supported with fervour. I thought he was unwise in his strong ideological prejudice against the Bank lending to publicly owned manufacturing industry and publicly owned development banks. I had objected to his failure to consult me adequately on the chairmanship of the special eighteen-member economic mission to India in 1964 and I had blocked two of his proposals for the chairmanship.

My doubts about George Woods were, I am sure, accompanied by doubts by Woods of my abilities as a senior officer of the Bank. At one time when we were having lunch together he suggested that I move from heading the South Asian Middle Eastern department to heading the Western Hemisphere department, which would have been a demotion. I said, 'Oh, no, George,' and that finished it.

At the end of my farewell talk I thanked Woods for requesting *Bank Notes*, the periodical circulated to the staff of the Bank, to print my advice to aspiring development diplomats:

The Bank official who is called upon to give advice to a low-income country will be a more effective diplomat of development if he constantly reminds himself of four things. Firstly, that human judgment is fallible. Secondly, that luck or providence or the unpredictable plays a large role in economic development. Thirdly, that while it is a good thing for poor people to have more to eat and to wear, better places to live in, more and better nurses, doctors and teachers, and less illness, it is a better thing for them to have these goods without sacrificing those ancient values of their society which can give them a feeling of belonging to a group, a sense of dignity and the possibility of serenity. The fourth thing which a giver of advice to a low-income country can usefully remind himself of is that, even if final truth has been revealed to him, he is not Moses laying down the law from Mount Sinai. He is a partner speaking to a free and equal partner. His task is one of persuasion. When he intervenes with advice his 'intervention should be in the least abrasive, the least corrosive, way possible.'

Abe Fortas, the distinguished American lawyer, had used these words about intervention with reference to intervention by the Supreme Court of the United States in the criminal proceedings of a state.[7] His wise advice on intervention applies, it seems to me, to almost all kinds of intervention, whether in private life or in the conduct of public affairs.

In my booklet on the future of the World Bank I developed my ideas

7 Quoted in Anthony Lewis, *Gideon's Trumpet* (New York: Random House 1964), 172

on the diplomacy of development. I said that those who participated on behalf of the Bank in dialogues with poor countries were better able to carry out their task of persuasion if they had compassionate hearts, imaginative sympathy, and a sense of history. They were better equipped if they had acquired the ability to feel in their bones something of what life was like for a poor man in a poor country and for the political leaders of poor countries 'who know that if their country is to lift itself out of its poverty they must hold down increases in consumption by the poor, they must put off doing much to reduce inequalities and inequities among regions and among groups within regions, they must sacrifice today's goods for tomorrow's hopes.' This did not mean, I hastened to add, that these leaders should never depart from policies and programs likely to result in the most rapid possible rate of economic growth. 'Even in the poorest countries the sole aim of policy cannot be [that] ... Some departures are required by the realities of politics and the demands of conscience.'

A novel feature of my booklet was that instead of talking of developed countries and developing countries (an absurd term since many so-called developing countries are not developing) I divided the nations of the world into four groups based on their per capita gross national products – very poor, poor, middle-income, rich – and for each nation I gave its population and the annual growth rate in its population. For members of the Bank I gave the amount of the loans they had received from the Bank and IDA and – this was most important – the net annual flow or transfer of resources to them resulting from the loans. (Net flow is the disbursement on the loans less the payment of interest on the loans and the repayments of capital.) I was confident that this would show that the countries which most needed help from the Bank and IDA were not getting it and it did. The net annual flow of resources to the very poor member countries with a total population of 860 million was only 10 cents a head, to the poor countries with a total population of 420 million a little less than nothing, and to the middle-income countries with a total population of 340 million, 43 cents a head.

The obvious conclusion was that, since most of the low-income countries (very poor and poor) had little or no creditworthiness for loans from the Bank, the only way of giving them the help they needed was to increase the resources of IDA. If IDA's resources were increased from the existing level of $300 million a year to $900 million, the annual net flow of resources to the low-income countries would go up from 6 cents a head to about 50 cents. Seven years were to go by before IDA was able to increase its lending to above $900 million.

My booklet drew management's attention to the failure of the Bank to publish such statistics and the following year the Bank started producing its annual World Bank Atlas. I was pleased that the introduction to the first Atlas in 1966 said: 'The statistics in this booklet carry on series of figures that aroused considerable interest when they were first presented in Mr. Escott Reid's essay, "The Future of the World Bank." ' The annual World Bank Atlas now divides countries into five income groups – very poor, poor, lower middle-income, higher middle-income, and rich. In 1978 the Bank in its annual report began to provide statistics on net transfer of resources.

My booklet was widely reviewed. I was especially pleased by the review in the London *Economist* which said that it was 'a masterly and deeply disturbing document' and that what I was basically saying was that the Bank's remarkable success hitherto gave little comfort for the future because the nature of its task was changing so drastically, from the finance of individual projects to the finance of major development programs. This called for greater use of quite sophisticated economic techniques, taxed the Bank's diplomatic skills, and increased the urgency of diluting 'its American content.'[8]

8 *The Economist*, 6 November 1965

20

Creating Glendon College
1965–1969

At the beginning of August 1964 when I was with the World Bank in Washington I received, much to my surprise, a letter from the president of York University in Toronto, Murray Ross, asking if I might be interested in becoming principal of Glendon College.

One part of our plan for the future of this university is the development of a fine residential undergraduate college for about one thousand students ... As you know, almost all universities in Canada are now fairly large and all are growing larger. We felt it quite important that there be in Canada a first-rate small residential college such as Swarthmore, Amherst, Reed, etc. (all colleges that have made a significant contribution to higher education in the United States) and have built our own college at Glendon Hall with this in mind. We thought also that our college might have as its distinctive ethos, both in its curriculum and outside, a compelling interest in public affairs – perhaps a college from which would come people interested in politics and the civil service. I think such a college will be in great demand, will win a very large measure of support from government and private individuals, and can acquire a considerable record for the quality of its work.

In a letter a few weeks later he added: 'Glendon College can become known nationally, if not internationally, as an outstanding undergraduate college that produces first-class candidates for public service.'

The World Bank once made a survey of a representative group of projects it had helped to finance. One of the principal conclusions was that if the Bank had known all the difficulties it would encounter in completing the projects it would not have undertaken most of them. If I had in 1964 known all the difficulties I would encounter in establishing

Glendon I would not have accepted the principalship. Murray Ross was the creator of York University, which is now one of the largest universities in Canada. He, like most people of creative vision, possessed the happy faculty of turning a blind eye to obtacles in the way of realizing the vision. He wanted Glendon to be like Swarthmore, Amherst, and Reed. He overlooked the fact that these colleges had substantial endowments, Amherst with less than twelve hundred students having an endowment of $50 million. (In 1987 its endowment was about $300 million.) Glendon could not hope to be like Amherst unless it had much more money than governments were ever likely to provide.

My younger son Timothy was at the time assistant to the president of York University. He wrote me that he had had nothing to do with the invitation. He described the principalship as 'one of, if not "the", plum, in Canadian universities.' I asked advice from two old friends, John Holmes and Norman MacKenzie. Holmes said that his impression was that there would be a good deal of autonomy in the job, that the Board of Governors of York University was first-rate, that there was a determination to create a liberal arts college of high quality, and that it could be one of the most fascinating jobs in Canadian university life. MacKenzie advised me to take the job: 'It should be a good show and great fun. Murray is an old and good friend of mine – and I foresee no trouble with him.' Then he added a warning, the full significance of which I did not appreciate at the time, 'save that he may not be able to deliver all he would like or has promised.' This is another of the attributes of successful creative visionaries: they promise more than they are able to deliver.

I visited the Glendon campus a few weeks after receiving Murray Ross's letter to have talks with members of the Board of Governors and faculty of the university. I fell in love with the campus, a beautiful, wooded, eighty-five acres of parkland. It had been a market garden when E.R. Wood, a wealthy Toronto businessman, had bought it shortly after the First World War. At that time it was miles beyond the northern limits of Toronto; now it is in the centre of Metropolitan Toronto. E.R. Wood added to the natural beauty of the estate by employing first-class landscape architects and he had an Edwardian mansion built, Glendon Hall, part of which was to be the residence of the principal of the college.

One of my great pleasures when I was principal of Glendon was to walk in the valley of the west branch of the Don River below the college, one of the few unspoiled bits of valley in Toronto. In my farewell talk to the students I said that Glendon because of the beauty of its surroundings 'can help its students discover for themselves the solaces of gardens, quiet walks and wooded hills.' When I left the college the students named the path from the college residences to the valley 'the Escott Reid walk.' This pleased me greatly.

E.R. Wood's widow left the estate in 1950 to the University of Toronto and the university's law school was established there from 1956 to 1961. When York University was founded the University of Toronto gave it the estate. After Glendon College had been established, Edgar MacInnes of its history department said that York University had turned the University of Toronto's white elephant into a nursery of future greatness.

The reason York University invited me to be the first principal of a college 'that produces first-class candidates for public service' must have been that I had been a senior public servant. The university did not realize that my qualification for the job was not my accomplishments as a public servant but my lack of accomplishment: I had never learned to speak French. My failure to become bilingual, my recognition that in future any Canadian contemplating a career as politician or public servant should be bilingual, made me determined that Glendon should be a bilingual college.

There was no suggestion in York University's approach to me in 1965 that Glendon should be a bilingual college; the university's ambition for Glendon was that a considerable number of its graduates would enter public life as politicians or civil servants. My contribution to Glendon was to insist from the beginning that this meant that Glendon must be bilingual. The day after my first visit to the Glendon campus in August 1964 I sent a memorandum to Murray Ross in which I said: 'All students should be given training throughout their four years in writing English. All students should acquire an ability to read and speak French.' If I had not been successful in my demand that Glendon be bilingual the college would have ceased to exist in any recognizable form some time in the seventies. The seventies were a period of great financial stringency for universities in Ontario. Glendon was a drain on York University's limited finances and the cost of Glendon to the university would be reduced if it were moved from its separate campus to the main campus of the university in North York thirteen miles away. But if it were moved to the main campus the possibility of it succeeding in becoming bilingual could cease to exist. This consideration saved Glendon from extinction. By insisting on bilingualism I builded better than I knew.

The recurrent threats in Glendon's first dozen years of existence that it be moved to the main campus helped to unite the college in its defence. Nollaig MacKenzie, who came to Glendon in 1967 as a professor of philosophy, has said: 'There was a recurring sense of crisis. Part of the

Glendon spirit came about because we had to defend the college constantly. We managed to keep the wagons drawn in a circle when that was necessary.'

The first mistake I made in my efforts to persuade the Senate of the university to approve of a special position for English and French in the curriculum of the college was to describe the objective as the acquisition of skills. In the middle of July 1965 I prepared a lengthy memorandum for submission to the Board of Governors and the Senate of the university, which began with the statement, 'My idea of Glendon College is that it should be a small, residential, undergraduate college of high scholastic standards where there would be a special emphasis on public affairs and on the acquisition of skill in the use and appreciation of the English and French languages.' I used the word 'skill' three times in the succeeding paragraphs on the place of English and French in the curriculum. Murray Ross patiently explained to me why my emphasis on the acquisition of skill had aroused apprehensions among the faculty of the university:

This relates to the fundamental purpose of the university: to deepen knowledge, understanding and insight. The teaching of a specific skill, be it to play the piano, to operate a computer, or to speak a language, is not a prime function of a university, but belongs in a special technical school of some kind. It is true that the university teaches skills, but this cannot be considered its prime function ... There is ... a good deal of reluctance to accept the idea that the teaching of a skill should have priority over education as it is conceived in a university setting.

In spite of this I continued to use the term skill in my description of the teaching of English and French at Glendon and in September 1965 the Senate of the university authorized my use of the term. Perhaps the faculty's apprehensions had been allayed by reading again the statement in my memorandum of mid-July:

The English and French languages are two of the greatest treasures of western civilization. It is the proud duty of universities in the western world to cherish and defend these treasures against their enemies who are legion ... Skill in the use of language is the key to efficient administration, whether in government or business. Clarity of language and clarity of thought go together. Sophistication of language and sophistication of thought go together. An appreciation of the beauty of the written and the spoken word is one of the great joys of life.

It was one thing to get the acquiescence of the university Senate in the goal of bilingualism; it was another and more difficult task to get acquiescence in a curriculum for the first two years at the college in which the study of English and French would take up almost half of the student's time at the expense of other subjects usually studied in the first two years. I argued that though the Glendon student who intended to specialize in his third and fourth years in history, economics, political science, philosophy, or sociology would know less about these subjects at the end of his second year than students who had not had to spend so much time on English and French, he would at the end of his fourth year know more about them because of his command of both languages.

At the beginning of May 1965 I presented my ideas on the curriculum to a joint committee of the Board of Governors and the Senate. The representatives of the teaching staff of the university attacked my proposals. Afterwards Douglas Verney, the leading political scientist at the university, told me that my difficulty with the teaching staff was that I naturally wanted to be the architect of the new college but they did not want to be relegated to the role of bricklayers. I, on the other hand, believed that what I was trying to do was to get agreement on the master plan for the curriculum before asking the architects, the chairmen of departments, to design the individual buildings.

The next month the Senate approved of much of what I had proposed, but added a joker: it requested the Glendon College Faculty Council to consider what further steps would be required 'to make the first two-year program identical to the present York curriculum.' I protested to Murray Ross that 'if the Senate request were acceded to, it would make impossible the emphasis on English and on French in the first two years which in my opinion is essential.' I said I could not take up my post if the Senate persisted in this view. Under pressure from Murray Ross the Senate agreed that the first two-year program at Glendon need not be identical to that on the main campus.

My views on the curriculum for Glendon were not limited to insisting that the students should master English and French. I wanted them in their final year to take a course in social ethics. In a letter in December 1967 to Marcel Cadieux, then under-secretary of the Department of External Affairs, I said:

One reason for my insistence on the importance of a course in social ethics is that I have found that a number of the younger members in the United States foreign service and in our own foreign service seem to have forgotten the first two pages or so or the first chapter of many of the books in the social sciences which they read at university, in which it was said that, for the purposes of the discussion in the book or chapter, value judgements or moral judgements would be disregarded. They thus graduated from university in the false and dangerous belief that in the making of great national decisions moral judgements or value judgements do not play and should not play an important role.

In my effort to help the students understand the nature of the ethical problems which people faced in their professional lives I persuaded the students who ran the Glendon College Forum to include in their program for 1967–68 three talks on social ethics. I started with a talk on the conscience of a diplomat. Norman Smith, the editor of the *Ottawa Journal*, spoke on the conscience of an editor, and Robertson Davies on the conscience of a writer. I hoped that during the next two years there would be another half-dozen or so 'conscience' talks, sufficient for a book of essays, but the next year, 1968, was the peak year of student radical unrest and no more conscience talks were given.

It seemed to me obvious that the first step in getting together a teaching staff for the college was to appoint the chairmen of the departments. They could then, in consultation with me, approach possible members of their departments. I consulted with friends who were particularly well informed in these matters and in July 1965 I submitted to Murray Ross my proposals for chairmen of the departments of economics, political science, and sociology and requested permission to write to them offering these appointments. (I already had chairmen of the departments of history and philosophy.) To my astonishment I found I could not do this. I had first to go through six steps: write a possible chairman asking if he might be interested in the post; if he was interested ask him to nominate persons to give me letters of reference; have him visit Glendon and meet members of the faculty; have him interviewed on the main campus of the university by the dean of the faculty of arts and science; secure the consent of the dean to the appointment; secure agreement from the university on salary, rank, and tenure. Murray Ross asked me how I could contemplate appointing people I had never met. I said Mackenzie King had asked St Laurent to join his cabinet even though he had not met him and that I had confidence in the judgment of the people I had consulted.

I think I might have persuaded the scholars I had nominated to accept appointment if I had been able to make a firm offer to them a year before they would take up the appointment and if they had been given authority to recruit the other members of their departments. The necessity of following the complicated process laid down by the university meant that I had to toil for two years to secure competent chairmen. I had learned that the red tape of universities was worse than the red tape of governments. My painful education in university affairs was proceeding apace.

I also painfully learned something about the bargaining abilities and professional ethics of some university teachers. I remember one case with some bitterness. I interviewed a possible professor twice; he met members of the staff; he was interviewed on the main campus; I informed him of the salary and other terms of his appointment. He then told me that when he had expressed an interest in coming to Glendon he had not realized how greatly the university at which he was now teaching valued him. So he was withdrawing his request to be appointed to the Glendon faculty. His gambit had succeeded. He had got a letter from me offering him generous terms. He had shown it to his university and had got from them an increase in his salary.

By the spring of 1966 I still did not have enough teachers of oral French. As a last resort I called on the French ambassador in Ottawa and asked his help. We had been colleagues in Bonn when I was ambassador and he the second-in-command of the French embassy. He explained that young Frenchmen, in place of doing compulsory military service, could apply to do national service and one form of national service was to teach French in foreign countries. He would see if he could get national service men for me. He got three. They were excellent. Two of them, Alain Baudot and J.-C. Jaubert, are still on the Glendon faculty.

My letters in 1965 to friends asking for advice elicited helpful replies. Frank Underhill urged that every student in residence have a room to himself:

The gregariousness of North Americans is one of the chief obstacles in the way of producing individuals who are accustomed to live for considerable periods on their own resources ... Most university residences today operate to discourage hard intellectual activity because they haven't got enough dons living in close contact with the students and giving a living demonstration every day of how interesting and inspiring the intellectual life can be. If you haven't this influence operating every day in the residence the students will settle down to talk about women and football.

T.W.L. MacDermot, formerly of the Department of External Affairs and at that time on the staff of Bishop's University, wrote:

The most revolutionary, and the most outstandingly original and valuable idea to me [in your proposal] is the establishment of the English language as the core of the whole scheme of learning ... Nearly all Canadian students are fundamentally handicapped by ignorance of the language. They have no respect for it, they are not curious about it, they have no knowledge of its origins, are unconscious of its range and power; they cannot use it to read or to write; they do not understand the text books they use nor are they stimulated by the masterpieces they are asked to criticize, analyse, and assess.

Doris Crowe, the wife of Marshall Crowe, formerly of External Affairs and at that time economic adviser to the Canadian Imperial Bank of Commerce, caught me out in a sexist statement. In my memorandum of July 1965 which I had sent to Marshall Crowe I had written: 'Only a relatively small proportion of the graduates of Glendon College would become politicians or civil servants. Most would go into business or a profession or the arts. Many would become university teachers and I hope they would be inquisitive, imaginative, creative, lively scholars. Most of the women would, no doubt, marry and I hope they would become inquisitive, imaginative, creative and lively wives and mothers.' Doris, according to her husband, 'took strong objection' to my statement about the women graduates. 'She does not object to their being wives and mothers, but objects to the assumption that they would not want to put their education to the same professional use as their male contemporaries.' I acknowledged my fault and amended my statement.

I thought that one way to attract good students to Glendon was to have a well-publicized opening ceremony in September 1966. The prime minister, L.B. Pearson, with his usual generosity to a friend and former colleague, gave the principal speech. His wife Maryon opened the new women's residence. The minister of education of Ontario, William Davis, and a cabinet minister from the province of Quebec spoke. I got much publicity for Glendon as the result, but it was not the kind calculated to attract good students to the college. The headlines in the three Toronto newspapers about the opening ceremony were: 'Students picket Pearson at college opening' (*Globe and Mail*); 'Students picket P.M. at York U., demand more money' (*Telegram*); 'York students demand more money as Pearson opens Glendon' (*Star*). The cause of the demonstration was the claim by the students that Pearson had failed to carry out a promise he had made in the general election campaign in 1965 to institute a system of federal scholarships to universities.

A year later I discovered the effect of these newspaper stories. In Glendon's first year Lisgar Collegiate in Ottawa, one of Ontario's best secondary schools, had provided Glendon with fifteen students with high marks in their grade 13 examinations, the next year with only four. I asked the principal if he could give me an explanation. He said that the Lisgar students had read of the demonstrations at the opening of the college and that first-class students did not want to come to a college which was subject to this kind of disturbance.

Another unexpected difficulty occurred at the end of our first year when about half of our first-year students deserted Glendon for the main campus of the university; Glendon had not lived up to their expectations. It had not lived up to mine either. More of them left the next year, with the result that in the autumn of 1968 of those who had entered the college two years before, only 40 per cent remained. These men and women saved the college. They saved it by sticking with it and by enriching the life of the college with the Glendon Student Forum and with activities in drama, music, and art. They who were the first graduates of the college in 1970 are an annus mirabilis.

Because so many of our students left Glendon, in order to reduce the deficit in the operation of the college we had to take overflow students who had applied for entry to the main campus of the university and could not be accommodated there. In my talk to first-year students that year I welcomed these students 'who did not choose Glendon but for whom Glendon was chosen.' They wanted to be on the main campus of the university but there was no room for them there and they had had to come to Glendon. 'You did not choose greatness. You have had greatness thrust upon you.' These students were not required to study French. In 1970 after I had left the college the procedure for dealing with students who were not required to try to become bilingual was regularized. Students applying for admission to Glendon could apply to enter the 'bilingual stream' or the 'unilingual stream.' Sixteen years later (in 1986) two-thirds of the first-year students chose the bilingual stream. In that year the unilingual option for first-year students was abolished and in the autumn of 1987 all incoming students were enrolled in the bilingual stream, with the result that by 1990 all the students at the college will be in the bilingual stream and Glendon will become a college in which all students will do their best to become bilingual in French and English. I had thought it would take ten years for Glendon to become bilingual. It is taking twenty-five.

Another unexpected difficulty was our failure to recruit French Canadians to the faculty of the college. I told Murray Ross at the end of 1964 and the beginning of 1965 that I wanted the vice-principal, the head of the French department, and most of the other members of the department to be French Canadians. I also hoped to secure French Canadians for the other departments at Glendon so that at least one-fifth of the teaching staff would be French Canadian. I wrote to many French-Canadian teachers at universities in Quebec; I entertained at the college about twenty French-Canadian scholars in the hope of persuading them to join our faculty; I offered senior posts including chairmanships of departments. I had not one favourable reply. Faced with this failure I tried to recruit from French Canadians who had graduated from Quebec universities and were studying in Europe. I appealed for help to my friend and former colleague in External Affairs, Jean Chapdelaine, who was the representative of the government of Quebec in Paris. He arranged for the Association of Quebec Students in France to send a circular to all its members about the openings for them at Glendon. There was no response. Chapdelaine wrote me: 'I have little encouragement to offer. I have myself spoken to many of the students. They are geared to a pole, the university, be it Laval or Montreal or Sherbrooke whence they come, for which they are preparing their doctorate, and in which they were more or less assured of a place before they left Canada.' I wrote individual letters to about twenty French-Canadian students who were studying in Britain. I asked the Canadian ambassadors in Brussels and Bonn to help me get in touch with French-Canadian graduate students. The following was a typical reply: 'I regret to say that I am not interested in seeking an academic post outside of Quebec.'

Still another unexpected difficulty resulted from the outbreak in Glendon in 1968 of student radicalism, part of the outbreak that year in most universities in the western world. In the mid-sixties when I came to Glendon, students at almost all universities in Canada were not consulted by university administrators on matters of direct concern to them. York University in 1965 was about to begin construction of a second residence on the Glendon campus similar to the existing residence. I discovered that the students who were living in the existing residence had not been consulted on the plans for the new residence though they were obviously in a better position than anyone else to know what deficiencies in the existing residence should not be repeated in the new building. I insisted that they be consulted and they came up with many intelligent recommendations. Students would know better than anyone else how the services provided by the library, the bookroom, and the catering service could be improved but they were not consulted. I had committees on these services set up on which students were represented.

The students at Glendon properly demanded more than this recognition of their right to be consulted on housekeeping matters. They wanted to participate in the making of decisions on academic matters. They had no representation on the faculty council or its committees. This grievance was remedied. Twelve students elected by the students were added to the faculty council and all eleven committees of the council were composed of an equal number of faculty and students, including those dealing with the tenure and promotion of members of the faculty, bilingualism, the curriculum, and examinations and academic standards.

On all these matters it was high time that students were given greater responsibility, but their demands, at Glendon as elsewhere, went far beyond this. Two weeks before the autumn term in 1968 the student council sent a letter to all the members of the college, faculty and students, and followed it up a few weeks later with a manifesto. These documents included a wise and eloquent statement of the aims of education and much less wise specific proposals on how these aims might be realized at Glendon College.

The aims of education are to enable the individual to think independently and critically, to appreciate and understand compassionately, to act courageously and knowledgeably. Education may be defined as a process of enlightenment by which one shuns the constraints of tradition, prejudice and ignorance in the search for a truly human existence, both for oneself and for one's fellow members of society. It allows the individual to acquire two basic things – one is knowledge, and that is a tool, the other is courage, and that is an immeasurable internal ability to relate that knowledge to human values and act accordingly.

The principal specific proposal was that 'every member of the College should be able to pursue his education in whatever manner is deemed best by him. This denies compulsory courses, evaluative processes, and any rule or regulation not agreed to by members of the College as individuals and as a group.' Some students 'will decide in all likelihood, not to register in courses at all, but to *continue to educate themselves within the university community*' (my italics). 'The aims of Glendon to create a bilingual college with a special emphasis on public affairs ... are we feel potentially exciting and worthwhile,' but the council did not attempt to explain how the college could hope to become bilingual if its anglophone students were free to decide not to spend any time studying French in their four years at the college.

In the words which I have italicized lies, I think, much of the explanation of the demands of the student council. Whereas only about one-third of Glendon's first-year students had received 75 per cent or more in their final examinations at secondary school, six out of the seven members of the student council had received 75 per cent or more. Students who are intellectually gifted can 'educate themselves within the university community.' The ordinary university student cannot; he or she needs the stimulus and discipline of lectures, tutorials, essays, and examinations. The intellectual elite in the student council, who prided themselves on their opposition to elitism, were prescribing for all the members of the college what was only possible for an elite.

The Toronto newspapers gave great publicity to the demands of the Glendon student council but this publicity, like the publicity when Pearson opened the college, was not the kind which would help us recruit first-class students. Some of the headings were: 'Student rebels are getting absurd'; 'Glendon dean, student president clash'; 'Glendon College warns of doom'; 'Students, faculty clash: search for role hurts Glendon.' The guidance director of Lisgar Collegiate in Ottawa told me later that it was unfortunate that the report in the *Globe and Mail* of the incidents at Glendon in the fall of 1968, and similar accounts in the Ottawa papers, 'conveyed the impression of hostility and student revolt on the campus ... Generally speaking, students from this school are interested seriously in studies, and I think some parents jumped to false conclusions about the above-mentioned incidents.'

Two occurrences in this period of student unrest stand out in my mind. At Glendon every member of the faculty was assigned half a dozen first-year students who would call on him for advice on the courses they might register for, and we had a meeting of the faculty at the beginning of each academic year to discuss administrative problems. Just as I was about to adjourn the meeting on administration a newly appointed assistant professor demanded that we should immediately discuss the demands of the student council, which it was clear he supported. He made his demand ten minutes before the faculty had promised to be in their offices to meet first-year students. I said, 'Punctuality is the politeness of professors as well as of princes. The meeting is adjourned.'

I learned in my first year at the college how easy it was to offend students by taking action on a matter of concern to them without consulting them. My bedroom in Glendon Hall faced the driveway leading to the student residence. My sleep was constantly disturbed by screeching cars delivering pizzas to the residence. I had the driveway closed at night by a chain put across it which meant that the deliverers of pizzas would have to walk 150 yards from their cars to the residence. The student newspaper attacked me with vigour. It said that few day students had met me: 'Escott Reid. Is he the guy who has the dog?' said one boy. Another commented, 'If York needs an English lord we've got the right man,' while in the Residence he is known as 'Escott Quatorze in Versailles.' When a Toronto newspaper interviewed me I said: 'One of my hopes at Glendon College is to encourage the undergraduates to write lucid, vigorous prose. I'm already having some effect.'

I agreed to take the chains down for two weeks while some sensible arrangement was worked out with the students. The *Globe and Mail*, which gave me constant support in its editorials and news columns while I was principal, tactfully ran a story two days after Christmas headed 'Rift healed. Principal host to students,' concluding with the statement: 'He removed the chain and set about rectifying the situation by meeting the students on an individual basis and at teas. And yesterday he invited all students spending their holidays at the college to his home for dinner. He, his wife and their dog, Bhuttu, entertained about 15 students.'

Every year I gave a talk to new students at the opening of the academic year and every year there would be some crisis at the college which made it desirable for me to give a talk to the whole student body. I talked about my ambitions for Glendon. I insisted that Glendon was not a professional college, not a school of administration, but a college dedicated to liberal education, and that there were two halves of a liberal education: undergoing the tough intellectual discipline required to gain an understanding of the world we lived in so that we might help to make the world a better place to live in; and, quoting from an English academic, 'breaking the influence of the world we live in and finding deliverance from the tyranny of the immediate, the novel and the transitory.' Those who wanted to change society for the better needed warm, compassionate hearts as well as cool, calculating brains. 'A revolution will diminish misery only if it is led by people who are moved to tears by the misery of their fellow men and, as Leonardo da Vinci has said, "Tears come from the heart not from the brain." ... I hope that today's student generation will undertake the task of making [the revolutionary changes that are needed in Canadian society] with fire in their bellies, excitement in their eyes, and a smile on their lips.'

A head of a college who gives advice to students is like the sower of seed in the parable. He does not know what seed will fall on fertile ground and flourish and what will be sterile. In my first talk to the students I gave them two texts to meditate on:

The first is a Sanskrit saying about the way the wealthy should give to the poor – and anyone who has had the privilege of studying at a university for three or four years is wealthy. The Sanskrit saying is sraddhaya deyang which means, Give with reverence, give with humility. The second are the last words of the founder of one of the world's great religions, Buddhism. The last words of the Lord Buddha were 'Work out your own salvation with diligence.'

One of the students later said to me that when as a first-year student he had heard me quote from Hindu and Buddhist scriptures he knew he had come to the right college: the talks to students at his high school had always been larded with quotations from Christian scriptures.

The unexpected setbacks, the unexpected challenges which Glendon faced in its first few years, produced unexpected creative responses. Glendon was saved by the creative responses of its faculty and its students. The most important of these responses was the organization by Glendon's first first-year students of the Glendon College Forum. The students and I would persuade a prominent Canadian to speak to the students after lunch or dinner in the dining-hall and his talk would be followed by discussion. Towards the end of our first year of existence a delegation from the forum, headed by David Cole, called on me. David Cole said that they proposed to hold in the following November a three-day conference focusing on events within Quebec and between Quebec and the rest of Canada since the death of Premier Duplessis in 1959. The conference would be given the title 'Quebec: Year Eight,' and would be addressed by leading spokesmen for Canadian federalism and for Quebec separatism. The students wanted my support. I was amazed that first-year students should contemplate such a difficult undertaking. Certainly first-year students at my time in the University of Toronto would never have dreamed of doing such a thing. I had, however, enough sense to agree to help them. The forum was attended by six hundred students. It was addressed by René Lévesque, Claude Ryan, Eric Kierans, Jean-Luc Pépin, Robert Cliche, Gilles Grégoire, Marcel Masse, Frank Scott, Michael Oliver, Ramsay Cook, and others. The proceedings were televised by the Canadian Broadcasting Corporation and were published by the corporation. The success of this first annual Glendon Forum infused new hope and vigour into the college.

The next year the annual forum was on the position of the Indian in Canadian society. In the following summer of 1968, the student council proposed that the third forum examine the nature of the current international radical student unrest and 'provide a clear exposition and critical study of the radical ideas and theories which underlie the student revolution.' Radical student leaders from many countries would be invited to participate, 'whether moderate, "New Left", Trotskyite, Maoist, Guevarist, Marxist-Leninist, "Marxist-Humanist", or Stalinist.' The Canadian students participating in the forum would be 'representative of *all* facets of student opinion.' The title would be 'The Year of the Barricade.' After prolonged discussions between the students and the executive committee of the faculty council I gave permission for the holding of the conference. Shortly afterwards I had my annual meeting with the board of governors of the university to present a progress report and to appeal for increased funds for the college. I was pleased by the favourable reception of my presentation. Then the chairman of the board raised the matter of 'The Year of the Barricade.' He suggested that the publicity which would be given to this forum would probably have a serious detrimental effect on obtaining financial support for Glendon from business and the public. Another member questioned the propriety of my giving permission for the holding of the forum without first referring the matter to the board which was responsible for the management of the university and in particular for the safety of the university buildings. I said that under the York University Act I had been given power 'to implement regulations governing the conduct of students and student activities.' A third member, commenting on my statement that student demonstrations or sit-ins might result from attempts to ban the conference, said that in his business the management had twice withstood the pressure of prolonged strikes in support of unacceptable demands and that he could not countenance demands backed up by threats. A fourth member feared that the students would not be able to control the conduct of the meeting and that matters would get out of hand.

In defending my support for the forum I said: 'My colleagues on the faculty and I have tried to divert student discontent, student radicalism into constructive channels. In doing this we have had to weigh risks. We have had to choose between the greater and the lesser risk, the greater and the lesser evil. In this kind of matter there can be no certainties. In this kind of matter one deals with possibilities and probabilities. So far we have been successful.'

The board did not press its objections. I was, however, afraid that influential members of the board, fearing for the safety of the college buildings, might arrange for large numbers of police to be provocatively in evidence near the entrance to the college grounds when the forum was in session. I therefore made an agreement with the police that they would intervene on the Glendon campus during the meeting only if I requested them to and they gave me a special telephone number which I should use to make such a request. They warned me that once they arrived on the campus I would have no control over what they did. Presumably they would beat up the leading rioters. I knew from reading about the student radicals in Western Europe that one reason they organized violent student demonstrations was that they hoped the demonstrations would result in brutal police intervention which would tear the liberal mask off the face of the university establishment and disclose the face of fascism. I spent the three days of the forum in October 1969 with my special telephone number to the police in my pocket and with the members of the Council on Student Affairs warned to be available for consultation. The council was composed of students elected by the students and members of the faculty elected by the faculty. There were no disturbances. If there had been, the Glendon students would have handled them. They appointed students as 'ushers' for the meetings, all muscular, large, and determined. They were not ushers but bouncers.

Towards the end of my time at Glendon I tried to assess some of the similarities and some of the differences between university students of the late sixties and my generation of students at Toronto and Oxford forty years before. The two generations, I said, were alike in the contempt and anger with which they regarded the previous generation for the mess it had made of the world. But there was one profound difference. My generation of young leftists was concerned with how to get power and what we would do with power when we got it; but

students at universities throughout the western world today talk much about student power, power for the student community, but the paradox is that the individual student today, unlike the student in my time, is reluctant to exercise power once he gets it ... They don't want to be labelled as members of the power elite at their college or university. They know from the bitter history of the last fifty years the danger that those who hold power will abuse it ... and be corrupted by it ... For them ... power has been invalidated by the monstrous uses to which it has been put in the last half century. Stalin's purges and mass murders, Hitler's murder of six million Jews, the holocausts of Dresden and Hiroshima, the destruction of Vietnam.

While previous generations of students might have been afraid of sex, 'The present generation is afraid of power. Perhaps the Puritan ethic is so deeply ingrained in the western world that you have to be a Puritan about something and if you cease to be a Puritan about sex you become a Puritan about power and in place of being over-scrupulous about sex you become over-scrupulous about power.'

There might in time be a student revolt against the power-Puritans just as there had been a student revolt against the sex-Puritans. And the new student rebels may say that it is natural to enjoy power, that the appetite for power is normal and healthy and that we must not frustrate ourselves and others by being afraid of power. But, I added, 'If such a rebellion should arise there is danger that it will go too far for there is no contraceptive pill to prevent power from giving birth to monstrosities.'

In the spring of 1969 I was greatly encouraged by news that there might be an article on Glendon in the most widely circulated weekly magazine in Canada, a weekend supplement to many of the leading Canadian newspapers. The English-language edition was called *Weekend Magazine*. It had a circulation of two million. The French-language edition, *Perspectives*, had a circulation of half a million. This publicity for Glendon would, I was confident, make it easier for us to recruit students from across Canada. The author of the article, Mike Cowley, came to Glendon to interview me and members of the faculty and students. I ordered in advance of publication a considerable number of copies to be used for publicity.

When the issue of *Weekend Magazine* for 4 October 1969 arrived I was dismayed. The article on Glendon was the leading article, taking up the first three pages of the magazine, but it was no paean of praise, rather it sounded like a death knell. The heading was 'Glendon's fading dream. Three years ago, Toronto's Glendon College enthusiastically set out to create a bilingual educational community. Unfortunately, the French-Canadians never came.' At the top of the next page were photographs of four pallbearers at Glendon's funeral: Georges-Paul Collet, chairman of the French department at McGill University; Hubert Guindon, a sociologist at Sir George Williams University in Montreal; Claude Ryan, editor of *Le Devoir*; and Bob McGaw, president of the Glendon student council. Under each photograph was a text for a funeral oration. Collet was reported to have said that 'few people believe Glendon will help unify Canada'; Guindon that Glendon is 'a damned good concept but should have been in Montreal'; Ryan that 'there are simply too many challenges for Quebecers within their own province for them to look elsewhere'; and McGaw that 'compulsory bilingualism must end before Glendon can be turned into an effective college.'

On the cover of *Perspectives* was 'Glendon. Les maux du tête du bilingualism', and the article was headed 'Bilingualisme universitaire à Toronto. Professeurs et étudiants Québecois se font tirer l'oreille.'

I immediately wrote a reply to the article:

French-Canadian students are coming to Glendon College. Glendon's dream to create a bilingual educational community in Toronto is not fading. Three years ago when the college opened we didn't have one French-Canadian from Quebec in our first year. This year we have 18 in our first year of 340, and we have 11 Franco-Ontarians instead of the one we had three years ago. Of our total student body of 885, 48 are French-Canadians ... I'm willing to bet we'll have at least fifty French-Canadians in our first year next year and a hundred by 1972. The French-Canadian yeast is working at Glendon. The French-Canadians have taken over the student coffee house and turned it into a centre of biculturalism. They've changed the whole atmosphere of the place. It's now *une boite à chansons*. You have only to enter L'Araignée in the evening to feel the French-Canadian fact at Glendon. Biculturalism is certainly an emerging reality at Glendon not a fading dream.

I went on to say that Glendon was the only college or university in Canada fully committed to having all its students become bilingual; it was a pilot project for the whole of Canada; compulsory courses at university were now unfashionable but at Glendon compulsory French for anglophones and compulsory English for francophones had a few months before been supported unanimously by the faculty council of the college, which included twelve students elected by the student body.

Weekend Magazine and *Perspectives* did not publish the reply.

I left Glendon at the end of 1969 when I was about to reach the retirement age of sixty-five, convinced that Glendon would succeed because of the creative responses of its faculty and students to the challenges posed by its setbacks. The teaching of oral French, which had not been first rate the first time it was tried in 1966–67, had greatly improved. The curriculum had been strengthened. There had been an outburst of extracurricular activities in drama, creative writing, music, and art. Within ten years of the establishment of the dramatic arts program by Michael Gregory in 1967, twenty-eight of the students involved in it had worked professionally for the stage as actors or technicians. Of these the most distinguished is Kate Nelligan. Among the graduates of the college who have received recognition for their creative writing are M.T. Kelly, who won the Governor General's award for fiction in 1987 and Greg Gatenby, a writer of prose and poetry, who has done much to make Toronto a centre of festivals of international writing. The Glendon Orchestra founded by Alain Baudot has evolved into the York Community Orchestra.

Glendon has gone through many crises since my time there. Periodically threats have been made that it would have to be moved to the main campus of the university in order to save money. My successors as principal of the college – Albert Tucker, David McQueen, Philippe

Garigue, and Roseann Runte – and their allies in the faculty and the student body and in the francophone community in Ontario have surmounted these threats and other setbacks.

The original goal for Glendon set by Murray Ross in 1964 was that it would be a first-rate residential college for about a thousand students. Glendon now (1988) has 1,373 full-time students and 354 part-time students; its numbers had to be increased in order to qualify for more money from the provincial government. Only a college with a large endowment could be limited to a thousand students. It is not a residential college; only one-quarter of its students live in residence. But it is a bilingual college and it has many bicultural activities. Every student who intends to graduate from Glendon is committed to acquiring skill in reading, speaking, and writing English and French. French is the language of instruction in about one-fifth of the courses given by departments other than the language departments, and the college is determined to increase the number of courses given in French. Of the 524 new students who enrolled in the autumn of 1988, 111 were francophones, 48 from Quebec, 55 from Ontario, and 8 from elsewhere. Among the bicultural activities are the film club which presents French and English films, the drama program which enables students to work on theatrical productions in French and English, and the student organization, Trait d'Union, which has as one of its goals to assist francophones to increase their appreciation of their own background and to initiate anglophones to French cultural activities. The increased size of the college has enabled it to increase the number of departments. Originally there were seven: English, French, history, philosophy, economics, political science, and sociology. Psychology, Spanish, mathematics, computer science, and translation have been added.

All this has made me proud and happy. And I know that Glendon will continue to develop. I hope that more and more first-class students will come to Glendon from all parts of Canada so that it will become a national college. This will be possible only if the federal government establishes a system of national scholarships or if Glendon raises an endowment from which it can grant scholarships to first-class students. The more students who come from beyond metropolitan Toronto and its vicinity the more need there will be for residences. I hope that more will be built so that eventually half the students will live in residence.

And above all I hope that the quality of teaching at Glendon, the depth of the scholarship of its faculty, and the quality of the students will continue to be high so that those who graduate from the college will have profited by the two mutually nourishing halves of a liberal education: gaining an understanding of the world we live in so that we may help to make the world a better place to live in, and 'breaking the influence of the world we live in and finding deliverance from the tyranny of the immediate, the novel and the transitory.'

21

*T*alks with L.B. Pearson
1963–1972

In earlier chapters I have discussed my association with L.B. Pearson up to 1962 when I left the foreign service. After that I had about a dozen private talks with him.

The first of these talks was at the end of May 1963, five weeks after he had become prime minister. He had invited me to have lunch with him in his office in the Parliament Buildings. When I was ushered into the office I said, 'Good morning, Mr. Prime Minister.' He said, 'Whenever anybody says that to me I still look over my shoulder.' In our talk he said that the Quebec problem was the most difficult and important problem before the government. He was afraid of the reaction of the rest of Canada to the demands of the French Canadians, demands which resulted from three factors: the creation of small independent French African states cast doubt on the contention that an independent Quebec would not be viable; the success of industrialization in Quebec drove home to the French Canadians that their industries were run by Americans or English-speaking Canadians; and the ferment among French-Canadian intellectuals.

Few people, he said in May 1963, recognized that his contribution as leader of the opposition in the previous Parliament had been to build the Liberal party up by persuading first-class men to stand as Liberal candidates. The new Liberal members of Parliament were mainly people he had chosen. He had hated the job of leader of the opposition in the House of Commons. (I am sure he said to me that every time he entered the House of Commons when he was leader of the opposition he had a sick feeling in his stomach but this remark does not appear in my notes of our talks.) Diefenbaker was better than he in the cut-and-thrust of parliamentary debate. Now as prime minister he could disregard

Diefenbaker's sallies in the House of Commons. The concluding sentence of my notes on this talk is, 'He remains obsessed by his hatred of Diefenbaker.' Three years later, in September 1966, he said to me, 'Diefenbaker is an evil man.'

In my talk with Pearson at the end of August 1964 he spoke for the first time about who his successor might be. He wanted Jean Lesage, the premier of Quebec. It was a great pity he could not be acknowledged as the heir apparent but this would weaken his position in Quebec. Six months later he gave me the impression that he had changed his mind about Lesage as his successor but that he thought he might join his cabinet. At the end of September 1966 he said he would resign after the centenary celebrations of confederation in 1967 and it might be that Jean Marchand would succeed him. He had been a success in the House of Commons though he had had no previous parliamentary experience. His trade union experience had made up for this. He might not, however, be able within twelve months to build up enough public support to enable him to secure the leadership. Was not this, I asked Pearson, a reason for his staying on as prime minister for two more years not just one? 'If Marchand cannot win a year from now, Paul Martin could become temporary leader.'

Five months later, at the end of January 1967, he said that Mitchell Sharp was now the leading candidate for the succession but, 'I've told him he must move to a bit left of centre ... Hellyer might be good but he is associated in the public mind with only one piece of legislation, the unification of the armed forces. Turner is the leading younger contender. Perhaps he will get the leadership. But he has never had a setback. He should be put in a place where he could demonstrate what his reaction would be to tough situations under fire.'

Four weeks before this talk he had brought Walter Gordon back into the cabinet. Gordon was the leader of the left wing of the Liberal party and Robert Winters the leader of the right wing. Pearson had no sympathy with Winters's views. He said in September 1966 that Winters properly belonged to the conservative wing of a Conservative cabinet. In January 1967 he had told some of his wealthy supporters in Montreal that they could criticize him for bringing Gordon back into the cabinet only if they preferred the New Democratic party to the Liberal party, for if he had not brought him back younger leftist Liberals would have left the Liberal party for the NDP. He had consulted Mitchell Sharp and Paul Martin about bringing Gordon back but not Winters who was away from Ottawa. 'I wasn't going to phone him.'

Our talk in August 1966 took place after Lesage had been defeated in the provincial elections in Quebec and Daniel Johnson had taken his place as premier. I said that the immediate reaction of some of my friends was that this was a good thing since Ottawa could now be tougher with Quebec. Pearson agreed. It was not just a matter of Lesage being a Liberal but also of his being a personal friend. After Lesage had said or done something which created difficulties for the federal government he would telephone him, explain why he had had to do it and ask for sympathetic consideration from a friend. 'Daniel Johnson will not be able to try this gambit.' 'The most difficult premier I have to deal with is a fellow Liberal, Thatcher, the least difficult a Conservative, Robarts.'

It was during this conversation at the beginning of September 1967 at the prime minister's summer residence at Harrington Lake that Pearson talked at some length about General de Gaulle. My notes read as follows:

General de Gaulle's continuing intervention in Quebec is making the situation much more dangerous. He has made separatism respectable. It is not so much what he said on his visit [his pronouncement at the end of his speech in Montreal of 'Vive le Québec libre'] as what he has been saying and doing afterwards. His latest act is to send a cabinet minister to Canada who personally wants to visit Ottawa but who has been instructed by de Gaulle not to visit Ottawa. De Gaulle told him in Paris some years ago that he respected him for his efforts to hold French Canada and English Canada together but it was hopeless. English Canada was going to join the United States ... France should help Quebec to survive. One reason that de Gaulle's intervention has made the situation much more difficult is the violent reaction in English Canada, particularly in the West, to de Gaulle's statements in Canada ... [a reaction which] has exacerbated opinion in French Canada. I now face the question whether I should conduct an open campaign against separatism in Quebec. One of my difficulties is that none of the French cabinet ministers from Quebec has a basis of political strength in Quebec. (I had said that they were much the best group of French Canadian ministers any prime minister in Canadian history had got together.) More and more they were acting as if they were ambassadors of Quebec in Ottawa.

A week before Pearson's farewell speech to the Liberal leadership convention I wrote him urging that after taking a long holiday he should devote his time to writing his memoirs, first memoirs on foreign affairs and then memoirs on his life as a political leader.

My plea to you is not to be modest about the importance of your memoirs. You have it within you to produce the most important book on foreign affairs of the last twenty years. You have more knowledge and understanding and perspicacity and wisdom about foreign affairs than any of your contemporaries ... But, just because you have gone through so much over so long a period and have so much to say, the task that faces you is inordinately difficult ... It means ... recollecting in tranquility, pondering and reflecting on the past, enlivening your wisdom with your wit and mingling your remembrance of things past with illuminating insights into what is likely to come, the kind of things that we might do to make the future somewhat less terrifying, more hopeful, more humane ... There will be many people who will want to use you during your retirement for one cause or another – some good causes, some indifferent, some very good, but I plead with you not to allow your energies to be diverted from your main task.

He thought he had plenty of time to write his memoirs and he did allow his energies to be diverted. He undertook tasks, some of great importance, some of none. He headed a World Bank commission on international development. He was chairman of the board of governors of the International Development Research Centre. He gave seminars on foreign affairs at Carleton University in Ottawa. He gave many speeches. He became president of the Rideau Club. The great memoirs he should have written were not written.

My last memory of Pearson is of a meeting with him in September 1972. He had in August sent me his draft of chapters three and four of the second volume of his memoirs, the chapters on the North Atlantic alliance. He telephoned me – I was at our farm in the Gatineau hills – to say he would like me to have lunch with him at the Rideau Club in Ottawa and give him my suggestions for revising the chapters. I was amused when I read the draft chapters to find at the end of the chapter on the negotiation of the treaty a passage, 'Escott Reid who had striven so long and with an almost feverish and single-minded intensity to bring into being the perfect North Atlantic Treaty.' In his own hand he had struck out 'an almost feverish.'

I decided that though I would not strive with feverish intensity to bring into being perfect chapters on the North Atlantic treaty in Pearson's memoirs, I would take seriously his request for suggestions on improving his draft. Knowing that Pearson, unlike some professional politicians, learned from the eye as well as the ear, I further decided, after reading the draft several times, that I would send him a memorandum on the chapters and give him a chance to study it before we had our talk and I sent him a four-thousand-word memorandum at the end of August. Two weeks later he and I with his two editors, John Munro and Alex

Inglis, supported by four bulky volumes of documents drawn from the files of the Department of External Affairs, had a two-hour talk in his office in Ottawa, followed by lunch at the Rideau Club. In the talk we went over my memorandum paragraph by paragraph. On every second paragraph or so Munro or Inglis would intervene with a quotation from an external affairs document either to support or to rebut one of my comments. It was for me a strange experience to hear them quote memoranda I had written more than twenty years before which I had completely forgotten. Pearson showed as always a generous and discerning welcome of criticism.

Pearson was at his happiest that morning. The first volume of his memoirs had just appeared and had been greeted with affectionate enthusiasm. He had clearly been nervous about how the book would be received. Now he was joyous. He looked at least five years younger than the last time I had seen him four months before. Two weeks later he learned that he was dying and three months later he died. I count it among the blessings of my life that my last memory of Pearson is this joyous occasion.

In my note to Maryon Pearson on Pearson's death I spoke of 'his zest for life, his courage, his cheerfulness, his ability to roll with the punches and never to show when he was under tension even when the tension was continuous. And above all, his refusal to be corrupted by power.'

22

*E*ssays in Persuasion
1965–1988

In November 1965 I wrote to L.B. Pearson: 'I have given my first public speech on a controversial matter since ceasing to be a civil servant, national or international. You must have found in 1948, as I have found now, that you feel somewhat naked when you can no longer suggest that your speech would have been brilliant if you had not been confined to the platitudes of a civil servant.' I soon got over this feeling and during the next twenty-three years I tried by many speeches and articles to influence the foreign policy of the Canadian government and other governments.

When at the beginning of 1968 it seemed that Pierre Trudeau was hesitating about whether to stand for the leadership of the Liberal party in succession to Pearson, I wrote him on 5 February: 'I hope you stand for the leadership. I hope you win. I hope you agree with the proposals on foreign policy which I make in the enclosed article. It will appear in about three weeks' time in *Maclean's* for March.' The same day I sent my son Timothy, then a Liberal member of the Ontario legislature, a contribution of $100 towards the expenses of the 'Draft Trudeau for Prime Minister Committee,' which Robert Stanbury, Donald Macdonald, and he had established. The committee needed money to rent a room in the Royal York hotel in Toronto for a news conference and reception by Trudeau. Ten days later Trudeau announced that he was running for the leadership. On 28 March, a week before the leadership convention, I sent Trudeau a memorandum 'on the main aspects of Canadian foreign policy which I hope you will deal with in your speech at the convention.' In this memorandum I made recommendations on Canadian policy on China, Vietnam, foreign aid, the North Atlantic alliance, the Commonwealth, France, and the United States.

CHINA

I used to say in the fifties that I knew when the United States would recognize communist China: it had taken sixteen years from 1917 to 1933 to recognize communist Russia; it would take the same time to recognize communist China. The communist government in China had come to power in 1949; United States recognition would therefore come in 1965. I was out by eight years; American opposition to recognizing communist China was accompanied by opposition to Peking occupying the Chinese seat in the United Nations; Peking did not occupy that seat until 1971.

When Pearson came back from the Colombo conference in February 1950 we expected that within a few months Canada would follow the example of Britain, India, and Pakistan by recognizing communist China. If it had not been for the outbreak of the Korean War in June Canada would have recognized communist China that summer. The Korean War made recognition at that time impossible, and when China entered the war in 1951 and American opinion became inflamed against China, the U.S. government put extreme pressure on friendly governments not to recognize.

When I visited Washington in the mid-1950s I had a glimpse of how the passionate contempt of so many Americans for the communist government of China warped the judgment of intelligent, well-informed men when Walter Robertson, the assistant secretary of state for far eastern affairs, said to me in a private conversation, 'I tell you that Mao Tse-tung is no more representative of China than William Z. Foster, and I repeat William Z. Foster, is representative of the United States.' Foster was then head of the minuscule American Communist party. Another indication of the feelings of the American administration in the fifties was the statement which President Eisenhower made to two successive Canadian prime ministers, St Laurent and Diefenbaker, whom he suspected of flirting with the idea of recognizing Peking and supporting the seating of its representatives in the United Nations. 'If communist China is admitted to the United Nations the United Nations will leave the United States and the United States will leave the United Nations.'[1] I have always considered that the second part of the warning was a bluff. I said in a despatch to Ottawa in July 1954 that 'I have myself too much respect for the intelligence of the American people to believe that they would be prepared to set in motion a series of events which might end

1 Sandra Djwa, *The Politics of the Imagination: A Life of F.R. Scott* (Toronto: McClelland and Stewart 1987), 352–3

by the Soviet bloc and the "peace area" powers getting control of the name, the goodwill and the assets of the United Nations.' I therefore regret that the United States' bluff was not called in the fifties, since it might have led to the happy result of the United Nations leaving the United States while the United States remained in the United Nations.

Eisenhower was not the only spokesman for the United States who confused the issue by talking about 'admitting' communist China to the U.N. when it was not a question of whether communist China should be admitted to the U.N. but whether the member state China should be represented there by the government in Taiwan or the government in Peking. This distinction was one which Americans of all people should have found easy to understand since at party conventions they occasionally faced two delegations from the same state, and the question the convention had to face was not whether to admit that state to the convention but which delegation from that state should be seated.

I sometimes wonder whether the ability of the policy-makers in Washington at that time to keep a clear mind when pondering the problem of China may have been affected also by their constant use of the term 'Chincoms' in telegrams between the State Department and American embassies to denote the communist government of China in Peking. If you think in terms of Chincoms it may be more difficult for you to keep constantly in mind that you are referring to the government of a great power with a rich ancient civilization.

In the General Assembly of the United Nations American tactics were first to have the Assembly adopt a resolution stating that any proposal to change the representation of China was an important question requiring a two-thirds majority and then to rally support for opposing a resolution to seat Peking. I said in a letter to Ottawa in the summer of 1958 that requiring a two-thirds majority meant that one-third plus one of the Assembly composed of 'the United States plus Latin America and the hard-core of its client states around the world' could frustrate the wishes of 'the Russian bloc, the uncommitted countries and almost all Europe.'

In 1966, eight years later, Canada was still supporting the Assembly resolution declaring that a two-thirds majority was required to seat the representatives of Peking; but that year, for the first time, instead of voting against the resolution to seat Peking it abstained. This was unfortunately the only advance towards a sensible policy on China made by the Pearson government.

Once I became principal of Glendon College in 1965 and was no longer inhibited from expressing my views on foreign affairs publicly, I pressed in speeches and articles for Canada to break its long-continued adherence to American policy on China. I made this one of the two themes in my speech to the annual dinner of the Canadian Centenary Council in February 1967, the other theme being that Canada should increase the quantity and quality of its foreign aid, and the speech was printed in the *International Journal*. In his memoirs Paul Martin, who is obviously defensive about the failure of the Pearson government in which he was foreign minister to recognize Peking and support the seating of its representatives in the United Nations, wrote that in that speech I said 'that our presence in Peking would restore Canada to her position as an international mediator' but that he 'had strong doubts that a Canadian embassy in Peking would achieve results very different from the British or French. The golden age of diplomacy, to which Escott had alluded, was long since gone.'[2]

I did not say what Martin says I said. I advocated more than the mere establishment of an embassy in Peking. I recalled that when the United States established diplomatic relations with the Soviet Union in 1933 it had sent to its embassy in Moscow some of the brightest young men in its foreign service, among them George Kennan, Charles Bohlen, and Llewellyn Thompson. They had contributed greatly to the long, slow, patient process of bringing about better understanding between the Soviet Union and the western world. We should maintain at our embassy in Peking four of our most brilliant foreign service officers so that the embassy might be a forcing ground for talent on China which could serve the interests of the western world. The universities in Canada should co-operate in establishing a first-rate institute for the study of contemporary China. The government should give the institute financial support. We should more than triple our expenditures on foreign aid. We should strengthen the personnel of the Canadian International Development Agency. We should embark on a tough intellectual exercise on how to increase the effectiveness of the international agencies concerned with the economic development of poor countries and press for these improvements. If we did all this, then 'the next ten years could become a golden decade in Canadian foreign policy comparable to the great decade of 1941 to 1951.' I continue to believe I was right in this statement. The decade 1967 to 1977 could have been a second golden decade in Canadian foreign policy. It wasn't.

2 Paul Martin, *A Very Public Life*, vol. II (Toronto: Deneau 1985), 529

The next step in my campaign on China was my article in *Maclean's* which I had sent Trudeau on 5 February 1968. *Maclean's* headed the article 'Escott Reid says: "It's time Canada worked boldly to seat Red China in the U.N. and *really* helped have-not nations." ' I followed this by recommending in the memorandum I sent Trudeau on 28 March that we should recognize Peking and support the seating of its representatives in the U.N. 'We should surely years ago have ended the farce that a government, which governs less than 15 million people on an island off the coast of mainland China, represents the 700 to 800 million people of China.'

During the general election campaign I attended an open-air meeting in Scarborough, on the eastern edge of Toronto, where Trudeau spoke. His speech was twice interrupted by applause: when he delivered a few sentences in French, and when he said that the time had come to recognize communist China. In May 1968 the Trudeau government announced that it intended to seek diplomatic relations with China and in 1970 Canada recognized Peking and voted in favour of the resolution to seat its representatives in the General Assembly. This resolution failed to secure a two-thirds majority but the next year it was carried by a vote of seventy-six to thirty-five with seventeen abstentions. Not a single fellow member of the North Atlantic alliance voted on the United States' side. After twenty-two years Peking took the place in the United Nations to which it had been entitled since 1949.

Some of the leaders of the campaign in Canada for a change in Canadian policy on China were unquestioning disciples of Mao Tse-tung. I met them at a conference on China held at the University of Guelph in April 1968. I was asked to give the final speech at the conference. I arrived with the text of a speech based on my *Maclean's* article. As I listened to the discussions I became more and more dismayed. The conference was taking place at the height of the excesses of the cultural revolution in China. Speaker after speaker dismissed criticisms of these excesses. Paul Lin, for example, said, 'All countries and peoples have a right to make their own experiments according to their own needs and aspirations.' I decided that I could not pass by these statements in silence and I added a new conclusion to my speech. I said that my generation remembered

the intelligent well-meaning men who told us in the thirties that it was unreasonable of us to expect from Germany – humiliated in 1919, plunged into depression – behaviour other than that of the Nazis – government-inspired disorders on the streets, government-inspired destruction of synagogues, government-inspired attacks on innocent people. Germany, they said, had the right to solve its own problems in its own way. They didn't know that the way Hitler intended to solve one of Germany's problems, the Jewish problem, was by the final solution of mass murder. They can be excused for not knowing that. They cannot be excused for arguing that every nation has the right to solve its own problems in its own way. No nation has the right to try to solve its problems by methods which involve the destruction of the fundamental rights and freedoms of its citizens. These fundamental rights and freedoms include the right to protection by the state from mob tyranny, and the right to a fair trial. This is what national and international declarations and statutes on fundamental rights and human freedoms are all about.

We of my generation remember the intellectuals who told us in the thirties that Stalin was right to execute the old Bolshevists who had made the revolution. We remember the intellectuals who told us that the Red Army had been strengthened by the liquidation of most of its officers. Because my generation has these nightmarish recollections we shudder when in 1968 we hear in statements by intellectuals about Peking, Mao and the Chinese cultural revolution echoes of what we heard from intellectuals in 1938 about Moscow, Stalin and the Russian revolution.

VIETNAM

The first time I recall talking to Pearson about Vietnam after he had become prime minister was on 27 March 1965, six days before he gave his Temple University speech in Philadelphia which provoked President Lyndon Johnson to anger. I said that six months before there had been good reason to believe there was going to be a progressive improvement in relations between the United States and the Soviet Union and that the United States might begin the long process of working out a *modus vivendi* with China. What was happening in Vietnam was destroying these hopes.

Pearson said: 'What the United States is doing is disastrous. They intend to carry their bombing of Vietnam further. The United States is doing itself great damage by the demonstration it is giving of the most powerful nation in the world laying waste a small Asian country. The United States is getting virtually no support from other members of the North Atlantic Alliance in confidential meetings of the Alliance. The United Kingdom may soon have to make a public statement showing its disquiet.' He went on to say that he was contemplating urging a suspension of American bombing of North Vietnam in the speech he was giving the following week in Philadelphia. What Pearson said delighted me and I encouraged him to do this. I regret that it did not occur to me, as it should have, that it is almost always unwise for a prime minister or foreign minister to criticize adversely the foreign policy of a friendly government in a public speech on its own territory. It would have been better if Pearson had made his criticism in a speech delivered in Canada.[3]

The language in which Pearson urged a suspension of American bombing of North Vietnam in his Temple University speech in Philadelphia could scarcely have been milder. He said: 'There are many factors which I am not in a position to weigh. But there does appear to be at least a possibility that a suspension of such air strikes against North Vietnam, at the right time, might provide the Hanoi authorities with an opportunity, if they wish to take it, to inject some flexibility into their policy without appearing to do so as the direct result of military pressure.'

I had another talk with Pearson about Vietnam in early 1967. He said then that the Department of External Affairs suffered from too many of its officers having served in Indo-China. I assume he meant that these officers were hawks on Vietnam, that they supported American policy to the hilt, and that this had resulted in the department's advice on Vietnam being biased in favour of the United States.[4] Certainly there was more opposition within the State Department to American policy in Vietnam that there was within the Department of External Affairs.

Instead of the situation in Vietnam getting better after 1966 it got worse. American bombing intensified. I became more and more unhappy that I was doing nothing to help rally opinion in Canada against what the United States was doing. The speech of my friend Walter Gordon on 13 May 1967 precipitated my decision to make a public appeal. If Walter Gordon, a cabinet minister, could risk his political career by urging that the United States stop its bombing, surely I could risk criticism from the board of governors of York University. I got in touch with my old friends and former colleagues in External Affairs who had also become principals of colleges in Toronto, Douglas LePan and Wynne Plumptre, and with John Holmes of the Canadian Institute of International Affairs. I went to Ottawa in the first week of June with a draft statement which I discussed with Paul Martin, Walter Gordon, and Ralph

3 Peter Stursberg states: 'Even Escott Reid, who strongly supported the call for an end to the bombing felt that it was unwise to give it in the United States.' He should have added after 'felt' 'on reflection after the event.' Peter Stursberg, *Lester Pearson and the American Dilemma* (Toronto: Doubleday 1980), 223.
4 Paul Martin told Peter Stursberg that Pearson and he were surprised at how many Canadians returned from Vietnam as hawks; ibid. 215.

Collins of the Department of External Affairs. I revised it in the light of their comments. Pearson had been unable to see me but wrote me on 12 June commenting on my revision:

I don't quarrel with your sentiments or your expression of them though, in present circumstances, I would not be able to go along with the advice in your last paragraph that Canada take the lead in endeavouring to secure a joint public statement urging the United States to stop the bombing as a first step toward negotiations. More than once I have told the Americans, confidentially, what I thought they ought to do about some phases of the Viet Nam conflict, most recently when President Johnson came to Ottawa, but, at this stage at least, I do not think it would help if I made any public declaration to this effect. Certainly at least three of the Commonwealth Governments, the United Kingdom, Australia and New Zealand, would not join in such a declaration nor, I suspect, would many of the European countries. In any event, this is no reason why you should not express your views.

LePan and Plumptre had dinner with me at my apartment at Glendon College on 21 June and we agreed on the final text of the statement which I sent the next day to Pearson, Martin, and Marcel Cadieux, the under-secretary for external affairs, telling them that we would be releasing it to the press for publication on 27 June. The statement reads as follows:

During recent months, the pace of destruction of Vietnam – both North and South – has speeded up. Casualties among the armed forces of all the belligerents and among the civilian population of Vietnam have increased. The ancient civilizations of South East Asia are being undermined. The danger of war spreading has become much greater ...

In these circumstances we believe that the Government of the United States should, as a first step towards the opening of negotiations on a cease-fire and a peaceful settlement, stop the bombing of North Vietnam without attaching any conditions. We consider that, when the United States Government announces this, it should express the hope that the Government of North Vietnam would respond by undertaking that, during the negotiations, it would not strengthen its armed forces in South Vietnam provided that the United States, Australia, New Zealand, the Philippines, South Korea and Thailand did not strengthen their armed forces there. We believe that the Government of North Vietnam should make this response.

We welcome the efforts which the Government of Canada has been making to promote a peaceful settlement in Vietnam. We believe that the people of

Canada would enthusiastically support the Government in making the most intensive efforts possible to enlist the support of other governments for peace proposals such as we have set forth above.

In question time in the House of Commons on 27 June T.C. Douglas asked Pearson what reply he was making to this appeal. Pearson said: 'These proposals do not in any way conflict with government thinking.' When I had a talk with him two months later at his house at Harrington Lake I thanked him for saying this. He said: 'I was surprised some one in the House of Commons didn't say, "Well, if you think that way, why don't you talk that way?" ' The government did talk that way twenty-five days later.

He asked me what more the government could do about Vietnam. What would I do if I were secretary of state for external affairs? I said that in the crisis in the mid-fifties over Quemoy and Matsu he had said publicly that if the United States got into a war with China over these islands Canada would not support the United States. He said the time might come when he would have to say this about Vietnam, perhaps if the United States went in for saturation bombing of North Vietnam. 'But,' smiling, 'at least I've said more than Harold Wilson.'

Three of my former colleagues in External Affairs who had left government service supported the statement which LePan, Plumptre, and I had issued. Dana Wilgress commended us for our 'timely and constructive statement on Vietnam.' R.A. MacKay wrote that he agreed with the statement. John Holmes said that the statement 'expresses exactly my own concern and if it had not been for my real anxiety about my right to entangle indirectly the Institute [of International Affairs] in the policy statement, I would have signed it.' I was relieved when one of the members of York University's board of governors, John Gray, the head of Macmillan of Canada, who had been worried when I had told him I would be issuing a statement on Vietnam, congratulated us, adding: 'If we could have more clear-headed and informed people contributing light where there is mostly heat, I am sure it would help.'

I sent the statement to Dean Rusk, then the American secretary of state, and to Ellsworth Bunker, the American ambassador in Vietnam. Rusk, as was to be expected, disagreed with our proposal that the United States should 'stop the bombing of North Vietnam without attaching any conditions':

We cannot, in fairness to those for whose safety we bear a major responsibility, cease our efforts to reduce the flow of armed men and weapons into South Viet

Nam from the North without some assurance that the other side will not exploit this cessation to secure military advantage ... Despite the discouraging experiences we have had so far, we are increasingly probing for some indication from the other side that our action will evoke a response which might lead to peace.

Bunker said much the same thing:

The crux of the matter is that mentioned in your third paragraph, i.e., any indication by Hanoi that with a cessation of bombing it would undertake not to strengthen its armed forces in South Viet Nam. Advantage has been taken of the five bombing cessations in the past to accelerate the movement of men and supplies to South Viet Nam on the part of the North Vietnamese.

LePan, Plumptre, and I were happy with the publicity and support which our statement received in Canada. The Toronto and Ottawa papers printed it in full and carried stories about it and its signatories, and elsewhere in Canada it was well reported. Perhaps this made it easier for the government to adopt our recommendation three months later. In a speech to the U.N. General on 27 September 1967 Paul Martin called on the United States to stop the bombing of North Vietnam without attaching any conditions.

In January 1968, when it seemed to me that there was a clear and present danger that the continued bombing of North Vietnam might result in the United States becoming involved in a war with China, I suggested to LePan and Plumptre that we might issue a second statement in which we would recommend that if the United States did not stop the bombing of North Vietnam the Canadian government should give the United States government the kind of warning Pearson had given them in the mid-fifties – 'a warning that Canada does not consider that a conflict between the United States and China arising out of the fighting between the United States and North Vietnam would require any Canadian intervention in support of the United States government.' I did not get support for this suggestion from LePan and Plumptre but I did recommend it in the memorandum I sent Trudeau at the end of March, a week before the Liberal convention which elected him leader of the Liberal party. Two days after the convention, when it was clear that Mitchell Sharp would be foreign minister in Trudeau's cabinet, I sent the memorandum to him.

In the opening paragraph of the memorandum I said:

As a result of the Vietnam war, Vietnam is being destroyed – the country, the civilization, the people. Tensions in the United States are mounting. The state of incipient civil war between black and white in the northern cities of the United States becomes more acute. International trade, international finance, are gravely affected. The have-not nations are deprived of resources for their development. Alliances are crumbling. The danger of the war spreading increases.

I went on to propose that the government should announce that it was seeking support from other members of the United Nations for a resolution by the General Assembly calling on the United States to cease the bombing of North Vietnam without attaching any conditions; if the General Assembly adopted the resolution and the United States did not accept it, 'Canada should cease to export armaments to the United States.' 'If a continuance of the bombing is followed by an extension of the fighting to China, Canada should remain neutral.' The conference of Commonwealth prime ministers to be held in the autumn should consider 'what the nations of the Commonwealth, acting individually and collectively, acting alone or in association with other countries, might do to try to bring the fighting in Vietnam to a close or, if the fighting cannot be ended, to reduce the evil consequences to us all of this obscene tragedy.' I concluded by saying:

Canadians and Americans are so closely linked that it is inevitable that public opinion in Canada should, like public opinion in the United States, be deeply and bitterly divided over the Vietnam war. Americans who attack their government for its policy on Vietnam are not being anti-American. Canadians who attack the United States government for its policy on Vietnam are not being anti-American. Both groups believe that if the United States government persists in its present policies on Vietnam the whole world may be engulfed in one of the greatest tragedies that has ever befallen the world. It is important that the government of Canada should make every effort to make this clear to the government and people of the United States. Certainly the new prime minister of Canada and his foreign minister should, as soon as possible after they take office, visit Washington for confidential discussions with the President and the Secretary of State.

According to Douglas Ross in his book on Canada and Vietnam, when Trudeau came to power a month later he had

repudiated the American bombing in Vietnam as 'an error in basic psychology.' But he was not on record in opposition to American war aims in Vietnam ... In late 1968 the government reaffirmed Canadian support of an indefinite halt to the bombing of the DRVN [North Vietnam]. This reaffirmation was made in language carefully phrased not to offend American authorities. Secretary of State for External Affairs Mitchell Sharp declared that henceforth the government would aim at 'balanced criticism' because Ottawa wanted both sides to 'contribute significantly to military de-escalation'.[5]

Having failed to move Trudeau by my memorandum of March 1968, I remained silent on Vietnam until June 1972 when I gave the convocation address at Glendon Colege. I began that address as follows:

When I was here with you as your principal I said that the war in Vietnam was the greatest tragedy the United States had undergone since the Civil War ... that the United States involvement in Vietnam was the greatest blunder in foreign policy committed by any great power since Napoleon's invasion of Russia ... This unnecessary war, this brutal, senseless, obscene war has demonstrated flaws in the society of the United States so profound in their possible implications as to be terrifying ... Insistently the question presents itself. Has the United States become not only the most powerful nation in the world but the most dangerous nation in the world?[6]

FOREIGN AID

In a speech in March 1969 to a conference of the Liberal party in Ontario I said: 'Expenditures on defence and expenditures on aid for the economic development of poor countries are both deterrents. One is a deterrent against armed attack. The other is a deterrent against anarchy, the anarchy into which much of the poor two-thirds of the world may be plunged if there is not a substantial speed-up in its rate of economic growth. Anarchy begets monsters – plague, pestilence, famine, war.'

I was happy when a month after I gave this speech Prime Minister Trudeau said: 'It's in our national interest to reduce the tensions in the world, tensions which spring from the two-thirds of the world's population who go to bed hungry every night, the two-thirds of the world's population who are poor whereas the other third are rich.'

At a conference I attended in New Delhi in 1971, I.G. Patel, the brilliant and witty senior officer in the Indian finance ministry, explained

5 Douglas A. Ross, *In the Interests of Peace: Canada and Vietnam 1954–73* (Toronto: University of Toronto Press 1984), 324, 328
6 The address was printed in the *Toronto Star* for 3 June 1972

why he, a Hindu and thus a believer in reincarnation, advocated foreign aid: since two out of three people in the world were poor, his chances of being born into a poor family in his next incarnation were two out of three; that was why he was determined in his present incarnation to do his best to improve the conditions of life of the poor. My speech followed immediately after his. I said that for a Christian the argument for supporting foreign aid was even more compelling, since Jesus had declared that those who did not feed the hungry would be punished by everlasting fire; the poor countries should support a revival of Christianity in the rich countries so that their citizens would take seriously this judgment of Jesus.

I was not content in my articles and speeches in the late sixties merely to urge an increase in the quantity of our foreign aid; I insisted that if aid was to be effective Canada would have to make substantial changes in the nature of its aid programs and in the policies it pursued in international aid agencies. I had an opportunity to put this argument at the end of 1969 to the policy conference of the Liberal party at Harrison Hot Springs in a paper which was subsequently published in the *International Journal*. I said that aid-giving countries should stop financing 'projects built in the wrong places at the wrong time ... projects calculated more to advance the prestige of the donor or the recipient than to speed up the rate of economic growth of the receiving country – for example, many of the steel plants, some nuclear power plants, many new capital cities, many big multi-purpose dams, many international airports and airlines built in poor countries in the past fifteen years.'

As important as, if not more important than, grants and loans and technical assistance for first-rate projects were 'the opening of markets in wealthy countries to the exports of poor countries, the securing of a higher selling price in wealthy countries for such exports of poor countries as tea, coffee, cocoa and bananas, and the stimulation of private investment in poor countries by corporations and individuals in wealthy countries.'

In a speech in March 1969 I had said that our aid should go to 'deserving poor countries.' I now defined deserving countries as those which were 'making sustained and disciplined efforts to mobilize their own material and intellectual resources for investment in their own economic growth and which were trying to correct grossly uneven distributions of wealth and power within their countries, unequal distributions as evil and dangerous as those between rich nations and poor nations.'

I had made another point about how to improve foreign aid in my speech to the Canadian Centenary Council in February 1967, subsequently published in the *International Journal*. It was that Canada should take a lead in international efforts to make the international development agencies more effective instruments of the world community in combating world poverty. These agencies, I pointed out, had been created at a time when the world was not as conscious as it later became of the importance of helping the governments of the poor nations in their efforts to improve the conditions of life of their poorer citizens, and of the difficulties involved in this endeavour. They had been created when most of the states now members of them had not yet gained their independence. Canada would make a significant contribution to the war against world poverty if the government were to instruct experts in the public service 'to examine in turn each of the international agencies concerned directly or indirectly with the economic development of poor countries and to draw up recommendations on what steps should be taken to make each of them more effective, by changes in their practices or management, by increasing their resources, if necessary by changes in their constitutions. The recommendations of the Canadian experts would constitute a basis for discussions with other countries.

Maurice Strong, then head of the Canadian International Development Agency, took me up on this. He invited me to join CIDA as a consultant and to prepare memoranda for it on how to make some of these agencies more effective, beginning with the World Bank, not because we believed it stood in most need of reform, but because it was the one I knew most about. After I had completed the study of the World Bank for CIDA, I decided not to try to cover any of the other international agencies but to use the voluminous material I had collected as a starting-point for a book on the Bank and I gave up my appointment with CIDA.

I had never written a book before, and I found writing this one a task of great difficulty. I was often tempted to give it up. But forty years before I had failed to write my book on Canadian political parties for submission to Oxford as a DPhil thesis and I was determined not to incur this humiliation again. I visited Washington for talks with officers of the World Bank. I sent them drafts of chapters for comments. They were generous with their help. I got help from experts on foreign aid in the United States, Britain, and India. I finished the book in the spring of 1973 and it was published in the autumn in time for me to present copies to the delegates and the senior officers of the Bank attending the annual meeting of the Bank in Nairobi that year.

While the book was going through the press Indira Gandhi, then prime minister of India, visited Ottawa. Trudeau invited my wife and me to the dinner he gave for her. He knew there was something I wanted from her and he asked me what it was. I said I wanted her to write a commendation of the book I had written on the World Bank. He said that prime ministers didn't have time to read books like that. I said that two of Indira Gandhi's principal economic advisers in whom she had great confidence admired the book and would advise her to commend it. This she generously did and her commendation appeared as a preface to the book. She wrote that I 'had not attempted merely an evaluation of the World Bank ... His plea for greater imagination and sympathetic understanding of the nature and urges of different societies should be heard by all those who influence international economic arrangements.'

My book on the World Bank made thirty-eight proposals for strengthening the Bank and its two sister institutions, the International Development Association and the International Finance Corporation. They ranged from making the Bank Group a less unequal partnership between its rich member countries and its poor member countries, to expanding its lending to poor countries for small-scale rural development works yielding a high real rate of economic return; this would put money into the hands of the poorer peasants, the underemployed artisans, and the landless labourers. I warned that the politically powerful rural elite in many poor countries, notably in India, Pakistan, and Bangladesh, would try to get control of rural development programs to abort or twist them to serve their own purposes and that the Bank would have to get assurances that the rural works projects would be so organized and monitored that they would in fact help the rural poor. In many very poor countries the governments would have to assist the rural poor to organize themselves against those who held power in the villages.

How much influence my book and my article in *Foreign Affairs* summarizing it may have had I do not know. I do know that the book influenced the report made four years later by the Willy Brandt commission on international development issues. Drag Avromovic, the head of the commission's research staff, told me that he had read my book four times while serving on the commission and Robert Cassen, a principal adviser to the commission, assured me that it was the commission's bible for the sections in the commission's report on reforming the World Bank.

My wife and I spent the winter of 1978-79 in India. I wanted to find out how far the events of the twenty-two years since I had ceased to be high commissioner had served to qualify or confirm the opinions I had expressed in my reporting to Ottawa from 1952 to 1957.

I found from talking to economists, officials, journalists, and politicians that there was general agreement that the conditions of life of the poorest two-fifths of the people of India had probably not improved in the preceding twenty years or so; it was indeed possible that their conditions had worsened. It seemed to me likely that what was true of the 250 million absolute poor of India was also true of the other 750 million absolute poor of the world. (Robert McNamara, the president of the World Bank, had defined the absolute poor as those 'severely deprived human beings struggling to survive in a set of squalid and degrading circumstances almost beyond the power of our sophisticated imaginations to conceive.') It seemed to me that their governments could raise the absolute poor out of their poverty if they set as a principal goal of national policy providing productive employment for those of them who were unemployed or underemployed. Rich countries had not been able to conquer unemployment; for poor countries to conquer it would be incredibly difficult. To succeed the poor countries would have to make profound changes in their policies, programs, and projects and they would need a greatly increased flow of real resources from the rich countries. If rich countries were to provide these resources they would have to be assured that the poor countries they were helping were doing their best to help themselves. Poor countries would be most reluctant to accept the necessary profound investigations into their affairs by an agency such as the World Bank, dominated by rich countries. An agency which was an equal partnership between rich and poor countries would be better able to undertake this invidious task, especially if it also conducted investigations into whether the rich countries were carrying out their promises to help. What was required was the establishment of a new agency, a new partnership between rich and poor countries. The new agency could draw upon the World Bank for administrative and other services, though it would have its own governing body and its own funds contributed by its rich member countries. Votes in the governing body would be divided equally between the rich and the poor member countries.

At the end of my visit to India I put down on paper my proposals for the establishment of this new agency and my memorandum was published in two of the leading international journals on development.[7] This memorandum constitutes my last will and testament on foreign aid. I continue to hope that the kind of new partnership between rich and poor nations which I advocated in 1979 will be established.

7 *U.N. Development Forum*, May 1979 and the *International Development Review*, 1979/3. Also in an appendix to my *Envoy to Nehru* (Delhi: Oxford University Press), 286–7

PALESTINE

In May 1988 I spoke at the annual conference of the Canadian Professors for Peace in the Middle East.

I said that the United Nations played a central role in the creation of Israel. What role should the U.N. now play in the tragic drama being enacted in the occupied territories of the West Bank and Gaza – and in Israel? Can it, more than forty years later, take steps to bring into effect the principal recommendations of the General Assembly's historic resolution on partition of 29 November 1947? I believe it can and should.

The members of the United Nations, by agreeing to the Charter, conferred on the U.N. Security Council primary responsibility for dealing with international situations which, like the situation in the West Bank, Gaza, and Israel, endanger the maintenance of international peace and security. To enable the Council to discharge this responsibility, the members gave it the power, in the last resort when all other efforts have failed, to decide on the terms of settlement of a dangerous international situation and to impose those terms by the threat or use of such sanctions as the complete interruption of economic relations. The members of the United Nations have undertaken to carry out the Council's decisions.

The Security Council can assume this responsibility only if its five permanent members agree that it should. Hitherto they have never reached such an agreement on any dispute or situation. May there not now, however, be ground for cautious hope that if by the end of 1988 the conflict between Israel and Palestine has not been settled, the permanent members of the Council may be prepared to recommend to the Council that it impose terms of settlement?

I speak of a conflict between Israel and Palestine, not of a conflict between Israel and the Palestinians, because it seems to me clear that though a Palestine nation may not have existed forty years ago, or twenty years ago, a Palestine nation exists today and that there can be no lasting peaceful settlement of the situation in the West Bank, Gaza, and Israel which does not include the creation of an independent sovereign state of Palestine which would recognize Israel's right 'to live in peace within secure and recognized boundaries' in return for Israel's recognition of the right of Palestine 'to live in peace within secure and recognized boundaries.'

The U.N. Charter provides that before the Security Council decides to impose terms of settlement it 'may call upon the parties concerned to comply with such provisional measures as it deems necessary or desirable' and the Council can impose sanctions against a party which refuses to comply. I suggest that the provisional measures should include the withdrawal of Israel from the West Bank and Gaza and the holding by the Security Council of an election in the West Bank and Gaza of a constituent assembly which would choose a provisional government of Palestine.

The Security Council would then take up the task of working out with the governments of Israel and Palestine measures to reduce occasions of strife between them and to increase the possibility of their co-operating in matters of common concern.

If the Security Council were to carry out in this way the responsibilities conferred on it by the Charter it could proclaim that, after a lapse of more than forty years, the principal recommendations of the General Assembly's partition resolution of 29 November 1947 had been brought into effect other than the recommendation for economic union: the establishment of what that resolution called an 'Independent Arab State' as well as of an 'Independent Jewish State'; the holding of elections in the Arab state followed by the formation of a provisional government; and the creation of a 'Special International Regime for the City of Jerusalem'.[8] Might we not hope that the creation of an international regime for Jerusalem might in time result in the fulfilment of the vision of the psalmist, 'Jerusalem that is built to be a city where people come together in unity'?

THE NORTH ATLANTIC ALLIANCE

In the memorandum I sent Trudeau on 28 March 1968 I wrote:

Canada's entry into the North Atlantic alliance in April 1949 did not result either in Canadian rearmament or in the sending of Canadian forces to Germany. A year after the alliance was created, Canadian defence expenditures were only about $300 million a year and there was no thought of sending Canadian armed forces to Europe. The increase of Canadian defence expenditures and the sending of Canadian armed forces to Europe were a consequence of the Korean war

---

8 The resolution on the Palestine question adopted by the U.N. General Assembly on 29 November 1947 reads in part as follows: 'Independent Arab and Jewish States and the Special International Regime for the City of Jerusalem, set forth in Part III of this plan, shall come into existence in Palestine two months after the evacuation of the armed forces of the mandatory Power has been completed but in any case not later than 1 October 1948 ... [Each state shall] hold elections to the Constituent Assembly ... [which] shall choose a provisional government ...'

which broke out in the summer of 1950. The world situation has changed since the summer of 1950 to an extent which would permit Canada to return at least part of the way to the situation which existed between the signature of the North Atlantic treaty in April 1949 and the Korean war in June 1950.

A year later I conducted a public campaign for reducing our defence expenditures from $1,800 million a year to $1 billion[9] and increasing our expenditures on foreign aid from $300 million a year to $2 billion. I advocated that Canada should negotiate with its North Atlantic allies the progressive withdrawal of Canadian armed forces from Europe, to be completed in about four years. I set forth my arguments in an article in the *Globe and Mail* on 17 March 1969, and I submitted a summary of the article to the House of Commons Committee on External Affairs and National Defence. On 28 March I presented my proposals in a speech to the annual meeting of the Liberal party in Ontario. The *Toronto Telegram* and the *Ottawa Journal* published virtually the whole speech and other papers published summaries. On 29 March the *Globe and Mail* in a lengthy editorial noted that the cabinet would that day begin discussion of Canada's future commitments to NATO, summarized the arguments I had been putting forward 'wherever and whenever he felt there was a possibility of the Cabinet hearing or reading his words,' and concluded by stating that my recommendations 'deserve the serious consideration of the Cabinet.'

The government decided to withdraw half the Canadian armed forces from Europe, but whether my arguments had helped the government to make that decision I do not know. The first announcement was made on 3 April when Trudeau stated that Canada had decided to 'bring about a planned and phased reduction of the size of Canadian forces in Europe' and in September the government announced that half the forces would be withdrawn.

I did not in my public statements at the time express views on the kind of consultation on foreign policy which should take place in the North Atlantic Council, but I did in a letter to Edmonton publisher Mel Hurtig, just before the policy conference of the Liberal party at Harrison Hot Springs in November 1969 which we were both to attend. He was the chairman of the task force on international relations at the conference and I presented a paper on foreign aid to the task force. I told Hurtig

9 The official NATO statistics on defence expenditures give Canada's expenditures in 1949 as $372 million Canadian, not $300 million, and in 1968 and 1969 as about $1,900 million, not $1,800 million.

that I did not agree with him that Canada should leave the Atlantic alliance. I believed that we could use the North Atlantic Council to encourage an ally to do sensible things and to discourage an ally from doing stupid things.

[W]ithin the North Atlantic Council we could do things to help the sensible people in the new administration in Bonn to break out of the confines of past German foreign policy. For ten years I have been arguing that the way to make an advance on the German problem and on easing tensions in central Europe is to have three Germanies, east, west and a united city of Berlin. All the parties concerned would enter into specific commitments to guarantee freedom of access to Berlin by air, road, rail, canal, for persons and goods ... [We could use] the North Atlantic Council, if our policy is firm enough and our diplomats shrewd enough, to make it impossible for the United States administration to pretend even to itself that it has the support of its North Atlantic allies when it does not. This is a matter of our arranging with our friends in advance of a North Atlantic Council meeting that one by one the allies get up and make clear that they are in disagreement with United States policy on such and such for the following reasons.

The organizers of the policy conference at Harrison Hot Springs did not require that those who led discussions there should be reliable members of the Liberal party. Hurtig, Pauline Jewett, and I led discussion at the meeting on foreign policy. Hurtig left the Liberal party shortly afterwards. Jewett became an NDP member of Parliament and I have always since 1933, whenever a candidate of the CCF or NDP was on the ballot paper, voted for him.

In 1977, eight years later, I published a book on the North Atlantic alliance, *Time of Fear and Hope: The Making of the North Atlantic Treaty 1947–1949*. I started writing this book in 1973 when I was Skelton-Clark Fellow of Queen's University, Kingston, Ontario, and I finished it three years later when I was a scholar-in-residence in the tranquil, luxurious Rockefeller villa on Lake Como. In both places I had intellectually stimulating colleagues. At the Rockefeller villa, scholarship was also stimulated by superb food and wine and beautiful surroundings.

I dealt in the book with what seemed to me to have been the obstacles in the way of the Atlantic alliance moving towards what Pearson had called in September 1948 'political and economic unification.' The principal obstacle had been the concentration on the military aspects of the alliance following the outbreak of the Korean War in the summer of 1950, fourteen months after the North Atlantic treaty had been signed, a concentration which Pearson deplored in 1951 because it would in his words 'endanger the "Article 2" idea of the Pact, the development of a North Atlantic community.'

Another obstacle was that from the beginning of the alliance most of the politically influential people in France and Belgium wanted greater western European unity rather than greater North Atlantic unity and opinion in the other member countries of the alliance was divided. Then from 1952 on, under both Republican and Democratic administrations, people who not only rejected the goal of a North Atlantic federation but who never really liked, or even understood, the very idea of an alliance secured great influence in the White House and the State Department. They were not anxious to learn the complex and subtle art of how the leader of an alliance conducts its relations with the other members. They hankered after unilateral declarations, unilateral decision-making, and unilateral actions. If they were out of step with their real allies, and in step only with their client states, they were inclined to believe that it was their allies who were out of step with them: in policy towards China up to 1973, in their war in Vietnam, in their policies in the Middle East and Central America, and in their policies towards the Soviet Union.

All this had meant that most United States administrations since the creation of the alliance had been reluctant to consult effectively with their allies at North Atlantic summit meetings, even though the treaty imposed an obligation to consult whenever an ally believed that the security of any of the allies was threatened in any part of the world by the actions of any country, whether potential adversary or ally. The blame for this breach by North Atlantic countries of their obligation to consult was shared between the United States, which had generally resisted effective consultation, and the other members of the alliance, which had not insisted on it.

Seven years after I made this argument in my book Pierre Trudeau confirmed the truth of what I had written about the lack of effective consultation when he stated that he had attended four of the six summit meetings the alliance had held since its foundation and that at none of them was there any real consultation.

NATO heads of state and of government meet only to go through the tedious motions of reading speeches drafted by others with the principal objective of not rocking the boat. Indeed, any attempt to start a discussion ... was met with stony embarrassment, or strong objection. Is it any wonder that the value of NATO as a political alliance is increasingly being questioned? ... NATO must be transformed into a vital political alliance, as had been intended in the beginning … NATO summits must be frequently held and sufficient time must be allowed for fruitful and creative exchanges.

In 1985 my apprehensions over President Reagan's policies towards the Soviet Union, Central America, and the Middle East, his proposals on Star Wars, and the refusal of the North Atlantic alliance to renounce the first use of nuclear weapons prompted me to resurrect many of the ideas I had previously put forward. In a number of articles I made the following points.

The first step in considering what Canadian policy should be towards the North Atlantic alliance is to clear up misconceptions about the alliance. The most serious misconception is that it is little more than a military alliance; it is much more. The treaty imposes eight obligations on the members of the alliance of which only two are military and the other six are non-military.[10] All eight obligations are equally binding. The architects of the treaty believed, and rightly believed, that the chances of a third world war would be reduced if the members of the alliance adhered strictly to both sets of obligations. Adherence to the military set would deter the Soviet Union from running risks of precipitating a world war. Adherence to the non-military set would reduce the risk that an ally's policy might increase the chances of a world war. Britain, the Western European countries, and Canada wanted the alliance not only because it would restrain the Soviet Union, but also because they hoped it would restrain the United States from pursuing impatient and provocative policies towards the Soviet Union.

Each ally is under the obligation to settle any international dispute in which it is involved by peaceful means in such a manner that international peace and security and justice are not endangered and to refrain in its international relations from the threat or use of force in any manner inconsistent with the purposes of the United Nations. When Britain and France invaded Egypt in 1956 they violated this undertaking. So did the United States when it intervened in Chile, Grenada, Libya, and Nicaragua and when it failed to pursue patient, unprovocative, and constructive policies in its relations with the Soviet Union.

Each ally has undertaken to promote conditions of stability and well-being in the world. Since there cannot be stability and well-being as long as one-fifth of the men, women, and children of the world live in the most squalid and degrading poverty, this means that each ally is under an obligation to give adequate aid to poor countries to help them speed

10 These are set out above, pp. 235–6.

up their economic and social development. This some of the allies, especially the United States, have failed to do.

The bad effects of members of the alliance not living up to their non-military obligations have been compounded by the insistence of some spokesmen for allied governments that the allies are bound by obligations which are not in the treaty and which are indeed inconsistent with their obligations under the treaty. One such erroneous belief is that once the North Atlantic Council has made a decision an ally is under an obligation not to question that decision. The council is not infallible. If an ally on reflection concludes that a decision in which it has concurred does not serve the interests of the alliance it is under an obligation as a loyal ally concerned with the strength of the alliance to use its best efforts to have the decision changed.

A variant of this error is the belief that decisions of the council are binding on the member countries. A decision of the council binds only those members who agree to be bound by it. The council was not given power by the treaty to commit its members to go to war if one or more of them is subjected to armed attack. Each ally decides for itself 'in accordance with [its] respective constitutional processes' whether an armed attack has occurred and, if so, what action 'it deems necessary [to take] to restore and maintain the security of the North Atlantic area.' The rule which applies to decisions on war applies with equal force to other decisions of the council.

Another erroneous belief is that loyalty to the alliance means that an ally should support the foreign policies of its allies. Loyalty to the alliance may mean the opposite. If an ally believes that a policy of one of its allies weakens the alliance or increases the risks of war, it is bound as a loyal ally to oppose that policy. When in December 1957 I was putting this point to the newly appointed Canadian foreign minister, Sidney Smith, I wrote:

If Great Britain had, after the war, tried to suppress the Indian independence movement, the friends and allies of Great Britain would have done Great Britain – and the whole free world – a disservice if they had given Great Britain diplomatic and other support for this policy. They would have strengthened both Great Britain and the free world as a whole if, by refusing to support such a suicidal British policy, they had put pressure on Great Britain to grant independence to India. Here would have been a case where strength did not lie in unity among Great Britain and its friends and allies. Unity would have been a source of weakness. In disunity lay strength.

There is one thing worse in an alliance than disunity. It is unity on an unwise policy. The most impressive demonstration in history of unity of purpose and collective action is that of the Gadarene swine who, with one accord, rushed down a steep place into the sea and were drowned.

Since the formation of the alliance its members have embarked on many unwise foreign policies from which they have been slow to withdraw. The world would be in better shape if France had withdrawn sooner from North Africa and Indo-China, if Britain and France had not invaded Egypt in 1956, if the United States had recognized the communist regime in China earlier and had got out of Vietnam sooner, if the United States had consistently pursued patient, unprovocative, and constructive policies in its relations with the Soviet Union. Is it not possible that if there had been frank discussion of these matters at confidential meetings of the heads of the North Atlantic governments some of these costly errors might not have been committed and others might have been corrected sooner? On issues like these a government which is committing an error cannot rely on a friendly government giving it a friendly warning in a confidential talk between the two governments. Governments are reluctant to say displeasing things to a friendly government on an issue that government considers important. This reluctance is especially great when the government whose policies are being questioned is the government of the United States for then other governments have to bear in mind that their criticism may make it less likely that they will get the support or sympathy they need from the United States on matters of great importance to them. One example which Alastair Buchan has given is the way in which '[President] Johnson brutally used the dependence of sterling on the dollar to exact [Prime Minister] Wilson's support for American policy in Vietnam, except for the bombing of the North. In the end, Wilson failed in both his objectives: to maintain the parity of sterling and to retain any leverage over American policy in Asia. Both countries suffered in the process.'[11]

The Atlantic allies of the United States would have found it easier to talk frankly to the United States about its Vietnam policy if they had sought safety in numbers, if they had agreed among themselves well in advance of a North Atlantic summit meeting that they would act together at that meeting in an effort to persuade the United States to reconsider its Vietnam policy. Faced with the arguments of its allies the American administration might have moved sooner to get out of Vietnam.

These were the arguments I put forward in 1985. Two years later I accepted an invitation to give the opening speech at a conference in

11 Alastair Buchan, 'Mothers and Daughters (or Greeks and Romans),' *Foreign Affairs* (July 1976), 666–7

Toronto in May 1987 on Canada, the United States, and the Atlantic alliance. I had reached the age of eighty-two. I decided to make this speech my swan song on the alliance.

I dealt in my speech with some of the similarities and some of the differences between the conditions in 1948 and 1949 which resulted in the North Atlantic treaty and conditions in 1987. One similarity is that in both periods the western governments dismissed the idea of a Soviet military invasion of western Europe. A difference is that four decades ago the Soviet Union could use strong communist parties in Western Europe as its subservient agents in undermining Western European governments by exploiting economic grievances, social unrest, and fear of vengeance in the event of the communists coming to power. Another difference is between the Soviet Union under Stalin and the Soviet Union under Gorbachev. We would certainly view the establishment in Western Europe of states similar to the Soviet Union under Gorbachev as abhorrent, but the prospect of such a development is not so revolting as was the prospect in 1948 of the establishment of states similar to the Soviet Union under Stalin. A similarity between the two periods is the fear that the United States might pursue impatient and provocative policies in its relations with the Soviet Union. From 1981 to 1987 under Reagan's presidency this fear was greater than it had been in 1948 and 1949.

A consideration of these differences and similarities led me to conclude my talk in May 1987 as follows:

It is a quarter of a century since I last lived in Western Europe so I do not know at first hand how the minds of the Western Europeans are moving but I do know that if I were living in West Germany ... I would support the idea that the governments of Western Europe should now launch confidential discussions with the Soviet government on its willingness to work out with its allies and with western Europe a comprehensive European settlement – a package deal, a trading of concessions. The comprehensive settlement might include the withdrawal of European countries from the Atlantic alliance and the Warsaw Pact, the withdrawal of American, Canadian and Soviet armed forces from Europe to their homelands, the termination of the special rights of the United States, the Soviet Union, Britain and France in Berlin, the unification of Germany with its capital in Berlin, and making Europe up to the Soviet border an area free of nuclear weapons.

It is easy to dismiss such a proposal as unrealistic. In 1947 all or virtually all experts on foreign affairs would have dismissed as unrealistic a proposal to create a military alliance of the North Atlantic countries; the inertia, scepticism, doubts, hesitations, fears and opposition were too great to be overcome. From

1947 to 1949 politicians and civil servants who knew that international politics is the art of the almost impossible overcame these obstacles by two years of patient, and impatient, secret soundings and secret diplomacy accompanied by public statements to rally support for an alliance. They wrought a miracle – the birth of the alliance.

May we not now plead that politicians and civil servants of vision and determination will work another miracle. For the North Atlantic alliance to give place to a comprehensive European settlement would be its crowning achievement.

When I was with the World Bank one of my colleagues who obviously considered that I was a stuffy diplomatic type said to me that he was surprised that someone like me had a daughter who was training for the stage in New York and a son who was a professional football player.

When Morna was at Queen's University she decided she wanted to be an actress and she went to New York to study acting. She had a few happy years there and then began to be afflicted by two terrifying diseases – schizophrenia and manic depression. For the last half of her fifty-three years she struggled against these diseases with stubborn courage. She loved our farm and at her request her ashes were scattered on it.

Timothy on his return to Canada from Oxford played professional football one season for the Hamilton Tiger Cats. The high point in his professional football career was playing in the Grey Cup 'fog-bowl game.' Later while he was assistant to the president of York University and assistant professor of economics he embarked on a political career, first as an unsuccessful Liberal candidate in a federal election and then as a successful Liberal candidate in a provincial election, which led to his being the spokesman for the Liberal opposition in the Ontario legislature on education and university affairs. Ruth and I admired his undertaking the hard work and running the risks of active participation in politics. Our regret that he did not throw in his lot with the party we had supported ever since it was established in 1933, the New Democratic Party, formerly the CCF, was balanced by our appreciation of the independence he had shown by not blindly following in the political footsteps of his parents.

After his defeat in a provincial general election he first worked for the Organization for Economic Co-operation and Development in Paris and then became a deputy secretary of the Treasury Board in Ottawa in 1978. I told him then that I was forty-three before I reached the rank of assistant deputy minister and that he had beaten me by a year. From 1985 to early 1989 he was dean of the faculty of business at Ryerson Polytechnic Institute in Toronto. He is now a professor there. He is also a commissioner of the Ontario Securities Commission. His wife Julyan is assistant deputy minister (operations division) of the Ontario Ministry of Environment.

Timothy and Julyan edited in 1969 a book on student power and the Canadian campus.[12] I was flattered that they included passages from five speeches or essays of mine and proud that they dedicated the book to Julyan's father and to me: 'Their life styles show that there need not necessarily be a generation gap.'

When I left the World Bank in 1965 Patrick came to it first as alternate executive director representing Canada, Ireland, and Jamaica and then as executive director. His knowledge of India and his studies at Cambridge of the problems of the development of poor countries enabled him to press for reforms in the principles and practices the Bank followed in lending to poor countries. On many of these issues his was then a minority voice. A few years later much of what he advocated became conventional wisdom. In 1971 Robert McNamara, the president of the World Bank, told me that Patrick had been most helpful in emphasizing two things: that the Bank was a development institution, and the importance of ensuring that the Bank's loans for agriculture benefited the poorer farmers and the agricultural labourers. On his return to Canada from Washington he worked first for the Canadian International Development Agency and then for the Department of Regional Economic Expansion, where he applied his insights into the problems of development of poor countries to the problems of development of the poorer regions of Canada, especially Newfoundland.

Now when Ruth and I are eighty-four we face old age with the support of our sons, grandchildren, and great-grandchildren, our daughters-in-law and grand-daughters-in-law. We watch with admiration, compassion, and love the unfolding drama of their struggles to deal with accomplishments and frustrations, hopes and fears, joys and sorrows.

---

12 Tim and Julyan Reid, eds, *Student Power and the Canadian Campus* (Toronto: Peter Martin Associates 1969)

Acknowledgments

I have received permission from Sandra Gwyn to quote from her letter to me in chapter one, from Douglas LePan to use his description of Nehru in chapter seventeen, and from Florence Bird for extracts from her memoirs in chapter eighteen.

The Social Sciences and Humanities Research Council of Canada gave me a grant toward my expenses in writing this book. The historical section and the library of the Department of External Affairs in Ottawa helped me to locate documents and books. W.C. Johnston and Paul Marsden gave me much help as research assistants. I have profited greatly from comments on drafts of the book which University of Toronto Press secured from two readers. Diane Mew edited the manuscript with care and intelligence. The Colbert Agency has served me well. Ernestine Hopkins, who has typed my last four books, has typed and retyped this one from my scarcely legible handwritten copy with her customary skill, accuracy, and patience. To all these I am most grateful.

I am indebted to the following with whom I have corresponded about the book: John R. Baldwin, John English, Duane Freer, J.L. Granatstein, Michael Gregory, H.S. Harris, Michael and Barbara Hicks, John W. Holmes, David Hopper, Michiel Horn, D.V. LePan, Peyton Lyon, Edward T. Pryor, Julyan Reid, C.P. Stacey, J.H. Taylor, and Douglas Verney.

For permission to quote from the poem 'The General' by Siegfried Sassoon thanks are due to: George T. Sassoon; Chatto and Windus, London, publishers of *Men Who March Away*, edited by I.M. Parsons, 1965; and to Viking Penguin for the same quotation from *Collected Poems* by Siegfried Sassoon (Copyright 1918, 1920 by E.P. Dutton & Co., Inc. Copyright 1936, 1946, 1947, 1948 by Siegfried Sassoon. All rights reserved. Reprinted by permission of Viking Penguin, a division of Penguin Books USA, Inc.)

Thanks are also due to: William Toye, Literary Executor for the Estate of A.J.M. Smith for permission to reprint the poem 'College $pirit' by A.J.M. Smith; and Professor Jack Granatstein for permission to quote passages from his book *The Ottawa Men: The Civil Service Mandarins, 1935–1957*.

Index